11-9

CHAUCER IN PERSPECTIVE

CHAUCER
IN PERSPECTIVE

Middle English Essays
in Honour of Norman Blake

edited by
Geoffrey Lester

Sheffield
Academic Press

Copyright © 1999 Sheffield Academic Press

Published by Sheffield Academic Press Ltd
Mansion House
19 Kingfield Road
Sheffield S11 9AS
England

Printed on acid-free paper in Great Britain
by Bookcraft Ltd
Midsomer Norton, Bath

British Library Cataloguing in Publication Data

A catalogue record for this book is available
from the British Library

ISBN 1-85075-988-X

Contents

Abbreviations

Briquet	C.M. Briquet, *Les Filigranes: Dictionnaire Historique des Marques du Papier dés leur Apparition vers 1282 jusqu'en 1600*. Facsimile of the 1907 edition, with supplementary material contributed by a number of scholars, edited by A. Stevenson (4 vols.; Amsterdam: Paper Publications Society, 1968)
Cal. Close Rolls	Public Record Office, *Calendar of the Close Rolls preserved in the Public Record Office: Richard II* (London: Public Record Office, 1920)
Cal. Pat. Rolls	Public Record Office, *Calendar of the Patent Rolls preserved in the Public Record Office: Henry VI* (London: Public Record Office, 1901–10)
CT	*Canterbury Tales*
CTP	The *Canterbury Tales* Project
DNB	L. Stephen and S. Lee (eds.), *Dictionary of National Biography* (63 vols.; London: Smith, Elder, 1885–1900)
EETS (ES, SS)	Early English Text Society (Extra Series, Supplementary Series)
GKW	*Gesamtkatalog der Wiegendrucke; hrsg. von der Kommission für den Gesamtkatalog der Wiegendrucke* (Leipzig: Hiersemann, 1925–)
IMEP	*Index of Middle English Prose* (Research project in progress. Publications to date are in the form of Handlists to individual manuscript collections. See also *IPMEP*.)
IMEV	C. Brown and R.H. Robbins, *The Index of Middle English Verse* (New York: Columbia University Press, 1943) (See also *SIMEV*)
IPMEP	R.E. Lewis, *et al.* (eds.), *Index of Printed Middle English Prose* (New York: Garland, 1985)
LALME	McIntosh, A., *et al.*, *A Linguistic Atlas of Later Mediaeval English* (4 vols.; Aberdeen: Aberdeen University Press, 1986)
MED	*Middle English Dictionary*
PMLA	*Publications of the Modern Language Association of America*
OED	*Oxford English Dictionary*

SIMEV   R.H. Robbins and J.L. Cutler, *Supplement to the Index of Middle English Verse* (Lexington: University of Kentucky Press, 1965)

STC   *A Short-Title Catalogue of Books Printed in England, Scotland, and Ireland... 1475–1640*, first compiled by A.W. Pollard and G.R. Redgrave, 2nd edn by W.A. Jackson and F.S. Ferguson, completed by K.F. Pantzer (3 vols.; London: The Bibliographical Society, 1986–91)

Unless otherwise stated, quotations from Chaucer's works are from L.D. Benson (ed.), *The Riverside Chaucer* (Boston: Houghton Mifflin, 1987). For standard abbreviations of the titles of Chaucer's works and sigils of the manuscripts of the *Canterbury Tales* see Benson (1987: 779 and 1118-19).

List of Contributors

Julia Boffey, Queen Mary and Westfield College, University of London, England.

David Burnley, University of Sheffield, England.

John Burrow, University of Bristol, England.

Graham D. Caie, University of Glasgow, Scotland.

T.P. Dolan, National University of Ireland, Ireland.

Brian Donaghey, University of Sheffield, England.

A.S.G. Edwards, University of Victoria, Canada.

Ralph Hanna III, Keble College, University of Oxford, England.

Luuk Houwen, University of Groningen, The Netherlands.

Geoffrey Lester, University of Sheffield, England.

Carol M. Meale, University of Bristol, England.

David Mills, University of Liverpool, England.

Linne R. Mooney, University of Maine, USA.

Daniel W. Mosser, Virginia Polytechnic Institute and State University, USA.

Derek Pearsall, Harvard University, USA.

Oliver Pickering, University of Leeds, England.

Peter Robinson, De Montfort University, Leicester, England.

John Scattergood, Trinity College, Dublin, Ireland.

Irma Taavitsainen, University of Helsinki, Finland.

Toshiyuki Takamiya, Keio University, Tokyo, Japan.

Ronald Waldron, King's College, University of London, England.

Foreword: Norman Blake and his Work

Geoffrey Lester

This book is dedicated to Norman Blake on the occasion of his sixty-fifth birthday and in advance of his retirement from his full Professorship at the University of Sheffield later in the year.

Norman was born on 19 April 1934 in Ceara, Brazil, where his father was manager of the Bank of London and South America.[1] His father was English, his mother half-Brazilian, half-German. Norman, together with his elder brother and sister, lived in Ceara until 1938, when the children were taken to England because their father wanted them to have an English education in a boarding school. The school, in Horley, Surrey, was called High Trees, and took boys up to 10 and girls up to 15 years of age. Their father was not often granted leave (a period of six months only once every three years), so visiting the children in England was not easy. The journey in those days had to be made by ship. Their mother visited them in 1939, but the outbreak of war meant that they did not see their parents again until 1946. It is one of Norman's early memories that while they were at High Trees a German pilot who had been shot down landed in the school grounds and was captured as the pupils watched.

In 1944 he and his brother went to Magdalen College School in Brackley, Northamptonshire, as boarders during term-time, spending the vacation in different places, including Sheffield, where they had an aunt and uncle. A devastating event in the life of 13-year-old Norman was the death of his brother in an accident at a school summer cadet camp.

1. I am grateful to Valerie Blake for the biographical information on Norman's early life and the years in Liverpool.

In 1952 he won a scholarship from Magdalen College School to Magdalen College, Oxford. Before going to university he took a year out, which he spent teaching in a private school and working in an uncle's office in London. His uncle was very interested in the family and asked him to research its history. Showing an early talent for historical research, Norman traced the family roots to Suffolk, and in particular to the village of Dallinghoo. An eighteenth-century ancestor who was a rich farmer was the first to breed the heavy horse known as the Suffolk Punch.

He went to Magdalen College, Oxford, in 1953. His tutors there were C.S. Lewis and J.A.W. Bennett, who together encouraged him to specialize in medieval English literature and language. He also studied Old Norse with E.O.G. Turville-Petre. Upon graduation he decided to do a BLitt degree in Old Icelandic, and in preparation for this spent 1956–57 in Copenhagen, studying the Icelandic manuscripts there under Jón Helgason. He travelled throughout Scandinavia and has had a very strong affection for that part of the world ever since. He returned to England in 1957, but stayed in contact with his resourceful former landlady, Else Damgaard Nielsen, with whom he later spent several vacations, travelling by car to Greece, Yugoslavia, Austria, Holland and Germany. In the summer of 1960 he visited Iceland and worked there on a farm.

Having obtained his BLitt in 1959 he became a lecturer at Liverpool University, where the Head of the English Language Department was Simeon Potter. The two professors of English Literature were Kenneth Muir and Kenneth Allott. In 1961 he met the woman who was to be his wife, Valerie, at a dance to which they had both been unwillingly dragged by friends. They were married in 1965. During this period Liverpool was a vibrant, lively city, famous for the Liverpool Poets, the Liverpool Philharmonic, its outstanding art galleries, the Everyman Theatre—and, of course, the Beatles. The university was expanding following the Robbins Report, which recommended the development of higher education in Britain. In these years Norman showed the same wide range of interests that have characterized him throughout his working life. He was an active member of various societies, particularly the Medieval Society. He played cricket, went walking with Valerie in the Lake District, and sometimes accompanied her on sketching expeditions, producing his own collection of sketches. He also tried his hand at acting in two plays for the English Literature Department. There was a flourishing local play-reading group to which they belonged, some of whose members they still count among their close friends.

After four years of lecturing in Liverpool Norman spent a year as Visiting Professor at University College, Toronto. On the return journey he travelled with a Canadian friend on a merchant ship from Montreal to Avonmouth. When they had left the St. Lawrence River the Norwegian captain decided to give the eight passengers a treat: he stopped the engines, issued lines and hooks, and instructed them to cast the lines overboard. The cod were so plentiful that they swallowed the hooks without bait, and the haul was sufficient for them to enjoy several meals. (Despite this success, however, Norman has never taken up fishing.)

1973 was a year of change, first because he was appointed to the Chair of English Language in the University of Sheffield, on the retirement of R.M. Wilson, and secondly because of the arrival of a daughter, Dorinda. Norman played an active role in bringing up Dorinda, and in the years that followed she was often to be seen with him at university social events.

His academic life was filled to the brim with university activities. He was head of the department (later expanded to the Department of English Language and Linguistics) for 23 years, serving also as Dean of the Faculty of Arts and Pro-Vice-Chancellor. He also served for a while as Chairman of the School of Modern Languages and Linguistics and of the School of East Asian Studies. He was Public Orator for five years, from 1991, and always wrote the orations himself. Once, when reading the oration for the former University Registrar, Alec Currie, he discovered on turning the pages that the final leaf was missing. He had to *ad lib*, and got most things right—apart from the fact that he presented Alec Currie for the wrong honorary degree. During his time as Public Orator he met and presented many famous people, from actors and athletes to academics and establishment figures. An unfortunate situation occurred when Sir Arthur Gold, President of the British Olympic Association, collapsed on stage during the oration. At first it was thought he had had a heart attack, but it turned out to be heat exhaustion and the effects of the long ceremony. When he came round and all the commotion had died down Norman had to continue with the oration—which he managed with typical coolness and humour.

Norman was a supportive and able Head of Department. He always seemed to have his finger on the pulse of things, and his colleagues could be confident that he would fight for their interests and for the subject. He was (and still is) quick-witted and unflappable, a demanding teacher who always took on a fair share of classes. He particularly enjoyed working with smaller seminar groups and with individual research students, and quite a few of the ideas which have emerged in his publications over the years have started in these situations. In view of his (self-imposed) heavy workload, it is a mystery how he found the time to produce such a long succession of books and articles, sometimes dealing with large and controversial subjects. Even his inaugural lecture generated heated disagreement, but later formed the basis of a book (*The English Language in Medieval Literature*, 1977) which is now often cited for its common sense. With typical disregard for what was expected of him (and to the consternation of the publisher, Edward Arnold), he decided to base his 1980 commissioned edition of the *Canterbury Tales* on the Hengwrt manuscript. In support of his decision he produced a succession of books, articles and lectures on the primacy of Hengwrt over the generally preferred Ellesmere manuscript. Although not everybody agrees, the issue remains central to *Canterbury Tales* scholarship throughout the world, and he has substantial support for his views.

He is at present a Research Professor in the Humanities Research Institute at Sheffield, with particular responsibility for the *Canterbury Tales* Project. The Project was set up in 1992 in collaboration with Peter Robinson (then of Oxford University Computing Services) with the aim of putting all the manuscript and early printed versions of the poem on computer. The texts are in the process of being transcribed and issued by Cambridge University Press as CD-ROMs (the first was issued in 1996). The project is supported by the University of Sheffield, the British Academy and the Leverhulme Foundation, and has won substantial funding.

Beyond Sheffield, in the wider field of English language and medieval literature Norman must surely be one of the best-known figures. He enjoys meeting people, and is therefore happy to accept invitations to national and international conferences, and to give invited lectures in Britain and other countries. He is a member of the Council of the Early English Text Society, Assistant Editor of the Index of Middle English Prose, Secretary of ESSE (the European Society for the Study of English), General Editor of Macmillan's Language of Literature series, and a member of the advisory boards of five academic journals. He has acted as external examiner for BA degrees at 14 British universities and has examined many PhD theses at home and abroad. He is an assessor in the current Teaching Quality Assessment of English in British Universities, and his knowledge of Denmark and the Danish language made him an ideal choice as a Teaching Quality Assessor there (with a reputation for toughness which has earned him the nicknames 'Norman the Conqueror' and 'Stormin' Norman'). In 1993 he was one of a panel appointed to report on the teaching of English in Finnish universities, and in the same year he acted as consultant on the teaching of Linguistics in the University of the South Pacific.

Because he is so widely connected, there may be friends and colleagues who are disappointed at not having been invited to contribute to this book. It was my first and most difficult task to draw up a list that would be of proportions acceptable to the publishers. My next difficulty was to choose the topic, since Norman has made himself an authority in several different subject areas over the years (as can be seen from his list of publications below). After consultations with various interested people it seemed in the end best to focus on the period with which he is most closely connected—that of Middle English—and on the author with whom he has become so intimately (and controversially) associated—Geoffrey Chaucer—(though it is appropriate and gratifying that the other figure on whom he has written extensively, William Caxton, is also well represented in the essays in this book).

'Retirement' is not a word that collocates very readily with 'Norman Blake'. Writing comes so naturally to him that he is sure to continue to produce books and articles in abundance. He will certainly remain a member of the University of Sheffield for many years, and will continue to be seen playing students and members of staff on the squash courts, eating hearty meals in the Senior Common Room, and queuing at the bus stop (for he is a great user of public transport). He also hopes to realize his ambition to walk some of the pilgrim route to Santiago in Spain. No doubt he will continue to travel widely, to attend conferences, and to give lectures, and colleagues in Britain and abroad will continue to value his company and his advice. It is therefore with genuine affection and respect that those of us who have collaborated to produce this book now dedicate it to Norman—whom we have all had the privilege to know as a genial scholar, an inspiring teacher, a supportive colleague, and a good friend.

Publications by Norman Blake

Books

1962	*The Saga of the Jomsvikings* (London: Nelson).
1964, 1990	*The Phoenix* (Manchester: Manchester University Press; Exeter University Press, 2nd edn, 1990).
1969	*Caxton and His World* (London: Deutsch).
1970	*William Caxton's History of Reynard the Fox* (EETS, 263; London: Oxford University Press).
1973a	*Middle English Religious Prose* (London: Arnold).
1973b	*Selections from William Caxton* (Oxford: Clarendon Press).
1973c	*Caxton's Own Prose* (London: Deutsch).
1975	*Quattuor Sermones printed by William Caxton* (Heidelberg: Winter).
1976a	*Caxton: England's First Publisher* (London: Osprey).
1976b	*Jacobus de Cessolis The Game of Chess, Facsimile Edition with Introduction* (London: Scolar Press).
1977, 1979	*The English Language in Medieval Literature* (London: Dent; London: Methuen).
1980	*The Canterbury Tales by Geoffrey Chaucer Edited from the Hengwrt Manuscript* (London: Arnold).
1981	*Non-Standard Language in English Literature* (London: Deutsch).
1983	*Shakespeare's Language: An Introduction* (London: Macmillan, [Reissued as *The Language of Shakespeare*, 1989; Italian translation (Florence, 1989); Japanese translation (Tokyo, 1990)]).
1984	*English Historical Linguistics: Studies in Development* (ed. with Charles Jones; Sheffield: University of Sheffield).
1985a	*The Textual Tradition of 'The Canterbury Tales'* (London: Arnold).
1985b	*William Caxton: A Bibliographical Guide* (New York: Garland).
1985c	*The Index of Printed Middle English Prose* (with R.E. Lewis and A.S.G. Edwards; New York: Garland).
1988	*Traditional English Grammar and Beyond* (London: Macmillan).
1990	*An Introduction to the Language of Literature* (London: Macmillan).
1991	*William Caxton and English Literary Culture* (London: Hambledon Press).

1992	*The Cambridge History of the English Language.* II. *1066–1476* (ed.; Cambridge: Cambridge University Press).
1993a	*Introduction to English Language* (with Jean Moorhead; London: Macmillan).
1993b	*The Canterbury Tales Project Occasional Papers,* I (ed. with P. Robinson; Oxford: Office for Humanities Communication).
1994	*A New Concordance to 'The Canterbury Tales' Based on Blake's Text edited from the Hengwrt Manuscript* (with D. Burnley, M. Matsuo and Y. Nakao; Okayama: University Education Press).
1995	*A New Rime Concordance to The Canterbury Tales based on Blake's Text edited from the Hengwrt Manuscript* (with D. Burnley, M. Matsuo and Y. Nakao; Okayama: University Education Press).
1996a	*William Caxton* (Aldershot: Variorum).
1996b	*Essays on Shakespeare's Language* (Misterton: Language Press).
1996c	*A History of the English Language* (London: Macmillan).
1997	*The Canterbury Tales Project Occasional Papers,* II (ed. with P. Robinson; London: Office for Humanities Communication).

Notes and Articles

1961a	'A Note on *hw* in Old English', *Notes and Queries* 206: 165-66.
1961b	'Originality in *The Phoenix, Notes and Queries* 206: 326-27.
1962a	'Two Notes on the Exeter Book', *Notes and Queries* 207: 45-47.
1962b	'The Seafarer, lines 48-49', *Notes and Queries* 207: 163-64.
1962c	'The Heremod Digressions in *Beowulf', Journal of English and Germanic Philology* 61: 278-77.
1962d	'The Scribe of the Exeter Book', *Neophilologus* 46: 316-19.
1962e	'Some Problems of Translation and Interpretation in the OE Phoenix', *Anglia* 80: 50-62.
1962f	'Cædmon's Hymn', *Notes and Queries* 207: 243-44.
1962g	'William Caxton and Suffolk', *Proceedings of the Suffolk Institute of Archaeology* 29: 139-53.
1963	'A Possible Seventh Copy of William Caxton's *Reynard the Fox* (1418)', *Notes and Queries* 208: 287-88.
1963–64	'William Caxton's *Reynard the Fox* and his Dutch Original', *Bulletin of the John Rylands Library* 46: 298-325.
1964a	'The Epilogue in William Caxton's Second Edition of *Reynard the Fox', Notes and Queries* 209: 50-51.
1964b	'William Caxton and Suffolk: A Supplement', *Proceedings of the Suffolk Institute of Archaeology* 30: 112-15.
1965a	'English Versions of *Reynard the Fox* in the Fifteenth and Sixteenth Centuries', *Studies in Philology* 62: 63-77.
1965b	'The "noble lady" in Caxton's *The Book of the Knyght of Towre'*, *Notes and Queries* 210: 92-93.
1965c	'The *Vocabulary in French and English* Printed by William Caxton', *English Language Notes* 3: 7-15.
1965d	'William Caxton: His Choice of Texts', *Anglia* 83: 289-307.
1965e	'*The Battle of Maldon*', *Neophilologus* 49: 332-45.

1966a	'William Caxton's Birthplace: A Suggestion', *Notes and Queries* 211: 52-54.
1966b	'Caxton's Language', *Neuphilologische Mitteilungen* 67: 122-32.
1966c	'Some Observations on William Caxton and the Mercers' Company', *The Book Collector*: 283-95.
1966–67	'Investigations into the Prologues and Epilogues by William Caxton', *Bulletin of the John Rylands Library* 49: 17-46.
1967a	'Two New Caxton Documents', *Notes and Queries* 212: 86-87.
1967b	'Caxton and Chaucer', *Leeds Studies in English*, NS 1: 19-36.
1967c	'Caxton's Copytext of Gower's *Confessio Amantis*', *Anglia* 85: 282-93.
1967d	'The *Mirror of the World* and MS. Royal 19 A ix', *Notes and Queries* 212: 205-207.
1968a	'Caxton and Courtly Style', *Essays and Studies*, NS 21: 29-45.
1968b	'Word Borrowings in Caxton's Original Writings', *English Language Notes* 6: 87-90.
1968c	'The Genesis of *The Battle of Maldon*', *Anglo-Saxon England* 7: 110-29.
1969a	'Some Low Dutch Loanwords in Fifteenth-Century English', *Notes and Queries* 214: 251-53.
1969b	'Wynkyn de Worde and the *Quatrefoil of Love*', *Archiv* 206: 189-200.
1969c	'Chaucer and the Alliterative Romances', *The Chaucer Review* 3: 163-69.
1969d	'The Biblical Additions in Caxton's *Golden Legend*', *Traditio* 25: 231-47.
1969e	'Rhythmical Alliteration', *Modern Philology* 67: 118-24.
1970a	'The Fifteenth Century Reconsidered', *Neuphilologische Mitteilungen* 71: 146-57.
1970b	'Late Medieval Prose', in W.F. Bolton (ed.), *The Middle Ages* (London: Sphere Books): 371-403.
1971a	'Wynkyn de Worde: The Early Years', *Gutenberg Jahrbuch*: 62-69.
1971b	'Lord Berners: A Survey', *Medievalia et Humanistica* NS 2: 119-32.
1972a	'Middle English Prose and its Audience', *Anglia* 90: 437-55.
1972b	'Wynkyn de Worde: The Later Years', *Gutenberg Jahrbuch*: 128-38.
1973a	'Chaucer in his Time', in W.C. Johnson and L.C. Gruber (eds.), *New Views on Chaucer: Essays in Generative Criticism* (Denver: Society for New Language Study): 1-7.
1973b	'Revelations of St Matilda', *Notes and Queries* 218: 323-25.
1974a	'500 Years of Printing', *Illustrated London News* 262: 31-34.
1974b	'Varieties of Middle English Religious Prose', in B. Rowland (ed.), *Chaucer and Middle English Studies* (London: George Allen & Unwin): 348-56.
1974c	'Caxton's First Edition of *Quattuor Sermones*', *Gutenberg Jahrbuch*: 77-82 (with L. Reffkin).
1974d	'Geoffrey Chaucer', 'English Prose of the Fifteenth Century', 'Miscellaneous and Anonymous Verse and Prose of the Fifteenth Century', in G. Watson (ed.), *The New Cambridge Bibliography of English Literature*. I. *600–1660* (Cambridge: Cambridge University Press): cols. 557-628, 663-80, 679-98.
1974e	'*The Form of Living* in Prose and Poetry', *Archiv* 211: 300-308.

1975a	'Reynard the Fox in England', in E. Rombauts and A. Welkenhuysen (eds.), *Aspects of the Medieval Animal Epic* (The Hague: Leuven University Press,): 53-65.
1975b	'Caxton's Reprints', *The Humanities Association Review* 26: 169-79.
1976a	'Coleridge's Poetic Language', in R.F. Davies and B.G. Beatty (eds.), *Literature of the Romantic Period 1750–1850* (Liverpool: Liverpool University Press): 72-81.
1976b	'The English Language in Medieval Literature', *Studia Neophilologica* 48: 59-75.
1976c	'Born in Kent', *Lore and Language* 2.5: 5 9.
1976d	'The Flyting in *The Battle of Maldon*', *English Language Notes* 13: 242-45.
1976e	'Caxton Prepares his Edition of the *Morte Darthur*', *Journal of Librarianship* 8: 272-85.
1976–77	'William Caxton: The Man and his Work', *Journal of the Printing Historical Society* 11: 64-80.
1977a	'William Caxton', *Lore and Language* 2.6: 7-15.
1977b	'The Dating of Old English Poetry', in B.S. Lee (ed.), *An English Miscellany Presented to W.S. Mackie* (Cape Town: Oxford University Press): 14-27.
1977c	'William Caxton as Publisher', *Book Auction Record* 74: 2-4.
1977d	'A New Approach to William Caxton', *Book Collector* 26: 380-85.
1977e	'Another Northernism in "The Reeve's Tale"?', *Notes and Queries* 222: 400-401.
1978	'Dating the First Books Printed in English', *Gutenberg Jahrbuch*: 43-50.
1979a	'The Relationship between the Hengwrt and the Ellesmere Manuscripts of the *Canterbury Tales*', *Essays and Studies*, NS 32: 1-18.
1979b	'"Astromye" in *The Miller's Tale*', *Notes and Queries* 224: 110-11.
1979c	'Middle English Alliterative Revivals', *Review* 1: 205-14.
1979d	'Continuity and Change in Caxton's Prologues and Epilogues: The Bruges Period', *Gutenberg Jahrbuch*: 72-77.
1979e	'The Northernisms in *The Reeve's Tale*', *Lore and Language* 3.1: 1-8.
1980a	'Continuity and Change in Caxton's Prologues and Epilogues: Westminster', *Gutenberg Jahrbuch*: 38-43.
1980b	'William Caxton after Five Hundred Years' (University of California at Davis: Library Associates of the University Library).
1981a	'The Textual Tradition of *The Book of the Duchess*', *English Studies* 62: 237-48.
1981b	'Critics, Criticism and the Order of *The Canterbury Tales*', *Archiv* 218: 47-58.
1981c	'Chaucer Manuscripts and Texts', *Review* 3: 219-32.
1981d	'On Editing the *Canterbury Tales*', in P.L. Heyworth (ed.), *Medieval Studies for J.A.W. Bennett* (Oxford: Clarendon Press): 101-19.
1982a	'Chaucer's Text and the Web of Words', in D.M. Rose (ed), *New Perspectives in Chaucer Criticism* (Norman, OK: Pilgrim Books): 223-40.

1982b   'The Wife of Bath and her Tale', *Leeds Studies in English*, NS 13: 42-
              55.
1982c   'The Text of the *Canterbury Tales*', *Poetica* (Tokyo) 13: 27-49.
1982d   'Ars Moriendi', in J.R. Strayer (ed.), *Dictionary of the Middle Ages*
              (New York: Scribner), I, pp. 547-48.
1982–83   'William Caxton Again in the Light of Recent Scholarship', *Dutch
              Quarterly Review* 12: 162-82.
1983a   'Reflections on William Caxton's *Reynard the Fox*', *Canadian Journal
              of Netherlandic Studies* 4: 69-76.
1983b   'Varieties of Language in Modern English Drama', *Journal of English
              Language and Literature* 29.1: 55-75.
1983c   'Philip Larkin's Language and Style with Reference to "Lines on a
              Young Lady's Photograph Album" [from *The Less Deceived*]', *Journal
              of English Language and Literature* 29.1: 341-45.
1983d   'Reflections on Old English Scholarship', *In Geardagum* 5: 77-83.
1983e   'The Editorial Assumptions in the Manly-Rickert Edition of *The
              Canterbury Tales*', *English Studies* 64: 385-400.
1983f   'Aspects of Syntax and Lexis in *The Canterbury Tales*', *Revista Canaria
              de Estudios Ingleses* 7: 1-19.
1984a   'Editorial Assumptions and Problems in *The Canterbury Tales*', *Poetica*
              20: 1-19.
1984b   'Geoffrey Chaucer: The Critics and the Canon', *Archiv* 221: 65-79.
1984c   'The Colloquial Strain in English Poetry: Byron, Auden, and
              Larkin', *Anglo-American Studies* 4: 169-83.
1984d   'William Caxton', in A.S.G. Edwards (ed.), *Middle English Prose: A
              Critical Guide to Major Authors and Genres* (New Brunswick, NJ: Rut-
              gers University Press): 389-412.
1985a   'John Lydgate and William Caxton', *Leeds Studies in English* NS 16:
              272-89.
1985b   'The Debate on the Order of *The Canterbury Tales*', *Revista Canaria de
              Estudios Ingleses* 10: 31-42.
1986a   'Jonathan Swift and the English Language', *Englisch Amerikanische
              Studien* 8: 105-19.
1986b   'Late Medieval Prose', in W.F. Bolton (ed.), *The Middle Ages* (Lon-
              don: Sphere Books, 2nd edn): 369-99, 420-21.
1986c   'The *Book of the Duchess* Again', *English Studies* 67: 122-25.
1986d   'Critical Approaches to Medieval Devotional Prose', *Anglo-American
              Studies* 6.2: 131-47.
1987a   'William Caxton: A Review', in H. Bekker-Nielsen *et al.* (eds.), *From
              Script to Print: a Symposium* (Odense: Odense University Press): 107-
              26.
1987b   'Beat cut's saddle', in *KM80: A Birthday Album for Kenneth Muir*
              (Liverpool: Liverpool University Press): 15-16.
1987c   'Fabliau(x)', in *Lexikon des Mittelalters* (Munich: Artemis): IV, 212-13.
1987d   'The Spread of Printing in English during the Fifteenth Century,
              Gutenberg Jahrbuch: 26-36.
1987e   'Reflections on Stylistics with Particular Reference to the Opening
              Paragraph of *Mrs Dalloway*', in M.J. Gomez Lara and J.A. Prieto

	Pablos (eds.), *Stylistica I Semana de Estudios Estilisticos* (Seville: Alfar): 15-29.
1987f	'Levels of Language in Shakespeare's *King Henry IV Part I*', in M.J. Gomez Lara and J.A. Prieto Pablos (eds.), *Stylistica I Semana de Estudios Estilisticos* (Seville: Alfar): 89-107.
1988a	'The Manuscripts and Textual Tradition of the *Canterbury Tales* Again', *Poetica* 28: 6-15.
1988b	'Literary and Other Languages in Middle English', in P. Boitani and A. Torti (eds.), *Genres, Themes and Images in English Literature* (Tübingen: Narr): 166-85.
1988c	'Another Reference to Chaucer', *Notes and Queries* 233: 159-60.
1988d	'Negation in Shakespeare', in G. Nixon and J. Honey (eds.), *An Historic Tongue* (London: Routledge): 89-111.
1988e	'Reflections on some Approaches to Style and Stylistics', *Revista Alicantina de Estudios Ingleses* 1: 5-18.
1988f	'An Early Reference to Morris Dancing', *Lore and Language* 7.2: 91-92.
1989a	'Standardizing Shakespeare's Non-Standard Language', in J.B. Trahern (ed.), *Standardizing English* (Knoxville: University of Tennessee Press): 57-81.
1989b	'The Chaucer Canon: Methodological Assumptions', *Neuphilologische Mitteilungen* 90: 295-310.
1989c	'Manuscript to Print', in J. Griffiths and D. Pearsall (eds.), *Book Production and Publishing in Britain 1385–1475* (Cambridge: Cambridge University Press): 403-32.
1990a	'Shakespeare's Language: Some Recent Studies and Future Directions', *Shakespeare Jahrbuch*: 61-77.
1990b	'Vernon Manuscript: Contents and Organisation', in D. Pearsall (ed.), *Studies in the Vernon Manuscript* (Cambridge: Brewer): 45-59.
1991a	'Fume/Fury in 2 Henry VI', *Notes and Queries* 236: 49-51.
1991b	'Gower's Vocabulary as a Guide to his Imaginative World', in A. Crépin (ed.), *The Medieval Imagination: L'imagination médiévale. Chaucer et ses contemporains* (Paris: Association des Médiévistes Anglicistes de l'Enseignement Superieur): 177-206.
1991c	'Modernising Language and Editing Shakespeare', *Poetica* (Tokyo) 34: 101-23.
1991d	'The Language of the Quarto and Folio Texts of *King Lear*', in M. Kawai (ed.), *Language and Style in English Literature: Essays in Honour of Michio Masui* (Tokyo: Eihosha): 3-26.
1992a	'Shakespeare, Discourse and the Teaching of English', in R. Ahrens and H. Antor (eds.), *Text–Culture–Reception: Cross-cultural Aspects of English Studies* (Heidelberg: Winter): 431-45.
1992b	'Geoffrey Chaucer: Textual Transmission and Editing', in A.J. Minnis and C. Brewer (eds.), *Crux and Controversy in Middle English Textual Criticism* (Cambridge: Brewer): 19-38.
1992c	'*Why* and *What* in Shakespeare', in T. Takamiya and R. Beadle (eds.), *Chaucer to Shakespeare* (Cambridge: Brewer): 179-93.

1992d   'Translation and the History of English', in M. Rissanen *et al.* (eds.), *History of Englishes* (Berlin: W. de Gruyter): 3-24.

1992e   'MS. Chetham 6709 and some Manuscript Copies of Caxton Prints', in C. Blank (ed.), *Language and Civilization: A Concerted Profusion of Essays and Studies in Honour of Otto Hietsch* (Frankfurt-am-Main: Lang): 239-54.

1992f   'Early Modern English', in C. Nocera Avila *et al.* (eds.), *Early Modern English: Trends, Forms and Texts* (Fasano:Schena): 13-37.

1993a   'Wynkyn de Worde: A Review of his Life and Work', in D. Buschinger and W. Spiewok (eds.), *Etudes de linguistique et de litterature en l'honneur d'André Crépin* (Greifswald: Reineke Verlag): 21-40.

1993b   '"Do the green sour ringlets make" (*The Tempest* V.i.37)', *Notes and Queries* 238: 201-202.

1993c   'From Old to Middle English', in T.F. Lema (ed.), *Papers from the IVth International Conference of the Spanish Society for Medieval English Language and Literature* (Santiago: University of Santiago Press): 19-33.

1993d   'Editing the Canterbury Tales: An Overview', in N.F. Blake and P. Robinson (eds.), *The Canterbury Tales Project Occasional Papers* (Oxford: Office for Humanities Communication): I, 5-18.

1993e   'Early Printed Editions of *Confessio Amantis*', *Mediaevalia* 16: 289-306.

1994a   'Periods and Premisses in a History of English', in F. Fernández *et al.* (eds.), *English Historical Linguistics 1992* (Amsterdam: Benjamins): 37-46.

1994b   'Antony and Cleopatra II.ii.56-58', *Lore and Language* 11.2: 223-26.

1994c   'Some Recent Developments in the English Language', in H.P Longo (ed.), *Atti del Seminario di Studi sul Lessico* (Bologna: CLUEB): 87-99.

1995a   'Speech and Writing: An Historical Overview', *Yearbook of English Studies* 25: 6-21.

1995b   'Shakespeare and Discourse', *Stylistica* 2/3: 81-90.

1995c   'The Canterbury Tales Project', *Archiv* 232: 126-33.

1995d   'The Ellesmere Text in the Light of the Hengwrt Manuscript', in M. Stevens and D. Woodward (eds.), *The Ellesmere Chaucer: Essays in Interpretation* (San Marino, CA: Huntington Library; Tokyo: Yushodo): 205-24.

1996a   'Lexical Links in Shakespeare', *Poetica* (Tokyo) 45: 79-103.

1996b   'Holofernes' Lyric in *Love's Labour's Lost* Act IV Scene II', in S. Horlacher and M. Islinger (eds.), *Expedition nach der Wahrheit: Poems, Essays and Papers in Honour of Theo Stemmler* (Heidelberg: Winter):177-91.

1996c   'Shakespeare's Language: Past Achievements and Future Directions', in J.P. Guerra (ed.), *Proceedings of the XIXth International Conference of Aedean* (Vigo: Universidade de Vigo): 21-35.

1997a   'The Project's Lineation System', in N.F. Blake and P. Robinson (eds.), *The Canterbury Tales Project Occasional Papers* (London: Office for Humanities Communication): II, 5-14.

1997b   'Chancery English and the Wife of Bath's Prologue', in T. Neval-
             ainen and L. Kahlas-Tarkka (eds.), *To Explain the Present: Studies in
             the Changing English Language in Honour of Matti Rissanen* (Helsinki:
             Societé Neophilologique): 3-24.
1997c   'Some Comments on the Style of Love's *Mirror of the Blessed Life of
             Jesus Christ*', in S. Oguro *et al.* (eds.), *Nicholas Love at Waseda: Pro-
             ceedings of the International Conference 20–22 July 1995* (Cambridge:
             Brewer): 99-114.
1997d   'Editing Shakespeare: The Role of Language Studies', *European
             Journal of Language Studies* 1.3: 329-53.
1997e   'Geoffrey Chaucer and the Manuscripts of the *Canterbury Tales*', *Jour-
             nal of the Early Book Society for the Study of Manuscripts and Printing
             History* 1: 96-122.
1997f   'The Phylogeny of the *Canterbury Tales*', *Nature* 394 [29 August]: 839
             (with A.C. Barbrook, C.J. Howe and P. Robinson).
1998a   'Standardisation of English and the Wife of Bath's Prologue', in
             M. Kanno *et al.* (eds.), *A Love of Words: English Philological Studies in
             Honour of Akira Wada* (Tokyo: Eihosha): 3-24.
1998b   'Reflections on the Editing of Middle English Texts', in V.P.
             McCarren and D. Moffatt (eds.), *A Guide to Editing Middle English*
             (Ann Arbor: University of Michigan Press): 61-77.
1998c   'Editing the *Canterbury Tales*': Preliminary Observations', *Anglia* 116:
             198-214.
1998d   'Prose, Middle English', in P.E. Szarmach *et al.* (eds.), *Medieval
             England: An Encyclopedia* (New York: Garland): 617-19.
1998e   'Shakespeare's Sonnet 69', *Notes and Queries* 243: 355-57.

Reports
1993   *Peer Review of the Teaching of English Studies in Finnish Universities*
             (with J. Svartik and G. Toury; Helsinki: Ministry of Education).
1998   *Engelskuddannelserne* (with G.D. Caie *et al.*; Copenhagen: Evaluer-
             ingscenteret).

Audio Material
1985a   *Life in Chaucer's England:* Audio Learning (with J.D. Burnley; cas-
             sette with supplementary notes).
1985b   *Courtly Love.* Audio Learning (with J.D. Burnley; cassette with sup-
             plementary notes).
1985c   *The Miller's Tale.* Audio Learning (with J.D. Burnley; cassette with
             supplementary notes).

Part I

Geoffrey Chaucer

Scogan, Shirley's Reputation and Chaucerian Occasional Verse

David Burnley

Medieval authors were perturbed by the fragility of the medium in which they were forced to operate. Parchment was durable, but they were well aware that scribal copying of their texts was likely to efface their achievement. Christine de Pizan took a defiant attitude, quoting Ovid on the indestructible nature of poetry, and interpreting it

> comme livres qui tost sont ventillés en plusieurs pars par diverses copies n'en puist estre distruitte la matiere (Solente 1940: II, 132) [in the sense that the subject matter of books quickly scattered by the wind in various quarters through multiple copying can never be destroyed].

However, her use of the word *matiere* 'subject matter' is significant, for she is talking of content rather than poetry. Robert Mannyng of Bourne had noted the fate which had befallen the work of Thomas of Erceldoune (Furnivall 1887: I, 3-4), and resolved to write more simply himself, hoping by this strategy to preserve his meaning. Chaucer expected *Troilus and Criseyde* to be mismetred, and had doubts about the ability of even its subject matter to survive in understandable condition, vanishing like the icy letters in the *House of Fame*. Such uncertainties of language and transmission were the occasion of Norman Blake's attempt to revise attitudes to the criticism of medieval poetry over 20 years ago. Linguistic and cultural contexts were considered to define what was possible in terms of literary effects and to constrain distribution and survival.[1]

In the light of posterity, these authors had some justification for their pessimism. Viewed from a modern perspective, a medieval poem is a whodunit with a cast of mutually unacquainted protagonists, any one of whom may have contributed to the demise of the author's meaning. The prime suspects, of course, have always been the scribes, who, although hard to distinguish from the early editors and commentators, are reckoned to be less responsible with regard to the author's text. Early editors may have been well disposed to the author's meaning but were sometimes so eager to help that they made additions to the text, or added marginal graffiti of dubious authority. But there are those among them who were less scrupulous, and may even have stolen the author's text and meaning for their own uses.[2] Modern editors and textual scholars have, of course, impeccable motives, but sometimes miss the wood among the trees, becoming embroiled in minor textual variants which are unlikely to have any interpretative significance. More recently literary critics have usurped the role of the scribes as chief suspects in the drama, and indeed some hide their crime by denying the very existence of the author's meaning. Nevertheless, although it may be difficult to find it alive and well, authorial meaning was the expressed purpose of medieval poetry.[3] Medieval poets wrote within a historical, social and linguistic context, in which they intended their meaning to emerge. The purpose of this essay is to try by examining the means of distribution,

1. The argument was presented in a strong form in Blake (1976) and in a more extensive but more attenuated fashion in Blake (1977).

2. Allusion and borrowings within a single literary tradition, such as that of courtly lyrics, is unsurprising and often unobtrusive, but there is often obvious but unashamed plagiarism. The prose *Julius Chronicle* (Kingsford 1905, 97-115) suddenly turns to verse as it quotes without acknowledgment Lydgate's poem on the entry of Henry VI into London following his coronation in Paris in 1430.

3. Medieval poets would have found the 'intentional fallacy' puzzling, since they regarded the transmission of their intended meaning as the major yardstick of their art. This perspective is mirrored in Chaucer's use of the verb *to mene*, which overwhelmingly has a personal subject (Burnley 1996: 229).

the authors, audience and language, to restore this meaningful context in a single interesting case.

Of all Chaucer's works, Christine's confidence in semantic survival is hardest to justify among his short poems, which are particularly tattered and windblown leaves, whose meaning depends so often on their relationship to uncertain occasions and authority. Among these there is a particularly intriguing nexus of historical incident, intertextuality, scribal graffiti, and manuscript variation in the case of the *Envoy to Scogan*, the moral balade *Gentilesse*, and Scogan's own *Moral Balade*, printed by Skeat in his collection of 'Chaucerian Pieces' (Skeat 1894–97: VII, 237-44). Without expecting to answer confidently all the questions of authorship, occasion, genre and purpose which these poems raise, it would seem appropriate to the dedicatee of this volume to raise some doubts about established opinions and to offer a few alternative interpretations which some may regard as rash, but which are nevertheless not entirely unsupportable.

Let us start with the case of Scogan's *Moral Balade*, a poem whose attribution depends on a very extended scribal annotation. John Shirley, as was his habit (Brusendorff 1925: 207-95; Hammond 1927: 191-97), writes an introductory note telling us at the beginning of his copy in Bodleian MS Ashmole 59 that:

> here foloweþe next a moral balade to my lord þe Prince, to my lord of Clarence, to my lord of Bedford and to my lorde of Gloucestre by Henry Scogan at a souper of feorþe [worthy] merchande in þe vyntre in london at þe hous of Lowys Iohan (Furnivall 1879: 427).

A similar introduction distinguishes Caxton's print of the poem:

> Here next foloweth a tretyse whiche Iohn Skogan Sente vnto the lordes and gentil men of the kynges hows exortyng them to lose no tyme in theyr yougthe, but to vse vertues (Boyd 1978: 19-24).

The two claims are broadly similar, but there are very significant differences. Shirley regards this as a *moral balade*, Caxton as a *tretyse*; Shirley connects it with a very specific occasion and personnel, Caxton with a social milieu. Most strikingly, Shirley attributes it to Henry Scogan, Caxton to Scogan's elder brother, John. If only one of these introductions had survived, we would have been disposed to accept it, but since the two contradict each other, who are we to believe? Norman Blake has taught us to regard Caxton's assertions of association with an aristocratic audience in the light of his business interests, but Caxton is after all the 'Father of English Printing' while most modern scholars regard Shirley as a scurvy scrivener, the sort who copies *thenkepe* as *then kepe*,[4] and has been repeatedly condemned as a 'gossip'.[5] Caxton made his reputation with the new technology; Shirley has never had much of one. Moreover, he seems to have written Ashmole 59 at the age of nearly 90 (Hammond 1907: 321). The fact is, however, that Shirley is probably the more reliable witness. John Scogan rarely visited London, and was dead by 1392, so that unless one believes that the author of the *Moral Balade* would commend the soul of a living man to God, he cannot be the author of the poem (Hallmundsson 1981: 131). But proving Caxton wrong does not prove Shirley right. Can we find evidence to support his opinion on authorship?

First of all, it is useful to try to develop a profile of the man himself, and here historical researches are crucial. According to Blomefield's history of Norfolk, Henry Scogan (more often *Scoggon*) was a *capellanus* who became lord of a cluster of manors about four miles south-west of Fakenham in about 1391–92 at the age of 30, and died in 1407 (Blomefield 1805–10: VII, 139-42).[6] Scogan seems to have shared mutual acquaintances with Chaucer in London as early as 1387 (Hallmundsson 1981: 132), but succession to his manor established him there, and he appears in the employ of Richard II perhaps as early as 1392/93 (Lenaghan 1975: 46), and certainly by 1394. He survived the deposition, accepting the role of tutor to the sons of Henry IV at about the same time as John Payne—an old family friend and another Norfolk man—became the king's butler. Payne was also known to Chaucer, and when he relinquished his post in 1402, he was

---

4.   The mistranscription is in MS Ashmole 59, line 57 (see Furnivall 1879: 427).

5.   The epithet 'gossiping', which seems to have originated with Bradshaw, is repeated in Hammond (1927: 191) and echoed in Pearsall (1970: 74). To term anyone a gossip does not necessarily mean that their evidence is discredited, but there is a tendency to understand gossip as vain.

6.   Blomefield is probably the source for Skeat's vague recollection of having 'seen it noted' that he died at the age of 46 (Skeat 1894–97: VII, xlii).

succeeded in it by the poet's son, Thomas. Scogan's own son, Robert, continued the family acquaintance with the Paynes, granting the Norfolk manors of Haviles and Rouse to Payne in 1410.

Historical records therefore associate Chaucer with a Norfolk circle in the final decade of the fourteenth century, but can Scogan's poem be attached to it? Perhaps it can, through its language. The poem survives in three manuscript and two early printed versions: **A**, **H³**, **C¹**, **Cx** and **Th**.[7] Copyists, editors and compositors have stamped their own linguistic usages on the various copies. **Th** achieves the greatest consistency, adopting some spellings of the Chaucer tradition, with some modernizing; **A** has imposed characteristic Shirley spellings (Brusendorff 1925: 218-19) found elsewhere in his copied works; and there are characteristic Caxtonisms in Caxton's text. **H³** exhibits a distinct North Midland colouring, whilst **C¹** preserves some more southerly forms in common with **A**, but generally updates the spelling with North Midland forms. Viewing the textual tradition as a whole, the

---

7. The following sigils are used in this essay:

A	Bodleian Ashmole 59 (Shirley's complete text of the *Moral Balade*, including *Gentilesse*. c. 1450)
A⁴	British Library Additional 22139 (first half of fifteenth century)
C	British Library Cotton Cleopatra D.vii (early fifteenth century)
C¹	Cambridge University Library Ff.4.9 (incomplete text of *Moral Balade*; later fifteenth century)
Cov	Coventry City Record Office (mid-fifteenth century)
Cx	Caxton's *Temple of Bras* (1478). Printed version of *Moral Balade*, which contains seven lines of *Gentilesse*.
H³	British Library Harley 2251 (contains two incomplete versions, one consisting of only two stanzas; later fifteenth century)
H⁴	British Library Harley 7333 ('Shirleian' manuscript of second half of fifteenth century)
H⁵	British Library Harley 7578 (late fifteenth century)
Hg	National Library of Wales Hengwrt 154 (very early fifteenth century)
Nott	Nottingham University Library Me LM 1 (second half of fifteenth century)
R²	Trinity College, Cambridge, R.3.20 (Shirley MS; mid fifteenth century)
R⁴	Trinity College, Cambridge, R.14.51 (second half of fifteenth century; contains seven lines of *Gentilesse*)
Th	Thynne's 1532 print of *Moral Balade*, which contains *Gentilesse*.

spellings are relatively colourless, and no text is very dialectally revealing. However, there is a method by which the texts in combination may be made more informative. We may assume that, if the poem were written by Scogan, then it would have been written in London. It is then possible to compare the forms found in all these early versions against the backdrop of forms found in contemporary London documents. By this means a picture of the status of the variants in the entire textual tradition will emerge. For example, if a particular form is revealed by this process to be rare in the London language of the time, then it must be assumed to be either a form introduced by a non-London copyist or else a non-London relict form descended from an earlier manuscript. If the form can then be paired with many other dialectally coherent forms, two possibilities arise: either we may be dealing with the work of a 'translating' scribe from outside the area, but resident in London; or, if these forms are sporadic in occurrence and alien in London but still form a dialectally coherentpattern across more than one text, then we may be justified in interpreting them as true relicts from the original version of the work.

The following table illustrates the occurrence of such forms as variant readings in the texts.

Cx	Th	H^3	C^1	A
of wylke	of whiche	of whiche	off whiche	of whiche
moche	moche	moche	moche	michil
gyue	yeue	gyve	yeue	gif
geue	yeue	yive	yeue	gyf
gyuen	yeue	-	-	give
gyue	yeue	yeve	yeue	gif
forgete	forget	foryete	foryete	forgete
gete	haue	gete	-	gete
to + h + V	to + V	-	-	til + V
our	hir	theyr	her	þeire
theire	her	theyr	-	þeire
can	can	-	-	wol
wil	wolde	wil	woll	wol
wil	wol	wil	will	wol
wil	wol	wil	-	wil
wil	wolde	-	-	wil

Caxton's form *wylke* is highly unusual, found in no other text of the *Moral Balade*, unparalleled in London texts, and not normally used by Caxton. Shirley's *michil* is equally notable. All other texts of the *Moral Balade* have the normal London form *moche* at this point. *Michel* is common in earlier London texts, and is for example the normal form of Hand 1 of the Auchinleck MS and of the Bodley version of *Kyng Alisaunder*, but the spelling in which the unstressed syllable contains <i> is unparalleled, and *mich-* or *mych-* forms are very rare in London by the end of the fourteenth century, when *moche(l)* and *mochil* predominate.

The forms of *give* exhibit an interesting degree of variation. The best Chaucer manuscripts show a marked preference for the South Midland spelling *yeue*, with a much lower incidence of the southern *yiue*. The more northerly form with an initial plosive, *gyue*, is rare in Chaucer, occuring once only in the Hengwrt manuscript (*CT* III.501). This Chaucerian distribution of forms is similar to that found in contemporary London documents, where the Scandinavian-derived <g-> spellings are relatively uncommon throughout the first half of the fifteenth century, appearing first in petitions about 1422. The word *forget* also had a palatal consonant in Old English (*forȝietan*, ME *foryit*), and the modern form is analogically restored from the simplex *get*, derived from the Scandinavian *geta*. All texts of the *Moral Balade* have *get*, except Thynne's, where the word has simply been replaced by *haue*. The reason for this substitution can only be guessed at: *get* is more common in northerly texts, but is quite widely used both by Chaucer and in other London documents. It may, however, have seemed to Thynne somewhat colloquial and unpoetic. The preposition *til* with the sense 'motion towards' is also generally considered to have descended from Scandinavian usage. It is very rare in this sense in documentary prose, but is exploited frequently by Chaucer in the *Canterbury Tales* as a syllabic variant of *to* used before a following vowel in order to avoid elision. Nevertheless, in the texts of the Auchinleck manuscript its association is most marked with works like *Sir Tristrem* and *Horn Childe* which have passed through a northern copying stage. Oblique forms of the third-person plural pronoun in <th-> were similarly associated with the North in Chaucer's time, but had already occurred rarely in the Auchinleck manuscript. By 1415, the word was becoming increasingly frequent in documentary sources, but now with the spelling <their> rather than <thair>. The variation between *wil* and *wol* likewise reflects the extension of a minority variant of northern origin which gradually replaced the London form *wol*. The latter is still more common in Hengwrt, but *wil* seems to be a deliberate choice in the context of the *Reeve's Tale*. However it is also used in the *Wife's Prologue*, and Ellesmere has an increased number of examples of *wil* throughout as compared with Hengwrt. In London documents there may be a social distinction, since *wil* is found quite early among Guild returns, and *wol* is characteristic of Signet documents.

To summarize, there appears to be in the textual tradition of the *Moral Balade* a certain northern colouring, which would be noticeable, but which would not seem outlandish, in London in the decades preceding and succeeding the turn of the century. The clerk of the tower ward in 1422 uses the form *gayt* for 'goat', and Thomas Usk, in his Appeal (1384), used northern forms of the third-person pronoun. Records of petitions in parliament, although not really standardized at this period, are mostly written in a colourless language of East Midland type, but a York petition of 1425 (*Rotuli Parliamentorum* IV.290) contains the words *agayn-*, *hafes, kyrke, mykell, qwos/qwat, theire/thaire* and the third-person singular *-es*, and a letter from the Bishop of Durham (c. 1417) has the forms *kirk* and *kist* (Fisher *et al.* 1984: no. 112). The will of Richard Roos of Beverley (1406) has the forms *kyrke* and *wylk* (Furnivall 1882: 12) and a petition from one Mydelton of Holderness (c. 1425) has a rich northern vocabulary: *agayn-, kyrke, lange, lyuand, mykill, qwhylk*, the third-person pronoun form *yair*, and third-person present tense verbal endings in *-es* (Fisher *et al.* 1984: no. 173). More striking than this are the accounts given in 1399 of Chief Justice William Thirnyng's words to Richard II at his deposition (*Rotuli Parliamentorum* III.424; 451-52). Thirnyng's origin is unknown, but according to *DNB* he had spent at least eight years as a Justice of Assize in the North before his appointment in London, and the reports contain a significant number of forms which contrast with their context: *agayn-, gif-, kyrk, mykel, sall, thair, wil*. It is unlikely that the Chancery scribe would have attempted to reproduce the actual manner of speech of the Chief Justice of Common Pleas, but he seems at the very least to have preserved some of the forms used by a long-serving secretary.

What is the implication of this for Scogan? The various texts of the *Moral Balade* contain a scattering of northern forms, and among these familiar northernisms there seem to have been two truly unusual forms, *wylke* and *michil*. If considered to be true relicts from the original, which Scogan says was *writen with myn owne hand* (4), they can be treated as a scribal profile. The only match which *LALME* can offer for this group of forms is that for British Library MS Harley 1035, a text of the *Scale of Perfection* which is localized in Fakenham, Norfolk. This may be pure chance, but there is a strong temptation to believe that this profile of relict forms in the textual tradition of the *Moral Balade* justifies Shirley in his attribution of the work to Henry Scogan, late of Fakenham, Norfolk.

His further remarks which place the poem on the occasion of a dinner given for the royal princes by the merchant Lewis John also sound plausible. John was a Welshman with premises in the Vintry, who had been trading illegally in wines, since the Welsh had been restricted by a statute of the second year of Henry IV from holding lands in England and from becoming burgesses. He was apparently tolerated and patronized, for in 1414 he petitioned Parliament in the company of Thomas Chaucer and John Snypston to recover 40 marks for the supply of wine to Henry IV (*Rotuli Parliamentorum* IV.37). A second petition in the same year (*Rotuli Parliamentorum* IV.44) was intended to regularize his legal position so as to enable his family to inherit his business. Both petitions proved successful, and it may be that influential contacts played some part in their success. On February 8 1423 he is described in the Ordinances of the Privy Council (iii.24) as *armiger* and became Seneschal and Receiver General of the Duchy of Cornwall. The probability that Shirley might have been aware of the career of Lewis John has been increased by Ian Doyle's demonstration that Shirley not only had aristocratic contacts, but that from 1429 at the latest he lived not half a mile from John's house in the Vintry, and mingled with much the same London society (Doyle 1961).

Scogan wrote his *Moral Balade* some time between Chaucer's death in 1400 and his own in 1407. This was at a time when Chaucer's literary reputation had been established, but before the great expansion in the copying of his works which took place after the accession of Henry V in 1413. He was at this time an author whose works were known and respected by a relatively limited circle of gentlemen in the royal court, functionaries, and wealthy London merchants. It was not simply a parochial reputation, however, since Deschamps had praised his translations of Boethius and the *Roman de la Rose*, and recognized him as a fellow author as early as 1386. *Boece* and *Troilus and Criseyde* were well known and alluded to by Usk (c. 1387 *Testament of Love* III.iv.254) and Gower (1390 *Confessio Amantis*, ed. Macaulay 1900–1901: 7598-602) (also 1376 *Miroir de l'Omme*, trans. Wilson 1992: 5249). By 1402 Hoccleve was referring to the *Legend of Good Women* (*Letter of Cupid*, 316-18) and was paralleled in this by Edward, Duke of York some time between 1406 and 1413 (Baillie-Grohman 1904). Although few of these allusions precede the death of Chaucer, it would be perverse to believe that many of Chaucer's works were not known in some form among his circle before 1400. The most striking example of this is that Scogan quotes the poem *Gentilesse* in its entirety.

His rendering of it is interesting in two ways: first because it illustrates how even a strong admirer of Chaucer, not long after his death, felt justified in adapting his text, and secondly because it suggests that Scogan may have had his own copy of the poem, which in some places contained superior readings. The table below cites significant variants in the 11 extant manuscript versions:

A	Cx	H³	H⁴	R²	R⁴
foundour	stok	stok	fynder	fynder	stokke
grounde of	ful of	fader of	ful of	grounde of	-
suwe	folowe	loue	shew	suwe	shewe
claymeþe	claymeth	claymeth	desirith	desyreþe	kleymyght
þou	men	man	ye	yee	-

C	H⁵	A⁴	Cov	Nott
stocke	strooke	stok	stokke	stokke
full of	ful of	ful of	ful of	ful of
loue	loue	loue	love	love
desireth	desireth	coucyteth	coueitith	cleymeth
men	men	men	men	men

These variants are not very helpful in developing a traditional stemma or deciding a base manuscript, although some readings are clearly much less satisfactory than others. But the nature of the variation is sometimes instructive in a different way. In the first row the reading of H^5 can obviously be discarded as an error. Since the rest of the manuscript tradition (omitting the 'Shirleian' H^4) asserts the reading *first stok (&) fader*, the Shirley readings *first fader and foundour* (A) and *first fader fynder* (R^2) seem to suggest Shirley's uneasiness with the word *stok*. What has been substituted at different copyings are two colourless phrases which *MED* (*foundour* 3[a] and *findere* 2[a]) reveals to be semi-formulaic. The first is often used to refer to founders of institutions, and the latter in characteristic aetiological statements like *Cereris...was e firste Fynder of wheete*. But Shirley's limitations are not so easily invoked to justify the variation in the second row (where we can discard H^3 as error). The majority of manuscripts, including the 'Shirleian' H^4, read *ful of*, but the two Shirley manuscripts A and R^2 read *grounde of*. There is little doubt that Shirley's is the more 'difficult' reading. In row three the Shirley texts both have *suwe*, for which *shew* (H^4 and R^4) must simply be an error. Most manuscripts have *love*, which may stem from a simple misreading earlier in a common ancestor; but Caxton, encountering the word *suwe* in his copy-text, characteristically substitutes a more familiar lexical item, *folowe*. The implication of these variants complements the argument of a more difficult reading with a clear evolutionary path for the variants, which again suggests the superior nature of Shirley's source for A.[8] Row four is mainly a fluctuation between *claymeth* and *desireth*, with *coueitith* as a sporadic variant, probably suggested by the latter. Like the variation in the final row between *þou*, *ye*, and *man/men*, it does not seem easily explicable within the limits of the poem *Gentilesse*. However, if the versions of the *Moral Balade* are also taken into account, the circumstances of the variation are more understandable. The poem contains a system of address to its imagined audience which

---

8.   Hammond (1907: 345-46) believed that Shirley wrote Ashmole 59 partly from memory because she could not come to terms with his freedom with his exemplar; but she did acknowledge that he may also have used an earlier manuscript of his own, which is now lost.

fluctuates between the general and the particular in various texts. For example, **C** reflects on the behaviour of young men in general: *But ye yonge men haue a manner nowe-a-dayes,* and Thynne refers broadly to the behaviour of the upper classes: *Many lordes haue a maner nowe-a-dayes.* Shirley's text **A** however stays true to its putative audience of the royal princes (*For yee lordes of coustume nowe-a-dayes*) and normally uses the address-forms *ye* and *ye lordes.* It deviates from this only in quoting *Gentilesse,* where line 16 reads: *But þere may no man as þou maist wele seeme.* The switch to the singular pronoun is justified by the singular context and the admonitory tone.[9] Within the *Moral Balade,* as reported by Shirley, the address forms of Chaucer's poem have been modified for a particular audience, the royal princes. This modification also neatly explains the substitution in line 2, where *claymeþe* in the *Moral Balade* text replaces *desireth* in most of the manuscript tradition.

The abuses of copyists and editors against the author's text are sins both of omission and commission. Shirley's careless errors seem to have been accompanied by the occasional deliberate change, in the same way that Caxton occasionally made lexical substitutions. Nevertheless, the evidence suggests not only that Shirley was probably justified in his introductory claims about the occasion of the *Moral Balade,* but that Scogan had privileged access to a copy of *Gentilesse* as well as knowledge of other works of Chaucer, some of which may not have been widely known at the time of the composition of his poem. He both refers to *Boece* and paraphrases Book I, Metre 6, turning it to his own purpose. The accumulation of the *exempla* of Nero, Balthasar and Antiochus forms a pattern which suggests familiarity also with the *Monk's Tale,* but most arresting is his evident knowledge of the *Wife of Bath's Tale.* In view of Chaucer's *Envoy to Bukton,* which refers to the *Prologue,* Scogan's ability to paraphrase the Wife's conventional teachings on *gentilesse* in the *Tale* may not be surprising, but his accurate quotation of two lines is more worthy of note. The various texts read as follows:

---

9.   Use of the singular form of the second-person pronoun is characteristic of admonitory discourse, and overrides considerations of relative rank when a clerk adopts an instructional role to princes (see Burnley 1986 and 1990).

H³   Thus by youre auncestris ye may nothyng clayme
As that my maister Chauncer sayde
But temporal thyng that man may hurt and mayme

A   By avncetrye þus may yee no-thing clayme
As þat my maistre Chaucier doþe expresse
But temporell thinge þat man may hurte and mayme

Cx   Thus by your eldres ye may nothing claime
As my maister chawcer seith expresse
But temperal thing that may hurte and mayme

These lines correspond to the reading of the Hengwrt manuscript lines 1105-106:

> For of oure eldres may we nothyng clayme
> But temporel thyng that man may hurte and mayme.

The variation here between *auncetr-* and *eldres* seems not to have been generated within the textual tradition of the *Moral Balade*, since it is reflected in the textual history of the *Wife of Bath's Tale* itself, where well-regarded early manuscripts such as Harley 7334 and CUL Dd.4.24 have this reading. It seems likely that *auncetr-*, found in all texts except **Cx**, was Scogan's original reading, in which case Caxton may have substituted *eldres* from his own copy of the *Canterbury Tales*, which he printed in the same year. In any case, it seems that Scogan had access to a version of the *Wife of Bath's Tale* which at this point had an early and independent ancestor distinct from Hengwrt and Ellesmere.

The final piece in this jigsaw of associated works and historical records is Chaucer's *Envoy to Scogan*, a poem of which the tone and purpose have been the subject of some dispute among critics. How does it fit into the relationships implied above, and can awareness of the implications of its language help to settle these questions? The poem, which is in the form of a brief verse epistle, is in some respects typically Chaucerian, commencing with elevated rhetoric and quickly descending to an ironic colloquialism. Scogan's behaviour has, it seems, caused a dislocation of cosmic law, to the extent that Venus, supposedly located beyond sublunary disturbance, has been moved to tears, which drench the earth. The cause of it seems to be Scogan's renunciation of a lady who has shown him no sympathy, and in this renunciation he has called Cupid as a witness. Chaucer mockingly points out that

Cupid is unlikely to waste arrows on such unpropitious targets as Scogan and himself, but he nevertheless fears that guilt by association may bring some other vengeance on all grey-haired old men of portly appearance. And just in case Scogan feels he is initiating a comic correspondence on this matter, he denies this intention, for his days of writing such verses are over. With a sudden change in tone, the envoy follows (lines 43-49), and is worth quoting in full:

> Scogan, that knelest at the stremes hed
> Of grace, of alle honour and worthynesse,
> In th'ende of which strem I am dul as ded,
> Forgete in solytarie wildernesse—
> Yet, Scogan, thenke on Tullius kyndenesse;
> Mynne thy frend, there it may fructyfye!
> Far-wel, and loke thow never eft Loue dyffye.

All the early manuscripts contain marginal glosses which seek to contextualize this envoy, identifying the *stremes/welles hede* as Windsor and either the *solytarie wildernesse* (Gg.4.27) or *thende of which streme* (Fairfax, Pepys) as Greenwich. These glosses are clearly quite early, and are apparently authoritative, belonging to two independent textual traditions. Despite the fact that the second gloss is evidently misplaced in Gg.4.27, the manuscript commands respect as an early attempt to make a collection of Chaucer's works. Furthermore, it is associated with East Anglia, and spells Scogan's name (*Scoggon*) in the manner of contemporary historical documents. Such marginal glosses are a fatal temptation to many modern critics, who seem prepared to believe that they can cast light on texts which themselves prove resistant to interpretation. But these glosses, unlike Shirley's commentaries, cannot be contextualized; they have no known history, nor can they be analysed linguistically. Despite Furnivall's opinion that the glosses descend from the author, and the acceptance of them as literally true in Benson (1987: 1087), it seems *a priori* rash to take them seriously. Rather, they read like the rationalizations of a peculiarly literal-minded critic congratulating himself on his knowledge that Chaucer had had a house in Greenwich until 1396 and that the royal court was sometimes at Windsor. Greenwich could scarcely be described as a wilderness, and it is no more at the end of the Thames than Windsor is at the head. The lines themselves make far better sense read as conventional metaphor (David 1968–69), and they can be shown to be so by a comparison of their language.

The phrase *stremes hede of grace* is a genitive construction paralleled In phrases like the *Wifes loue of Bathe*, and is best understood as a reference to the 'head or source of the stream of grace'. Grace and favour spring from the king before whom Scogan is said to kneel at court, wherever that may be situated. The liquid metaphor of grace is a ubiquitous one: it is imagined as a *welle* in the *Parliament of Fowls*, 129 (Cambridge University Library Gg.4.27) and Gower's *Confessio Amantis* VIII.1900. Hoccleve refers to the *spryng and sours* of grace in his *Balade for Chichele*, 105. Scogan, it seems, is in favour; Chaucer is out, beyond the furthest reaches of the stream of grace in a *solytarie wildernesse*. Here the word *solytarie* potentially carries with it powerful associations not just of separateness, but of voluntary withdrawal from the world for the purposes of religion. If so, the figure of Chaucer as a recluse with Scogan as the successful entrepreneur is not without irony, for although it glances back to Scogan's treachery in love, the purpose of the envoy is a serious request, based upon friendship, for help in re-establishing worldly credit. The instruction to remember a friend where it may bear fruit would be unmistakable even if the associations of the verb *fructifie* were not as they are. In fact, before it became an item of aureate diction the root *fruct-* was rare, but is associated in various contexts with benefit, usually of a moral or religious kind, though in administrative prose *fruct-* and *fruit* had a much more practical significance associated with profit. It has here a subtly ironic tinge, in key with the inflated language of much of the poem and the society from which it arose. Chaucer seems to be asking a well-placed friend to fix something for him. Although he received the arrears on his pay as Clerk of the Works and an annuity of £20 in February 1394 and a further gift of £10 in January 1393, it is impossible to relate a poem such as this to such specific occasions, since the poem itself cannot be securely dated. It is tempting to read North Petherton for *solytarie wildernesse*, but there is no evidence that Chaucer ever went there, and it is as well to avoid falling into the trap which captured the early annotator, and to remember that we are dealing with images rather than factual information. All that is necessary for a poet to figure himself and his friend in the relative positions imagined in the envoy is a minor and temporary reversal of fortunes.

It is usually assumed that the injunction to *thenke on Tullius kyndenesse* is a reference to the author of *De amicitia*, which it may indeed be (Scattergood 1995: 507-508); but this would be inappropriate in an explicit request for profit from friendship. The more elevated kind of friendship is that between equals in which profit is not the motive. It is therefore equally possible that Chaucer is referring to another Tullius who was much less well known, but mutually familiar to Chaucer and his addressee: this is that Tullius Hostilius who is quoted in the *Wife of Bath's Tale*, 1140 and later by Scogan (*Moral Balade*, 166) as an exemplum of one who rose to power through merit (Phipps 1943). It is tempting to believe that in addition to recalling their friendship Chaucer is alluding to Scogan's own rise in fortune by an allusion to the *Wife of Bath's Tale* which he knew that he had read.

A detailed intertextual reading of the scattered remains of the poems which medieval poets wrote can thus help us to restore the meanings which they intended for their earliest audience. In order to do this, however, we need to be able to draw upon the variants made available by modern textual scholarship, and to combine that with a knowledge of the social history of the period; but most of all we need an awareness of the subtler meanings of the language, drawn from the contexts in which it was used. And to feel confident in reconstruction we need sufficient data of two or more of these different kinds.

Finally, the demonstrable tone of the *Envoy to Scogan* is sufficient to imply the known historical circumstances. Contrast it with the highly situated, informal and relaxed *Envoy to Bukton*, in which Chaucer seems unambiguously the senior partner patronizing a less experienced man. In *Scogan* the references are cosmological and apocalyptic, but undercut by comic disproportion and inappropriateness. It begins with an emphatic inversion of clause order to bring the violent word *tobroken* into initial prominence. A similar vehemence of expression is found in the emphatic negation (8-9) which asserts the eternity of the stability which Scogan's monstrous crime has disrupted. There is both a philosophical and a legal element in the poem's lexicon, and this is most significant in the sudden stylistic plunge of the allegation that Scogan 'gave up' his lady at Michaelmas. In this context the very phrase *gave up* sounds dismissively colloquial, but its associations are perhaps even more churlish. This phrasal verb is very rare in late.fourteenth-century London literature. Chaucer uses it on four other occasions, most comparably in *Anelida and Arcite* (*I yeve hit up for now and evermore* [343]), where it forms part of Anelida's renunciation of love. Elsewhere it occurs sparingly in administrative documents, meaning 'to offer up judgments, accounts or other documents'. Accounts were, of course, presented at Michaelmas by all kinds of officials, and government servants' salaries became due then. It was also the end of the farming year, when reeves completed their terms of office and new hirings were made.

The third stanza of the poem is focused on the couplet:

> That, for thy lady sawgh nat thy distresse,
> Therfore thow yave hir up at Michelmesse (18-19).

It is easy to read this simply as a conventional breach of the 'law of love' through inconstancy, but the first and final lines of the stanza make it clear that Scogan's offence is something he has *said* rather than *done*. It can only be that he has shared with Chaucer and his circle a *défiance* of love in which, using their common administrative language, he has called Cupid to witness as irrevocable (*to recorde*, 22) his dismissal of an unsatisfactory lady. He has simply renounced his love, but has used the language of the termination of a servant's contract at Michaelmas to do it. Penetrating the mythopoeic fabrications of Chaucer's poem, then, is the unsentimental voice of the practical administrator replying to Scogan and reminding him of their shared world of work and poetry before challenging him with the implied question of whether he has renounced a friend as well as a lover.

Works Cited

Baillie-Grohman, W.A., and F. Baillie-Grohman (eds.)
1904   *The Master of Game by Edward, Second Duke of York* (London: Ballantyne, Hanson).

Blake, N.F.
1976   'The English Language in Medieval Literature', *Studia Neophilologica* 48: 59-75.
1977   *The English Language in Medieval Literature* (London: Dent).

Blomefield, F.
1805–10   *An Essay towards a Topographical History of the County of Norfolk* (11 vols.; London: Miller).

Boyd, B. (ed.)
1978   *Chaucer According to William Caxton: Minor Poems and Boece, 1478* (Lawrence, KS: Allen Press).

Brusendorff, A.
1925   *The Chaucer Tradition* (Oxford: Clarendon Press).

Burnley, J.D.
1986   'Christine de Pizan and the So-called Style Clergial', *Modern Language Review* 81: 1-6.
1990   'Langland's Clergial Lunatic', in H. Phillips (ed.), *Langland, the Mystics and the Medieval English Religious Tradition: Essays in Honour of S.S. Hussey* (Cambridge: Brewer): 31-38.
1996   'Chaucer's Literary Terms', *Anglia* 114: 202-35.

David, A.
1968–69   'Chaucer's Good Counsel to Scogan', *Chaucer Review* 3: 265-74.

Doyle, A. I.
1961   'More Light on John Shirley', *Medium Aevum* 30: 93-101.

Fisher, J.H. *et al.*
1984   *An Anthology of Chancery English* (Knoxville: University of Tenessee Press).

Furnivall, F.J. (ed.)
1879   *Parallel Text Edition of Chaucer's Minor Poems* (London: Chaucer Society, 1st series 58, Part 3).
1882   *The Fifty Earliest English Wills* (EETS, 78; London: Trübner).
1887   *The Story of England by Robert Manning of Bourne* (2 vols.; London: Eyre & Spottiswoode, Records Commission IV.87)

Hallmundsson, M.N.
1981   'Chaucer's Circle: Henry Scogan and his Friends', *Medievalia et Humanistica* 10: 129-39.

Hammond, E.P.
1907   'Ashmole 59 and other Shirley Manuscipts', *Anglia* 30: 320-48.
1927   *English Verse between Chaucer and Surrey* (Durham, NC: Duke University Press).

Kingsford, C.L.
1905   *The London Chronicles* (Oxford: Clarendon Press)

Lenaghan, R.T.
1975   'Chaucer's *Envoy to Scogan*: The Uses of Literary Conventions',
            Chaucer Review 10: 46-61.
1983   'Chaucer's Circle of Gentlemen and Clerks', *Chaucer Review* 18: 155-
            60.
Macaulay, G.C. (ed.)
1900–1901   *The English Works of John Gower* (2 vols.; EETS ES, 81 and 82;
            London: Routledge & Kegan Paul).
Pearsall, D.
1970   *John Lydgate* (London: Kegan Paul, Trench, Trübner).
Phipps, T.M.
1943   'Chaucer's Tullius', *Modern Language Notes* 58: 108-109.
Scattergood, V.J.
1995   'The Shorter Poems', in A.J. Minnis (ed.), *Oxford Guide to Chaucer:
            The Shorter Poems* (Oxford: Clarendon Press): 455-512.
Skeat, W.W. (ed.)
1894–97   *The Complete Works of Geoffrey Chaucer* (7 vols.; Oxford: Clarendon
            Press).
Solente, S. (ed.)
1940   *Christine de Pisan: Le Livre des Fais et Bonnes Meurs du Sage Roy Charles
            V* (2 vols.; Paris: Champion).
Wilson, W.B. (trans.)
1992   *John Gower: Mirour de l'Omme* (East Lansing: Colleagues Press).

'This was a thrifty tale for the nones': Chaucer's Man of Law

Graham D. Caie

The *Man of Law's Introduction, Prologue* and *Tale* are undoubtedly among the most enigmatic works in the *Canterbury Tales*, presenting major problems of a textual and literary nature, as Norman Blake has clearly shown (1985: 84-86). In the *Introduction*, for example, we learn that a prose tale will follow, whereas the *Tale* is in rhyme royale (see Benson 1987: 854). Some critics feel that it was meant for another pilgrim, such as the Prioress or the Merchant, while others see it as a satire exposing either the teller or fourteenth-century middle-class sentimentality.[1] One can find a wide range of ironic interpretations and as many literal readings of this work, that has been called a hagiography, romance, folktale, romantic homily, religious exemplum, and Christian comedy (see Benson 1990a; 1990b; David 1967; Wood 1967; and Sullivan 1953). Such diversity in perception suggests an exceptionally subtle work that requires very careful reading. The Man of Law's performance would probably have been met by Chaucer's contemporary audience with as many conflicting interpretations as today. Some might have been greatly moved by an eloquent tale of the tribulations of an aristocratic saint, while others might have been offended by the narrator's theologically and morally questionable apostrophes on divine providence and his emphasis on worldly wealth. The upbeat conclusion that replaced Trivet's more

---

1. Ann W. Astel claims that the tale is about the 'popular piety of the time, with its misdirected veneration of the saints [which] threatened to obscure the true, exemplary power of their holy lives through "golden legends" and sensational displays' (1991: 96).

sombre ending would have been welcomed by those wishing to
see the saint live happily ever after, while those who were aware of
the narrator's debt to Innocent III's *De miseria* might have been
suspicious of such a prosperous end in this world for Custance.

The contemporary audience, however, was afforded some guidance in its reading of this complex tale by the glosses in the
manuscripts. The prominent appearance of the glosses on the
manuscript page would have demanded the attention of the
fifteenth-century reader and ought therefore to make us pause to
examine them today. The glosses certainly are not 'marginal' in
any sense of the word and are found in around 30 of the fifteenth-
century manuscripts containing the *Man of Law's Tale*. In the
Ellesmere and Hengwrt manuscripts they are placed centrally,
and have been given the same visual prominence as the text. In
the case of Ellesmere the text itself is placed to the left of the page
in order to give way to the glosses, while in both manuscripts they
are in the same hand and in as large a hand as the text, with the
same size of initial capitals. They are not simply source references,
but many are extended quotations which divert the reader's attention from the text to the source material. They were present in
the earliest versions of the *Canterbury Tales*, and were faithfully
copied throughout the fifteenth century. The glosses have never
been given their rightful place by editors; Manly and Rickert
transcribed some of the glosses 'when they seem important' in
their edition (Manly and Rickert 1940: III, 525). Robinson (1957)
gave a selection in the 'Explanatory Notes' to his edition,[2] while
the *Riverside Chaucer* (Benson 1987) translates most of the glosses
in the notes. It is only with the advent of electronic editing, such
as the Sheffield *Canterbury Tales* Project, that there is the possibility of restoring them to their correct place beside the text and not
hidden in endnotes.[3]

The majority of critics who have studied the glosses in detail
seems to agree that most were written by Chaucer himself. This

2.   In the explanatory notes to the *Man of Law's Tale* he adds comments
such as 'Four lines of the Latin [of Bernardus Silvester] are quoted in the
margins of several MSS' (693).

3.   Information about the Project is available on the Web at
http://www.shef.ac.uk/uni/projects/ctp/index.html and in the two volumes
CTP 1993 and *CTP* 1997.

might also explain why they were given such prominence on the page and were faithfully copied for a century. As they appear in manuscripts of the first decade of the fifteenth century, such as Ellesmere, Hengwrt and Cambridge University Library Dd.4.24, they were probably written during Chaucer's lifetime. Robert Enzer Lewis (1967: 13) has shown that the glosses in the *Man of Law's Tale* from Innocent III's *De miseria humane conditionis* probably came from the same source manuscript as that used by Chaucer when translating sections of this work in the *Tale*, and he also suggests that Chaucer was their author.[4]

The *Man of Law's Tale* is one of the most heavily glossed works in the *Canterbury Tales*; Manly and Rickert state that this tale has 'the most widely distributed glosses [and] the most learned' (1940: III, 525). They come from Bernardus Silvestris's *Cosmographia*, Pope Innocent III's *De miseria humane conditionis*, Ptolemy's *Almagest* and Zael's *Liber Electionum*, as well as the Vulgate. Even the briefest glosses have interpretative functions, such as the moral admonition in *cave ebrietatem*. Simple glosses such as *nota bene* arrest our reading, while the marginal *descripcio constancie* does more than signal the entrance of Custance. As the phrase generally appears in popular romances to signal the description of the conventional romance heroine, there is a suggestion that the glossator considered the tale a romanticized saint's life, such as those criticized by Wycliffe.[5]

4.   Lewis states that 'It is therefore extremely likely, and in fact the only reasonable conclusion, that not only is the manuscript used for Chaucer's paraphrase *practically* identical to the one used for the glosses, but they are one and the same manuscript. And if this is so, the glosses were written either by Chaucer in his autograph copy of the *Man of Law's Tale*, or by a scribe under Chaucer's supervision from Chaucer's own manuscript of the *De Miseria*, or by a scribe shortly after Chaucer's death from that same manuscript found among Chaucer's papers.' Lewis in the same article (1967: 2-3) lists the critics who support the argument of Chaucerian authorship. See also my comments on the possibility of Chaucer's authorship of some of the glosses (Caie 1977: 354-55).

5.   See Keiser (1990: 125) and Astel (1991: 96). Wycliffe warns about these 'fals prophetis, techinge fals cronyclis & fablis to colour here worldly lif therby...for thei louen welle to telle hou this seynt or this lyuede in gay & costy clothis & worldly aray, & yit is a grete seynt. But they leuen to teche the grete penaunce & sorow that thei diden after ward, for which thei pleseden god & not for here worldly lif, & thus thei make the peple to wene that

In this essay I shall examine the first three major glosses in the tale, all of which are of an astrological nature, to demonstrate their function as commentary on the narrator. The first major gloss in the tale is at line 197: it gives examples of patterns of human behaviour that can be read in the stars:

> Ceptra Phorenei fratrum discordia Thebe fflammam Phetontis Deucalionis Aque In stellis Priami species Audacia Turni Sensus Vlixeus Herculeusque vigor.

This comes from the first book of Bernardus Silvestris's *Cosmographia*, the *Megacosmos*. In Peter Dronke's edition (Dronke 1978) this passage appears as:

> Sceptra Phoronei, fratrum discordia Thebe,
> Flamme Phetontis, Deucalionis aque;...
> In stellis Priami species, audatia Turni,
> Sensus Ulixeus, Herculeusque vigor (39-40, 43-44).

> [The scepter of Phoroneus, the conflict of the brothers at Thebes, the flames of Phaeton, Deucalion's flood... In the stars are Priam's pomp, the boldness of Turnus, Odyssean cleverness, and Herculean strength (trans. Wetherbee 1973: 76).]

The gloss appears beside the following section of the *Man of Law's Tale*:

> For in the sterres, clerer than is glas,
> Is writen, God woot, whoso koude it rede,
> The *deeth* of every man, withouten drede.

> In sterres, many a wynter therbiforn,
> Was writen the *deeth* of Ector, Achilles,
> Of Pompei, Julius, er they were born;
> The strif of Thebes; and of Ercules,
> Of Sampson, Turnus, and of Socrates
> The *deeth*; but mennes wittes ben so dulle
> That no wight kan wel rede it atte fulle (II.194-203: italics mine).

Had it not been for the gloss, it would have taken the most diligent student of Bernard in the fifteenth century to spot the

worldly lif of prestis & veyn cost of hem...plesith god & is vertuous lif...For crist seith that men schullen be blissed of god whanne men schullen curse hem & pursue hem & seie alle euyl ayenst hem falsly for the loue of crist & his trewthe' (*The Office of Curates* in Matthew 1880: 153-54).

source of this passage in Chaucer, if indeed it is a direct source, as it is so contorted and truncated by the Man of Law.

The *Cosmographia*, however, was extremely influential through-out the Middle Ages and beyond. Peter Dronke (1978: 12-15) and Brian Stock (1972: 12) list the many authors who quote or make use of this twelfth-century *magister* of Tours, such as his pupil Matthew of Vendome, Giraldus Cambrensis, Alexander Neckam, Vincent of Beauvais, Jean de Meun, Dante and Boccaccio.[6] C.S. Lewis has shown how Bernard played an important part in the creation of the courtly love tradition (1936: 90-98). Chaucer, who also quotes from Bernard in the *Knight's Tale*, would probably have come across this author not only at second hand through Boccaccio but also directly, as many texts of the *Cosmographia* are found in the same manuscripts as treatises on composition, such as the *Poetria Nova* of Geoffrey of Vinsauf, Chaucer's 'deere mais-ter soverayn' (Stock 1972: 12, 275). Chaucer, then, is quoting from a well-known work, although he makes alterations to it.[7] The major difference is that of tone and purpose, as Bernard's aim is to show that 'the stars inscribe the patterns of human behaviour—all that man can come about through the law of fate' (Dronke 1978: 34). The passage culminates in the advent of Christ when 'earthly existence realises true divinity' (Wetherbee 1973: 76). The tone of the passage is positive and concludes on 'the divine shaping of the universe'.[8]

Both authors start with the metaphor of the heavens as a book in which the future may be read. Then Chaucer mentions the *death* of Hector, Achilles, Pompey, Julius Caesar, Hercules, Samson, Turnus and Socrates, and the strife of Thebes—9 names, only 4 of which appear in Bernard's list of 30. Not only is the list different, but there is no mention of the *virtues* of these characters that Bernard states are seen in the stars, such as the rhetorical powers of Cicero, but only their deaths. It is not the *strength* of

6. For further information about Bernardus and his influence see Dronke (1974), Silverstein (1948–49: 92-116), Gilson (1928: 5-24) and Rat-kowitsch (1995).

7. Some of these points I have made in Caie (1984); see also Wood (1970: 208-19).

8. See also the explanatory notes to the *Man of Law's Tale* by Patricia Eberle in Benson (1987: 858).

Hercules and the *boldness* of Turnus in his opposition to Aeneas, but their demise that the Man of Law says can be read in the heavens. Omitted also are the characters whose *good* fortune was predestined, such as Deucalion, son of Prometheus who, as a Noah-figure, survived the Flood and helped repopulate the earth. The passage begins with 'the deeth of Ector...' and concludes '...and of Socrates/The deeth'. 'Deeth' appears no fewer than four times in the two stanzas, lines II.190-203. A passage of hope in humanity is turned into one of fatalistic death (Wood 1970: 218).

Therefore, had there been no marginal gloss, there would have been little to associate the passage with Bernard. The gloss, then, is much more than a source reference. Cosmic order, rationality and freedom of will mark Bernard's philosophy, which is diametrically opposite to the Man of Law's fatalistic view that one's death is predetermined. One imagines that Chaucer would have supported Bernard rather than the deterministic view of the character he created. What did Chaucer intend to achieve by these misquotations and why should the glossator—possibly Chaucer himself—wish to provide a counterbalance?

The reader's attention is thus shifted from the hagiography to the teller. The spotlight at this early stage of the tale is not on the heroine but on the Syrian merchants and the Sultan. Custance is the *object* of the Sultan's desire: he must possess her or, like a courtly lover, he will die (II.209). At this point the Man of Law interrupts with this hyperbolic apostrophe on fate. He is worried about the poor Sultan's fatal attraction to Custance: 'That he for love sholde han his deeth, allas!' (II.193). But there is no mention of Custance, the rightful heroine of this tale, or any suggestion of what ought to be the underlying theme, namely the need to trust in God's providence and turn one's back on the things of this world.

It is significant that the characters that the Man of Law substitutes in Bernard's list, Hercules, Samson and Socrates, figure in another list, namely in the 'Book of Wicked Wives' that the Wife of Bath's Jankyn reads to her; these are all men who are deceived and afflicted by women. It could be a case of the Man of Law's bad memory that he has already demonstrated when he listed in his introduction the names of lovers he claims are in Chaucer's works, a list that does not tally with Chaucer's surviving writings (Sullivan 1953: 2-5). Whatever the reason, we are led to sympathize with the poor Sultan, who is in love with someone who will cause his death, and are presented with a deterministic view that is diametrically opposite to the philosophy of Bernard and to the sources of this tale about a heroine who trusts in divine providence.

The suggestion that the glossator's aim is to show the reader how the narrator manipulates texts is strengthened by the next gloss in the manuscript, which comes from Ptolemy's *Almagest:*

> Vnde Ptholomeus libro 1° capitulo 8° Primi motus celi duo sunt quorum vnus est qui mouet totum semper ab Oriente in Occidentem vno modo super orbes et cetera Item alter vero motus est qui mouet orbem stellarum currencium contra motum primum videlicet ab Occidente in Orientem super alios duos polos et cetera.

> [Whence Ptolemy in Book 1, chapter 8: 'The primary motions of the heavens are two, of which the first is that which continually moves the whole from east to west in one way above the spheres' and so forth. 'Moreover there is indeed a second motion which impels the sphere of the moving stars, running contrary to the first motion, that is to say, from west to east above the two other poles' and so forth (trans. Benson 1987: 858).]

At first sight this would appear to have nothing to do with the text. Custance is to marry the Sultan, who is willing to convert to Christianity for her sake. She is 'with sorwe al overcome' at the prospect, but with exemplary, saintly obedience agrees to this unwelcome marriage in 'the Barbre nacioun' (II.281), lamenting: 'Wommen are born to thraldom and penance/And to been under mannes governance' (II.286-87). As she is about to experience the domination of her new mother-in-law over the Sultan, there is perhaps a hint of irony here. In a hyperbolic outburst the weeping at her departure is compared with other tragic historic events that were the cause of equal displays of extravagant lamentation (II.292-93); this highly rhetorical tone continues with an apostrophe that again attempts to shift our sympathies away from Custance and on to the poor Sultan:

> O firste moevyng! crueel firmament,
> With thy diurnal sweigh that crowdest ay
> And hurlest al from est til occident

> That naturelly wolde holde another way,
> Thy crowdyng set the hevene in swich array
> At the bigynnyng of this fiers viage,
> That crueel Mars hath slayn this mariage (II.295-301).

The tirade against the planets is not because of their cruelty in *creating* this unwanted marriage but because they *destroy* it, presumably what both reader and Custance would have wished. But the fickle narrator has reverted to sympathizing with the merchants who instigated the marriage deal and the Sultan. It is significant that this passage is not in any of Chaucer's sources and seems, therefore, to have been added as another clue as to the character of the Man of Law.

Much has been written about this astrological interpolation (e.g. Wood 1970: 231; Curry 1960: 164-94; North 1969: 427-31; Eade 1982: 76-82). The crux of the matter is that, according to Platonic and Aristotelian teaching, the *Primum Mobile* ('the firste moevyng') in its daily motion from east to west is associated with order and rationality, as in the rising and setting of the sun, and was traditionally equated with God's power and harmony. The second movement is that of the planets in their annual motion from west to east and is associated with irrational desire, as the planets struggle against the *Primum Mobile*. Boethius Book I, Metre 5 clearly refers to God as the First Mover, as does Theseus in his Boethian 'hymn' to the First Mover who made 'the faire cheyne of love' (*Knight's Tale* I.2988). The Man of Law, however, berates the First Mover for 'hurling' (a curious verb to express the natural, God-ordained cosmic movement) all from east to west, thus *causing* 'that crueel Mars' to kill the marriage.

The gloss will, therefore, remind the reader that what the Man of Law is saying is both blasphemous and reflects a totally incorrect grasp of the basic principles of God's firmament. It parallels the fatalistic view which the despairing Troilus also held, namely that his personal predicament is the fault of the stars, but there is no way the movement of the *Primum Mobile* could have a direct effect on the sublunary fortunes of this world. So once again the Man of Law's sympathies are misplaced, as what he sees as a tragedy, the wrecking of a financially solid marriage deal, is in fact to be Custance's salvation; tragedy for one is escape for another.

This gloss is immediately followed by, and in some manuscripts connected to, another astrological quotation, this time from the ninth-century Arab astrologer Zael Benbriz, who wrote the *Liber Electionum:*

> Omnes concordati sunt quod elecciones sint debiles nisi in diuitibus habent enim isti licet debilitentur eorum elecciones radicem .i. natiuitates eorum que confortat omnem planetam debilem in itinere et cetera.

> [All agree that elections are uncertain except concerning the rich. Although elections concerning them are uncertain as well, these persons possess a fundament/root, that is their nativities which serves to conform all weak planets in respect to the journey, etc. (translation mine)].

It glosses this passage in the tale:

> Imprudent Emperour of Rome, allas!
> Was ther no philosophre in al thy toun?
> Is no tyme bet than oother in swich cas?
> Of viage is ther noon eleccioun,
> Namely to folk of heigh condicioun?
> Noght whan a roote is of burthe yknowe?
> Allas, we been to lewed or to slowe! (II.309-15).

The thrust of the argument in the gloss is that astrological elections cannot be certain unless the 'root', or one's personal astrological configuration at birth, is known; of course, an emperor's daughter would surely have had her astrological 'root' determined at birth. The narrator's extended diatribe of over three stanzas against the 'imprudent Emperour of Rome' who failed to enlist astrological advice concerning the journey, is totally pointless, unless one sympathizes with the sultan; the journey is a success in spite of the disastrous astrological signs that the narrator notes. The reader, however, is caught up in the frenzy of accusations against the planets and the emperor that overwhelms the calm voice of Custance, who is allowed the single line: 'Now Jhesu Crist be with yow alle' (II.318). She at any rate places her faith in Christ, unlike the Man of Law who regrets that 'Allas we been to lewed or to slowe' (II.315) to be guided by astrologers.

Why did the Man of Law devote so much time and energy to this material that is not in his source and that detracted from his heroine? Did he wish to appear superior and more learned than the Emperor and his astrologers? The presence of the gloss, however, reminds us of the misconstrued source and the limitations of the narrator's spiritual vision. In addition to the glosses we have some clues in the *General Prologue to The Canterbury Tales* and the *Introduction* to the *Tale* that corroborate this interpretation by the narrator.

In the *General Prologue* the Sergeant of the Lawe is described as follows:

> Discreet he was and of greet reverence—
> He semed swich, his wordes weren so wise...
> Nowher so bisy a man as he ther nas,
> And yet he semed bisier than he was (I.312-14, 321-22).

Assuming that the Man of Law is the same character as the Sergeant of the Lawe, we are presented with a judge of considerable status who talks of fees and clients' gifts, and has unrestricted possession (*fee symple*) of estates. He wishes to appear wise, discerning and *of greet reverence* (I.312), an attribute which the Man of Law claims is absent in the poor ('If thou be povre, farwel thy reverence', *Man of Law's Prologue* II.116). *Bisy* here can have the meaning of 'anxious' or 'concerned'. Here, then, is a wealthy and powerful man, whose status is secure, and who is keen to be considered wise and worthy of reverence, as well as concerned about humanity. The image is slightly undercut by the repetition of 'semed' and the curious assertion that 'He semed bisier than he was'. He places weight on appearance, therefore, and wishes to project the image of a man of high esteem who is also caring.

In spite of the Man of Law's protestations in the *Introduction* that 'I kan right now no thrifty tale seyn' (II.46), the tale is summed up by Harry Bailey in the *Epilogue*: 'This was a thrifty tale for the nones!' (II.1165).[9] It appears an insultingly brief comment that seems to damn with faint praise, if one compares it to the Host's fulsome remarks about other tales. *Thrifty* means 'useful', 'profitable', 'prosperous', 'worthy', and Modern English 'profitable' retains the financial and moral ambiguity. To win the prize for the best story the Man of Law attempts to woo his audience with a sentimental, at times romantic, story of saintly and patient Custance that ends happily and is guaranteed to leave

---

9. The *Epilogue* of the *Man of Law's Tale* occurs in 35 of the *Canterbury Tales* manuscripts.

not a dry eye in the audience. 'Moving' or 'emotional' would surely have pleased the Man of Law more than *thrifty*.

His concern for worldly prosperity and his fear of poverty permeates the tale, which was narrated to the Man of Law originally by a merchant, who in turn begins with 'chapmen riche, and therto sadde and trewe' (II.135). No wonder, then, that it was considered by Harry Bailey a 'profitable' tale. This undoubtedly explains the long description of the merchants' *thrifty* wares (II.138), their satins, cloths of gold and spices, but one wonders about its place in a Saint's Life (II.134-40). There are also many other details that reflect the narrator's interest in worldly goods: for example, he is careful to note that Custance's treasure, food and clothes follow her on her travels and that, although she was in exile,

> Vitailled was the ship, it is no drede,
> Habundantly for hire ful longe space,
> And othere necessaries that sholde nede
> She hadde ynogh (II.869-72).

Before this Custance herself was a mere object that is described by the merchants to the Sultan along with marvels and wonders, while the details of the dowry interest the teller considerably: the dowry not only comprised gold but also *suretee*, 'security', a detail that financiers, not pilgrims, might want to know. The pomp and dignity of her entourage that includes bishops, lords and knights are described as well as the rich array (II.393), and, by dwelling on the fateful wedding feast, the Man of Law is distracted from his tale into the hyperbolic outbursts mentioned above.

In the *Prologue* the Man of Law clearly expresses his hatred of poverty in his partial quotations from and misunderstanding of Innocent III's *De miseria*:

> O hateful harm, condicion of poverte!
> With thurst, with coold, with hunger so confoundid!
> To asken help thee shameth in thyn herte;
> If thou noon aske, with nede artow so woundid
> That verray nede unwrappeth al thy wounde hid! (II.99-103).

This is a faithful rendition of the section of *De miseria* 1:14, entitled *De miseria pauperis et divitis*:[10]

---

10. This was not only a work that Chaucer frequently quoted and was well

> The poor are indeed oppressed by starvation, tortured by need, hunger, thirst, cold, nakedness; they become worthless and waste away, are despised and confounded. O miserable condition of a beggar. If he begs he is confounded with shame and if he does not beg, he is consumed with want... (trans. Lewis 1978: 114).

As the title of the section implies, Innocent then addresses the evils of the rich:

> The rich man flies away to his pleasure and falls into unlawfulness and they become the instruments of his punishments that had been the pleasures of his sins (trans. Lewis 1978: 114, 116).

But at this the Man of Law balks, deciding to change his source and abruptly launch into a eulogy on riches and merchants in particular:

> O riche marchauntz, ful of wele been yee,
> O noble, o prudent folk, as in this cas!...
> Ye seken lond and see for yowre wynnynges;
> As wise folk ye knowen al th'estaat
> Of regnes; ye been fadres of tidynges
> And tales, bothe of pees and of debaat (II.122-24, 127-30).

Innocent's theme in *De miseria* (in 83 manuscripts aptly entitled *De contemptu mundi*) is that the Christian must acknowledge the miserable state of mankind, as true and eternal joy is only in heaven. The Man of Law's theme in the *Prologue* is equally clear: those who have no worldly possessions are miserable, friendless, beggars, thieves, without reverence, and despised. It is therefore not by chance that he makes the rich merchants who 'seek winnings over land and sea' (II.127) the ones who convey this *thrifty* tale, and it is they who create the mercantile tone in the first part of the tale.

The Man of Law, then, gives the impression of being wise, worthy of reverence and concerned about humanity. He is not a *bad* person or the type of evil lawyer that Wycliffe, Gower and Langland portrayed. In fact he is described as modest and

acquainted with, but also a work that he claimed in *Prologue G* to the *Legend of Good Women* to have translated:

> He hath in prose translated Boece,
> And of the Wreched Engendrynge of Mankynde,
> As man may in pope Innocent yfynde (413-15).

'hoomly' in the *General Prologue*. His only fault is that his spiritual vision is limited, as he cannot give up his worldly baggage or allow his heroine to do so either. What better tale to promote himself as a concerned and dignified judge, wise, reverential and diligent, as we learn in the *General Prologue*, than a sentimental legend about a saint that will bring a tear to a pilgrim's eye and help him win the prize for the best tale? The glosses, then, warn us of the fact that this *bisy* man with his *thrifty* tale places too much emphasis on the things of this world and is spiritually lacking.

WORKS CITED

Astel, A.W.
1991   'Apostrophe, Prayer, and the Structure of Satire in *The Man of Law's Tale*, *Studies in the Age of Chaucer* 13: 81-97.

Benson, C.D.
1990a   'Poetic Variety in the *Man of Law's* and the *Clerk's Tales*', in Benson and Robertson 1990: 137-44.
1990b   'The Aesthetic of Chaucer's Religious Tales in Rhyme Royal', in P. Boitani and A. Torti (eds.), *Religion in the Poetry and Drama of the Late Middle Ages in England* (Cambridge: Brewer): 101-19.

Benson, C.D., and E. Robertson (eds.)
1990   *Chaucer's Religious Tales* (Cambridge: Brewer).

Benson, L.D. (ed.)
1987   *The Riverside Chaucer* (Boston: Houghton Mifflin).

Blake, N.F.
1985   *The Textual Tradition of the Canterbury Tales* (London: Arnold).

Blake, N.F., and P. Robinson (eds.)
1993   *The Canterbury Tales Project Occasional Papers*, I (Oxford: Office for Humanities Communication).

Caie, G.D.
1977   'The Significance of the Early Chaucer Manuscript Glosses (with special reference to the *Wife of Bath's Prologue*)', *Chaucer Review* 10: 350-60.
1984   'The Significance of Marginal Glosses in the Earliest Manuscripts of *The Canterbury Tales*', in D.L. Jeffrey (ed.), *Chaucer and the Scriptural Tradition* (Ottawa: Ottawa University Press): 337-50.

Curry, W.C.
1960   *Chaucer and the Mediaeval Sciences* (London: George Allen & Unwin, rev. edn).

David, A.
1967   'The Man of Law vs Chaucer: A Case in Poetics', *PMLA* 82: 217-25.

Dronke, P.
1974   *Fabula: Explorations in the Uses of Myth in Medieval Platonism* (Leiden: E.J. Brill).

Dronke, P. (ed.)
1978   *Bernardus Silvestris: Cosmographia* (Leiden: E.J. Brill).
Eade, J.C.
1982   ' "We ben to lewed or to slowe": Chaucer's Astronomy and Audience
              Participation', *Studies in the Age of Chaucer* 4: 76-82.
Gilson, E.
1928   'La cosmonogie de Bernardus Silvestris', *Archives d'histoire doctrinale
              et littéraire du Moyen Age* 3: 5-24.
Keiser, G.
1990   'The Spiritual Heroism of Chaucer's Custance', in Benson and
              Robertson 1990: 121-36.
Lewis, C.S.
1936   *The Allegory of Love* (Oxford: Oxford University Press).
Lewis, R.E.
1967   'Glosses to the *Man of Law's Tale* from Pope Innocent III's *De Miseria
              Humane Conditionis*', *Studies in Philology* 64: 1-16.
Lewis, R.E. (ed.)
1978   *De Miseria Condicionis Humanae* (Athens, GA: University of Georgia
              Press).
Manly, J.M., and E. Rickert (eds.)
1940   *The Text of the Canterbury Tales, Studied on the Basis of All Known
              Manuscripts* (8 vols.; Chicago: University of Chicago Press).
Matthew, F.D. (ed.)
1880   *The English Works of Wyclif* (EETS, 74; London: Trübner).
North, J.D.
1969   ' "Kalenderes enlumyned ben they": Some Astronomical Themes in
              Chaucer', *Review of English Studies* NS 20: 418-44.
Ratkowitsch, C.
1995   *Die Cosmographia des Bernardus Silvestris: Studien zur Literatur und
              Gesellschaft des Mittelalters und der Frühen Neuzeit* (Cologne: Böhlau).
Robinson, F.N. (ed.)
1957   *The Complete Works of Geoffrey Chaucer* (London: Oxford University
              Press, 2nd edn).
Silverstein, T.
1948–49   'The Fabulous Cosmogony of Bernardus Silvestris', *Modern Philology*
              46: 92-116.
Stock, B.
1972   *Myth and Science in the Twelfth Century: A Study of Bernard Silvester*
              (Princeton: Princeton University Press).
Sullivan, W.L.
1953   'The Man of Law as a Literary Critic', *Modern Language Notes* 68: 1-8.
Wetherbee, W. (trans.)
1973   *The Cosmographia of Bernardus Silvestris* (New York: Columbia Univer-
              sity Press).
Wood, C.
1967   'Chaucer's Man of Law as Interpreter', *Traditio* 23: 149-90.
1970   *Chaucer and the Country of the Stars: Poetic Uses of Astrological Imagery*
              (Princeton: Princeton University Press).

Chaucer's Sense of Wealth

T.P. Dolan

In this essay I wish to examine some of the social and literary
implications arising from contemporary theories about the relative merits and prestige of wealth and poverty during Chaucer's
writing life. In the *Canterbury Tales*, from the *General Prologue* to the
Parson's Tale, Chaucer seems to have taken the traditional and
orthodox view that the poor were to be protected since they were
precious in the sight of God. At the same time he appears to recognize that there is nothing wrong with wealth, not least because
it enables him to maintain his own position in society. Understandably, where poverty is claimed, and at the same time wealth
enjoyed, he exposes the hypocrisy. The Friar, who in his mendicant vocation should have espoused poverty, absolute or at least
conditional, is implicitly criticized in the classic irony of:

> It is nat honeste; it may nat avaunce,
> For to delen with no swich poraille,
> But al with riche and selleres of vitaille (I.246-48).

By contrast, the Parson is especially attentive to the poor in his
parish:

> But rather wolde he yeven, out of doute,
> Unto his povre parisshens aboute
> Of his offryng and eek of his substaunce (I. 487-89).

The *Parson's Tale* similarly confirms the special quality of the poor
and their right to protection:

> Wherefore I seye that thilke lordes that been lyk wolves, that
> devouren the possessiouns or the catel of povre folk wrongfully,
> withouten mercy or mesure, / they shul receyven by the same

mesure that they han mesured to povre folk the mercy of Jhesu
Crist, but if it be amended (X.774-75).

There is nothing wrong with being a lord, presumably in possession of wealth; the iniquity consists in not behaving mercifully to
the poor.

The contrast between the Friar and the Parson is obviously
deliberate, the polarity being perhaps acknowledged by the fact
that theirs are the two longest portraits in the *Prologue*. In some
respects, though, the contrast is specious, especially as regards
their respective wealth. The Parson is not a poor man (see
Swanson 1991)—references to his *offrynge, substaunce,* and *benefice*
call into question the validity of the label 'povere persoun of a
toun'; he is a man of substance to whom we are first introduced as
'a good man...of religioun' (I.477). The term *religioun* is problematical. A 'religious', up to the present day, is a member of a
religious order, monastic or mendicant, not a secular:

> id quod communiter multis convenit, antonomastice attribuitur ei
> cui excellentiam convenit...Religio autem...est quaedam virtus per
> quam aliquis ad Dei servitium et cultum aliquid exhibet. Et ideo
> antonomastice *religiosi* dicuntur illi qui se totaliter mancipant
> divino servitio (Thomas Aquinas, *Summa Theologiae* 2a2ae.186.1)

> [A name common to many things is sometimes appropriated to
> that one to which it belongs in an eminent degree...Now, religion
> is the virtue by which a man does something for the service and
> worship of God. And so by transference of epithet, they are said to
> be religious who have devoted themselves entirely to the service of
> God]

In *Piers Plowman* Langland's use of the term 'religion' with
reference to Haukyn the Actif Man indicates that he, like Thomas
Aquinas, distinguishes members of religious orders from the secular clergy by reason of their strict observance of a rule in order
to serve God exclusively:

> Yhabited as an heremyte, an ordre by hymselve—
> Religion suanz rule and resonable obedience (B Text, XIII, 284-
> 85).

By contrast, Chaucer's understanding of the term *religioun* may be
a significant factor in establishing his position in the contemporary disputes over the validity of different sections of the

priesthood and may suggest that he is offering his own solution
to these difficulties: he may have felt that the distinction drawn
between religious and secular was a false one. There can be no
doubt that he favours the Parson, and yet he describes him in
terms which are ambiguous. Indeed, many of his qualities are
those which are normally and specifically demanded of, and
claimed by, friars:

> But Cristes loore and his apostles twelve
> He taughte; but first he folwed it hymselve (I.527-28).

The Franciscans, in particular, insisted that they were imitating
Christ's lifestyle and Gospel to the letter. The beginning of the
Franciscan Rule, in the *Regula Bullata* text, reads:

> Regula et vita Minorum Fratrum haec est, scilicet Domini nostri
> Iesu Christi sanctum Evangelium observare (*Regula Bullata,* in Esser
> 1978: 226).

It is also significant that the Parson walks round his parish, as
friars were enjoined to do, although his wealth and position
would have enabled him to ride:

> Wyd was his parisshe, and houses fer asonder,
> But he ne lefte nat, for reyn ne thonder,
> In siknesse nor in meschief to visite
> The ferreste in his parisshe, muche and lite,
> Upon his feet, and in his hand a staf (I.491-95).

Chaucer is comfortable with the wealth of the Parson, because
he is a secular, but critical of the Friar's, because he is a mendicant. In the *Summoner's Tale* the Friar is critical of the secular
clergy's efficiency as pastors and confessors:

> Thise curatz been ful necligent and slowe
> To grope tendrely a conscience
> In schrift (III.1816-18)

but careful to point out his own vow of poverty:

> We lyve in poverte and abstinence (III.1873)

In his singleminded use of the anti-mendicant *topos* and his
support for the Parson, Chaucer is signalling his position as a
defender of the secular clergy and, most importantly, he indicates
that the wealth of the Parson is no barrier to his being regarded as
a good priest:

A bettre preest I trowe that nowher noon ys (I.524).

Chaucer's attitude on this matter conforms with the argument advanced by some earlier commentators, including Ælfric, that there is nothing inherently immoral about wealth: despite being a monk, Ælfric is anxious 'to defend the rich from the criticism of the Bible' (Godden 1990: 61). Chaucer's support for the Parson is also signified in the length and the quality of his *Tale*, which has attracted some reservations as to its function within the context of the series of *Tales*:

> The Parson's Tale is not actually a tale nor even a sermon. The language is vigorous and thus suited to the Parson, who would 'snybben sharply' the wrongdoers of his parish, and the subject and its treatment are appropriate to this character. But beyond that, the tale has no dramatic or even fictional qualities, and if (as is possible) it was written for some purpose other than inclusion in the Tales, it shows no signs of adaptation to the larger work beyond the opening paragraph (Benson 1987: 21).

> *The Parson's Tale*, a prolix call to repentance with a punctilious cataloguing of the various forms of sin and their dangers, seems to the modern mind exceedingly tedious (it may have seemed so to the pilgrims as well) (Swanson 1991: 41-42).

Such reservations about the *Tale*, focusing particularly on the tediousness caused by its length and content, may not be wholly valid. The length of the *Tale*, even if it is regarded as a sermon, should not necessarily compromise its efficacity. Many contemporary preachers, speaking in the vernacular, held the attention of audiences, even when they spoke at great length. It is recorded, for instance, that some of St Bernard of Siena's vernacular sermons, which were taken down by stenographers in the congregation, sometimes lasted for as long as three or four hours (Mazzarella 1944: 320-21), and Richard FitzRalph's vernacular London Sermons, especially the last, on the theme 'Nemo vos seducat inanibus verbis', preached at St Paul's Cross on 12 March, 1357, was uncompromisingly long and complicated (no modern edition; see British Library MS Lansdowne 393, ff.124v, 11-136, 34).

The underlying preoccupation with wealth which informs much of the *General Prologue* portrait of the Parson mirrors that of the secular clergy in general, as witnessed by FitzRalph in various references in his London sermons, and it will be useful at this stage to note what the Archbishop has to say on the subject of wealth and the necessity to have it in order to maintain an efficient priesthood with stable and regular offerings, such as Chaucer's Parson seems to have enjoyed. Chaucer does not mention FitzRalph by name, nor may he have heard the Archbishop preaching in London on 18 December 1356, 22 January 1357, 26 February 1357, and 12 March 1357. It should be noted , however, that Chaucer appears to have been in London during that period: there is an early reference to a payment to Chaucer to buy clothes for his attendance at Easter ceremonies in London in 1357 (Pearsall 1992: 34). During his earlier years at court he may have become acquainted with FitzRalph (c. 1299–1360), whose controversial career on several occasions brought him into conflict with Edward III—for instance, on 31 March 1357 the king ordered FitzRalph not to leave the country, but he did so, arriving in Avignon in the summer (Walsh 1981: 420-21). Langland does not mention FitzRalph in the A, B or C versions of *Piers Plowman*, but Wendy Scase (1989: 31) plausibly suggests that the line 'Ant sworen be seynt Rycher a schent the rewme' (Z Text, IV, 152, ed. Rigg and Brewer 1983) refers to Archbishop FitzRalph with his local title of 'St. Richard of Dundalk' (he was born in the town of Dundalk, County Louth). Such evidence of FitzRalph's notoriety, and the high opinion which Wyclif and the Lollards later came to hold of him, suggests that Chaucer could well have been familiar with his writings and the controversy they caused.

FitzRalph was chiefly famous for his defence of the secular clergy, in particular their rights to moneys which the friars were sequestrating. His London sermons constitute the fullest statement of his position in the vernacular, and form the basis of his famous Latin address known as the *Defensio Curatorum*, preached in Avignon on 8 November 1357. (There are no modern editions of the London sermons or of the *Defensio*; citations here are taken from British Library MS Lansdowne 393 [paper, early fifteenth century]). Much of his defence depended on definitions of poverty and wealth, within the context of his application of the theory of Dominion and Grace. FitzRalph states that before the Fall no-one was in a state of destitution since such a state is a situation of distress:

nunquam eorum aliquis fuisset mendicus, inops, aut pauper, quonian hee sunt condiciones miserie (Sermon I, 'Dirigite viam Domini', f.110, 14-15).

He sees no intrinsic spiritual value in poverty (cf. the views on poverty expressed in the *Prologue to the Man of Law's Tale*, beginning 'O hateful harm, condicion of poverte!', II.99-127), and in the second London Sermon, in arguing that Christ never begged deliberately or wilfully (*spontanee*), he avers that poverty is an effect of sin:

nullus effectus peccati est propter se diligibilis cum omnis effectus peccati sit propter se aut per se odibilis; paupertas uero non dubium quantum ad priuationem diuitiarum...est effectus peccati (Sermon II, f.113, 23-25).

He uses the Bible selectively to prove his general misgivings about the poor:

Omnino egens et mendicus non erit inter vos (Deut. 15.4: Sermon II, f.117, 7).

In the third sermon he draws attention to the way that the income of the parish clergy under his care is being damaged by the failure of the parishioners to pay their tithes (f.120, 29-30), and refers elsewhere to the 'periculosa subtraccio decimarum' (f.123, 9).

The longest of the London sermons reiterates and expands his criticism of the friars' hypocritical pursuit of wealth and the possessions which come with it—their fine houses, churches, libraries, etc. (f.128r, 33–f.128v, 2). It seems to him that the possession of such wealth is not compatible with the claim that they are professing absolute poverty, especially as the wealth is used to enjoy the *temporalia commoda* bought from the dues and offerings arising from burials, confession and preaching, which, in his view, are means of income for the secular clergy, who are entitled to moneys generated by their ministry from their parishes. The delinquency of the friars is rendered even more objectionable because they receive money *per receptorem*, rather than handling it themselves (f.131v, 5-8). His constant position is that the secular clergy have the right to enjoy the income from their profession as ministers: he does not want them to be poor. He insists that the parish clergy are efficient in their calling because they, as stable, non-peripatetic members of the community, get to know all their parishioners, rich and poor (as does Chaucer's Parson), and minister to them as a doctor to his patients (Sermon III, f.122, 4-8, 11-15, 18-20). The friars, he says, associate only with the rich and powerful: 'imperatores, reges, et reginas, duces, ducissimas, comites, comitissas, et nobiles alios', f.130, 27-28), the implication being that his own clergy deal with the spiritual problems of both rich and poor.

It is clear that of the many themes and arguments treated in the London Sermons one of FitzRalph's major concerns is the income of his clergy. He is happy for them to have a reasonably comfortable ministry, and Chaucer's Parson seems to fit this context, from the image of him we are given in the *General Prologue*.

With regard to the sources of wealth available to his clergy, FitzRalph is constantly sensitive to the fact that a significant proportion of the income from preaching (as well as from administering the sacrament of Penance in confession and the conducting of burials) which should be enjoyed as of right by his (secular) clergy was being taken by the friars. It is important to note that the parish clergy regarded all the duties of the priesthood as part of their ministry, including preaching. It may therefore be a reasonable presumption that Chaucer would give his Parson a sermon to deliver in order to demonstrate his craft as a learned man and to show one means by which he generates income, just as the Pardoner displayed his expertise as a preacher with the intention of making money.

As far as his *Tale* is concerned, there has been some discussion as to whether it is a sermon at all. Norman Blake's note on the Parson's reference to 'this meditacioun' ('*meditacioun*: sermon; an unusual sense of the word which usually had a contemplative connotation': Blake 1980: 595, gloss on line 55) has been challenged by Thomas H. Bestul, who argues for Chaucer's 'obligation to the meditative tradition' (Bestul 1989: 601). Lee Patterson says that it is 'not a typical medieval sermon' but 'an instance of a clearly defined and recognizable genre, the manual intended exclusively for penitential use...the form of the whole is that of treatise rather than a sermon' (1978: 339; cf. Wenzel 1984: 2-9). These observations are certainly plausible, although the disputed *Epilogue* to the *Man of Law's Tale*, in which both the Host ('we schal han a predicacioun', II.1176) and the Shipman ('Heer schal he nat preche', II.1179) clearly state that they expect a sermon, seems to confirm that the Parson was expected to deliver a sermon.

The density of the material in the *Parson's Tale* need not necessarily compromise Norman Blake's gloss of 'meditacioun' as 'sermon'. Vernacular sermons, which were actually delivered in some form, could be substantial and even ostensibly 'drab' (to use an epithet applied in Patterson 1978: 331 to the *Tale*). As an example, one might cite the last of Richard FitzRalph's London Sermons on the theme 'Nemo vos seducat inanibus verbis'. Admittedly, it seems that the surviving Latin version of the vernacular was written up after the actual delivery. It is probably too far-fetched to excuse the formality of the presentation of the *Parson's Tale* as an attempt on Chaucer's part to conclude the *Canterbury Tales* with a type of written-up vernacular sermon, with the casualness attendant on oral delivery removed. The oral quality of the *Tale*, which has been understandably denied or queried because of the nature of the content, is not entirely absent if attention is paid to the rhetorical figures embedded in the text. Recently Helen Cooper has drawn attention to some of the rhetorical features of the *Tale* (in particular the similes and the use of enumeration), in the light of her statement that 'The treatise is written in the plain style appropriate to exposition, where understanding is more important than persuasion' (1996: 408). The significant word here is 'persuasion', the key factor in determining the presence or effectiveness of rhetoric. An audience is persuaded by the use of carefully chosen rhetorical devices (as Chaucer so well displayed in the *Tales* of the Nun's Priest and of the Pardoner). The range of rhetorical devices in the *Parson's Tale* is wider and more sophisticated than Cooper's necessarily brief account discloses—so much so that one might question her claim that it is 'written in the plain style' and that 'understanding is more important than persuasion'.

The rhetoric of the *Parson's Tale* includes a range of Figures of Speech (as well as Figures of Thought) which indicate that, if it were delivered as a sermon, it would have been stimulating, or, at least, that the attention of the listeners would have been courted by the use of different effects. Alliteration occurs frequently, for example,

> The thridde cause that oghte moeve a man to Contricioun is drede of the day of doom (X.157)

> that I may a while biwaille and wepe, er I go withoute returnyng to the derke lond, covered with the derknesse of deeth (X.175).

There is subtle use of wordplay, for example,

> For right as resoun is rebel to God, right so is bothe sensualitee rebel to resoun and the body also (X.265).

Repetition of key words in prominent locations in clauses (e.g. at the end, with the device of Antistrophe) emphasizes what the Parson wishes his listeners to concentrate on at different stages in the address, for example,

> the repentaunce of a synguler synne, and nat repente of all his othere synnes, ore elles repenten hym of all his othere synnes and nat of a synguler synne, may nat availle (X.299).

In this sentence the rhetorical level further rises with the addition of repetition of the root 'repent' (the device of Polyptoton).

The register of the spoken voice is further indicated by the frequent inclusion of Apostrophe (e.g. 'O goode God, muchel oghte a man to drede swich a juggement', X.161) and Exclamation (e.g. 'Allas, allas, nedeles is he recreant and nedelees despeired', X.697).

General repetition of words is ubiquitous (e.g. 'and more sharp and poynaunt for he hath agilt hys Fader celestial; / and yet moore sharp and poynaunt...' (X.130-31).

A sophisticated effect is achieved by the use of the rare figure of Climax:

> God sholde have lordshipe over resoun, and resoun over sensu-alitiee, and sensualitee over the body of man (X.261).

Throughout the *Tale*, the Parson is very sensitive to the rhythm achieved by balancing clauses, which is particularly effective at the end of the *secunda pars Penitencie* ('and eek whan...eke whan... etc., X.372-75).

As a well-tried means of arresting the attention of the listeners, whose attention tends to drift, he uses the device of Rhetorical Question at strategic moments in the text to focus their minds back on his words, for example,

> Whare been thanne the gaye robes, and the softe shetes, and the smale shertes? (X.196).

> What seye we of hem that bileeven on divynailes…? (X.604).

All these figures are classified as Figures of Speech—they derive their effectiveness from the response of the listener, and their presence in such volume in the *Tale* may indicate that Chaucer envisaged that such a tale, though ostensibly off-putting in its contents, would be told in such a forceful way that the listeners would respond to it as they would to any serious homily. The presence of many types of Figures of Thought and tropes in the *Tale* (e.g. metaphors such as 'Penaunce is the tree of lyf' [X.126] or 'Thilke manere of folk been the flyes that folwen the hony, or elles the houndes that folwen the careyne' [X.440]) further enhance the stylistic register of the *Tale*. If they constituted the main type of rhetorical device in the *Tale*, that fact might perhaps support the view that the *Parson's Tale* is primarily a manual of penance or meditation—but the wide range of Figures of Speech help to support the case for regarding the *Tale* as something to be delivered to an audience, not just read, in which case Norman Blake's gloss of *meditacioun* as a sermon may be correct.

If the *Tale* is a sermon, its highly important position at the close of the *Canterbury Tales* may support the view that Chaucer seems to take sides in the secular-mendicant controversy, at the basic level of giving the Friar a populist tale involving a domestic squabble with a Summoner, whose own tale rehearses well-known features of the anti-mendicant *topoi*, while giving the Parson an elevated address, enhanced by sophisticated rhetorical figures which further raise his prestige. There is nothing mercenary in his *Tale*. It does not seek superficial applause or laughter from content or style. It is not idealistic about the conditions of the poor, nor critical of the condition of being rich, if people in the higher strata of society behave responsibly to those lower down. It is the considered address of the type of comfortably-off priest that Richard FitzRalph celebrated and attempted to defend.

WORKS CITED

Aumann, J. (ed.)
    1973   *St Thomas Aquinas Summa Theologiæ*. XLVII. *The Pastoral and Religious Lives (2a2æ. 183-9)* (London: Eyre & Spottiswoode).
Benson, L.D. (ed.)
    1987   *The Riverside Chaucer* (Boston: Houghton Mifflin).
Bestul, T.H.
    1989   'Chaucer's *Parson's Tale* and the Late Medieval Tradition of Religious Meditation', *Speculum* 64: 600-619.
Blake, N.F. (ed.)
    1980   *The Canterbury Tales by Geoffrey Chaucer, Edited from the Hengwrt Manuscript* (London: Arnold).
Cooper, H.
    1996   *The Canterbury Tales* (Oxford: Oxford University Press, 2nd edn).
Esser. C. (ed.)
    1978   *Opuscula Sancti Patris Francisci Assisiensis* (Grottaferrata, Rome: Editiones Collegii S. Bonaventurae ad Claras Aquas).
Godden, M.R.
    1990   'Money, Power and Morality in late Anglo-Saxon England', *Anglo-Saxon England* 19: 41-65.
Mazzarella, B.
    1944   'St. Bernardine of Siena, a Model Preacher', *Franciscan Studies* 25: 320-21.
Patterson, L.W.
    1978   'The *Parson's Tale* and the Quitting of the *Canterbury Tales*', *Traditio* 34: 331-80.
Pearsall, D.
    1992   *The Life of Geoffrey Chaucer, A Critical Biography* (Oxford: Basil Blackwell).
Rigg, A.G., and C. Brewer (eds.)
    1983   *William Langland, Piers Plowman: The Z Version* (Toronto: Pontifical Institute of Mediaeval Studics).
Scase, W.
    1989   *'Piers Plowman' and the New Anticlericalism* (Cambridge: Cambridge University Press).
Schmidt, A.V.C. (ed.)
    1987   *William Langland, The Vision of Piers Plowman: A Complete Edition of the B-Text* (London: Dent).
Swanson, R.N.
    1991   'Chaucer's Parson and Other Priests, *Studies in the Age of Chaucer* 13: 41-80.

Walsh, K.
    1981   *A Fourteenth-Century Scholar and Primate: Richard FitzRalph in Oxford,
                  Avignon and Armagh* (Oxford: Clarendon Press).
Wenzel, S. (ed.)
    1984   *Summa Virtutum De Remediis Anime* (Athens, GA: University of
                  Georgia Press).

Caxton's Printing of Chaucer's *Boece*

Brian Donaghey

When one considers the amount of research done in recent years on Caxton, his career and his output, most notably by the dedicatee of this festschrift, one can only conclude that a reassessment of his printing of Chaucer's *Boece* (**Cx**) is long overdue, for it has been largely neglected by comparison with others of his books. This is so even though a facsimile has been available for some time[1] and the text has been published verbatim in transcribed form (Boyd 1978). It has survived, remarkably, in more than 20 complete or fragmentary copies, including two copies in their original bindings from Caxton's shop (and a detached binding from another copy), and one in a different but contemporary binding. The Appendix below lists the known copies.

Apart from in the pioneering work of Blades (1861–63: II, 69-71; 1877: 211-16), **Cx** has not often been studied as an artefact in its own right. The view taken of it has been almost exclusively textual. Indeed, the *Boece* itself has hardly been held in high regard by Chaucer scholars, though that perspective has begun to alter because of several important studies over the past few years.[2] Earlier editors, from Thynne in 1532 onwards, approached the task by regarding **Cx** (printed near the end of 1478) as more or less equivalent to the extant manuscripts. They found little of

1. *Anicius M.T.S. Boethius: Boecius De Cosolacione Philosophie Tr. by G. Chaucer. Westminster (W. Caxton) (1478?)* (Amsterdam, 1974; The Eng. Experience, no. 644).

2. See, for example Machan (1985), Gleason (1987), Minnis (1987a), Machan (1987), Minnis (1993); also the discussion of the *Boece* by Copeland (1991).

interest in the *Boece*, including it dutifully but perfunctorily in the
collected works. Even in the more serious work of Skeat (1894–97:
II, 1-151) and Liddell in the Globe edition (Pollard *et al.* 1898:
352-437), where some manuscripts were examined, a place in the
textual tradition was assigned to **Cx** and it was hardly considered
further. After that the standard of editing was rather woeful,
reflected in the careless work of both Robinson editions (1933
and 1957) and Fisher (1977 and 1989), neither of whom consulted the manuscripts at first hand, misnumbering Salisbury
Cathedral MS 113 and remaining ignorant of Pembroke College
MS 215 although its existence had been signalled by Aage Brusendorff in 1925 (1925: 174). Only in more recent times has attention turned to the textual problems, the matter of Chaucer's
dependence on the French translation by Jean de Meun and
the Latin commentary of Nicholas Trevet, and the reception of
Chaucer's work by readers and copyists. The discovery of the Mis-
souri manuscript fragment (published in Pace and Voigts 1979)
and the new Riverside edition (Benson 1987), mark important
advances in this field; and the completion of the Variorum
edition, now in preparation, should further enhance the status of
the *Boece* as a work to be taken seriously.

So, what of the status of **Cx** in all this? As the *editio princeps*, it
must have manuscript copy-text behind the version as printed,
though none of the extant manuscripts can be the one Caxton
used. Editors have been led not only to fit **Cx** into a relationship
with the extant manuscripts, but also to note some editorial inter-
ference (not as extensive as in the *Morte Darthur* of 1485) and to
view the compositor(s) in the workshop as equivalent to scribes
transferring the written word into type. Deliberate editorial intervention shows up chiefly in the modernization of Chaucer's language, which may point to an annotated copy-text. Where readings are anomalous or plainly erroneous, especially in the way of
omissions and clearly wrong settings, these are attributed to unintentional error, or faulty or difficult copy-text. But viewing the
compositors as 'scribes', without some knowledge of the processes
of composition, imposition and presswork, can, I believe, distort
the true picture, causing omissions in particular to be considered
as careless and due to the common causes such as eyeskip and
haplography.

One conspicuous feature of **Cx** that has puzzled commentators is the high proportion of Latin text quoted to Chaucer's translation. Following a familiar pattern, as in some manuscripts, Latin text is quoted at the start of each Prose and Metre in order to identify it, though the Proses and Metres are not numbered, unlike the manuscript practice. The headings are all the more conspicuous because Caxton used a textura type (his no. 3 according to Blades 1861–63) to distinguish them, as against the bastard cursive (no. 2) of the same body size, used for the English text (see Figs. 1 and 2). It is the extent of such quotation which has seemed odd, for in most instances it exceeds the requirements of mere identification, as may be shown from a few examples. Many two- and three-line headings appear, but the greatest number are of four lines, verse being set continuously as prose. There are some of five lines: the headings to Bk. I, M.5 (f.10v), Bk. II, M.2 (f.17v), Bk. III, M.4 (f.37v), Bk. III, Pr.12 (f.52v), for instance. More striking are even longer examples, such as Bk. III M.2 (f.34) of six lines, and Bk. III M.5 and III Pr.6 together on f.39, of five and six lines respectively (see Fig. 3); Bk. III M.11 (f.51v) of six lines, and Bk. IV M.2 (f.61) of no fewer than nine lines, reproducing the whole Metre, for only 16 lines of English text (see Fig. 4); and lastly, Bk. IV M.5 (f.69), of eight lines, in which the compositor has also clearly misunderstood the layout of the Metre in the copy-text (see Fig. 5). In most cases a space of one line, made by setting 16 quads in a row, is left before and after the headings, though a few instances occur where one or both spaces are absent, as in f.61.

These vagaries of the settings of headings have assumed some significance in the eyes of bibliographers. The imprecise descriptions by Joseph Ames (1749: 57-58), William Herbert's revision of Ames's book (Ames 1785–90: I, 75-76) and Thomas Dibdin in his further revision (1810–19: I, 303-306, no. 42)[3] could give the impression that whole sections of Latin and English text were printed alternately, an inference picked up by Continental bibliographers who had not seen the book (such as Graesse 1858-69, I, 465), and even repeated later (Lowndes 1857–64: I, 229).

---

3.   A useful summary of Caxton studies in the eighteenth century is also given by Hellinga (1982: 25-28).

Chaucer in Perspective

Figure 1: Caxton's Type 2 (after Blades 1861–63)

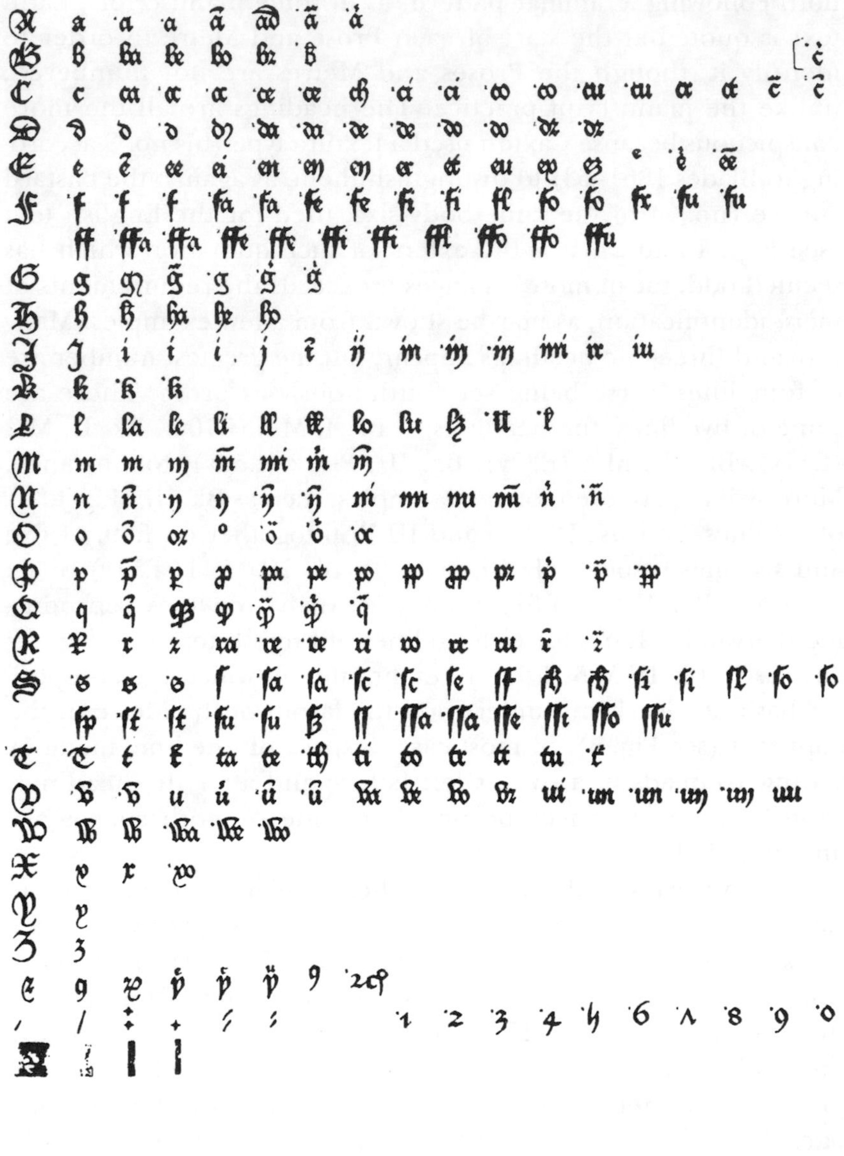

Figure 2: Caxton's Type 3 (after Blades 1861–63)

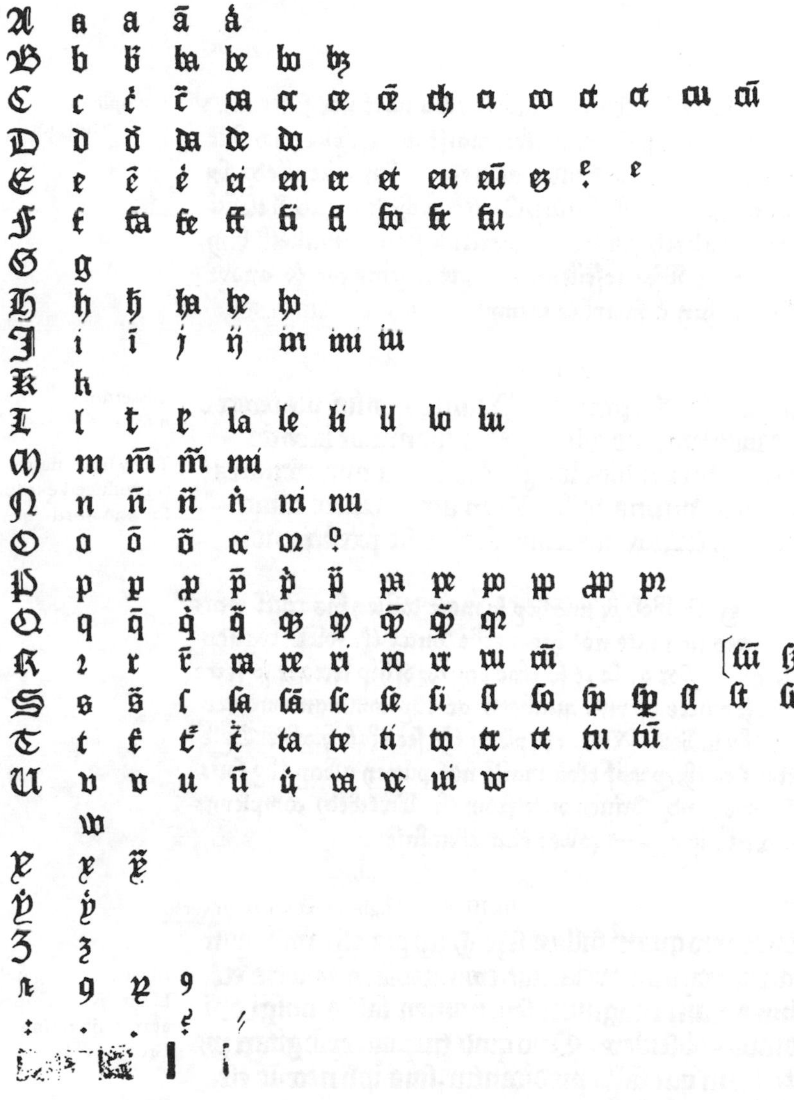

Figure 3: Disproportionately long quotations on f.39

And Whan thou Woldest haue it thou nast not siker, and
if thou Woldest forleten it thou maist not eschewen it, but
Whether suche men be frendes at nede as ben counseilled by
fortune, and not by vertue, Certes suche folke as weleful
fortune maketh frendes, contrarious fortune maketh hem
ennempes, & What pestilence is more mighty for to anoye
a Wight than a famylier enempe   (end of Bk.III Pr.5)

example of
broken full stop

Bk.III, M.5

Qui se wolet esse potentem Animos domet ille feroces
Nec victa libidine colla Fedis submittat habenis
Et enim licet indica longe Tell9 tua iura cremiscat
Et seruiat vltima thile Tum atras pellere curas
Miseralqz fugare querelas Non posse potencia non

missetting—
u for n

The whole metre
reproduced except
for one word

W   Ho so Wole be mighty he mote daunten his cruel cora-
            ges ne putte not his necke Vnder the folke regnes
of lecherie, For al be it so that thy lordship streche so ferre
that the countre of ynde quaketh at thy commandementes
or at thy lawes, And the yle in the see that highte Tyle
be thral to the, yet if thou maist not putten away thy foule desires, and driuen oute from the Wretched compleyn-
tes, certes it nys no power that thou hast

Bk.III, Pr.6 (English text starts on verso)

Gloria vero quam fallax sepe q turpis est. vnde non
iniuria tragicus exclamat. eros. azosa. myplocia etc
Plures enim magnum sepe nomen fallis vulgi opi
nionibus abstulere . Quo quid turpius excogitari po-
test. Nam qui falso predicantur. suis ipsi necesse est.
laudibus erubescant etc

Illustrates 'vulgate'
Latin text attempts
at transliterating
Greek

Figure 4: Excessive quotation on f.61

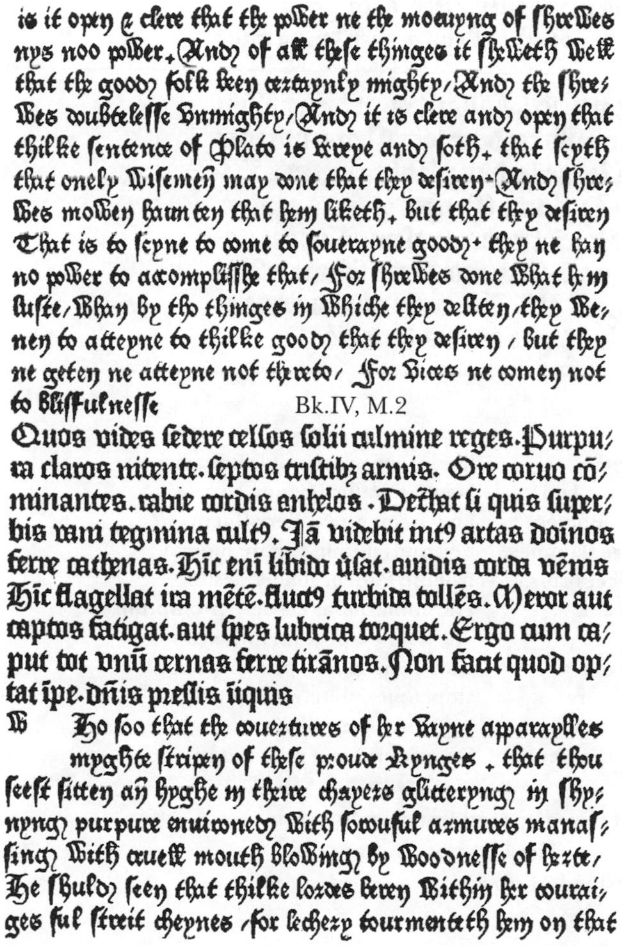

is it open & clere that the power ne the moeuyng of shrewes
nys noo power. And of alle these thinges it sheweth well
that the goode folk been certaynly mighty, And the shrewes doubtelesse vnmighty, And it is clere and open that
thilke sentence of Plato is sooth and soth. that seyth
that onely wisemen may done that they desiren. And shrewes mowen haunten that hem liketh. but that they desiren
That is to seyne to come to soueraine good+ they ne han
no power to accomplisshe that, For shrewes done what hem
luste, whan by tho thinges in whiche they delyten, they we-
nen to atteyne to thilke good that they desiren / but they
ne geten ne atteyne not therto. For vices ne comen not
to blisfulnesse   Bk.IV, M.2

Quos vides sedere cellos solii culmine reges. Purpu-
ra claros nitente. septos tristibz armis. Ore toruo co-
minantes. rabie cordis anhelos. Dethat si quis super-
bis vani tegmina cult9. Ia videbit int9 artas doinos
ferre cathenas. Hic eni libido vsat. auidis corda venis
Hic flagellat ira mete. fluc9 turbida tolles. Meror aut
captos fatigat. aut spes lubrica torquet. Ergo cum ca-
put tot vnu cernas ferre tiranos. Non facit quod op-
tat ipe. dñis prmis iiquis

¶   Ho soo that the couertures of her vayne apparaylles
        myghte stripen of these proude kynges . that thou
seest sitten an hyghe in thire chayers gliterynge in shy-
nynge purpure enuironed with sorowful armures manas-
synge with cruel mouth blowinge by woodnesse of herte,
He shulde seen that thilke lordes beren within her courai-
ges ful streit cheynes /for lechery tourmenteth hem on that

The whole Metre
is reproduced

Figure 5: Long, erroneously set verse on f.69

the cause of so grete a disposicioy. Natheles for as meche
as godly the goode gouernour attempteth andly gouerneth
the Worlde, ne doubte ye not that al thinges ben done a right

Si quis arturi sidera nescit. Lassant ꝫ crebris pulsibꝫ
aera. Propinqua summo cardine labi. Nemo miratur
flamina chori. Cur legat tardus plaustra boetes . Li⁄
tus frementi tundere fluctu. Mergat ꝫ seras equore
flamas. Nec nimis dura frigore molem. Cur nimis
sceleres explicet ortus . Feruente phebi soluier estu.
Legem stupebit etheris alti. Hic enim causas cernere
promptum. Palleant plene cornua lune etc

Si quis Arcturi sidera nescit	lassantque crebris pulsibus aera.
propinqua summo cardine labi,	Nemo miratur flamina cori
cur legat tardus plaustra Bootes,	litus frementi tundere fluctu,
mergatque seras aequore flammas,	nec niuis duram frigore molem
cum nimis celeres explicet ortus,	fruente Phoebi soluier aestu.
legem stupebit aetheris alti.	Hic enim causas cernere promptum est,
Palleant plenae cornua lunae	illic latentes pectora turbant.
infecta metis noctis opacae	Cuncta quae rara prouehit aetas
quaeque fulgenti texerat ore	stupetque subitis mobile uulgus,
confusa Phoebe detegat astra,	cedat inscitae nubilis error,
commouet gentes publicus error,	cessent profecto mira uideri

The lines of Bk. IV, M.5 as disposed in two columns in
the exemplar manuscript. The compositor has read
across the columns instead of down.

They may have made a comparison with George Colville's translation of Boethius, printed in 1556, where the texts are in parallel;
it cannot be said with certainty that any of them knew of the
manuscript, now Cambridge University Library MS Ii.3.21, which
does indeed have Latin and English texts alternating. Unfortu-
nately, even William Blades in 1863 and 1877, who knew the book
well, does not clarify the nature and extent of the 'Latin quotations' (his phrase) very precisely. He was, after all, more interested
in the typography than in the text and arrangement of the book.
The more recent pronouncements on the subject still reflect puz-
zlement, the more so since the fluctuating nature of the Latin text
itself in the Middle Ages has been recognized. Here is an example
of more recent critical opinion:

> An interesting characteristic of the manuscript copies of Chaucer's
> *Boece* is that they usually give quotations from the Latin text at the
> head of each prosa and metrum...Some Latin headings are a word
> or two; some are quite long. One manuscript (Ii.3.21, University
> library, Cambridge, 1430–50) alternates the complete Latin text
> with Chaucer's translation; only Caxton's edition approaches its
> generosity with Latin headings. Chaucer's translation, however,
> does not match the Latin of the headings, and it does not do so in
> Caxton's edition. Whether the printer took his copious headings
> from the same manuscript that was his source for the translation it
> is impossible to say on the basis of textual evidence. His dealings
> with the text of the first edition of *The Canterbury Tales* suggest that
> he did, though his patron—assuming that he had one, since he
> says in his epilogue that *Boece* is printed at the request of an
> unnamed friend—may have wanted the headings from some other
> source agreed upon in advance. But that Caxton would have done
> this sort of thing on his own during the period of his early Chaucers
> appears unlikely. Caxton's edition is still important in the editing
> of *Boece.* It belongs to the first of two textual traditions, alpha and
> beta, which do not differ greatly. Scholars have wavered between
> one and the other as the better text, and the case is not yet closed.

These are the words of Beverly Boyd in her chapter on Caxton in
Editing Chaucer: The Great Tradition (1984: 28); they are a condensed version of her description of the matter in her transcription of 1978. Setting aside the misdating of the Cambridge manuscript, which can be shown to have been in the medieval university
library already by 1424, these remarks serve as an index to the

reaction of many observers who have noted this inconsistency in Caxton's practice in the book.

Admittedly the situation *is* puzzling, and it poses a challenge to examine the book more critically to look for some explanation. Might the problem be more amenable to solution by adopting a bibliographical approach?

In an attempt to answer this question, I began by examining one copy of the state of the text presented in the print. From this there is a distinct impression that Caxton's workmen had no great respect for Chaucer's text. There are many wrong settings which could have been corrected during presswork, indicative either of no care to proofread during the printing runs, or of no concern to make corrections if errors were noted (see Fig. 6).[4] I then proceeded to collate in full a dozen copies on the chance of finding variant states which might have been significant—variation does occur in other books of Caxton's—but none were found except minor disturbances of type reflecting purely mechanical factors in operation, such as loosening and pulling of type in the formes, and the common enough problem of rising quads. This strengthened my belief that the printers preferred to disturb the text, once set, as minimally as possible during the production of the book (the edition size is not known, but probably not more than several hundred copies).

Though one hesitates to call the workshop attitude a cavalier one, nevertheless it is tempting to wonder whether the integrity of the text might have been compromised by the demands of the production process. Collation of the print against the manuscripts discloses not only textual affinities, but also instances to be expected of compositorial error comparable to scribal error, and evidence of the editorial intervention already mentioned. But when all such explicable readings are accounted for, there is a residue of unique features not so explicable, especially certain omissions, and one or two extensions of text, which do not seem attributable to the common causes of mechanical error to which scribes and compositors are subject. Perhaps the **Cx** readings are

4.   Around 60 such examples have been noted, in both the English text and the Latin headings. They include the common faults such as turned letters, and types returned to the wrong compartments in the cases after distribution.

Figure 6: Typical misprints not corrected during the printing run

Turned letters

81r, l.3   67v, l.5

ꝭꝭ it ꝭy ueꝭꝭ ite   tꝭe maladie of ſynne

purueaꝭ , to ꝭꝭiche purneaꝭ   71r, l.12

ye men tꝭat ꝭee ſemblable to God   24r, l.24

Errors perhaps due to faulty distribution

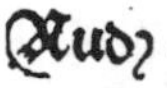

ꝭuꝭ = And   feſtynaly = festyualy   29v, l.8

   29v, l.5, and 51v, l.3

ſo grete a ſemble of ſenatours,   = a(s)semble   19r, l.1

ꝭlſſfulnes = blissfulness   concluſion = conclusion

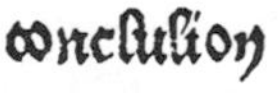

   56v, l.29   65r, l.8
     (= bottom line)

not all just the accidental results of localized compositorial error.

In the light of these findings, I considered that a fuller bibliographical investigation was desirable. But, before I proceed with these more technical matters, it may be helpful for me to give a general description of the physical make-up of the book. It consists of 94 leaves in folio format, made up of 11 gatherings of eight leaves (i.e. four sheets quired and folded inside one another), and a final one of six leaves. The initial leaf is an integral blank in the first gathering. All gatherings are unsigned and unpaginated (or foliated), though at least one copy has evidence of manuscript signatures, which I follow here, so the collation is: fol.: a-l^{8}m^6.

An uncut copy measured 300×215 mm, so sheets of about 300×430 mm were used. The type area occupies 190×127 mm, with fairly ragged right-hand edges because of rough justification. There are 28 lines to a full page. Two type styles (Types 2 and 3), of the same body size, were used. There is an initial heading, but no running titles or numbering in the text. Within sections, there is no paragraphing: the type is set solid. Space is left at the start of sections for large initials to be supplied by a rubricator, and this has been done in some copies. The paper stock in all copies, of laid pattern, has the same watermark (a pair of scissors), identifiable as Italian, and consistent with the date 1478 as assigned to this book; it is rather thick and rough in most copies, with long fibres, showing that the 'stuff' in the vat into which the moulds were dipped was coarse and thickly concentrated. The marks of the felt on which it was couched from the mould are often evident.

When the book is considered as a commercial venture, its appearance yields obvious information about the printer's choices of size, types, layout and design, format, and provision for rubrication. We even have Caxton's 'advertisement' in the epilogue, including observations on the nature of the book, accompanied by a fulsome poem on Chaucer by Surigonus.[5] But a closer study, to be pursued here, can provide further evidence of production details from the printer's type, that is, the inked shapes which had left their impression on the paper. Since I have no means of knowing how many readers of this article are familiar with the

5.   These are put in context in Blake (1980: 38-43).

procedures of analytical bibliography applied to early printed books, I pause here briefly to describe the compositor's method of setting, while begging the indulgence of those to whom this subject is already familiar.

The first observation is that the format is relevant here. In many of his books Caxton used quired folios rather than the more complex formats of quarto and octavo, which involve more folding, and the placing of more type pages in the formes in positions which appear odd to a layman's eye. Figure 7 may illustrate this format: it shows that each gathering of four sheets requires eight printings, two formes per sheet (inner and outer), in which, all except for one, the type pages set side by side (this is called imposition) are not in sequential numerical order. Unlike the copying of a manuscript gathering, the pages were not printed one by one from sheet to sheet, but in pairs, a whole side of the sheet being impressed at one time, probably in two pulls in the press.

It used to be a common assumption among historians of early printing that in order to impose the pages of successive formes compositors set the text *seriatim* from the copy-text, that is, in numerical order, because it is difficult to know in advance the exact content of each page. In Caxton's format the implication is that nothing could be printed until the ninth page was set in each gathering (the seventh, in the final gathering), so the inner forme of the innermost sheet could be imposed. Work could then proceed to the outermost sheet by setting the rest of the pages, and imposing, as appropriate, with those standing ready. Such a procedure requires a sufficient quantity of type and space to keep standing type-pages safe from accident or confusion.

There are, however, alternative possibilities to overcome the disadvantages of this system. It has been maintained, for instance, that in the *Recuyell of the Histories of Troy*, printed in Bruges in 1473–74, a half-sheet system was used to set and print single pages in sequence (i.e. as in manuscript copying).[6] This is cumbersome and would need rigorous control to avoid confusion and spoiling

6.   See Hellinga (1976–77: 19-32), where the division of the work among several compositors is also pointed out. The single-page system might also be confirmed by the variant Bodleian copy of the *Recuyell*, where unlike other copies the verso on the twenty-ninth leaf has not been printed, though the corresponding other page on the same side of the sheet has been done.

Figure 7: The makeup of Caxton's Print

Collation: Fol.:   a – 1^8, m^6 = 94 leaves
              (NB: j is not used in the signing alphabet)

Structure of a typical gathering:

Quired folio in eights ('sig.' = any signature)
Viewed as if from top of book.

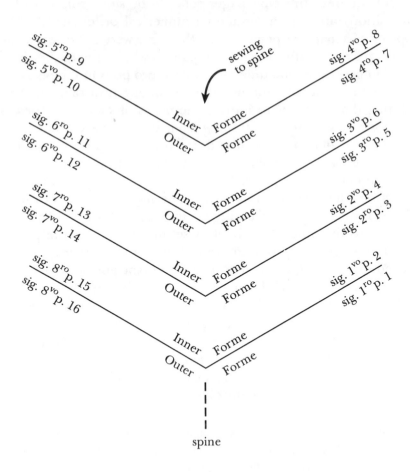

of sheets, but may have been forced upon the printers as a result
of their having only a small quantity of type. If Caxton was forced
by limitations to use this method, it was superseded when he
began his Westminster career, for he produced small books in
quarto format which could not have been printed in this way. A
better method is that of setting by formes, a practice amply
attested in later books but not suspected in incunabula by earlier
bibliographers. However, evidence has been steadily accumulating of its widespread use in this period. It consists of setting and
placing the appropriate pages directly into the formes for each
sheet regardless of numerical order. The advantages are great: an
easier balance is achieved between composition (and distribution) and presswork; only a small stock of type is needed; and
there are no standing pages to be damaged or pied.

This method of setting can be detected, often by type-evidence.
If in each gathering the pages had been set *seriatim* up to the
middle of the gathering, any individual type could not recur
within those pages, but might appear again in the conjugate
leaves of the rest of the gathering, depending on how soon the
machined type was distributed back into the cases for reuse.
Obviously it is best to look for conspicuously broken types, since a
recurrent one can more easily be noticed. Several can indeed be
identified, one in particular, a damaged full stop or period, which
appears frequently, in enough positions within the first halves of
gatherings, to prove the point sufficiently.

Caxton's workmen undoubtedly used this method of non-
sequential setting. The chief difficulty of this method, however, is
that preliminary calculations are necessary to determine what
parts of the text will occupy the pages in each forme. This process
of estimating what type-pages correspond to the copy-text is called
casting-off. The difficulty varies with the nature of the text: prose is
harder than regular verse. The copy-text must be marked up for
the compositor, and there is only a small margin of play to adjust
calculation errors by crowding up the type (if there is more text)
or driving it out, and possibly leaving blank spaces (if there is too
little), or making other accommodations such as varying spelling
or using contracted forms. Once a commitment has been made to
printing one or more formes, the others must tally. In recent
years a considerable number of copy-texts so marked-up has been

identified, throwing light on workshop practice, and confirming
the earliness of the method of setting by formes from cast-off
copy. These include the manuscript of the *Nova Rhetorica* from
which Caxton printed the text in the following year, 1479. George
Painter (1976: 97) even asserts that setting by formes was the
norm rather than the exception.[7]

With this bibliographical evidence in mind, the puzzling features of the *Boece* construction fall into place. First, the *Boece*
presents long passages of continuous prose, which increase the
problems of casting-off. Clearly this explains instances of cram-
ming text, or driving it out, observable in some pages. Where a
resulting underestimation of space was serious, it is not too fanci-
ful to suggest that the compositors merely adopted the expedient
of omitting a convenient portion of text, the explanation of the
oddities mentioned earlier. The most glaring instance of this
occurs on f.83v, at the beginning of Book V, Pr.4, where a substantial portion of text is omitted at the end of the page, before
the start of f.84. Secondly, and more important, at last the full
significance of those Latin headings is plain. The *Boece* is also
broken up into many sections of unequal length. Although the
headings may incidentally identify the successive sections, their
primary purpose is to aid the compositors in coping with casting-
off problems, by providing a 'stock' or 'pool' of text from which
variable fillers could be extracted to fit whatever space resulted
between sections of English text, following the page calculations.
It is entirely possible that in each page where they occur they were
set and inserted *after* the setting of the English text showed what
space needed filling. The obvious question is: 'Why was the matter
not resolved simply by leaving larger blank spaces?' The answer
may be that a full page of type was preferred so as to get an even

7.   This is echoed by Hellinga (1982: 46-47); see also her discussion
(Hellinga 1974: 64-69). The method is also described by Blake (1976: 55-58),
and he gives some examples of serious miscalculation in other Caxton books
(60); see also his later, more detailed treatment of the subject (1989: 407-10)
repr. in Blake (1991: 275-303). As for copy-texts known to have been used by
early printers, a good example is discussed by Meale (1982: 156-71), and a
convenient list with references is given on p. 156 n. 1. To these may now be
added the early fifteenth-century manuscript demonstrable as the copy-text
for the 1525 Tavistock printing of John Walton's translation of Boethius: see
Donaghey and Taavitsainen (forthcoming).

distribution of pressure in the forme during presswork. Blades and others refer to early printers' use of 'blind types' as bearers, that is, either uninked, or blocked out by the frisket in the press.[8] These types serve the same function.

In the context of Caxton's productions at Westminster, the printing of **Cx** in 1478 may be viewed as the culmination of the workshop's experience in printing several larger works (the first edition of *Canterbury Tales, History of Jason, Dictes and Sayings of the Philosophers,* and *Moral Proverbs of Cristyne*) and 14 smaller items in quarto format, either in his Type 2 (peculiar to Caxton) or a combination of his Types 2 and 3 (the latter a type which the founder, Veldener, sold commercially to other printers),[9] before other jobs were undertaken with Type 2* as a recasting of Type 2. The quantity of output in that period was remarkable, and so the personnel of the workshop can be imagined as struggling to keep up a rate of production which must have led to pressure to adopt expedient methods and not to be too conscientious about lapses in calculation and in typesetting.

A case in point is the first edition of the *Dictes and Sayings of the Philosophers* (1477),[10] certainly set by formes, in which the work appears to be divided between two compositors, one characterized by his rough justification of lines, leaving a generally ragged right-hand edge, and preferring punctuation between phrases in the form of full stops (though sometimes virgules), the other taking more care over even justification, more inclined to use hyphens in splitting words, and preferring the virgule as punctuation. There are many errors of setting by both which have not been corrected. There do not seem to have been any special difficulties in casting off the copy-text for the pages, but crowding is

8. See Paisey (1986: 220-33). It has been observed that the *Court of Sapience* (assignable to 1483), also printed in folio, ends with a miscellany of prose unrelated to the preceding verse text. This may likewise have been intended to fill up the forme so as to ensure even pressure under the platen.

9. See Barker (1976–77: 114-33 [and illustrations]); Hellinga (1982: 54-76) also has some pertinent observations on Caxton's use of these types (and the mixing and combination of them), including (p. 68) a revised chronology of the early books. The most recent listing of all Caxton's known imprints (111 items) is by Needham (1986: 83-91).

10. Hellinga (1982: 77-80) has some observations on the problems of dating the *Dictes.*

evident in some, and it is clear that in others, where a more generous allocation of space had occurred, the device was adopted of leaving gaps of varying widths between sentences (all starting with 'And') where paragraph marks could be supplied by hand (as was done in some copies) so as to drive out the text into the full space.

If Caxton's use of the Latin headings in **Cx** represents a refinement on the devices used in the *Dictes* (where there are no chapter headings), then the signs are that with experience he exercised an increasing degree of sophistication in adapting his printing methods for difficult texts, even though unfortunate errors occurred from time to time. Some work has been done on his ambitious undertaking of printing the *Morte Darthur* (1485; also printed by formes) to show how he proceeded. For a start, the very act of presenting the text redivided into a greater number of books, and in marked chapters within them, by comparison with the Winchester manuscript which is known to have been present in the workshop (twenty-one books and 506 chapters in total), is not only calculated to make the text more user-friendly, but also to facilitate adjustment of space within pages. Yet even where some licence was given to the compositors to deal flexibly with text, especially at page breaks, in order to create a seamless flow from page to page, there are indications of many difficulties.[11] It has also been suggested that the irregular pattern of use of paragraph marks (types on the same body as the letters of Type 4* used throughout the book) served the same purpose of helping in adjustment of space rather than strictly being used to show emphasis or to draw attention to text.[12] This would be an extension of the expedient already used in the *Dictes and Sayings*.

To return to **Cx**: here, then, within a vernacular text, we see the ultimate reduction of a Latin text to the status of a convenient aid to fit the constraints of a mechanical process, without regard to the intrinsic value of that text, or any necessary connection with the translation of it. The same conditions led to the taking of liberties with the English text, thereby reducing its value as a

11. Illustrated in the important article in Takamiya (1996: 63-78), though the matter had already been anticipated in Hellinga (1982: 92-93).

12. (Kato 1996: 1-13). I am grateful to Miss Kato for personal discussion and for drawing my attention to her article.

witness to the textual tradition. Finally, it must be concluded that Caxton's praise of the *Boece*, and his account of undertaking to print it, cannot be taken at face value to represent entirely his reception of the work. At the least, his allowance of rather hit-and-miss practices in his workshop almost constitutes a positive disrespect to Chaucer, in not respecting the integrity of his text so far as the limitations of his manuscript would allow. Chaucer might well have been as displeased with Caxton over the way his book got into print as he was with the laxity of his scribe Adam's copying.

APPENDIX

List of Known Copies of Caxton's Boece

Since the list by Seymour de Ricci (1909: 11-14) is now out of date, the following may serve as a finding list. Caxton's *Boece* is *STC* 3199 and *GKW* 4576.

1. British Library IB.55018 (de Ricci no. 5). Reverend Cracherode's copy, bequeathed to the British Museum in 1799.

2. British Library c.11.c9 (de Ricci no. 10). From the Royal Library, passed on to the British Museum in 1829. Made perfect by supplying the initial blank leaf and f.81 from another copy (see no. 19 below).

3. British Library IB55020 (de Ricci no. 6). From the Grenville Library, bequeathed to the British Museum in 1846. Partly rubricated by hand. A serious misbinding of sheets in sig.i happened in the rebinding of c. 1808.

4. Sion College, London (de Ricci no. 15). Given in 1644 by the London bookseller Henry Holland. Almost complete, lacking the initial blank and part of f.2. Partly rubricated by hand.

5. St Bride Printing Library, London (de Ricci no. 29). Bought by William Blades before 1879 and passed on to the Library. Fragmentary: de Ricci recorded 38 leaves, but three more have since been lost; one sheet from this copy is now in the Pierpont Morgan Library, New York (see no. 22 below). Rubricated by hand. This copy had its original binding from Caxton's workshop, but detached. The fragment was newly bound and the original binding put on exhibition, but it was temporarily misplaced in 1939 and rediscovered in 1967; it is now described as no. 5 in Nixon (1976–77: 92-113). A photograph of it was included in an anonymous article (1912: 21). It

bears some resemblance to the binding on the Colchester copy (no. 16 below). Fragments of printer's waste from *The Lyf of Our Lady* had been used to make up the boards.

6. English private collector (de Ricci no. 28). Once in the collection of Maurice Johnson (1688–1755), an antiquary of Spalding, Lincolnshire, it was sold at the dispersal of his library in 1898. It survived World War II in France in a private library, then passed to John Worth, then was sold in 1974. Incomplete, only 55 leaves. Rubricated by hand. Striking for being in its original binding from Caxton's workshop, as noted in Painter (1963: 73-80), and described in Nixon (1976–77: no. 4).

7. Bodleian Library, Oxford, Auct. QQ. sup. I.20 (de Ricci no. 11). Not quite complete: lacks initial blank and f.57. Rubricated by hand throughout.

8. Bodleian Library, Oxford, Auct. QQ. sup. I.21 (de Ricci no.12). Given in 1680 by the London bookseller Moses Pitt. Now bound with several other Caxton imprints. Amost complete, lacks f.9 (but not f.40 as de Ricci says) but the initial blank is intact.

9. Magdalen College, Oxford, B.III.2.12 (de Ricci no. 1). There from at least the mid-eighteenth century, but c. 1600 was in Hereford. A fine, complete, uncut copy, rubricated throughout, in a stout contemporary binding (but not from Caxton's workshop). The *Boece* is preceded by a copy of the *De Consolatione Philosophiae* in Latin, part of *GKW* 4530, from Cologne, 1482. Marks of chaining on the binding. Listed in Rhodes (1982: 78, item 402 [b]).

10. Exeter College, Oxford, 9.M.4815 (de Ricci no. 7). Bound up since the late seventeenth century with *The Orcharde of Syon* (Wynkyn de Worde, 1519), Caxton's *Cato* (1483) and *The Lyf of Our Lady* (1484). Complete except for the initial blank. Listed in Rhodes (1982: 78, item 402 [a]).

11. Wadham College, Oxford, A.6.11 (de Ricci no. 16). Owned by John Sepper, early seventeenth century, Thomas Martin, early eighteenth century, Francis Blomefield (the Norfolk antiquary), 1736, then Richard Warner, 1770, who bequeathed it to the College. Incomplete, now 69 leaves, but the missing text has been supplied in manuscript, on late eighteenth-century paper, from a later edition of the *Boece*. Rubricated by hand. Bound with an incomplete copy of the *Speculum Vitae Christi* (Pynson, c. 1495). The volume is noted in Wheeler (1929: 12) and listed in Rhodes (1982: 78, item 402 [c]).

12. Cambridge University Library, Inc. 3.J.1.1. (de Ricci no. 14). From Bishop Moore, to the Royal Library in 1714, then presented to the Cambridge library in 1715. Almost complete, lacking the initial blank and ff.3-4. Noted in Sayle (1900–1907: I, 3, item 2) and Oates (1954: 672, item 4064).

13. Manchester, John Rylands University Library (de Ricci no. 2). De Ricci confuses this with the Ripon copy (no. 15 below) so the names he lists there belong here: Francis Shewarde (not Howard), Ambrose Niclas, Nicholas Morgan. The known provenance begins with the sale of Thomas Staunton, April 1785. It was bought by Stanesby Alchorne of the Mint, sold to the bookseller Thomas Payne, who sold it to Johnes of Hafod, from whom it passed to the collection of Earl Spencer before 1823, when it was described by Thomas Dibdin. In 1892 much of the Spencer collection (including 3,000 incunabula) was acquired for the new John Rylands Library. Complete, with rubrication throughout, but much disfigured by many later inscriptions. Noted in Guppy (1930: 10-11).

14. Longleat, Wiltshire, Marquis of Bath's Library (de Ricci no. 9). This copy (though now in a nineteenth-century binding) may have been in the ownership of the Thynnes (the family name of the Marquises) for a long time, as it has been shown by Blodgett (1979: 97-113) to have been part of the copy-text for the *Boece* in William Thynne's folio edition of Chaucer's works in 1532: see also remarks in Donaghey (1997: 150-64). Complete, except for the initial blank, and rubricated throughout.

15. Ripon Cathedral Library, Yorkshire (de Ricci no. 13). Various early names are inscribed in this copy: Francys Kelsone (possibly in 1566), Davye Calvard of Monk Fryston, Jhon Wadward, Wyllyam Clerk, Thomas Erll. If a mid-sixteenth century date is indicated, the mention of Monk Fryston may mean that the volume was in West Yorkshire by that time. Later owned by Anthony Higgin, second Dean of Ripon under James I's foundation of 1608, and bequeathed by him in 1624 to the Cathedral Library. Nearly complete, lacking the initial blank and f.79, but not two leaves in the middle, as de Ricci asserts; as noted above, he also confused this with the Rylands copy. Bound, until c. 1815 with a copy of Caxton's *Vocabulary* (this was sold separately by the Dean and Chapter in 1960). This copy has been noted in Dibdin (1810–19: III, 419), Botfield (1849: 386), Fowler (1871–72: 371-402), Harrison (1892: 211), Smith (1914: 282), Wilkinson (1960: 13-14). This copy has now been deposited, with other material from the Library, on loan in the Brotherton Collection at the University of Leeds.

16. Colchester, Essex, Public Library. Not known to de Ricci. Listed in Ramage (1958: 14). Owned by Thomas Banckton, 1613, and probably by Archbishop Harsnett, who bequeathed books to the town in 1631. The neglected collection was rescued by Charles Gray, who restored the Castle and started the Castle Society Book Club in Colchester in 1750. When the Castle was acquired by the town in 1920 as a museum the books were transferred to the Public Library. The volume is listed in a mid-Victorian printed catalogue (anon. 1856: 6). An uncut copy, almost complete, lacking the initial blank and f.81, and rubricated throughout. Notable for being preserved

in its original binding from Caxton's workshop (though rather fragile), as noted in Painter (1963: 74), and described in Nixon (1976–77, no. 3).

17. San Marino, California, Huntington Library (de Ricci no. 3). Sold to the Library from the Duke of Devonshire's collection in 1914 as part of a block purchase of 25 Caxton prints. Almost complete, but lacking the initial blank. Listed in Mead (1937: 239, item 5222) and Goff (1964: B.813).

18. New York, Pierpont Morgan Library, no. 775 (de Ricci no. 4). From the Earl of Westmoreland to Quaritch in 1887, then to Lord Amherst of Hackney, and in 1908 to J. Pierpont Morgan. Almost complete, lacking the initial blank. Some leaves have been transposed in rebinding. Listed in Thurston and Bühler (1939: 166) and Goff (1964: B.813). On the last page, in an early sixteenth-century hand, is a copy of a late fifteenth-century lyric, beginning 'Love that is powre it is with pyne' (*SIMEV* 2013; also listed in Ringler [1992: 151]). A pre-1500 copy is also found on the rear flyleaves of British Library MS Cotton Vitellius C.xiii, added to Lydgate's *Pilgrimage of the Life of Man*.

19. Jenkintown, PA, Lessing J. Rosenwald Collection, Library of Congress (de Ricci no. 8; his report is inaccurate). Blades found this neglected and damaged copy at St Albans Grammar School in 1858, evidently in its original binding from Caxton's workshop. In 1859 he removed the binding, along with the fragments of printer's waste making up its boards, and had a plain binding applied, including the fragments at the end. By 1871 this bound copy was sold to the British Museum, where f.81 was removed to make perfect no. 2 above, and the fragments were also removed. The book was eventually exchanged for other rare books, and went to Sir Thomas Brookes' collection. It passed to the bookseller Rosenbach in 1891, and was bought by Mr Rosenwald in the 1940s. Not only was f.81 made up in facsimile, but an actual leaf was then supplied, by arrangement, from another copy (no. 20 below). Nothing has been heard of the original binding since 1859, and it must be presumed destroyed. Nixon (1976–77: no. 6) gives an account of the matter. This copy is now almost complete, lacking the initial blank.

20. Huio, Meisei University Library, Japan (de Ricci no. 17, identical with his no. 24). Offered in a catalogue in 1829, then in a catalogue by Pickering in 1834. Sold to John Dunn Gardner in 1844, then from his sale in 1854 to Upham. It then figured in the Earl of Ashburnham's sale in 1897, where it went to Tregaskis, then to Richard Bennett. J Pierpont Morgan bought the Bennett collection intact in 1902. The Pierpont Morgan Library offered this copy for sale in 1971 (through Charles Traylen) and in 1974; it was eventually bought by Meisei University. Incomplete, lacking the initial blank, and ff. 5, 81 and 94. As noted above, f.81 was abstracted by permission to supply the want in no. 19, the St Albans copy. This has been a made-up copy

since Gardner supplied ff. 6, 7 and 93 from another (unidentified) copy , and ff. 5 and 94 were supplied in facsimile late last century. Noted in Thurston and Bühler (1939: 166) and Yukishima (1995: 49-50, no. 086).

21. Private ownership, USA? (de Ricci no. 26). Duke of Hamilton's sale, 1884, to Quaritch. Complete.

22. New York, Pierpont Morgan Library (de Ricci no. 30). A fragment, being the inmost sheet of gathering e (i.e. sig.e4-e5). This was removed by William Blades from the copy which eventually went into the St Bride Printing Library (no. 5 above), and presented by him, with leaves from the *Lyf of Our Lady*, to W.H. Dutton in 1879. Acquired by Quaritch, all these leaves, bound together, were sold to W.C. van Antwerp in 1905 and in turn sold to Tregaskis in 1907. By 1926 the New York bookseller Gabriel Wells had them, from whom the Library bought them.

23. St Bride Printing Library (de Ricci no. 31). Another fragment, ff.85-8 (i.e. sig.l5-l8), of another copy. This belonged to Blades and was presumably passed on to the Library with other Blades material.

Works Cited

Ames, J.
  1749   *Typographical Antiquities: Being an Historical Account of Printing in England; with some Memoirs of our Antient Printers, and a Register of the Books Printed by them, from the Year MCCCCLXXI to the Year MDC* (London: Faden & Robinson).
  1785-90   *Typographical Antiquities: or an Historical Account of the Origin and Progress of Printing in Great Britain and Ireland: containing Memoirs of our Ancient Printers, and a Register of Books Printed by them. Considerably Augmented... by W. Herbert* (3 vols.; London: Payne & Son).
anon
  1856   *A Catalogue of the Library of the Colchester Castle Society Book Club* (Colchester).
  1912   'The Oldest English Bindings', *British and Colonial Printer and Stationer (Bookbinding Supplement)* 14 March: 21.
Barker, N.
  1976-77   'Caxton's Typography', *Journal of the Printing Historical Society* 11: 114-33.
Benson, L.D. (ed.)
  1987   *The Riverside Chaucer* (Boston: Houghton Mifflin).
Blades, W.
  1861-63   *The Life and Typography of William Caxton* (2 vols.; London and Strasbourg: J. Lilly).
  1877   *The Biography and Typography of William Caxton* (London: Trübner).

Blake, N.F.
1976   *Caxton, England's First Publisher* (London: Osprey).
1980   'Continuity and Change in Caxton's Prologues and Epilogues: West-
              minster', *Gutenberg Jahrbuch*: 38-43.
1989   'Manuscript to Print', in J. Griffiths and D. Pearsall (eds.), *Book
              Production and Publishing in Britain 1375–1475* (Cambridge: Cam-
              bridge University Press).
1991   *William Caxton and English Literary Culture* (London: Hambledon
              Press).
Blodgett, J.E.
1979   'Some Printer's Copy for William Thynne's 1532 Edition of
              Chaucer', *Library*, 6th series 1: 97-113.
Botfield, B.
1849   *Notes on the Cathedral Libraries of England* (London: Whittingham).
Boyd, B.
1984   'William Caxton (1422?–1491)', in P.G. Ruggiers (ed.), *Editing
              Chaucer: The Great Tradition* (Norman, OK: Pilgrim Books): 13-34.
Boyd, B. (ed.)
1978   *Chaucer According to William Caxton: Minor Poems and Boece 1478*
              (Lawrence, KS: Allen Press).
Brusendorff, A.
1925   *The Chaucer Tradition* (London: Oxford University Press).
Copeland, R.
1991   *Rhetoric, Hermeneutics and Translation in the Middle Ages: Academic
              Traditions and Vernacular Texts* (Cambridge: Cambridge University
              Press).
Dibdin, T.F.
1810–19   *Typographical Antiquities: Or the History of Printing in England Scotland
              and Ireland: containing Memoirs of our Ancient Printers, and a Register of
              the Books Printed by them. Begun by the late Joseph Ames, F.R. and A.SS.
              Considerably augmented by William Herbert... and now greatly enlarged...*
              (4 vols.; London: Miller).
1817   *The Bibliographical Decameron* (London: printed for the author).
Donaghey, B.S.
1997   'William Thynne's Collected Edition of Chaucer: Some Biblio-
              graphical Considerations', in J. Scattergood and J. Boffey (eds.),
              Texts and their Contexts: Papers from the Early Book Society (Dublin: Four
              Courts Press): 150-64.
Donaghey, B.S., and I. Taavitsainen
  forthcoming 'Walton's Boethius: From Manuscript to Print', *English Studies*.
Fisher, J.H. (ed.)
1977, 1989   *The Complete Poetry and Prose of Geoffrey Chaucer* (New York: Holt,
              Rinehart & Winston, 1st and 2nd edns).
Fowler, J.T.
1871–72   'Ripon Minster Library and its Founder', *Yorkshire Archaeological and
              Topographical Journal* 2: 371-402.

Gleason, M.J.
1987   'Clearing the Fields: Towards a Reassessment of Chaucer's Use of Trevet in the *Boece*', in Minnis 1987b: 89-105.

Goff, F.R.
1964   *Incunabula in American Libraries: A Third Census of Fifteenth-Century Books Recorded in North American Collections* (New York: Bibliographical Society of America).

Graesse, J.G.T.
1858–69   *Trésor de Livres Rares et Précieux, ou Nouveau Dictionnaire Bibliographique, contenant plus de Cent Mille Articles de Livres Rares* (8 vols.; Dresden).

Guppy, H.
1930   *English Incunabula in the John Rylands Library* (Manchester: Manchester University Press).

Harrison, W. (ed.)
1892   *Ripon Millenary: A Record of the Festival: Also a History of the City* (Ripon: Harrison).

Hellinga, L.
1974   'Notes on the Order of Setting a Fifteenth-Century Book' *Quaerendo* 4: 64-69.
1982   *Caxton in Focus: The Beginning of Printing in England* (London: British Library).

Hellinga, L., and W. Hellinga
1976–77   'Caxton in the Low Countries', *Journal of the Printing Historical Society* 11: 19-32.

Kato, T.
1996   'A Role of Paraph Marks in Caxton's *Morte Darthur*: Text Lengthiness', *Round Table* 11: 1-13.

Lowndes, W.T.
1857–64   *The Bibliographer's Manual of English Literature* (6 vols.; London: Bohn, 2nd edn).

Machan, T.W.
1985   *Techniques of Translation: Chaucer's Boece* (Norman, OK: Pilgrim Books).
1987   'Glosses in the Manuscripts of Chaucer's *Boece*', in Minnis (ed.) 1987: 125-38.

Mead, H.R.
1937   *Incunabula in the Huntington Library* (San Marino: Huntington Library).

Meale, C.M.
1982   'Wynkyn de Worde's Setting-Copy for *Ipomydon*', *Studies in Bibliography* 35: 156-71.

Minnis, A.J.
1987a   '"Glosynge is a Glorious Thyng": Chaucer at Work on the *Boece*', in Minnis (ed.) 1987: 106-24.

Minnis, A.J. (ed.)
1987   *The Medieval Boethius: Studies in the Vernacular Translations of the De Consolatione Philosophiae* (Cambridge: Brewer).

1993   *Chaucer's Boece and the Medieval Tradition of Boethius* (Cambridge: Brewer).

Needham, P.
1986   *The Printer and the Pardoner: An Unrecorded Indulgence Printed by William Caxton for the Hospital of St. Mary Rounceval, Charing Cross* (Washington: Library of Congress).

Nixon, H.M.
1976–77   'William Caxton and Bookbinding', *Journal of the Printing Historical Society* 13: 92-113.

Oates, J.C.T.
1954   *A Catalogue of the Fifteenth-Century Printed Books in the University Library, Cambridge* (Cambridge: Cambridge University Press).

Pace, G.B., and L.E. Voigts
1979   'A *Boece* Fragment', *Studies in the Age of Chaucer* 1: 143-50.

Painter, G.D.
1963   'Caxton through the Looking-Glass: An Enquiry into the Offsets on a Fragment of Caxton's *Fifteen Oes*, with a Census of Caxton Bindings', *Gutenberg Jahrbuch*: 73-80.

1976   *William Caxton: A Quincentenary Biography of England's First Printer* (London: Chatto & Windus).

Paisey, D.L.
1986   'Blind Printing in Early Continental Books', in A.L Lepschy *et al.* (eds.), *Book Production and Letters in the Western European Renaissance: Essays in Honour of Conor Fahy* (London: Modern Humanities Research Association).

Pollard, A.W, *et al.* (eds.)
1898   *The Works of Geoffrey Chaucer* (London: Macmillan).

Ramage, D.
1958   *A Finding-List of English Books to 1640 in Libraries in the British Isles* (Durham: Council of the Durham Colleges).

1982   *A Catalogue of Incunabula in all the Libraries of Oxford University outside the Bodleian* (Oxford: Oxford University Press).

Rhodes, D.E.
1982   *A Catalogue of Incunabula in all the Libraries of Oxford University outside the Bodleian* (Oxford: Clarendon Press).

Ricci, S. de
1909   *A Census of Caxtons* (Bibliographical Society Illustrated Monographs, 15; Oxford: Oxford University Press,).

Ringler, W.A., Jr
1992   *Bibliography and Index of English Verse in Manuscript 1501–1558* (London: Mansell).

Robinson, F.N. (ed.)
1933, 1957   *The Complete Works of Geoffrey Chaucer* (London: Oxford University Press, 1st and 2nd edns).

Skeat, W.W.(ed.)
1894–97   *The Complete Works of Geoffrey Chaucer* (7 vols.; Oxford: Clarendon Press).

Sayle, C.E.
  1900–1907   *Early English Printed Books in the University Library, Cambridge, 1475 to 1640* (4 vols.; Cambridge: Cambridge University Press).
Smith, L.
  1914   *The Story of Ripon Minster* (Leeds: Jackson).
Takamiya, T.
  1996   'Chapter Divisions and Page Breaks in Caxton's *Morte Darthur*', *Poetica* 45: 63-78.
Thurston, A., and C.F. Bühler
  1939   *Checklist of Fifteenth-Century Printing in the Pierpont Morgan Library* (New York: no publisher given).
Wheeler, H.A.
  1929   *A Short Catalogue of Books Printed in England and English Books Printed Abroad before 1641 in the Library of Wadham College, Oxford* (London: Longmans).
Wilkinson, A.M.
  1960   *The Ripon Caxtons* (Ripon: Harrison).
Yukishima, K.
  1995   *Union Catalogue of Incunabula in Japanese Libraries* (Tokyo: Yushodo).

Exemplum et Similitudo: Natural Law in the *Manciple's Tale* and the *Squire's Tale*

L.A.J.R. Houwen

Although over the years Gower's use of natural law in its various disguises and facets has received considerable attention, it is only relatively recently that critics have expressed a similar sort of detailed interest in Chaucer which has resulted in articles on the *Book of the Duchess*, the *Parliament of Fowls*, *Troilus and Criseyde*, and the *Canterbury Tales*.[1] So far the *Manciple's Tale* and the *Squire's Tale*, or rather the animal *exempla* in these tales, have been largely overlooked.[2] It will be argued here that the medieval Aristotelian theory of natural law may help us understand why Chaucer chose to insert these *exempla* in these two narratives. Since Thomas Aquinas presented not only the most influential but also probably the most coherently argued theory of natural law among the

---

1. See, for example, Erzgräber (1988), for a discussion of natural law in the *Book of the Duchess*, the *Parliament of Fowls*, and *Troilus and Criseyde* from an Aquinian perspective; Collins (1981) concentrates on Chaucer's (and Gower's) use of legal imagery and its connections with Thomas of Aquinas's definitions of eternal, natural and positive law in *Troilus and Criseyde* and several of the *Canterbury Tales* (but not the *Manciple's Tale* and the *Squire's Tale*); Ruud (1988) takes a much broader view of natural law; Ruud (1986) discusses various aspects of natural law and universal harmony. Natural law has, of course, been discussed in earlier studies as well, although these have been somewhat overshadowed by Neo-Platonic interpretations of the goddess Natura: see, for example, Bennett (1957: 194-212, Appendix on 'Natura, Nature, and Kind'), and Lewis (1936: 87-111).
2. One exception is Economou (1975).

Aristotelian philosophers and theologians, his ideas about natural law will be discussed in some detail.

In the *Manciple's Tale* the aetiological fable of the tell-tale bird so familiar from classical antiquity is ostensibly told to argue restraint in speech, that is, if we accept the 54 line *moralitas* at the end of the tale as the axis upon which the interpretation of the tale turns. Within this larger framework appears an apparently incongruous aside in which the Manciple demonstrates the unnaturalness of Phoebus's attempt to keep his wife Coronis (not mentioned by name in the tale) under lock and key by means of three *exempla* which establish the power of the laws of *kynd* in animals: those of a bird in a cage who longs for the woods, a cat who will pursue a mouse despite being fed choice morsels, and a she-wolf who will choose the worst member of the pack as her mate:

> Taak any bryd, and put it in a cage,
> And do al thyn entente and thy corage
> To fostre it tendrely with mete and drynke
> Of alle deyntees that thou kanst bithynke,
> And keep it al so clenly as thou may,
> Although his cage of gold be never so gay,
> Yet hath this brid, by twenty thousand foold,
> Levere in a forest that is rude and coold
> Goon ete wormes and swich wrecchednesse.
> For evere this brid wol doon his bisynesse
> To escape out of his cage, yif he may.
> His libertee this brid desireth ay.
> Lat take a cat, and fostre hym wel with milk
> And tendre flessh, and make his couche of silk,
> And lat hym seen a mous go by the wal,
> Anon he weyveth milk and flessh and al,
> And every deyntee that is in that hous,
> Swich appetit hath he to ete a mous.
> Lo, heere hath lust his dominacioun,
> And appetit fleemeth discrecioun.
> A she-wolf hath also a vileyns kynde.
> The lewedeste wolf that she may fynde,
> Or leest of reputacioun, wol she take,
> In tyme whan hir lust to han a make (IX.163-86).

The *exemplum* of the caged bird also appears in the *Squire's Tale* as part of the love-struck peregrine falcon's lament that she has been abandoned by her tercelet, whose desire for *newefangelnesse* made him fly off with a kite, a bird of an 'inferior' species:

> Men loven of propre kynde newefangelnesse,
> As briddes doon that men in cages fede.
> For though thou nyght and day take of hem hede,
> And strawe hir cage faire and softe as silk,
> And yeve hem sugre, hony, breed and milk,
> Yet right anon as that his dore is uppe
> He with his feet wol spurne adoun his cuppe,
> And to the wode he wole and wormes ete; (V.610-17).

This passage highlights the dichotomy between the animal and the human world which runs through this part of the *Squire's Tale* and on which some of the (bleak) humour depends, when a bird rather than a human being expresses sorrow for something that is entirely natural to animals.[3]

The ultimate inspiration for these similes is the second poem in book three of Boethius's *De Consolatione Philosophiae*. Having demonstrated to Boethius the Aristotelian notion that the ultimate end of all human endeavour is the pursuit of the Good, Lady Philosophy sings the praise of the power of Nature and her laws with which she controls all creation:

> It liketh me to schewe by subtil soong, with slakke and delytable sown of strenges, how that Nature, myghty, enclyneth and flytteth the governementz of thynges, and by whiche lawes sche, purveiable, kepith the grete world; and how sche, byndynge, restreyneth alle thynges by a boond that may nat be unbownde (*Boece* Bk. III, M.2, 1-7).

In harmony with her shift to the lyric mode, Lady Philosophy does not logically argue this notion but illustrates it by means of four *exempla*: that of the tamed Carthaginian lions who turn on their tamer once the spirit of nature is revived in them after having tasted blood, the cooped-up bird which longs for its original habitat in the woods once it catches sight of the shade of trees, the sapling bent down to earth by human hands which takes on its

3.   See below. By providing the peregrine falcon and her tercelet with a voice Chaucer humanizes these birds and places them firmly in the human rather than the animal realm. This is also borne out by their concerns and behaviour. In the rest of this article I shall therefore treat them as if they were human.

former straight shape the moment it is no longer restrained, and the sun which may sink in the ocean in the west but nevertheless resumes its ordered course the next day.

As has long been acknowledged, Chaucer is not just indebted to the *Consolation* for his *exempla* but also to the *Roman de la Rose*.[4] In an attempt to justify Venus's adulterous affair with Mars, Jean de Meun in his continuation of the *Roman de la Rose* is both inspired by and indebted to this passage in the *Consolation* when he has La Vieille argue that women, despite the constraints placed upon them by positive law, are unable to resist the power of natural law which gave them their desire for freedom (13845-68, ed. Lecoy 1965–70). As Boethius did before him, Jean exemplifies the power nature wields over all creation by means of several examples drawn from the natural world, in the process of which he repeats the Boethian *exemplum* of the caged bird and adds two further examples of his own, namely that of the kitten who, despite never having seen a rat or a mouse, still prefers them over the choice food prepared for it by man, and the horse that neighs as soon as it spots a mare, even though it has never seen one before.[5] La Vieille concludes that just as all men desire all women so the converse, that all women desire all men, is also true, and she laments the constraints placed upon (wo)mankind by positive law, which forces people to limit themselves to one partner for life.[6]

That Chaucer is also thinking about natural law in the illustrative stories in the *Manciple's Tale* is revealed by the Manciple's own declaration which immediately precedes the *exempla* and in which he, with reference to Coronis, notes that nature cannot be restrained:

4.   Koeppel (1892: 261-62), Bryan and Dempster (1941: 720-21), Benson (1987: 894 [n. to V.607-20] and 952). Koeppel also notes that, apart from being influenced by Boethius in the bird *exemplum* of the *Squire's Tale*, Chaucer is also indebted to the *exempla* in the *Manciple's Tale* for the straw as soft as silk, the milk fed to the bird (both derived from the *exemplum* of the cat) and the worms in the wood, which do not appear at all in either the *Consolation* or the *Roman de la Rose*; from this he concludes that the *Squire's Tale* must have been composed after that of the Manciple.

5.   *Roman de la Rose* 13911-36 (bird), 14009-22 (kitten), 14023-56 (horse).

6.   Cf. also Economou (1975: 680-81).

> But God it woot, ther may no man embrace
> As to destreyne a thyng which that nature
> Hath natureelly set in a creature[7] (IX.160-62).

Similarly, in the *Squire's Tale* Chaucer refers to the law of nature which has as its source God's eternal law when he has the peregrine falcon exclaim that 'alle thyng, repeirynge to his kynde, / Gladeth hymself' (V.608-609), which words, like those of the Manciple's above, echo the conclusion of Bk. III, M.2 of Boethius's *De Consolatione Philosophiae*, to which Chaucer was also indebted for the caged bird simile. In this passage Boethius refers not only to natural law but also to eternal law from which it springs:[8]

> Alle thynges seken ayen to hir propre cours, and alle thynges rejoysen hem of hir retornynge ayen to hir nature. Ne noon ordenaunce is bytaken to thynges, but that that hath joyned the endynge to the bygynnynge, and hath maked the cours of itself stable (that it chaunge nat from his propre kynde) (*Boece* Bk. III, M.2, 39-46).

Chaucer may indeed have been familiar with Aristotelian ideas and perhaps even Aristotelian scholarship, since we know he was acquainted with the works of such Dominican scholars as Nicholas Trevet and Robert Holcot and the Oxford scholar, logician and lawyer Ralph Strode, to whom Chaucer dedicated *Troilus and Criseyde* (Erzgräber 1988: 119). Strode rejected Wyclif's ideas about predestination, and it is not unlikely that, apart from discussing such issues as predestination and free will with Chaucer, as Pearsall suggests, he may have also discussed various aspects of law and theology with him as well, since they were near neighbours at one point (Pearsall 1992: 134; see also North forthcoming).

The theory behind the notion of natural law is set out most cogently by Thomas Aquinas in his *Summa Theologiae* and it was his definition which became the *locus classicus* for later philosophers and legal scholars. For Thomas, for whom the terms *jus naturale*

---

7.   These lines, as Scattergood observes in his note to lines 160-62 in Benson (1987), probably echo the *Roman de la Rose* 13989-94, which in turn borrowed them from Horace (*Ep.* 1.10.24), to whom they are duly attributed.

8.   See also Thomas Aquinas, *Summa Theologiae*, XXVIII, 1-2, *quaestio* 91, *articulus* 1; also Collins (1981: 114-15).

and *lex naturis* are virtually interchangeable (Gilby 1966: 170), natural law as it applies to human beings is essentially a *moral* law based on the Aristotelian (teleological) principle also encountered in Boethius that the ultimate end of living things is the Good. This moral stance is hardly surprising, since for Thomas natural law follows logically from his discussion of Aristotle's moral theory in his *Commentary on the Nicomachean Ethics* (Lisska 1996: 84). In his introduction to his threefold division of natural law in the *Summa Theologiae* Thomas states the moral basis of this law quite unambiguously:

> Now since being good has the meaning of being an end, while being an evil has the contrary meaning, it follows that reason of its nature apprehends the things towards which man has a natural tendency as good objectives, and therefore to be actively pursued, whereas it apprehends their contraries as bad, and therefore to be shunned.[9]

Thomas's definition of natural law which follows immediately hereafter distinguishes between three hierarchical levels among the precepts of natural law: self-preservation, instinct and 'rational' behaviour:

> Let us continue. The order in which commands of the law of nature are ranged corresponds to that of our natural tendencies. Here there are three stages. There is in man, first, a tendency towards the good of the nature he has in common with all substances; each has an appetite to preserve its own natural being. Natural law here plays a corresponding part, and is engaged at this stage to maintain and defend the elementary requirements of human life.
>
> Secondly, there is in man a bent towards things which accord with his nature considered more specifically, that is in terms of what he has in common with other animals; correspondingly those matters are said to be of natural law which nature teaches all animals, for instance the coupling of male and female, the bringing up of the young, and so forth.
>
> Thirdly, there is in man an appetite for the good of his nature as rational, and this is proper to him, for instance, that he should

9. 'Quia vero bonum habet rationem finis, malum autem rationem contrarii, inde est quod omnia illa ad quae homo habet naturalem inclinationem ratio naturaliter apprehendit ut bona, et per consequens ut opere prosequenda, et contraria eorum ut mala et vitanda.' (Gilby 1966: 80-81, *quaestio* 94, *articulus* 2)

know truths about God and about living in society. Correspondingly whatever this involves is a matter of natural law, for instance
that a man should shun ignorance, not offend others with whom
he ought to live in civility, and other such related requirements.[10]

In this definition of natural law Thomas lays down the fundamental preconditions for human life. The first precept of Thomas's
hierarchical arrangement defines the preconditions at the lowest
level without which all life would be impossible, namely self-preservation. This, in turn, depends on such activities (not necessarily
conscious) as nutrition and growth. The second precept relates to
sense experiences which human beings share with all animals and
which manifests itself in procreation and the care for one's
offspring. The third precept sets mankind apart from animals and
is pertinent both on the level of the individual and of society. As
long as human beings act in conformity with these precepts they
will reach what Aristotle in the *Nicomachean Ethics* has defined as
eudaimonia and which Thomas renders as *beatitudo*, or 'well-being'.
The violation of any of these precepts consequently leads to
unhappiness. In Christian moral terms this means that one should
pursue virtue and avoid vice, and this can only be achieved by
allowing reason to govern will.

It would be mistaken, however, to insist that Chaucer must have
had these precise precepts in mind when he wrote the *Manciple's
Tale* and the *Squire's Tale*. He may well have come across them in a

10. 'Secundum igitur ordinem inclinationum naturalium est ordo praeceptorum legis naturae. Inest enim primo inclinatio homini ad bonum
secundum naturam in qua communicat cum omnibus substantiis, prout
scilicet quaelibet substantia appetit conservationem sui esse secundum suam
naturam; et secundum hanc inclinationem pertinent ad legem naturalem ea
per quae vita hominis conservatur, et contrarium impeditur.

Secundo inest homini inclinatio ad aliqua magis speciala secundum naturam in qua communicat cum caeteris animalibus; et secundum hoc dicuntur
ea esse de lege naturali quae natura omnia animalia docuit, ut est commixtio
maris et feminae, et educatio liberorum, et similia.

Tertio modo inest homini inclinatio ad bonum secundum naturam
rationis quae est sibi propria: sicut homo habet naturalem inclinationem ad
hoc veritatem cognoscat de Deo, et ad hoc quod in societate vivat; et secundum hoc ad legem naturalem pertinent ea quae ad hujusmodi inclinationem
spectant, utpote quod homo ignorantiam vitet, quod alios non offendat cum
quibus debet conversari, et caetera hujusmodi quae ad hoc spectant' (Gilby
1966: 80-83). For an alternative translation see Lisska (1996: 274).

slightly different context, namely that of the tripartite division of the soul, which enjoyed a considerable popularity in the Middle Ages. Thomas's theory of natural law is intimately connected to this theory of the soul, as he himself acknowledges when he observes that 'the order in which commands of the law of nature are ranged corresponds to that of our natural tendencies' (*ordinem inclinationum naturalium est ordo praeceptorum legis naturae*). In *De Anima*[11] Aristotle divided the human soul into three parts and this division became the dominant one in the Middle Ages. The vegetative soul, like Thomas's first precept, was thought to be responsible for such involuntary processes as nutrition and growth; the sensitive soul, which affects animals and human beings only, was held to cater for the transference of an image, or *similitudo*, on to the five senses which, as many a medieval moral-didactic treatise admonishes, is one of the chief causes of sin; and the *anima rationalis*, or rational soul, unique to human beings, was thought to control thought (*intellectus*) and will (*voluntas*).[12]

St Thomas, like Boethius, allows for a certain amount of variation in human nature in the pursuit of the Good, but what is most important in Thomas's (imprecise) conception of natural law is that, as far as human beings are concerned,

> natural law…applies to *agere per voluntatem*, not to *agere per naturam*, that is to say, to actions which choose particular goods within the analogical comprehension of the universal good, not to actions impelled by determinism or nature as a principle of fixation (Gilby 1966: 170-71).

Consequently, when people follow those natural inclinations which they share with animals without allowing them to be controlled by reason, they are denying their true nature—in

11. 3.9.432a-b; cf. also Plato, *Rep.* 9.580d-81a and 4.435-42.
12. The concept of the threefold division of the soul was disseminated even before Jacob of Venice's translation of Aristotle's *De Anima* in c. 1150 by St Augustine and Latin doxographers. Many refinements were suggested by medieval theologians but their discussion falls outside the scope of this paper. That Thomas's definition of natural law is indebted to Aristotelian notions about the soul is also noted by Lisska when he observes that Thomas's account 'is based on Aristotle's philosophical anthropology as developed in the *De Anima*'. Lisska, however, does not comment on the 'Secundum…legis naturae' passage, which he leaves untranslated (1996: 100-101, 274).

Aristotelian and Aquinian terms they fail teleologically to reach the perfect state of which their species is capable, and it is precisely this behaviour, I would suggest, that characterizes the tercelet and Coronis in the *Squire's Tale* and the *Manciple's Tale*.

By embedding the animal *exempla* in a narrative which deals firmly with the human world and hence with human law rather than natural law Chaucer, like Jean de Meun, invites his readers to compare both worlds. As Collins observes:

> Animal-imagery in discussions of the 'law' of Kind has Boethian implications of irrationality and can also be further considered in the light of Aquinas' statements on the laws of nature, for man behaving like a beast is not actually a beast (Collins 1981: 118).

In order to enhance and underline this contrast Chaucer introduces two additional themes that feature prominently in both the *Squire's Tale* and the *Manciple's Tale*, namely the protagonists' craving for something new and their fulfilment of this desire by means of a socially inferior lover.

The peregrine falcon in the *Squire's Tale* rather gloomily observes that 'Men loven of propre keynde newefangelnesse' (V.610) and the Manciple squarely blames the lechery of men[13] on the yearning for the novelties of the 'flessh':[14]

13. The readers, however, know better than to reproach only men, not only because if we were to take the Manciple seriously the *exempla* would serve no purpose at all in the larger context of a narrative in which the motive force is that of adultery, but also because his last *exemplum* of the she-wolf and her lover belies it. In fact, Chaucer here appears to follow the narrative strategy of Jean de Meun in the *Roman* closely, since there too La Vieille skilfully (re-)introduces the topic of the lechery (and insatiability?) of women, when in her last example she deliberately shifts the focus of attention away from the natural inclinations of the male bird, the tomcat and the stallion to that of a mare. In fact, although La Vieille emphasizes the lustfulness of women, she is quite careful to point out that her arguments apply just as much to men, and her examples bear this out as well.

14. The Manciple's use of 'flessh' might also have reminded a medieval audience of the first of the three temptations of mankind identified by St Bernard (the other two being the world and the devil). Indeed, if this had been Chaucer's intention he would thereby have stressed man's personal responsibility rather than laying the blame on external factors.

Alle thise ensamples speke I by thise men
That been untrewe, and nothyng by wommen.
For men han evere a likerous appetit
On lower thyng to parfourne hire delit
Than on hire wyves, be they never so faire,
Ne never so trewe, ne so debonaire.
Flessh is so newefangel, with meschaunce,
That we ne konne in nothyng han plesaunce
That sowneth into vertu any while (IX.187-95).

Like Jean de Meun in the *Roman*, Chaucer motivates the use of these examples in terms of a natural inclination for freedom on the part of the tercelet and Coronis. As La Vieille explains, Nature implanted this inclination in both animals and humans, but in the latter case it has been curtailed by human law. But this is only part of the truth, because positive law is the result of encoding in human laws the general principles that follow from natural law. This is not to say that every human law has its equivalent in natural law, for human laws tend to differ from place to place, but natural law does provide the moral foundation of positive law, and cannot contradict it, as Thomas observes in the *Summa*:

> The first rule of reason is natural law, as appears from what has been stated. Hence, in so far as it derives from this, every law laid down by men has the force of law in that it flows from natural law. If on any head it is at variance with natural law, it will not be law, but spoilt law.[15]

Unlike Jean de Meun, Chaucer does not exploit the possibilities for irony that lie behind La Vieille's seemingly rational argument in favour of incontinence in the way that he did in the *Wife of Bath's Prologue*. He avoids a possible misinterpretation and underlines the immorality of this 'freedom' by calling it *newefangelnesse* instead. Chaucer consistently uses the idea of newfangledness in the context of love to characterize the culpable desire of either male or female lovers for new things, a desire which, if acted

---

15. 'Rationis autem prima regula est lex naturae, ut ex supra dictis patet. Unde omnis lex humanitus posita intantum habet de ratione legis inquantum a lege naturae derivatur. Si vero in aliquo a lege naturali discordet, jam non erit lex, sed legis corruption' (Gilby 1966. 104-105, *quaestio* 95, *articulus* 2).

upon, inevitably leads to the vice of inconstancy.[16] In the *Prologue* to the *Legend of Good Women*, for example, most birds sing the praise of St Valentine, save for some, like the small bird known as the *tydif*, which has to beg forgiveness for its *newfangelnesse*. Appropriately, this bird (together with *tercelettes and owles*) is also depicted as an example of disloyalty in love on the mew which Canace prepares for the wounded peregrine falcon (V.646-50). In *Against Women Unconstant* (attributed to Chaucer) the rejected lover complains about his lady's *newefangelnesse*. Her longing for *newe thing* (6) renders her incapable of holding on to a lover for very long. Similarly, when *false Arcite* in *Anelida and Arcite* tires of Anelida and runs off with another lady *proud and new* (144), his inconstancy is contrasted with Anelida's *stidfastnesse* (143). The narrator's exhortation to women to heed the example of Arcite and to beware of the lecherous nature of men (200-203) reminds us of the words of the Manciple, but his is an even bleaker vision. The Manciple's argument that men can only find pleasure in things that are not conducive to virtue (IX.194-95) further emphasizes the more general message in this passage which presents newfangledness as the cause of an incontinence which may be natural to animals but which is not conducive to virtue and by implication cannot lead to *eudaimonia* and *beatitudo*. The peregrine falcon may be thinking of this when, after she relates to Canace how she realized that she had been abandoned by her tercelet, she ruefully sighs that 'alle thyng, repeirynge to his kynde, / Gladeth himself' (V.608-609), thereby offering us another glimpse of her true, animal, nature (cf. n. 3 above).

   The choice for an irrational 'beastly' course of action rather than a rational and virtuous one, with its concomitant breach of both natural and human law, is also evident in the tercelet's and Coronis's choice of lovers, neither of whom matches their own standing in society. In the *Squire's Tale* this is expressed in avian terms when the tercelet flies off with a kite;[17] the hierarchical

16. For *newefangel* and *newefangelnesse* see the *Canterbury Tales* V.610, V.618, IX.193, *Legend of Good Women, Prologue F,* 154, *Anelida and Arcite* 141, and *Against Women Unconstant* 1.
   17. Although the term 'tercel' or 'tercelet' is occasionally used to denominate the male of any member of the hawk family, in literary works it is often used for the male peregrine falcon and the goshawk, both of which were

arrangement of birds of prey here mirrors the human social hierarchy, as it does in the *Parliament of Fowls* and elsewhere.[18] The choice of a kite as the tercelet's new lover in this context is an apt one, in part because the kite was generally considered morally depraved, but even more so because it was often looked upon as an inferior bird of prey which at best could only try to emulate its betters. Despite the fact that the *Boke of St Albans* rather fancifully suggests that it is a bird fit for an emperor, the kite was not actually used in falconry at all (Van den Abeele 1990: 59; see also Van den Abeele 1988). The kite's almost proverbial reputation for moral depravity is touched upon by Chaucer when he calls the kite a coward in the *Parliament of Fowls* (349) and associates it with thievery in the *Knight's Tale* (I.1177-80). In an early fifteenth-century manuscript of the *Canterbury Tales* the kite is associated with Gluttony, who is depicted holding a kite feeding on entrails (Rowland 1971: 20), and, according to Hugh of Fouilloy's *Aviarium*, the kite feeds on corpses *quia carnalibus desideriis voluptuosi delectantur,* 'because hedonists delight in the desires of the flesh' (Clark 1992: 206-207). Bernardus Silvestris regards the kite as both a morally and a socially inferior bird of prey when he classifies it as quarrelsome and mentions it in one breath with the greedy vulture as an example of a degenerate in the *Cosmographia* (1, 3), and in the *De Planctu Naturae* (Prose 1) Alan of Lille accuses the kite of trying to act the part of a hawk. Lydgate, in the envoy to the *De casibus*-tragedy of the low-born tyrant Agathocles in the *Fall of Princes,* notes that although a man may rise to power he cannot hope that his good fortune will endure:

regarded much more highly than the kite. In terms of social status the tercelet, unlike the kite, would have made a good match for the peregrine falcon. That the nomenclature for different types of hawks and falcons was somewhat confused in medieval times is also revealed in the *Squire's Tale,* where the peregrine falcon is referred to as a falcon (V.411, 424, 630, etc.), a peregrine falcon (V.428, 437, 440, etc.), and a hawk (V.446, 478, 632, 641), and the tercelet (V.504, 621) is also given its more general name, falcon (V.654).

18. Frederick II of Hohenstaufen categorized the predatory birds and correlated avian and human hierarchies in his *De Arte Venandi cum Avibus*; a similar classification appears in the *Boke of St Albans* (Hands 1975: 54-55). Cf. also Cummins (1988: 187-94) and Oggins (1989: 43-55).

Sum man forthred of sodeyn auenture,
Set in a chaier of roial dignite,
Wenyng his empire euer sholde endure,
Neuer to be troubled with non aduersite:
With roial egles a kite may nat flee,
A iay may chatre in a goldene cage,
Yit euer sum tech mut folwe of his lynage.
(IV.2948-54, ed. Bergen 1924–27).[19]

More than a century earlier the author of *Kyng Alisaunder* had
pointed out that one cannot make a hardy knight from a coward,
just as one cannot make 'a goshauk...of a kete' (3044, ed.
Smithers 1952).

Coronis fares even worse in the *Manciple's Tale* when she
deceives Phoebus Apollo with 'a man of litel reputacioun, / Nat
worth to Phebus in comparisoun' (IX.199-200). Although it seems
likely that the tercelet will eventually come to realize the errors of
his ways and return to his peregrine falcon, for Coronis the wages
of sin is death. The animal examples which precede the disclosure
of her adultery do not just underscore her beastly appetite, they
are also suggestive of her complete loss of humanity, which may
well explain why Apollo subsequently slays her with an arrow as if
she were an animal being hunted. The final simile, moreover, of
the she-wolf, whose *vileyns kynde* makes her choose the wolf *leest of
reputacioun*, also emphasizes her culpability in social terms. It
seems likely that Chaucer derived this simile from the *Roman*,[20]
which may also have suggested the idea of an animal's sexual urge
being so strong that it will not even distinguish between different
mates as long as they are readily available. La Vieille's last example of the warhorse, which will neigh despite never having seen a
mare before, is suggestive of social status in its use of colour
symbolism: she observes that, just as a black horse mates not only
with a black mare but also with those of other colours, so will a
mare mate with any stallion, irrespective of its colour 'si con sa
volanté li art':

19. Cf. also *Fasciculus Morum* I.120-29 (Wenzel 1989: 54-55).
20. Reid argues that this story had some currency in the Middle Ages and
thereafter but he also notes that its popularity in France and elsewhere down
to the sixteenth century was 'largely...through the *Roman de la Rose*' (1955:
16).

Li prumiers qu'ele troveroit,
c'est cil qui ses mariz seroit,
qu'ele n'en ra nus espiez,
fors qu'el les truisse desliez (14043-46).

Coronis's adultery, in fact, so upsets the Manciple that it leads him to refer to her lover as a *lemman*, for which he apologizes with reference to Plato that 'the word moot cosyn be to the werkyng' (IX.210) but which in fact resembles Reason's excuse for lewd speech in the *Roman* (7069-72. Cf. also 15160-62, and *Boece*, Bk. III, Pr. 12, 205-207). The Manciple's use of *lemman* clearly expresses his moral disapproval of the affair. As David Burnley has argued, the Manciple switches to a discourse here which is more akin to that of a preacher, in the process of which 'the social distaste felt by the *gentils* for *wenches* and *lemmans* is being converted to revulsion for a breach of the moral code' (1983: 196-97).

In their choice of socially inferior lovers the tercelet and Coronis also reveal their moral corruption. They have allowed their lust free reign instead of allowing reason to keep it in check, and thus they have not just breached positive law but also natural law.[21] Although Thomas argues that natural law cannot be cancelled in the human heart, 'it can be missing from a particular course of action when the reason is stopped from applying the general principle there, because of lust or some other passion'.[22] In the *Confessio Amantis* Gower puts this theory into practice when, in one of the few *exempla* drawn from the Bible (the story of Tobias), Genius relates the fate of Sara's seven suitors who were all killed by the devil Asmodeus because they were motivated by lust rather than procreation. Tobias survives this ordeal because 'he his lust so goodly ladde, / That bother lawe and kinde is served' (VII.5362-63). The narrator concludes this tale by drawing a distinction between 'instinct' and 'reason' and natural and positive law just as the *Summa Theologiae* does (*quaestio* 25, *articulus* 2),

21. Marie Collins shows that 'the disruption of positive law by the laws of love and kind is a notable motif with both Gower and Chaucer' (1981: 124).
22. 'Deletur tamen in particulari operabili, secundum quod ratio impeditur applicare commune principium ad particulare operabile, propter concupiscentiam vel aliquam aliam passionem' (Gilby 1966: 96-97, *quaestio* 94, *articulus* 6).

and (conventionally[23]) suggests marriage as the way out of the dilemma:

> For god the lawes hath assissed
> Als wel to reson as to kinde,
> Bot he the bestes wolde binde
> Only to lawes of nature,
> Bot to the mannes creature
> God yaf him reson forth withal,
> Wherof that he nature schal
> Upon the causes modefie,
> That he schal do no lecherie,
> And yit he schal hise lustes have.
> So ben the lawes bothe save
> And every thing put out of sclandre (VII.5372-83, ed. Macaulay 1900).

Similarly, Langland touches upon natural law in the famous Middle-Earth scene in *Piers Plowman*, in which the dreamer is taken to Middle-Earth, whence he regards all of creation and learns 'thorugh ech a creature kynde my creatour to louye' (B-Text, XI.326). In this scene Langland actually inverts the process we encountered in the *Manciple's* and *Squire's Tales* when, instead of revealing how beastly human behaviour can be, the animals set the standard for rational behaviour whereas man must forego reason:

> Reson I seiʒ sooþly sewen alle beestes,
> In etynge, in drynkynge and in engendrynge of kynde.
> And after cours of concepcion noon toke kepe of ooþer,
> As whan þei hadde ryde in Rotey tyme anoon [reste þei] after;
> Males drowen hem to males [al mornyng] by hemselue,
> And [femelles to femelles ferded and drowe].
> Ther ne was cow ne cowkynde þat conceyued hadde
> That wolde [bere] after bol[e], ne boor after sowe;

23. Cf. *Parson's Tale*, X.920-21: 'Trewe effect of mariage clenseth fornicacioun and replenysseth hooly chirche of good lynage, for that is the ende of mariage; and it chaungeth deedly synne into venial synne bitwixe hem that been ywedded, and maketh the hertes al oon of hem that been ywedded, as wel as the bodies. This is verray mariage, that was establissed by God, er that synne bigan, whan natureel lawe was in his right poynt in paradys; and it was ordeyned that o man sholde have but o womman, and o womman but o man, as seith Seint Augustyn, by manye resouns.' Cf. also Ruud (1988: 35).

Boþe hors and houndes and alle oþere beestes
Medled noȝt wiþ hir makes, [saue man allone].
Briddes I biheld þat in buskes made nestes;
Hadde neuere wye wit to werche þe leeste.
...
And siþen I loked on þe see and so forþ on þe sterres;
Manye selkouþes I seiȝ ben noȝt to seye nouþe.
I seiȝ floures in þe fryth and hir faire colours
And how among þe grene gras growed so manye hewes,
And some soure and some swete; selkouþ me þouȝte.
Of hir kynde and hir colour to carpe it were to longe.
Ac þat moost meued me and my mood chaunged,
That Reson rewarded and ruled alle beestes
Saue man and his make; many tyme [me þouȝte]
No Reson hem [ruled, neiþer riche ne pouere].
(XI, 335-72, ed. Kane and Donaldson 1988)

In keeping with Thomas's first two precepts of natural law, nutrition and procreation are singled out in this passage (XI.336) as the elements which ought to be governed by reason, thus avoiding gluttony and promiscuity.

In short, it appears that Chaucer, like his contemporaries, used the natural world in the *Squire's Tale* and the *Manciple's Tale* in order to invite his readers to contrast it with the human and 'humanized' world in the narrative by which the *exempla* are enclosed. The *exempla* also enable him to comment on an aspect of human morality without going into the sort of theorizing we find in the *Tale of Melibee* or the *Parson's Tale*. In the process he does not need to resort to such a technique as the addition of a ready-made *moralitas* (popular among medieval preachers, fable writers, and the compilers of bestiaries and moralized encyclopaedias), but uses the illustrative stories in such an imaginative and poetic way as to imply the moral rather than make it explicit.

At the narrative level Chaucer's *exempla* provide the motivation for the immoral behaviour of the tercelet and Coronis, but at an ethical level they question and criticize these same actions. In order to achieve this Chaucer introduces such elements into the narrative as *newfangelnesse* and social status which are either entirely lacking in Boethius's *Consolation* and the *Roman de la Rose*, or are only hinted at.[24] The final result of all his efforts at a literal,

24. The extent to which Chaucer is indebted to the *Roman* for these brief

narrative level perverts Boethius's original message, while endorsing it on a moral plane.

passages, not just for narrative details, but especially for ideas, rhetorical and theological/philosophical, is quite striking, and so is his use of details from his other poems.

WORKS CITED

Bennett, J.A.W. (ed.)
    1957   *The Parlement of Foules* (Oxford: Oxford University Press).
Benson, L.D. (ed.)
    1987   *The Riverside Chaucer* (Boston: Houghton Mifflin).
Bergen, H. (ed.)
    1924–27   *Lydgate's Fall of Princes* (EETS ES 121-24; London: Oxford University Press).
Bryan, W.F., and G. Dempster
    1941   *Sources and Analogues of Chaucer's Canterbury Tales* (Chicago: Chicago University Press).
Burnley, D.
    1983   *A Guide to Chaucer's Language* (London: MacMillan 1989 [reissued as *The Language of Chaucer*]).
Clark, W.B. (ed. and trans.)
    1992   *Medieval Book of Birds: Hugh Fouilloy's Aviarium* (Binghamton, NY: Center for Medieval and Early Renaissance Studies).
Collins, M.
    1981   'Love, Nature and Law in the Poetry of Gower and Chaucer', in G.S. Burgess *et al.* (eds.), *Court and Poet: Selected Proceedings of the Third Congress of the International Courtly Literature Society* (Liverpool: Cairns): 113–28.
Cummins, J.
    1988   *The Hound and the Hawk: The Art of Medieval Hunting* (London: Weidenfeld & Nicolson).
Economou, G.
    1975   'Chaucer's Use of the Bird in the Cage Image in the *Canterbury Tales*', *Philological Quarterly* 54: 679–84.
Erzgräber, W.
    1988   '"Kynde" und "Nature" bei Chaucer: Zur Bedeutung und Funktion des Naturbegriffes in der Dichtung des ausgehenden Mittelalter', in G.W. Weber (ed.), *Idee, Gestalt, Geschichte* (Festschrift Klaus von See; Odense: Odense University Press): 117–35.
Gilby, T. (ed. and trans.)
    1966   *Thomas Aquinas: Summa Theologiae* (London: Blackfriars).

Hands, R. (ed.)
1975   *Boke of St Albans* (London: Oxford University Press).
Kane, G., and E.T. Donaldson (eds.)
1988   *William Langland, Piers Plowman: The B version* (London: Athlone, 2nd edn).
Koeppel, E.
1892   'Chauceriana', *Anglia* 14: 227–67.
Lecoy, F. (ed.)
1965–70   *Roman de la Rose* (3 vols.; Paris: Champion).
Lewis, C.S.
1936   *The Allegory of Love* (Oxford: Oxford University Press).
1967   *Studies in Words* (Cambridge: Cambridge University Press, 2nd edn).
Lisska, A.J.
1996   *Aquinas's Theory of Natural Law: An Analytic Reconstruction* (Oxford: Oxford University Press).
Macaulay, G.C. (ed.)
1900–1901   *The English Works of John Gower* (EETS ES 81, 82; 2 vols.; London: Oxford University Press).
North, J.D.
forthcoming 'Ralph Strode', in H.C.G. Matthew (ed.), *New Dictionary of National Biography*.
Oggins, R.S.
1989   'Falconry and Medieval Social Status,' *Mediaevalia* 12: 43-55.
Pearsall, D.
1992   *The Life of Geoffrey Chaucer: A Critical Biography* (Oxford: Basil Blackwell).
Reid, T.B.W.
1955   'The She-Wolf's Mate', *Medium Ævum* 14: 16-19.
Rowland, B.
1971   *Blind Beasts: Chaucer's Animal World* (Kent: Kent State University Press).
Ruud, J.
1986   'Chaucer's *Envoy to Scogan*: "Tullius Kyndenesse" and the Law of Kynde', *Chaucer Review* 20: 323–30.
1988   'Natural Law and Chaucer's *Physicians's Tale*', *Journal of the Rocky Mountain and Renaissance Association* 9: 29-45.
Smithers, G.V. (ed.)
1952   *Kyng Alisaunder* (EETS OS 227; London: Oxford University Press).
Van den Abeele, B.
1988   'L'«escoufle»: Portrait d'un oiseau', *Reinardus*, 1: 5–15.
1990   *La Fauconnerie dans les lettres françaises du xiie au xive siècle* (Leuven: Leuven University Press).
Wenzel, S. (ed. and trans.)
1989   *Fasciculus Morum* (University Park, PA: Pennsylvania State University Press).

The Tale and the Book: Readings of Chaucer's *Legend of Good Women* in the Fifteenth Century

Carol M. Meale

'And whan this boke is made, yif it the queene,
On my bihalue, at Eltham or at Shene'
(*Legend of Good Women, F*, 496-97).[1]

With these words Alceste, in the more commonly preserved version of the two prologues to the *Legend of Good Women*, concludes her instructions to the dreamer/poet as to the 'penaunce' he is to undergo—to write 'of women trew in louyng all her lif' (438, 479). Their interest, however, resides as much in their suggestion of Chaucer's conception of his work's circulation—the form it would take, and the audience(s) to which it would be exposed—as in their immediate narrative context. Where form and dissemination are concerned, the ostensible implications of Alceste's words are, first, that the *Legend* was to form a substantial whole, a 'book', and, secondly, that part, at least, of its intended primary readership (or audience) was courtly, and included women—

---

1. All quotations from the *Legend* are taken from Cowen and Kane (1995). They discuss (pp. 124-42) the priority of the two versions of the *Prologue*, and of the status of the one extant manuscript which contains version *G*, Cambridge University Library MS Gg.4.27. They are of the opinion that the changes between *F* and *G* are 'presumably authorial' (p. 133), and, on the question of antecedence, that they 'have found...nothing against the assumption that *G* is the revised version...' (p. 140). In spite of their employment of a manuscript other than Oxford, Bodleian Library MS Fairfax 16 as copy-text, I retain the customary designation *F* to distinguish the common text of the *Prologue* from that of Cambridge University Library MS Gg.4.27.

perhaps, though not necessarily, Queen Anne herself.[2] But we know nothing of this possible initial phase in the history of the work: the earliest extant manuscript, Cambridge University Library MS Gg.4.27, dates from late in the first quarter of the fifteenth century, probably some 40 years after the collection was begun (Parkes and Beadle 1979–80: III, 6-7). But the 12 manuscripts surviving from the period up to c. 1500 provide substantial evidence relating to the reception of the *Legend* by its secondary readership or audience. They are relevant, for instance, to such questions as: Did the work retain its textual integrity, that is, was it read as a coherent whole, a secular legendary prefaced by a prologue? Or were individual tales excerpted for the purposes of creating an anthology, as the tales of the Clerk, the Man of Law, the Second Nun and the Prioress were extracted from the Canterbury framework to play a role within collections of saints' lives and other exemplary materials?[3] Did it circulate as a 'book' by itself, or

2.   For discussion of this point see Wallace (1997), esp. 365-70, and Taylor (1997). The connection made in the text between Alceste's command and the queen of Richard II is an ambivalent one. On one level Alceste's direction to the poet associates in exemplarity of wifely affection a living queen with a mythical one. But on another, Alceste herself is an ambiguous figure within the text (see Meale 1992: 65-66; and, for a more extensive analysis, Delany 1994: 103-14), which renders her association with Anne more problematic. While, then, superficially, the textual linkage of the two women is complimentary to the living Anne, such a reading is compromised by the critical unease over how Alceste should be 'read'. Take, for example, Delany's judgment that Alceste's 'instructions [to the dreamer/poet] are to produce a propagandist work' (p. 114), but that the enterprise fails through the *author's* intention of undermining the work's stated agenda, in its emphasis upon the paganism of the women (including Alceste herself) who are the ostensible subjects of celebration. Such an interpretation could support the view that the lines implicitly *praise* Anne, who, by virtue of her Christianity, is shown to be innately morally superior to Alceste. But, equally, as Wallace and Taylor suggest (from differing literary/critical perspectives), the connection which Chaucer makes between the two women and the fictional dreamer/poet could refer to the *real* author's own complex relationship with the world of the court and aristocratic culture: in this reading, therefore, it is the figure of Chaucer who becomes the subject of his own discourse—and thus, it could be argued, both Alceste and Anne are marginalized.

3.   For descriptions of manuscripts in which these tales are excerpted see Manly and Rickert (1940: I): on the *Clerk's Tale* 339-42 (Longleat MS 257),

was it read alongside works by other writers? Did women or individuals associated with the court form a significant constituency as reader/owners? In attempting to answer some of these questions it may be feasible to indicate ways in which Chaucer's poem took its place within the then-escalating literary debate over the role and status accorded to women by the writers of love poetry, a debate around which he organized the fiction of the *Prologue* to the *Legend* (if fiction, and not a fictionalized account of contemporary responses to his writing, it was)[4] in which the dreamer is famously rebuked both for his translation of the *Roman de la Rose* and for supposedly traducing women in *Troilus and Criseyde* (*Legend of Good Women, F,* 328-34).

Strong support for the theory that the *Legend* did, to begin with, circulate independently as an integrated series of tales is offered by the text's presence in manuscripts of the so-called Oxford Group: Oxford, Bodleian Library MSS Tanner 346, dating from the 1440s (used by Cowen and Kane as the copy-text for their edition); Fairfax 16, of *c.* 1450; and Bodley 638, for which a date nearer the end of the century has been suggested (Robinson

376-80 (Naples, Biblioteca Nazionale MS XIII.B.29) and 433-38 (San Marino, Huntington Library MS HM 140); for the *Man of Law's Tale* 82-84 (Manchester, Chetham's Library MS 6709); for the *Second Nun's Tale* 245-48 (London, British Library MS Harley 2382, in which it is described as 'Vita Sancte Cecilie'). The *Prioress's Tale* is also included in both these latter two codices: for accounts of manuscripts in which it appears as a single excerpt see Manly and Rickert (1940: I, 238-49 [British Library MS Harley 1704], 241-44 [British Library MS Harley 2251], 302-303 [Cambridge University Library MS Kk.1.6] and 472-75 [Oxford, Bodleian Library MS Rawlinson C.86]).

4.   A degree of support for the notion that Chaucer may have been referring to contemporary audience response is offered by the furore occasioned by Alain Chartier's poem *La Belle Dame sans Mercy*. Cf. the conclusion [sig.Z.vii v], purportedly by 'The auctour', to Wynkyn de Worde's 1517 edition of *Troilus and Criseyde* (*STC* 5095) which 'reads' Criseyde as the type of fickle woman, just as Cupid does:

> As touchynge Cresyde / to hym ryght vnkynde
> Falsly forsworn / deflouryng his worthynes
> Of feminine gendre / ye woman most vnkynde
> …
> The faythe of a woman / by her now maye you se…

See Benson and Rollman (1980–81: 275).

1980: xix; Norton-Smith 1979: vii; Robinson 1982: xxii-xxiii). There is a notable coincidence of contents between these volumes, each of which contains a number of Chaucer's shorter poems, together with other, later, poems in a similarly courtly vein, many of which testify to Chaucer's influence on the writers of subsequent generations. The conclusion arrived at in the 1920s by Aage Brusendorff, that there were in existence in the early-fifteenth century a number of separate booklets of Chaucer's works, comprising either one text, such as the *Legend*, or a number of his less substantial ones (1925: 182-207), has been affirmed in more recent years by the scholars named above in their researches into the history and make-up of the individual Oxford codices. These small, independent booklets, it is suggested, were combined and arranged by later book-producers into larger units within weightier volumes. There are strong textual affiliations between the three Oxford manuscripts (in the case of the *Legend*, for example, between Fairfax and Bodley; see Cowen and Kane 1995: 21, 26), but Brusendorff's pioneering dismissal of Eleanor Hammond's theory that there was a common archetype for the group necessitates recognition of the fact that an unquantifiable number of these booklets, which served as exemplars, have been lost (Hammond 1908: 337-39; Cowen and Kane 1995: 16 n. 28). Such a loss is of itself not surprising, given that smaller books, whether in manuscript or in print, are more subject to wear than larger ones. But the survival of fragmentary copies of the *Legend* which date from the second half of the century seems to indicate that the work continued to be produced and to circulate as an single entity. For instance, in London, British Library MS Additional 28617 (mid-fifteenth-century?), which lacks the opening 512 lines of the poem and contains other lacunae (Cowen and Kane 1995: 4), the ending of the text appears to be coincident with the end of the codex.[5] British Library MS Additional 9832 (third quarter

5.   Cowen and Kane (1995: 3-4) suggest a date of the first half of the fifteenth century for this manuscript: it may be possible to narrow this dating to the second quarter, since the watermark of a candlestick which appears on ff.5-8, 12, 14, 18, 21-22, 27-29, 32-33 and 36-37 is similar, though not identical, in appearance and measurement to Briquet 4350 and 4351, recorded respectively at Colonne, 1427, and Verceil, 1451. The text of the *Legend* finishes on f.38, and the verso of this leaf contains the inscription (along with

of the fifteenth century?), another incomplete copy, now inter-
leaved with pages from the 1542 edition of Chaucer's works
printed by William Bonham (*STC* 5069; Cowen and Kane 1995:
2), may also have been a self-contained booklet, although the
evidence for this is less clear.[6]

From an early stage of the *Legend's* history, however, it was
copied alongside a number of other texts by Chaucer and may
reasonably have been designed to be read in this context. In
Cambridge University Library MS Gg.4.27, for example, where it
is placed between the *Canterbury Tales* (ff.132-443v) and the *Parliament of Fowls* (ff.480v-490v), it forms part of an early Chaucerian
'collected works'. Yet the tendency to elaborate and expand upon
the Chaucer canon—to include within it other pieces of courtly
verse—is already in evidence here, as Lydgate's *Temple of Glass*
(*SIMEV* 851), which occurs in a number of the codices containing
the shorter poems, follows on ff.490v-509v.[7]

The Oxford Group manuscripts themselves, and others which
can be linked with them on the basis of varying textual affiliations—Cambridge University Library MS Ff.1.6 (the 'Findern
Manuscript', after 1446) and Cambridge, MSS Trinity College
R.3.19 (c. 1480) and Magdalene College Pepys 2006 (perhaps
slightly nearer the end of the fifteenth century; see Beadle and
Owen 1978: viii; Fletcher 1987: xxix; and Edwards 1985: xxii)—
established what may be loosely described as collected editions of

lines of music accompanied by verses, and fragments of other 'courtly' lyrics)
'Henricus dei gracia / Rex Anglie & ffrancie.' This latter could obviously
refer to either Henry VI or Henry VII, although the extreme neatness of the
secretary script and the elaborate strapwork of the initial *H* might point to
the later Henry as the monarch named. My reading of the marginal annotation on f. 27v, possibly in a different hand, as 'R ?ensued kyng' (which differs
from Cowen and Kane's interpretation as 'Reigned kyng'), could conceivably
be a reference to Richard III. Whatever the truth of the matter, it is clear that
the manuscript continued to be used—whether as a reading text or as a jot-
ting pad—after production.

6.   Cowen and Kane are more cautious in their dating, suggesting the
second half of the fifteenth century, although they characterize some aspects
of the script as 'a very common type of later fifteenth-century informal secretary with occasional anglicana forms' (1995: 1-2). They do not note the
curious mixture of folio and quarto in the make-up of the codex.

7.   See below for other occurrences of the *Temple* with the *Legend*; see also
SIMEV 851 and Boffey (1993).

the shorter poems. Thus the *Legend* is frequently found in the company of the dream poems and with the complaints of Anelida, Venus and Mars (*SIMEV* 3670, 3542, 913), as well as in juxtaposition with pieces in the Chaucerian style, such as Clanvowe's *Boke of Cupide* and Lydgate's *Complaint of the Black Knight* (*SIMEV* 3351, 1507) as well as his *Temple of Glass*. British Library Additional MS 12524, dating from the last quarter of the fifteenth century, is a particularly interesting example of the early-established 'authority' of some of these collocations of texts: although the codex now breaks off incomplete on f.28v, it does include the *incipit* to 'the compleynte of / mars and venus', and this in spite of its otherwise idiosyncratic inclusion as one of the 'Legend of Ladyse', Boccaccio's tale of *Guiscardo and Ghismonda* in the version of c. 1472 by Gilbert Banester (*SIMEV* 4082), from 1478 until his death in 1487 Master of the Children of the Chapel Royal (Wright 1937; Green 1978: 299-300).[8]

The regularity of these groupings of these shorter poems together with the *Legend* is not sufficient evidence of itself to offer proof as to how the latter text was received by its audiences, but in some instances it may be justifiable to trace an interest in the genre of the lyric complaint: compare the positioning of the *Legend* in MS Tanner 346, for example, where the text heads the present first booklet, which is composed almost exclusively of such verses (Robinson 1980: vii, xvii-xviii). In two other codices, Bodley 638 and Trinity College Cambridge R.3.19, the *Legend* is accompanied by the *Complaint unto Pity* (*SIMEV* 2756): the lyric precedes the *Legend* in the same booklet in the former manuscript (ff.46-47v), and follows it, as the only other component of the *Legend* booklet, in the latter (ff.151-152v). And, although non-scribal annotation of copies of the poem is far from common, one medieval reader of MS Tanner 346 has noted 'letera' and 'lettera'

---

8.   Interestingly, Banester's adaptation of Boccaccio's story appears in another *Legend* manuscript, Oxford, Bodleian Library MS Rawlinson C.86 (discussed below) in section 2 (Boffey and Meale 1991: 144-45, 165). The other (anonymous) Middle English version (*SIMEV* 3258) occurs in Trinity College Cambridge MS R.3.19; copied in the hand of the principal scribe it opens booklet 4 (ff.26-40v; see Fletcher 1987: xvii). In neither of these codices is the tale incorporated in the *Legend* in the same way as it is in British Library MS Additional 12524.

in the margins opposite Dido's and Phyllis's Ovidian laments on ff.20v and 37v.[9]

A more specific and revealing association of texts may link the *Legend* with Hoccleve's *Lepistre de Cupide* (*SIMEV* 666), a 1402 adaptation of Christine de Pizan's *Epistre au Dieu d'Amours* (Furnivall and Gollancz 1970; Fenster and Erler 1990). Hoccleve's poem is preserved in ten manuscripts, and is found together with the *Legend* in five of these. *Lepistre* follows the *Legend* on ff.41-48v in the first booklet of MS Tanner 346, the earliest of the Oxford group; and it precedes the *Legend* in MS Bodley 638, on ff.38v-45v, separated only by the short poem 'The Complaint unto Pity', ff.46v-47; in MS Cambridge University Library Ff.1.6 it follows the *Legend*, separated by the *Complaint of Venus* and a short filler lyric (*SIMEV* 2279) on ff.68-69v. It occurs in the same booklet in MS Fairfax 16, though here the separation is greater, the intervening texts being the game of *Ragman's Roll* (*SIMEV* 2251, ff.47-50), the English translation of Alain Chartier's *La Belle Dame sans Mercy* (*SIMEV* 1086, ff.50v-62v) and the *Temple of Glass* (ff.63r-82v). In Bodleian Library MS Arch. Selden B.24, an anthology of Chaucerian and courtly verse copied perhaps in the last decade of the fifteenth century, the *Legend* is followed on f.192 by the *Kingis Quair* (*SIMEV* 1215) and then *Lepistre*, ff.211v-217. The copyists were two Scottish scribes, of whom the second began his stint at line 1240 of the *Quair* (Edwards 1996: 55 n. 4, 67; Boffey and Edwards 1997). The most striking example of the perceived connection between Chaucer's and Hocccleve's poems is found in Findern, where the tale of *pyramus & tesbe* appears on leaves inserted into the quire containing *litera Cupidinus*, ff.64-67v (Beadle and Owen 1978: ix; Harris 1983: 314; Hanna 1987: 65, 67). The conjunction of texts is a meaningful one. Hoccleve invokes Chaucer's work in his reference to Cupid's *legende of*

9.   For the Ovidian source see Isbell (1990: 10-18, 56-66); for the popularity in Middle English of the subgenre of the 'letter' see Camargo (1991) (and, for Chaucer's deployment of it, specifically Chapter 3). The whole issue of the annotations within copies of the *Legend* is a fascinating but complex one, as is the question of the attribution of such textual apparatus to author, or individual scribes. Such an analysis, however, lies beyond the scope of this present essay but, together with a discussion of the hierarchy of decoration within individual manuscript copies, it offers a rich field for future investigation.

Martres, devoting a stanza (316-22) to the examples of male per-
fidy which, he claims, may be found within it. Hoccleve's poem
resembles Chaucer's in its tone of studied ambivalence—an
ambivalence which may have been taken by contemporary readers
to demonstrate hostility to women (cf. the fictional situation
dramatized in the later *Dialogue with a Friend* (*SIMEV* 299) of 1419-
21, in which the poet is taken to task by a friend for writing *large-
lich* about women (755). Even if, as with the encounter between
Cupid and the poet/dreamer/narrator in the *Legend*, the alternative interpretation—that Hoccleve is here 'fictionalizing' for
literary effect—is preferred, the debt he owed to his *Maister* is not
to be underestimated. Hoccleve, then, through both his reference
to Chaucer's text, and his later, extended, discussion as to the
representation of women, is placing himself firmly in a tradition
of pro- and anti-feminine literary debate. Hoccleve's ostensible
condemnation of Jean de Meun for his continuation of the *Roman
de la Rose* (*Lepistre* 281-87), based upon, though less biting than,
that of Christine de Pizan (*Epistre* 389-406), strengthens the work's
connection with the *Legend* by recalling Cupid's rebuke to the
dreamer/poet in the *Prologue* to the latter work, in which he
describes the *Romance of the Rose* as 'an heresie ayeins my lawe'
(*F*, 330).

Other collocations, although lacking this dimension of intertextuality, are equally suggestive of contemporary modes of reading.
In Findern, for instance, quire E, which contains the inserted
narrative of Thisbe, has a pronounced slant towards expressing
the concerns of women in love. It opens with the *Complaint of
Anelida*, which occupies ff.61-63v; the next text within this gathering is the *Complaint of Venus*, on leaves now numbered 68-69; and
the concluding item, on ff.71-76v, is Hoccleve's *Lepistre*. As indicated above, a lyric lament beginning 'My woo full hert this cled
in payn', uttered by a woman for her absent lover, was added
beneath the ending of Venus's complaint, on f.69v. Ff.64-67 in the
present numbering comprise the inserted quire on which the
Legend is copied. Conventional or routine though this grouping of
items may initially appear to be, their purposeful selection and
ordering should alert us to the possibility that the compiler(s) of
this section of the manuscript were concerned with issues other
than the simple reproduction of a well-known sequence of texts.

Findern, for example, is one of only two codices in which the *Complaint of Venus* is not accompanied by that of Mars, while the added lyric *My woo full hert* is one of four poems in the manuscript which is spoken—and possibly written—by women (Robbins 1954; Barratt 1987 and 1992: 268-74; McNamer 1991). Within this context the story of Thisbe, divorced from its narrative frame, reads simply as a further expression of the vicissitudes suffered by loving women.[10]

There is only one other manuscript surviving which contains an extract from the *Legend*, and this is Bodleian Library MS Rawlinson C.86, a late fifteenth/early sixteenth century miscellany of secular and devotional texts produced in London (Griffiths 1982; Boffey and Meale 1991). Here the story of Dido appears in the third of four booklets (now ff.90-140; Boffey and Meale 1991: 145), through-copied with other narratives which centre upon the fortunes of women: *Sir Landevale*, which is the earlier of the two Middle English translations of Marie de France's *lai* of *Lanval* (*SIMEV* 3203; Bliss 1960; Shepherd 1995: 351-64), and the romance of the *Weddyng of Sir Gawain and Dame Ragnell* (*SIMEV* 1916; Shepherd 1995, 243-67), an analogue to the *Wife of Bath's Tale* which has tentatively been attributed, as an apprentice work, to Sir Thomas Malory (Field 1982; 1993: 2, 131; Boffey and Meale 1991: 145, 153, 169). The eclecticism of the other contents of the booklet, however, disturbs any sense there might be of an overriding interest in women's experiences of love, for the account of Dido's betrayal by Aeneas is preceded by Lydgate's verses on social morality, the *Debate of the Horse, Goose and Sheep* (*SIMEV* 658), and by the scatalogical and obscenely punning tales of *Piers of Fulham* and *Colyn Blowbol's Testament* (*SIMEV* 71 and 4020). There is, in other words, no coherent emphasis throughout the booklet on female amatory biography, although the sequential ordering of the pieces dealing with this subject, even if their exemplars were

---

10. Harris (1983: 316) notes that neither the hand of the copyist of this *Legend* extract nor the paper-stock occur elsewhere within the manuscript: there is no scribal indication of the tale's place within a larger narrative sequence, and it concludes with the words 'nicholaus plenis amoris', one of the few scribal attributions within the codex. These facts emphasize the singularity of the text within the compilation, and strengthen the case for its having been deliberately chosen for inclusion in this quire.

obtained by somewhat arbitrary means, may well represent a fortunate arrangement of materials on the part of the scribes
involved in the volume's complex compilation.

A similar generic range to that of Rawlinson C.86 is exhibited in
the contents of Trinity College Cambridge R.3.19, which include
secular and religious poems by Lydgate, courtly lyrics (a number
by Chaucer), the *Monk's Tale* (copied from Caxton's edition of
1477; see Manly and Rickert 1940: I, 533; Fletcher 1987: xxix;
Blake 1989: 419), the *Parliament of Fowls*, the *Legend*, a series of
anti-feminist lyrics, *Piers of Fulham*, and an unpublished short
chronicle justifying Edward IV's claim to the throne of France.
But within this apparent diversity the placing of the 'the Boke
called the Legend of Ladyes' is suggestive. On f.114 it opens what
now constitutes booklet 8 of the volume (the *Complaint unto Pity* is
the sole other item). Booklet 6 contains the *Assembly of Ladies*
(*SIMEV* 1528), and booklet 7 the Middle English translation of *La
Belle Dame sans Mercy*, a poem instructing women on 'The .x.
Commaundment*es* of loue' (*SIMEV* 590, which a seventeenth-
century hand also copied into Fairfax 16, f.184r-v [see Norton-
Smith 1979: xvi, xvii]), and a uniquely-occurring nine-stanza
rhyme-royal poem on 'The .ix. Ladyes worthy' (*SIMEV* 2767)—a
text, deriving ultimately from French sources, detailing the
achievements of various Amazonian champions (Utley 1944: 224-
25; Mcmillan 1979; Boffey forthcoming; cf. Wimsatt 1991: 67-69).
All these items are copied in the hand of the principal scribe.
While the absence of continuous medieval foliation within the
codex necessitates caution as to the date at which these three
booklets were conjoined (the present binding bears the arms of
George Wilmer, who matriculated from Trinity in 1598), the
thematic links within them were evidently not lost on whoever was
eventually responsible for the ordering of the sections within the
volume.

The *Assembly of Ladies*, for instance, is one of the few Middle
English poems of any length which, it has been suggested, may
have been the work of a female writer (Barratt 1987; 1992: 262-63
and 295-300; Evans and Johnson 1991; Chance 1994),[11] and its set-

---

11. Derek Pearsall, in his edition of the text, remains sceptical as to the
possibility that the dream poem may have been female authored; see Pearsall
(1962: 14-15 and 19, and 1990: 31).

piece climax, in which women come together at the Court of Lady Loyalty in an attempt to gain redress for the wrongs done to them by men, owes much to the tradition of female complaint popularized in England by Chaucer. Indeed, the list of women unhappy in love depicted on the walls of the council chamber at Pleasaunt Regard may well have been drawn in the main from his poetry: they include 'Phyllis of wommanly pite / Deyd pitously for the love of Demophon' (457-58); Thisbe; Cleopatra, slain 'for Antony' (462); and 'Anelada the quene', complaining 'sore' 'Upon Arcite' (456-57). *La Belle Dame*, in contrast, shows a woman's defence against love: in words which recall the writings of Christine de Pizan the Lady satirizes the deceits and flatteries of men in such a way as to invite comparison with the laments of the female protagonists of the *Legend*.[12] The short poem *The .x. Commaundmentes of loue* is a conventional restatement of the virtues which women were expected to hold in relation to the men who treated them as objects of desire, while that on the nine female worthies is a remarkable defence of women as self-reliant individuals. None of these nine Amazons actually figure in the *Legend*, but their independent status allies them with women such as Cleopatra and Dido, whose stories Chaucer does recount but whose roles as successful leaders and conquerors are undermined, not to say censored, in his text in their encounters with the men who betray them. These three booklets taken together, therefore, offer a range of materials through which the nature and roles of women may be debated, and it is, perhaps, no coincidence that *La Belle Dame sans Mercy*, a poem which when it was first circulated in France sparked a socio-literary controversy (Laidlaw 1974: 39-40; Green 1983: 95, 98, 99-101), should appear in another two of the *Legend* manuscripts: Fairfax 16, ff.50v-62v, and Findern, ff.117-134v. (In the latter the poem is written in the hand of the scribe who was responsible for copying out Hoccleve's *Lepistre*.) It is apposite to note at this point, too, that in one of the books owned by Sir John Paston and described by him in an inventory sometime around 1479, 'The Legende off Lad<...>', is followed

---

12. See Skeat (1894–97: VII, 299-326), and, among the many works of Christine which could be cited for comparison, *Lepistre au Dieu d'Amours* (Fenster and Erler 1990) and the 1405 *Treasure of the City of Ladies* (Lawson 1985: 100-105).

by '...saunce Mercye', which must be a reference to the English translation of Chartier (Davis 1971–76: I, 517; Lester 1987).[13]

If this evidence as to the contexts in which the *Legend of Good Women* survives may be taken as representative, it seems that much of the appeal of the text to its fifteenth-century audiences dervied from its pertinence to the literary controversy concerning women which had fuelled debate among many European writers—from Jehan le Fèvre and Boccaccio to Christine de Pizan—during the preceding hundred years or so (Phillippy 1986; Meale 1992; Phillips 1995). Both Boccaccio and Christine made a point in their historics of women of dedicating their work to members of that sex: Boccaccio's *De Claris Mulieribus* is prefaced by a dedicatory letter to Andrea, countess of Altavilla (Guarino 1964: xxxiii-xxxv), and Christine uses the final chapter of her *Cité des Dames* to address its putative inhabitants as 'My most honored ladies...all of you who love glory, virtue and praise' (Richards 1983: 254).[14]

13. The volume cited in the text is item no. 3 in the inventory (which also contained 'Þe Parlement off byr<...>' and what must have been Lydgate's *Temple of Glass* (cf. Robinson 1982: xxxv); but Paston clearly owned more than one copy of several of these poems: no. 5, 'a boke lent Midelton', contained 'Bele Da<...> / Mercy', followed by 'Þe Parlement off Byrdys' and a collection of miscellaneous texts. Such replication of material within different volumes or booklets may well indicate the beginnings of a speculative mode of book production, whereby selections of texts were ready-prepared by a stationer, and the potential client therefore had reduced choice in terms of the exact contents of any particular book or booklet, by comparison with earlier purchasers who acquired books through commission.

14. Despite, however, the coincidence of the invoking of female patronage by Christine and Boccaccio, the latter's dedication of his work to a woman poses a problem for the modern reader which is not dissimilar to that posed by Chaucer's reference to Anne of Bohemia (cf. n. 2 above). Just as Chaucer's primary audience is likely to have been composed to some extent of educated men, who may have picked up satirical or joking references to women, so is that of Boccaccio. The Italian author wrote in Latin, itself principally a masculine preserve of learning, and his conclusion, in which he asks that 'for the glory of honorable studies, that wiser men tolerate with kindly spirit what has not been done properly', adding that 'if anyone has a charitable soul, let him correct what has been improperly written...' (Guarino 1964: 251), implies that he anticipated—perhaps just as Chaucer did—a learned response to his text. Issues of intended and primary audience for individual texts did not, of course, necessarily have any bearing upon

And both of these writers numbered women among their readers: the anonymous early-fifteenth-century French translation of *De Claris Mulieribus*, for instance, appears to have been read in England by Margaret Beaufort, the likely owner of British Library MS Royal 20.C.v (Meale 1992: 59 n. 17), while two queens of France—Isabeau of Bavaria (d. 1435) and Charlotte of Savoie (d. 1483)—are known to have owned Christine's *Cité*, as are, in England, Jaquetta of Luxembourg (to whom Isabeau's manuscript of Christine's collected works, British Library MS Harley 4431, passed), and Alice, Duchess of Suffolk (d. 1476), Chaucer's grand-daughter (Meale 1989: 208 and 229 n. 52; Tuetey 1864–65: 359; Meale 1996a: 86-87).

The appeal which Chaucer made to a female and courtly audi-ence was, by comparison, more indirect. Alceste, for example, protests against generalizations as to the infidelity of women articulated in the opening pages of the *Cité des Dames* by the author herself (Richards 1983), while the complimentary verses addressed to Anne of Bohemia were excised in the *G* version of the *Prologue*, revised presumably after the Queen's death in 1394. I would hesitate to claim that this lack of specific audience-address to women explains the relative lack of evidence of their ownership of the text, but it is a factor which should be borne in mind when considering patterns of ownership in which men figure more largely. Two copies seem to have been commissioned and/or owned by male members of the nobility: MS Selden B.24, on f. 230v at the end of the manuscript proper, bears the ownership mark of Henry, Lord Sinclair (c. 1460–1513), whose arms appear at the conclusion of *Troilus and Criseyde* on f.118v (Norton-Smith 1981: xxxiii-xxxiv; Lyall 1989: 250-52; Edwards 1996: 64; Boffey and Edwards 1997: 21-22); and the name 'JGraystok' in MS Tanner 346, f.131, following the colophon to the *Parliament of Fowls*, suggests secondary ownership of this volume by Sir John Greystoke of Yorkshire (d. 1501), and the possibility that it was made for one of his ancestors, perhaps his father, Ralph, Lord Greystoke (d. 1487) cannot be dismissed entirely (Robinson 1980: xxvi). Other owners of the codices in which the *Legend* is extant include members of the landed gentry. Manly and Rickert's

dissemination amongst secondary audiences, but cf. for additional comment on the first two categories Meale (1992: 59 and n. 15).

proposal that MS Cambridge University Library Gg.4.27, together with MS Selden one of the two most lavish productions, was made for Jacqueline of Hainault, first wife of Humphrey, Duke of Gloucester, has been rejected in favour of the theory that it originated in a country-house milieu in East Anglia (Manly and Rickert 1940: I, 181; cf. Parkes and Beadle 1979–80: III, 54-56, 63-65). And John Stanley of Hooton in Cheshire, gentleman, JP, MP and royal servant, was the purchaser and probable commissioner of MS Fairfax 16 (Norton-Smith 1979: xiii). The 'humfrey Kyryel', whose name is found among many sixteenth-century scribblings in the margins of MS Bodley 638 (f.127), may perhaps be identified as belonging to the long-established Kent family of Kyriel or Crioll, although it has also been proposed that the book could at this date have been used as a grammar school textbook (Robinson 1982: xxxix-xl). A member of an earlier generation of this family, John Kyriel (d. 1490), has been associated with the latter of the two originally distinct portions of MS Pepys 2006, as has the son of a London draper, William Fetplace; however, neither of these names occurs in the section of the manuscript which contains the *Legend*, and it is unclear whether the two separate codices, in which there is some overlap of materials, were joined prior to their being bound together in the seventeenth century (Edwards 1985: xxix). Two remaining manuscripts, MSS Rawlinson C.86 and Trinity College Cambridge R.3.19, are more likely to have been in the possession of the urban middle classes than the gentry. Rawlinson contains references to the London mercantile families of Warner, Callawey and Sampson (Griffiths 1982: 386; Boffey and Meale 1991: 157-58); and, while Trinity does not itself bear any indication of ownership, the fact that its principal scribe was also responsible for much of the copying of Trinity College Cambridge R.3.21, a book owned by the London mercer and collector Roger Thorney (d. 1515; see Bone 1931–32), and which is complementary to R.3.19 in its contents—in that its textual bias is towards religious, rather than secular matters—that the same scribe contributed to both volumes, and that the methods of production and compilation are similar, lends credence to the suggestion that it, too, was in his possession (Bone 1931–32: 303; Fletcher 1987: xxx; Boffey and Thompson 1989: 288-89). Of the three manuscripts in the British Library only one, Additional

9832, offers any indication of ownership in the Middle Ages, although I have not as yet managed to identify the 'William Dene' whose name is prominent in the margin of f.13v.

While it is dangerous to argue from negative evidence and assume that because the names of women do not appear in any of these books they did not read them or have access to them in some other way—for example in the context of a household, however constituted[15]—it remains the case that in only one copy of the *Legend*, the Findern Manuscript, is there incontrovertible evidence of women's apparently active perusal of the text. Although named, anachronistically, after the Derbyshire gentry Finderns because of sixteenth-century references to a male member of that family in one memorandum on f.59v and a list of household goods 'at fyndern' in another on f.70 (Robbins 1954), all the earliest annotations (leaving aside scribal attributions) name women. Thus the names 'Elisabet koton' and 'Elisabet frauncys' are placed at the conclusion of the earliest datable item in the volume, *Sir Degrevaunt* (f.109v), in the hand of the romance's second scribe, and that of 'margery hungerford' appears on f.20v, a page containing one of the women's lyrics mentioned above. A refrain from this lyric, 'withowte variaunce', is copied alongside her name, suggesting its use as a kind of motto—an echo of the practice of adopting such phrases as an indication of amatory fidelity enshrined in literary terms in such texts as the *Assembly of Ladies* (400-404, 489, 582-83, 589-90, 597-98, 615-16, 627, 645, 666, 675-76). Elsewhere, the signature? of 'Anne Schyrley' accompanies the text of *La Belle Dame sans Mercy* (f.118) and, from a slightly later date, that of 'ffraunces kruker' on f.65v, in the bottom margin of the second leaf of the extract from the *Legend* and on f.95v, a blank page following the tale of Apollonius of Tyre, VIII.271-846, of one of the two extracts from the *Confessio Amantis* (*SIMEV* 2662). These women belonged to families which had close local connections, and, although the exact nature of their association with the manuscript remains obscure in the sense that it has yet to be determined whether they acted as scribes, compilers, readers

15. I am deliberately leaving open the nature of individual households—whether noble, gentry or urban, nuclear or extended—within this discussion, since continuing research emphasizes the diversity, then as now, of potential models and actual examples.

or users,[16] their evident interest in the tale of Thisbe from the *Legend*, and in other courtly poetry, stands as an important witness to women's involvement with contemporary literature and with Chaucer's writing. But the question of why a greater number of women apparently did not own or commission copies of the *Legend*—and particularly, perhaps, the kind of women who were reading Christine and Boccaccio[17]—remains open.

The distinctions that I have drawn between the history of Chaucer's *Legend* in the later Middle Ages and that of other contemporary encyclopaedic collections of stories about women suggest three different strands in the work's reception. In some instances Chaucer's apparent intention that the *Prologue* and the tales should be taken together as a discrete entity seems to have been honoured. On a second level, though, readers of the poem—whether book-producers or their clients—engaged with the literary issues which it raised through judicious excerpting of material. On a third, the deliberately controversial, dialogic aspect of the *Legend*—that which renders it problematic to present-day audiences—is underplayed, to the extent that the legendary of love's martyrs as a whole can be interpreted as an exercise in sentimental complaint. This is nowhere so clearly illustrated as in British Library MS Additional 12524, the volume in which the *Legend* breaks off in its usual incomplete state prior to the conclusion of the story of Hypermnestra, only to be followed by the incipit to the 'llegenda Sismond'. In Banester's adaptation of this story from the *Decameron* (Day Four, no. 1; McWilliam 1972: 332-42), whether via the Latin and French intermediary sources suggested by the English text's editor (Wright 1937: xxv) or from the Italian (Green 1978: 300), much of the overt sensuality of Boccaccio's work is toned down. In the English writer's hands it becomes one in which the heroine, crossed in love by the unrealistic and unreasonable demands of a parent, is 'a m[i]roure to

---

16. Both Harris (1983: 303, 306-307) and Hanna (1987: 63) make the assumption of women scribes having been responsible for copying at least the romance of *Sir Degrevaunt*, but the evidence is circumstantial.

17. On female readers of Chaucer's works in general see Meale (1996b: 142); and cf. the will of William Banks, gentleman of Yorkshire, who in 1458 bequeathed to one 'Elenae Marshall unum librum Anglicum vocatum Trolias in manibus J. Manfeld existentem' (Raine 1855: 217-18).

women all, / Ensample of treue and stedfast lowe gyffyng' (605-606). While it is true that these lines echo Alceste's speech to Cupid, and that the comparison drawn at the opening of the story between Sismond's virtues and graces and those of women invoked by Chaucer—Penelope, Lucrece, Ypolita and Emelye—establishes the poem's credentials and suggests why it became associated with the *Legend,* its ethos of unrelenting and unambiguous 'courtliness' serves only to emphasize the surface simplicities of Chaucer's work, indicating a certain lack of literary discrimination on the part of whoever decided to combine the texts in this way. This absence of recognition of the tonal ambiguities of the *Legend* should not, perhaps, be a cause of surprise in a century which, in Paul Strohm's formulation, saw the narrowing of the Chaucer tradition (1982). But, in compensation, it offers a valuable opportunity through which to attempt the recovery of reading practices and literary reception in the years following Chaucer's death.

WORKS CITED

Barratt, A.A.T.
  1987   ' "The Flower and the Leaf" and "The Assembly of Ladies": Is There a (Sexual) Difference?', *Philological Quarterly* 66: 1-24.
Barratt, A.A.T. (ed.)
  1992   *Women's Writing in Middle English* (London: Longman).
Beadle, R., and A.E.B. Owen (introds.)
  1978   *The Findern Manuscript: Cambridge University Library MS. Ff.1.6* (London: Scolar Press).
Benson, C.D., and D. Rollman
  1981   'Wynkyn de Worde and the Ending of Chaucer's *Troilus and Criseyde*', *Modern Philology* 78: 275-79.
Blake, N.F.
  1989   'Manuscript to Print', in Griffiths and Pearsall (eds.) 1989: 403-32.
Bliss, A.J. (ed.)
  1960   *Thomas Chestre: Sir Launfal* (London: Nelson).
Boffey, J.
  1993   'The Reputation and Circulation of Chaucer's Lyrics in the Fifteenth Century', *Chaucer Review* 28: 23-40.
  forthcoming   ' "Twenty Thousand More": Some Fifteenth- and Sixteenth-Century Responses to *The Legend of Good Women*', in A.J. Minnis (ed.), *Middle English Poetry: Texts and Traditions in Honour of Derek Pearsall* (Cambridge: Brewer).

Boffey, J., and A.S.G. Edwards (introds.)
1997 *Bodleian Library, MS Arch. Selden B.24: A Working Facsimile* (Cambridge: Brewer).
Boffey, J., and C.M. Meale
1991 'Selecting the Text: Rawlinson C.86 and Some Other Books for London Readers', in F. Riddy (ed.), *Regionalism in Late Medieval Manuscripts and Texts* (Cambridge: Brewer): 143-69.
Boffey, J., and J.J. Thompson
1989 'Anthologies and Miscellanies: Production and Choice of Texts', in Griffiths and Pearsall (eds.) 1989: 279-315.
Bone, G.
1931–32 'Extant Manuscripts Printed from by W. de Worde, with Notes on the Owner, Roger Thorney', *Library*, 4th series 12: 284-306.
Brusendorff, A.
1925 *The Chaucer Tradition* (Oxford: Clarendon Press).
Burrow, J.A.
1994 *Thomas Hoccleve* (Aldershot: Variorum).
Camargo, M.
1991 *The Middle English Verse Love Epistle* (Tübingen: Niemeyer).
Chance, J.
1994 'Christine de Pizan as Literary Mother: Women's Authority and Subjectivity in "The Floure and the Leafe" and "The Assembly of Ladies"', in M. Zimmermann and D. de Rentiis (eds.), *The City of Scholars: New Approaches to Christine de Pizan* (Berlin: W. de Gruyter): 245-59.
Cowen, J., and G. Kane (eds.)
1995 *Geoffrey Chaucer: The Legend of Good Women* (East Lansing, MI: Colleagues Press).
Davis, N. (ed.)
1971–76 *Paston Letters and Papers of the Fifteenth Century* (2 vols.; Oxford: Clarendon Press).
Delany, S.
1994 *The Naked Text: Chaucer's Legend of Good Women* (Berkeley: University of California Press).
Edwards, A.S.G.
1996 'Bodleian Library MS Arch. Selden B.24: A "Transitional" Collection', in S.G. Nichols and S. Wenzel (eds.), *The Whole Book: Cultural Perspectives on the Medieval Miscellany* (Ann Arbor: University of Michigan Press): 53-67.
Edwards, A.S.G. (introd.)
1985 *Magdalene College, Cambridge, MS Pepys 2006: A Facsimile* (Norman, OK: Pilgrim Books).
Evans, R., and L. Johnson
1991 '*The Assembly of Ladies*: A Maze of Feminist Sign-Reading?', in S. Sellers (ed.), *Feminist Criticism: Theory and Practice* (New York: Harvester Wheatsheaf): 171-96.
Fenster, T.S., and M. Erler (eds.)
1990 *Poems of Cupid, God of Love* (Leiden: E.J. Brill).

Field, P.J.C.
  1982   'Malory and *The Wedding of Sir Gawain and Dame Ragnell*', *Archiv für das Studium der neueren Sprachen und Literaturen* 219: 374-81.
  1993   *The Life and Times of Sir Thomas Malory* (Cambridge: Brewer).
Fletcher, B.Y. (introd.)
  1987   *Manuscript Trinity R.3.19: A Facsimile* (Norman, OK: Pilgrim Books).
Furnivall, F.J., and I. Gollancz (eds.)
  1970   *Hoccleve's Works: The Minor Poems* (EETS ES 61 and 73; London: Oxford University Press; revised by J. Mitchell and A.I. Doyle and reprinted in 1 vol. [1892, 1897]).
Green, R.F.
  1978   'The Date of Gilbert Banester's Translation of the Tale of Guiscardo and Ghismonda', *Notes and Queries* 223: 299-300.
  1983   'The *Familia Regis* and the *Familia Cupidinis*', in V.J. Scattergood and J.W. Sherborne (eds.), *English Court Culture in the Later Middle Ages* (London: Gerald Duckworth): 87-108.
Griffiths, J.J.
  1982   'A Re-examination of Oxford, Bodleian Library, MS Rawlinson c.86', *Archiv für das Studium der neueren Sprachen und Literaturen* 134: 381-88.
Griffiths, J., and D. Pearsall (eds.)
  1989   *Book Production and Publishing in Britain 1375–1475* (Cambridge: Cambridge University Press).
Guarino, G.A. (trans.)
  1964   *Boccaccio: Concerning Famous Women* (London: George Allen & Unwin).
Hammond, E.P.
  1908   *Chaucer: A Bibliographical Manual* (London: Macmillan).
Hanna, R.
  1987   'The Production of Cambridge University Library MS. Ff.1.6', *Studies in Bibliography* 40: 62-70.
Harris, K.
  1983   'The Origins and Make-Up of Cambridge University Library MS Ff.1.6', *Transactions of the Cambridge Bibliographical Society* 8: 299-333.
Isbell, H. (trans.)
  1990   *Ovid: Heroides* (Harmondsworth: Penguin Books).
Laidlaw, J.C. (ed.)
  1974   *The Poetical Works of Alain Chartier* (Cambridge: Cambridge University Press).
Lawson, S. (trans.)
  1985   *Christine de Pisan: The Treasure of the City of Ladies* (Harmondsworth: Penguin Books).
Lester, G.A.
  1987   'The Books of a Fifteenth-Century English Gentleman, Sir John Paston', *Neuphilologische Mitteilungen* 88: 200-15.
Lyall, R.J.
  1989   'Books and Book Owners in Fifteenth-Century Scotland', in Griffiths and Pearsall (eds.) 1989: 239-56.

Manly, J.M., and E. Rickert
1940   *The Text of the Canterbury Tales: Studied on the Basis of All Known
                Manuscripts* (8 vols.; Chicago: University of Chicago Press).
McMillian, A.
1979   'Men's Weapons, Women's War: The Nine Female Worthies, 1400-
                1640', *Mediaevalia* 5: 113-39.
McNamer, S.
1991   'Female Authors, Provincial Setting: The Re-Versing of Courtly Love
                in the Findern Manuscript', *Viator* 22: 279-310.
McWilliam, G.H. (trans.)
1972   *Giovanni Boccaccio: The Decameron* (Harmondsworth: Penguin
                Books).
Meale, C.M.
1989   'Patrons, Buyers and Owners: Book Production and Social Status',
                in Griffiths and Pearsall (eds.) 1989: 201-38.
1992   'Legends of Good Women in the European Middle Ages', *Archiv für
                das Studium der neueren Sprachen und Literaturen* 229: 55-70.
1996a   'Reading Women's Culture in Fifteenth-Century England: The Case
                of Alice Chaucer', in P. Boitani and A. Torti (eds.), *Mediaevalitas:
                Reading the Middle Ages* (Cambridge: Brewer): 81-101.
1996b   '"...alle the bokes that I haue of latyn, englisch, and frensch":
                Laywomen and their Books in Late Medieval England', in C.M.
                Meale (ed.), *Women and Literature in Britain 1150–1500* (Cambridge:
                Cambridge University Press, 2nd edn): 128-58.
Norton-Smith, J. (introd.)
1979   *Bodleian Library MS Fairfax 16* (London: Scolar Press).
Norton-Smith, J. (ed.)
1981   *James I of Scotland: The Kingis Quair* (Leiden: E.J. Brill).
Parkes, M.B., and R. Beadle (introds.)
1979–80   *Poetical Works: Geoffrey Chaucer, A Facsimile of Cambridge University
                Library MS Gg.4.27* (3 vols.; Cambridge: Brewer).
Pearsall, D.A. (ed.)
1962   *The Floure and the Leafe* and *The Assembly of Ladies* (London: Nelson).
1990   *The Floure and the Leafe, The Assembly of Ladies, The Isle of Ladies*
                (Kalamazoo, MI: Medieval Institute Publications).
Phillippy, P.A.
1986   'Establishing Authority: Boccaccio's *De Claris Mulieribus* and
                Christine de Pizan's *Le Livre de la Cite des Dames*', *Romanic Review* 77:
                167-93.
Phillips, H.
1995   'Chaucer and Jean Le Fèvre', *Archiv für das Studium der neueren
                Sprachen und Literaturen* 232: 23-36.
Raine, J. (ed.)
1855   *Testamenta Eboracensia*, II (London: Surtees Society 30).
Richards, E.J. (trans.)
1983   *The Book of the City of Ladies: Christine de Pizan* (London: Pan Books).
Robbins, R.H.
1954   'The Findern Anthology', *PMLA* 69: 610-42.

Robinson, P.R. (introd.)
  1980   *Manuscript Tanner 346: A Facsimile* (Norman, OK: Pilgrim Books; Woodbridge: Boydell & Brewer).
Robinson, P.R. (introd.)
  1982   *Manuscript Bodley 638: A Facsimile* (Norman, OK: Pilgrim Books; Woodbridge: Boydell & Brewer).
Shepherd, S.A.H. (ed.)
  1995   *Middle English Romances* (New York: Norton).
Skeat, W.W. (ed.)
  1894–97   *The Complete Works of Geoffrey Chaucer* (7 vols.; Oxford: Clarendon Press).
Strohm, P.
  1982   'Chaucer's Fifteenth-Century Audience and the Narrowing of the "Chaucer Tradition"', *Studies in the Age of Chaucer* 4: 3-32.
Taylor, A.
  1997   'Anne of Bohemia and the Making of Chaucer', *Studies in the Age of Chaucer* 19: 95-119.
Tuetey, M.
  1864–65   'Inventaire des Biens de Charlotte de Savoie', *Bibliothèque Ecoles des Chartes* 26: 338-442.
Utley, F.L.
  1944   *The Crooked Rib: An Analytical Index to the Argument about Women in English and Scots Literature to the End of the Year 1568* (Columbus: Ohio State University Press).
Wallace, D.
  1997   *Chaucerian Polity: Absolutist Lineages and Associational Forms in England and Italy* (Stanford: Stanford University Press).
Wimsatt, J.I.
  1991   *Chaucer and His French Contemporaries: Natural Music in the Fourteenth Century* (Toronto: University of Toronto Press).
Wright, H.G. (ed.)
  1937   *Early English Versions of the Tales of Guiscardo and Ghismonda and Titus and Gisippus from the Decameron* (EETS, 205; London: Oxford University Press).

Chaucer and Interest in Astronomy at the Court of Richard II

Linne R. Mooney

In 1379–80, when Geoffrey Chaucer wrote the *House of Fame,* he described in his dialogue with the Golden Eagle of Book II his supposed resistance to learning the science of astronomy.[1] The Eagle introduces the subject of astronomy in the course of their discussion about how high they are above the earth:

> 'Now turn upward,' quod he, 'thy face,
> And behold this large space,
> This eyr, but loke thou ne be
> Adrad of hem that thou shalt se...' (*House of Fame* II.925-28).

He points out the Milky Way and tells the story of Phaeton forming it. The Eagle then offers to teach Chaucer astronomy:

> 'Lat be,' quod he, 'thy fantasie!
> Wilt thou lere of sterres aught?' (II.992-93).

But Chaucer shouts up, 'Nay, certeynly...ryght naught...For y am now to old' (II.994-95). The Eagle then explains that he would have taught Chaucer the names of the stars and signs of the zodiac, arguing that Chaucer should know them to understand poetic allusions to them in classical literature. But Chaucer asserts that he need not learn of them himself, because, first, he is willing

---

1.   I use the term 'supposed' here because there is certainly a possibility that Chaucer's resistance there is a fiction, to be associated with the character of narrator in the *House of Fame* rather than with the poet. But if his resistance to learning the science is a fiction, even a comic fiction, in the *House of Fame,* it is nevertheless a fiction he could carry off in 1379–80 with himself as narrator of the poem.

to believe 'Hem that write of this matere' (II.1013) as if he had
seen the stars himself, and, second, that they are so bright that it
would blind him to look at them. This silences the Eagle, but it
obviously did not silence other influences on Chaucer; for within
five years after writing these lines he was already well acquainted
with the stars and the zodiac, and was beginning to make astronomical observations himself. And this fascination with astronomy
would be witnessed again and again in the poet's writings over the
next decade.[2]

The works that Chaucer wrote after the *House of Fame*—the *Parliament of Fowls*, the *Complaint of Mars*, *Troilus and Criseyde*, the
Legend of Good Women, the *Treatise on the Astrolabe*, and some tales
of the *Canterbury Tales*—all contain allusions to the sciences of
astronomy or astrology, and many are dependent upon an understanding of the sciences for full appreciation of the plot and interpretation of the theme. Editors of these works from Skeat to the
present day note references to specific astronomical events or
calculations that can be interpreted in no other way than as
scientific references (Skeat 1894–97; cf. Curry 1960; Wood 1970;
and Eade 1984).

Some scholars have used the dates of the actual, fourteenth-
century astronomical events to date works by Chaucer in which he
alludes to such astronomical events (e.g. North 1988; O'Connor
1956; Root and Russell 1924; Manly 1896). Such dating of
composition seems questionable for two reasons. First, Chaucer
could have looked up some phenomena in tables, and thus
known of their occurrence beforehand. Second, and more likely,
Chaucer could well have written or revised the works after the
astronomical phenomena occurred.[3] Astronomical phenomena,

---

2. In the *Miller's Tale* I.3451-61 Chaucer has John the carpenter speak
disparagingly of the study of astronomy, but he is characterized as ignorant
and suspicious of all learning. In the *Treatise on the Astrolabe* II.4.57-60,
Chaucer, describing the ascendant planets and nativities, wrote: 'Natheles
these ben observaunces of judicial matere and rytes of payens, in whiche my
spirit hath no feith, ne knowing of her horoscopum', which Wood (1970: 15-
18) interprets as expressing Chaucer's lack of faith in astrology; but Smyser
(1970: 359-73) argues convincingly that Chaucer is here merely finding fault
with the inaccuracy of astrological measurements, as can be inferred from
the text that follows (II.4.60-9; also II.3.63-81).

3. This is even an argument North makes in dating the composition of

like any other historical event witnessed by an author, can be included in a work written after the event—provided that the author has recalled it or taken notes. We know that astronomers did take notes of astronomical observations or calculations; there are even such notes written by 'Hand C' in Cambridge, Peterhouse MS 75, part 1, thought by some scholars to be Chaucer's hand (Price 1955: 145; North 1988: 157-81; Robinson 1988: I, 83). Chaucer could also have added references to astronomical phenomena in revising works years after original composition, for he does seem to have been a poet who revised again and again over years of composition.[4] The references to astronomical events, then, could have been written (or added) either prior to or following the actual, historical occurrences of the natural phenomena.

Given these possibilities, the specific astronomical references in Chaucer's writings give us dates not so much for Chaucer's work on those writings as for his active interest in astronomy. That is, Chaucer's references to specific phenomena that would require use of sophisticated astronomical tables, and possibly observation of the heavens on a specific date, demonstrate that, around the time when the phenomena occurred Chaucer was interested in those astronomical occurrences, and may have observed them himself. He may even have gone so far as to take notes on them, or consider their astrological implications in relation to the characters and events of the works that were in his mind at the time.

Chaucer may have had the idea for including astronomical and astrological allusions in his writings from Dante, to whose works we believe he may have been exposed during his second journey to Italy in 1378. Dante frequently described or referred to the astrological properties of the planets in *Paradiso* 1-22 (Kay 1994).

the *Parliament of Fowls* in May 1385, more than a year after some of the astronomical events he claims are described therein (North 1988: 341, 365).

4.   Evidence in point is his revision of the *Prologue* to the *Legend of Good Women*, his apparent revision of the *General Prologue* to the *Canterbury Tales* to change the structure of the work as a whole, and his apparent revision of individual tales, as witnessed for instance by the apparent change in gender of the narrator of the *Shipman's Tale*. For the two versions of the *Prologue* to the *Legend of Good Women* as evidence of Chaucer's revising see Benson (1987: 1060); for revision of the *General Prologue* to the *Canterbury Tales* and the *Shipman's Tale* see Benson (1987: 798, 872, 910).

He does not, however, use a description of an astronomical occurrence to set a time of day or a date in the events of his tale, as Chaucer does. Where he has his Pilgrim being instructed by various authorities concerning the influence of the heavens on terrestrial events (as the Eagle offered to do for Chaucer in the *House of Fame*), Chaucer shows the effects of this influence on the characters in his stories.

Another explanation for Chaucer's inclusion of astronomical and astrological allusions in his writings is the interest of his aristocratic patrons in the sciences. Chaucer would then be including allusions to astronomical phenomena for the same reasons that he included references to the Trojan War or to classical myths with which the learned in his audience would be familiar. Their meaning and the implications of their inclusion in his texts would not be essential to an understanding of the storyline, but would add a depth and richness of meaning that the learned in his audience would appreciate.

Hilary Carey has argued that there was little interest in astrology at the court of Richard II. She writes:

> Reviewing the case so far, what conclusions can we reach concerning the practice of astrology at the court of Richard II? The example of his father and grandfather might have inclined Richard to ignore astrology as theologically unsound. As far as we can judge from the various contemporary chronicles, the English had not yet acquired a taste for the complex Arabic sciences of divination, such as astrology or geomancy, and preferred the verses of prophets... So far as Richard II is concerned, he seems to have known little about astrology, and was cautious even in commissioning a book on the less controversial subject of geomancy (1992: 98, 116).

However, the evidence of Chaucer's writings and of other books compiled in Richard's reign contradicts Carey's statements about the court's lack of interest in astrology. Richard and Anne of Bohemia were married in January 1382. Anne was the daughter of the Holy Roman Emperor Charles IV and the sister of Wenceslaus IV, who was king of Bohemia from 1378 to 1419 and emperor from 1378 to 1400, when he was deposed by the German Electors.[5] Carey herself drew attention to Wenceslaus IV's interest in

5.   Carey (1992: 106) names Wenceslaus as Richard's 'father-in-law', whereas he was his brother-in-law; she also errs in calling him 'Wenceslaus

astrology, as witnessed by a number of books on the subject owned by him (Carey 1992: 34, 116; North 1988: 237, citing Krása 1971). It seems likely that Richard and others in his court became interested in astronomy and astrology from the influence of Anne and her Bohemian followers.[6] In the years immediately following the marriage of Richard and Anne in 1381–82 Chaucer was writing *Troilus and Criseyde*, including among other astronomical references the reference to the conjunction of Saturn and Jupiter in Cancer (III.624-28), a historical parallel which North and others before him have dated as occurring in 1385 (North 1988: 369-78; Root and Russell 1924).[7] In the first half of 1385, too, occurred specific astronomical or astrological phenomena described in the *Complaint of Mars* (North 1988: 304-18; Manly 1896). Another, which occurred in 1386, is described in the *F* version of the *Prologue* to the *Legend of Good Women*, which was to be given to the queen;[8] others, which occurred in 1387–88, are described in the *Franklin's Tale*, the *Merchant's Tale* and the *Knight's Tale* (North 1988: 422-43, 433-55, 402-21); horoscopes dateable to 1392 figure

II'. Nevertheless, the points she makes about the connection between the Bohemian interest in astrology and Richard's interest after his marriage to Anne carry the same weight whether one is talking of Anne's father or her brother.

6.   In commenting on Richard's book of geomancy, Bodleian Library MS Bodley 581, completed 1391, in relation to Wenceslaus's book of geomancy, Oesterreichischen Nationalbibliothek MS 2352, illuminated in 1392–93, North comments: 'Within a year or so, another fine copy of geomancy was done for the Emperor, Wenceslaus IV of Bohemia, and it is tempting to suppose that Richard's having taken Anne of Bohemia as his queen was in some way responsible for this link between the tastes of the two monarchs' (North 1988: 237 and n. 58), without specifying in which direction he believes the influence might have acted. For Anne's and Bohemian influence on English manuscript illumination see Rickert (1965: 152) and Mitchell (1965: 37). For Anne's influence on vernacular translations of the Bible see Bell (1988: 176-78) and Deanesley (1922: 248, 445.)

7.   Other astronomical references in *Troilus and Criseyde* include that to the rising of 'Lucifer' and 'Fortuna Major' (III.1415-21), the rising of Venus in her Seventh House (II.679-86), and positions of Venus, Mercury and Mars (IV.29-39).

8.   In May 1386 Venus was in Trine aspect with Mars, as described in the *Prologue*; see North (1988: 537).

in the *Nun's Priest's Tale* (North 1988: 456-68). In the early 1390s Chaucer was writing the *Treatise on the Astrolabe,* and a *radix* for astronomical calculations found in Cambridge, Peterhouse MS 75. Part 1 is associated with his name.

Besides these references to astronomical occurrences in Chaucer's works, there is other evidence of interest in astronomy, astrology and related sciences at the court of Richard II in these years. Perhaps as early as 1380 Richard's mother, Joan of Kent, commissioned John Somer to write a kalendar of astronomical events for the years 1387–1462; the earliest surviving copies of Somer's *Kalendarium* date from 1383 and 1384 (see Mooney 1998: 58-59, 81). In 1386 John of Gaunt commissioned Nicholas of Lynn to produce a similar calendar, to include still more astronomical tables than Somer's (Eisner 1980: 2, 29). From other works attributed to him it is clear that Somer was knowledgeable about nativities and horoscopes: to him is ascribed a brief text on 'Ille Days in the Yere' in Oxford, Bodleian Library MS Digby 88, rules for forecasting life from the positions of the planets at birth (*Regule ad sciendum nati vitam*) in Oxford, Bodleian Library MS Laud Miscellaneous 674, and a horoscope figure in Corpus Christi College Cambridge MS 420 (Mooney 1998, Appendix D). From royal records and from his own chronicle in British Library MS Cotton Domitian A.ii (see Catto and Mooney 1998), we know that Somer was attached to the royal court in the 1390s.

Richard II's own interest in astrology and the occult can be dated to the same period. Richard himself apparently commissioned a Latin compilation of geomantic works, now Oxford, Bodleian Library MS Bodley 581, which was completed by its anonymous Irish compiler in March 1391. Richard's interest in astronomy and astrology is also witnessed by his possession of a golden quadrant, enamalled and pearl-studded, among the treasury objects inventoried at the accession of Henry IV (Carey 1992: 97 n. 37, citing Palgrave 1836: III, 41). His interest in the related subject of alchemy is witnessed by a text, the *Essentia Lapidis,* written by a monk of Cirencester in Latin in 13 chapters and dedicated to the king, '*summo gloria regi*', in 1390.[9] Furthermore,

---

9.   In Trinity College Cambridge MS R.14.38, Part II, beginning f.6. The epilogue ends in verse:

various chroniclers record that Richard depended upon divination to have predetermined the outcome of the trial-by-combat encounter of Henry, Duke of Hereford, and Thomas Mowbray, Duke of Norfolk, in 1398. Adam of Usk, for instance, records that 'because the king had it by divination that the duke of Norfolk should then prevail, he rejoiced much, eagerly striving after the destruction of the duke of Hereford'.[10]

Other English manuscript collections of astronomical and astrological texts from the late fourteenth century demonstrate interest in these subjects during Richard's reign. These manuscripts include Bodleian Library Digby 57, Latin texts on astronomy and astrology; Boston Public Library med. 100, which includes a Middle English verse text on divination by casting dice; Cambridge, Trinity College O.5.26, a collection of Middle English translations of Greek and Arabic texts on astronomy and astrology; and Cambridge, Peterhouse 75, Part 1, a collection of astronomical tables together with the Middle English *Equatorie of the Planetis*. And there are several more written in Latin and dateable to the 1380s and 1390s. The *Equatorie* text itself must have been written, if not by Chaucer, probably by or for a member of the court circle, for the size and materials of this astronomical instrument are such that it could only have been intended to be built by a person of enormous wealth, like the king himself. All in all, the manuscript evidence suggests an increasing interest in astronomy and related sciences in England in the late fourteenth century.

There is a striking coincidence between Chaucer's references to

> Hoc opus egi sit summo gloria regi
> Gloria sit illi finem ponendo labori
> Circa natale quod est tempus nonogeno
> Sit celo locatus author cirencestria natus
> pro ipso cari puries curate precari.

The sixteenth-century scribe of the Trinity copy notes, 'Mensse Maii per Fretwell 1594 ex libro autentico authoris manu scripto 1390 membrana.' See James (1900–1904: II, 322-23).

10. Thompson (1904: 24 and 171) (for the translation). The Latin text is:

> quia rex a sortilegio habuerat quod dux Northfolchie tunc prevaleret, ducis Herefordie destructionem affectando multum gaudebat (1904: 24).

specific astronomical and astrological phenomena and his residence in Kent during this same period. Such references begin
with the *Complaint of Mars*. Arguments that this poem describes
astronomical or astrological phenomena—the conjunction of
Venus and Mars in Taurus, and, after Venus passed out of Taurus
into Gemini, the approach of the sun to Taurus, burning Mars—
are particularly convincing for this work (North 1988: 304-18;
Manly 1896). These historical astronomical events occurred
between 14 February and 12 April 1385, and this dating corresponds to the literary scholars' accepted date for composition of
the *Complaint of Mars* (Benson 1987: 1079). A month later, in June
1385, occurred the conjunction of the moon, Jupiter and Saturn,
causing rain, that is featured in Book III of *Troilus* (Root and
Russell 1924: 48-63; North 1988: 369-78). These are much more
specific references to astronomical and astrological phenomena
than any of earlier date mentioned by Chaucer. It would seem
that something had occurred at or around this time that allowed
Chaucer to begin to calculate the times of astronomical events or
to make astronomical observations.

   In early 1385 Chaucer was serving as Controller of the Wool
Custom and Subsidy in London, and residing in the rooms over
Aldgate that he had occupied since 1374. This is what the biogra-
phies tell us; but the *Life Records* also tell us other things about this
period that cast doubt both on his activities and on his place of
residence in 1385. In 1383 Chaucer had received permission to
appoint a deputy controller of the Wool Custom and Subsidy for
over four months, from 23 June to 1 November—not, however,
with any known royal mission as the reason: the Close Rolls record
reads, 'shewing that he is like to be so much occupied upon
particular business that for a certain time he may not without
grievous disturbance attend to that office' (*Cal. Close Rolls 1381–
85*, 322). Again, a year later, in 1384, he received permission to
appoint a deputy for the month between 25 November and 25
December; and seven weeks after the end of this deputation, on
17 February 1385, he was permitted to appoint a permanent
deputy controller (Crow and Olson 1966: 168-69). Although he
did not officially relinquish his office until December 1386, he
had been relinquishing its daily duties virtually from November
1384, and permanently from 17 February 1385. He would have

continued to check on the activities of his deputies from time to time, and would have continued to appear in person at the Exchequer to testify to the accuracy of the accounts, but he need not have continued to reside in London to do that. By 12 October 1385 he was clearly residing in Kent, for he was named a Justice of the Peace for Kent at that date. In August of the following year, 1386, he was elected as one of the Knights of the Shire to represent Kent in the Parliament that would meet in October. Both of these appointments suggest that Chaucer was a resident or landowner of significant means and status in Kent. Although he did not officially relinquish his rooms over Aldgate until October 1386, he had by then clearly established his residence in Kent for over a year—since at least 12 October 1385. His desire to appoint a permanent deputy to the Wool Custom and Subsidy in February 1385 suggests that already by then he was anxious to spend more of his time in his residence in Kent, whence a daily commute to the Customs wharf would have been not impossible but certainly inconvenient. Meanwhile the Aldgate rooms could continue to serve as his *pied à terre* in London when he needed to be there overnight. In sum, the appointment of a permanent deputy suggests a wish or a need to retire from daily labours at the Customs wharf; and this, together with his established residence in Kent only seven months later, suggests an earlier move to the country than has usually been assigned to him.

This date in mid-February 1385, marking his semi-retirement from the Controllership of the Customs and possible move to Kent, coincides with the earliest specific references to astronomical and astrological phenomena described in his writings. If Chaucer had been actively interested in astronomy before 1385, one can imagine him making what observations of the heavens he could from the top of Aldgate, just as Oxford astronomers had done from the top of Oxford's Aldgate (at the town side of Folly Bridge) from the time of Roger Bacon (Hobhouse 1939: 4); but this conjectured move into Kent just at the time of the earliest specific astronomical phenomena described in Chaucer's writings suggests rather that his new residence in Kent afforded him opportunities for observation he had lacked in London.[11]

11. For an illustration showing the London Aldgate that Chaucer had occupied see Colvin (1963: 2), Pl. 44, A. van den Wyngaerde's sixteenth-

This theory that in Kent Chaucer had found a site for making astronomical observations stands the test of comparing Chaucer's references to astronomical phenomena with times when he was known to be out of the country, or in London, or elsewhere than in Kent (see North 1988: 516-17). For instance, we know from the *Life Records* that he served in the Parliament from 1 October to 28 November 1386 and that from 5 July 1387 he was in Calais with William Beauchamp, Captain of Calais (Crow and Olson 1966: 364-69, 61-62). He must have returned to Kent by 1 August 1387, when he served as Justice *Ad Inquirendum* at Dartford regarding the abduction of Isabella Hall (Crow and Olson 1966: 376). Thus far the theory holds, since there are no references to astronomical phenomena in his writings from either the autumn of 1386 or the summer of 1387. Astronomical references also show a break of almost three years around Chaucer's two-year service as Clerk of the Works: astronomical references cease in the spring of 1389; Chaucer was appointed Clerk of the Works on 12 July (Crow and Olson 1966: 402-406); he ceased to serve as Clerk of the Works on 17 June 1391 (Crow and Olson 1966: 462-66); and Chaucer began writing the *Treatise on the Astrolabe* in the spring of that year or within the year following (Benson 1987: 1092). Astronomical references continue from then into the mid-1390s, and perhaps beyond.

The table in the Appendix below compares dates of astronomical occurrences with historical dates and with the accepted dates for Chaucer's writings.[12] Some of John North's dates for astronomical phenomena described in Chaucer's writings, from *Chaucer's Universe*, Appendix 6 (North 1988: 539-40) are in ordinary print; historical dates and events, taken mostly from the *Life Records* (Crow and Olson 1966) are in bold print; and the accepted dates of writings, from Benson (1987), are in italic print. At the beginning of the table are a few dates of importance that

century sketch of the Tower of London, with Aldgate behind it, near the center of the picture. Above the gateway is a large rectangle of rooms, with two windows facing the City, and a large tower above one end of the rectangular gatehouse structure, rising at least another two stories above the roof of the gatehouse.

12. The 'accepted' dates for Chaucer's writings in this case are those given in the notes to Benson (1987).

relate to Chaucer's connection with Kent or with astronomy. The table is more inclusive from the arrival of Anne of Bohemia in December 1381. We see a flurry of astronomical activity in the spring and summer of 1385, followed by a lull in 1386–87 as Chaucer serves as MP for Kent in Parliament in the autumn of 1386, testifies in the Scrope-Grosvenor trial, resigns his Controllership, looks after his dying wife, and travels abroad for the king one last time. Then there is another flurry of activity, particularly in the spring of 1388, followed by only a few references in the spring of 1389 before Chaucer is appointed Clerk of the Works. We can then imagine him for the next two years too busy to sit over his astronomical tables in Kent. In the spring of 1392 he picks up activity again. In the early 1390s, as I have already noted, his interest is particularly strong, or rather particularly scientific, or technical, when we find a reference to a *radix* calculated by him in a book of astronomical tables and texts, and when he writes his treatise explaining the use of the primary instrument of astronomers, the astrolabe, for his son Lewis. According to North the last references to specific astronomical occurrences relate to the spring and early summer of 1394, only one, an anniversary, postdating Anne's death on 7 June 1394 (North 1988: 517).

To finish this table, I have also noted in 1397 the inability of the Sheriff of Kent to find Chaucer or his goods to distrain and the reassignment of collection of that debt to the Sheriffs of London and Middlesex, which may indicate that Chaucer had sold up and moved back to London or Middlesex 'more than a year before he took the lease of the house at Westminster' (Crow and Olson 1966: 513).

If Chaucer's active interest in astronomy coincides with his residence in Kent, as appears from this table, then where was the tower or point of high ground from which he would make his observations? Of course, we can imagine that he never watched the conjunction of two planets, or an eclipse of the moon, but only worked from the Alfonsine Tables and other books of astronomy. But we have the *Treatise on the Astrolabe* as evidence that he knew how to make observations: in Part II he describes in detail how to 'fynde the degre in which the sonne is day by day after his cours aboute,' how 'to knowe the altitude of the sonne or of othre

celestial bodies,' and how to perform 38 other operations with the
astrolabe (*Treatise* II.1, II.2, II.3–II.40). Even without the evidence
of the *Treatise*, who can imagine the writer of so many astronomical allusions not witnessing the events for himself?

Chaucer is usually assumed to have lived in Greenwich in these
years. In the Prologue to the *Reeve's Tale* Harry Bailey calls out,
'Lo Grenewych, ther many a shrewe is inne!' (*Canterbury Tales*
I.3907); and this is taken as one of Chaucer's characteristic self-
deprecations (Benson 1987: xxii). A woman sometimes identified
as Chaucer's sister, Katherine, was married to a Simon Manning,
who owned properties in both Cudham and East Greenwich
(Crow and Olson 1966: 288-89). Chaucer was named as Commissioner of Walls and Ditches along the Thames between Woolwich
and Greenwich in 1390 (Crow and Olson 1966: 490-93). He served
as justice, witness, attorney, and mainprise in cases involving persons and property from the towns around Greenwich (Crow and
Olson 1966: 512-13). Much more conclusive, though to date
largely ignored, is evidence from the well-known early fifteenth-
century manuscript anthology of Chaucer's works, Cambridge
University Library MS Gg.4.27, where the scribe has added marginal notes to his copy of *Lenvoy de Chaucer a Scogan*: 'id est Wyn-
disore' in the margin beside the first two lines of the envoy
proper:

> Scogan, that knelest at the stremes hed
> Of grace, of alle honour and worthynesse (43-44),

indicating that Scogan was with the court at Windsor, and 'id est a
Grenewych' beside the third and fourth lines:

> In th'ende of which strem I am dul as ded,
> Forgete in solytarie wildernesse (45-46),

indicating that Chaucer was at Greenwich.[13] With Chaucer's
Kentish residence possibly established at Greenwich, it is interesting to note that an unascribed lyric, consisting of two stanzas in
rhyme royal, found in Leiden University Library MS Vossius
Germ. Gall. Q.9, f.112, which contains many works of Lydgate and

---

13. These glosses are repeated in later manuscript copies of the *Envoy*,
Oxford, Bodleian Fairfax 16 (ff.192v-3) from the second quarter of the fifteenth century, and Cambridge, Magdalene College Pepys 2006 (pp. 385-86)
from the late fifteenth century. See Pace and David (1982: 150, 159).

the short lyrics *Truth* and *Fortune* from the accepted Chaucer canon, begins: 'Vpon temse fro london myles iij / In my chambir...' (*SIMEV* 3844.5; ed. Van Dorsten 1960). Greenwich is three miles downriver from London, and Chaucer is the only writer during that period who is known to have lived in Greenwich or in any other riverside town that could be said to be three miles from London.

It would certainly be one of the most remarkable coincidences of all time if Chaucer had been making astronomical observations in Greenwich more than 250 years before the founding of the first Royal Observatory there. Consider if you will, though, the geographical situation of Greenwich: the high ground behind the town at the edge of Blackheath, its placement close to the river, and its proximity to London were the very attributes that drew Sir Christopher Wren to select it as the site for Charles II's observatory in 1675 (Howse 1980: 28-29; Forbes 1975: I, 21-22). For that matter, its high ground below the U-bend in the river that forms the Isle of Dogs, with a commanding view of both curves of the river to sight ships approaching London from the sea, must have been a watch-place from the earliest settlement of London. There are no known records of its use as a watch-place from Chaucer's time or earlier, but in 1433 Humphrey, Duke of Gloucester, obtained by license under the Privy Seal a large parcel of land including this high ground from the Prior of Sheen in exchange for some of his lands, and a further license to build a tower on this high ground behind the town of Greenwich which was later to be the site of the first Royal Observatory (Nicolas 1834–37: IV, 138; Streatfield and Larking 1886: 54; Howse 1980: 31).

The royal manor house beside the Thames at Greenwich, to which the tower and its extensions on the hill were attached from Humphrey's time, is described by R.A. Brown and H.A. Colvin. It had been the manor house of an estate in Greenwich, given by Henry V to his uncle, Thomas Beaufort, Duke of Exeter, for life (Streatfield and Larking 1886: 54).[14] At his death in 1426 it was given to Humphrey, Duke of Gloucester, who in 1433 obtained a license to rebuild and crenellate the house and to build a stone

14. Sir William Dugdale (1675–66: II, 126), notes that Thomas Beaufort both wrote his testament and died 'at his Mannor of Grenewich' in December 1426.

tower in the park, as mentioned above (Nicolas 1834–37: IV, 138; *Cal. Pat. Rolls 1429–36*, 250). At his death in 1447 the house reverted to the crown, and was extensively altered by and for Henry VI's queen, Margaret, at a cost of almost 300 pounds. In her time its name was changed from 'Bella Court' to 'Plesaunce' (Streatfield and Larking 1886: 54-55; Brown and Colvin 1963: II, 949). Brown and Colvin describe the manor house in the time of Queen Margaret, but the core of the house, and its gardens, had existed from at least Thomas Beaufort's occupancy only 15 years after Chaucer's death:

> The buildings appear to have been largely of brick and timber, and stood in a garden close to the Thames. There were two courts or 'wards', one for the king, the other for the queen and her household. The accommodation in the Queen's ward [the older portion] included a great chamber, a parlour and a gallery overlooking the garden, and there was heraldic glass in the windows, some of it dating from the time of the Duke of Gloucester… The garden was hedged round and contained an arbour for the queen to sit in. It [that is, the garden] was probably on the south side of the house, away from the river, for in 1432 a brick wall was built 'between the manor and the Thames' (1963: II, 949).[15]

I have been unable to trace the ownership or occupancy of this manor house before Thomas Beaufort's time. The garden described by Brown and Colvin, with its arbour bench, reminds one of the 'little herber' beside the dreamer/narrator's house in the *Prologue* to the *Legend of Good Women*:

> Hom to myn hous ful swiftly I me spedde…
> And in a litel herber that I have,
> That benched was on turves fressh ygrave,
> I bad men sholde me my couche make;
> For deyntee of the newe someres sake,
> I bad hem strawen floures on my bed.
> Whan I was leyd and had myn eyen hed,
> I fel on slepe within an houre or twoo (*F* 200-209; cf. *G* 96-103).

Chaucer must have resided in such a house, if not this very one, to

15. Brown and Colvin note that Humphrey spent Christmas there in 1428. He later obtained leave to construct an aqueduct (see Brown and Colvin 1963: II, 949 n. 1 and [for information on the manor in Queen Margaret's time] n. 2).

establish his standing as a resident of significant importance in Greenwich from 1385 onwards.

Wherever he lived in Greenwich, Chaucer would have used the high ground at the edge of Blackheath as the site for whatever astronomical observations he may have made there. The high ground was not enclosed as part of the royal estate until Humphrey's time, but there may have been a wooden, or brick and timber, tower on the hill where Humphrey would later build his of stone. Chaucer may also have just used the open fields of Blackheath, near where the Royal Observatory would later be built, as an observation site. This was the practice of the clerk mentioned in the *Miller's Tale* (I.3451-61), who fell in a marl-pit while making observations in the open fields. Like that clerk, Chaucer would have had to be careful of falling into a marl-pit while making observations in the open fields, since the towns of Deptford, Lewisham and Greenhithe, which surround Greenwich, were centers of chalk (or marl) mining.[16]

On the other hand, another possible Kentish site for Chaucer's astronomical observations would have been the king's manor at Eltham, three miles south-east of Greenwich. Eltham, an easy walk from Greenwich, and Sheen, in present-day Richmond and thus an easy ride from Greenwich, were Richard's and Anne's two favorite residences. Richard had been characteristically extravagant in refurbishing them, and records show that the king and queen spent more time there than in Westminster or Windsor.[17]

16. 'Pits are situated at Lewisham, Charleton, Deptford, Camden Park, Greenhithe, Northfleet and Gravesend. The great chalk excavations known as the Chistlehurst Caves...are known to extend under the greater part of Chistlehurst Common, [and] are, at some points, 130 ft. below the surface... The Chistlehurst chalk was worked as early as 1250–74...' (Page 1932: III, 396).

17. Given-Wilson (1986: 31) describes the accomodations at Eltham: 'Here there were at least two halls...a "great chapel", and a host of private chambers. The king and queen both had chambers with chapels attached, and there was a bath-house and dancing chamber, as well as a wardrobe for the king with a fireplace in it. An account of repairs undertaken at Eltham in the years 1384–88 reveals that the "personalization" of private apartments had occurred here as well as at Sheen: John of Gaunt, Robert de Vere, Thomas Mowbray, the chamber knights Baldwin Bereford and Nicholas Sharnesfeld, controller of the household Baldwin Raddington, and one of

It was to Eltham that the king retired in response to the accusations made against his councillors at the Parliament of 1386 in
which Chaucer served; it was at Eltham that he and the Queen
celebrated Christmas with such extravagance in 1389 and 1392 as
attracted the notice of the chronicler monk of Westminster
(Steele 1941: 173 and n.; Barron 1971: 195 and n.). The manors
of both Eltham and Sheen were included among the royal residences whose repair and maintenance Chaucer had in charge as
Clerk of the Works in 1389–91. In the earlier version of the
Prologue to the *Legend of Good Women*, Alcestis instructs Chaucer to
write a book

> 'Of goode wymmen…
> And whan this book ys maad, yive it the quene,
> On my byhalf at Eltham or at Sheene' (*F* 484, 496-97),

as if these would be the most likely places to find the Queen—and
specifically for Chaucer to find the Queen, which suggests that he
had ready access to these manors. Not only Chaucer but others in
the royal circle were interested in astronomy and astrology (John
Somer, for instance), and the King and Queen may have allowed
one of the towers at their out-of-town manors like Eltham to be
used for making astronomical observations. Perhaps they witnessed such observations themselves, for among the faults with
which his contemporary detractors villified Richard was his habit
of remaining watchful sometimes halfway through the night, occasionally all night long, as they claimed in drinking and other
unspeakable acts;[18] others speak of his reliance on 'pseudo-
prophets' (Carey 1992: 93-97).

the queen's ladies in waiting, Lady Luttrell, all had their own chambers, to
which evidently they would always be assigned when the household was at
Eltham. There were also chambers for the steward of the household, the
keeper of the wardrobe, and the chaplains of the king's chapel.' For evidence that Edward II and Richard II spent much time at Eltham see Tout
(1967: III, 286-87; and IV, 176, 222, 483); and for evidence that Eltham and
Sheen were Richard's favorite residences see Given-Wilson (1986: 34).

18. The author of the *Historia Vitae et Regni Ricardi Secundi* writes that
Richard was, among other things, 'vigilator maximus, ita ut aliquando
dimidium noctem, non nunquam usque mane totam noctem in potacionibus
et aliis non dicendis in sompnem duceret' (Stow 1977: 166).

There does, then, seem to be a pattern of Chaucer's astronomical activity to link it with his residence in Kent, and perhaps also to the years in which Anne was Queen of England. From the evidence of his own writing, Chaucer had become an astronomy/astrology enthusiast by 1385, when he apparently moved from his rooms over Aldgate to something more like permanent residence at Greenwich. It seems probable that for at least a decade he was making astronomical observations at Greenwich, long before the Royal Observatory was founded there in the seventeenth century. Apart from the intervals taken to pursue the king's business, he maintained an interest in the science through the end of the 1380s and into the 1390s, having become an active amateur astronomer calculating his own *radices* and writing instructions for use of the astrolabe by 1393. Evidence of his interest in the science ends sometime in the mid-1390s, perhaps with the death of Anne in June 1394, or perhaps not until his return to London four or five years later. Given these conclusions, we should now return with new eyes to the records of Greenwich and Blackheath to look again for evidence of Chaucer's residence, associates and activities there.

APPENDIX

Table of Chaucer's Activities in Relation to the Royal Court

1375	**8 November and 28 December. Chaucer given wardship of two Kentish heirs.**
1377	**End of Chaucer's wardship of William Soles.**
1378–80	*Chaucer writes* House of Fame *in which he refuses to learn astronomy.*
1380	**1–4 May. Chancery enrolls releases re Cecily Champain.**
1380–82	*Chaucer writes* Parliament of Fowls.
1381	**December. Arrival of Anne of Bohemia in England.**
1382	**January. Marriage of Richard II and Anne.**
1382	**13 October. End of Chaucer's wardship of Edmund Staplegate.**
1382–86	*Chaucer writes* Troilus and Criseyde.
1383	**John Somer composes his *Kalendarium*.**
1383	**23 June to 1 November. Chaucer appoints deputy Controller.**
1384	14 February. Astronomical reference in *Parliament of Fowls.*
1384	**25 November to 25 December. Chaucer appoints deputy Controller.**

1385	15 February. Earliest specific astronomical phenomenon described in *Complaint of Mars*.
1385	**17 February. Chaucer appoints permanent deputy Controller.**
1385	*Chaucer writes* Complaint of Mars.
1385	12 March. Astronomical reference in *Complaint of Mars*.
1385	17 March. Astronomical reference in *Complaint of Mars*.
1385	27 March. Astronomical reference in *Complaint of Mars*.
1385	3 April. Astronomical reference in *Complaint of Mars*.
1385	8 April. Astronomical reference in *Complaint of Mars*.
1385	12 April. Astronomical reference in *Complaint of Mars*.
1385	4 May. Astronomical reference in *Troilus and Criseyde*.
1385	9–10 June. Astronomical references in *Troilus and Criseyde*.
1385	**7 August. Death of Joan of Kent at Wallingford. Chaucer receives black cloth for mourning as King's esquire.**
1385	**12 October. Chaucer appointed Justice of Peace for Kent.**
1386	**19 February. Philippa Chaucer admitted to Fraternity, Lincoln Cathedral.**
1386	1 May. Astronomical reference in *Legend of Good Women* (F version).
1386–87	*Chaucer writes Prologue to* Legend of Good Women (*F* version).
1386	**24 May to 28 June. Chaucer omitted from list of JPs for Kent.**
1386	**Nicholas of Lynn writes his *Kalendarium*.**
1386	**August. Chaucer returned as Knight of the Shire for Kent.**
1386	**1 October. Parliament in which Chaucer is MP for Kent.**
1386	**15 October. Chaucer testifies in Scrope-Grosvenor trial.**
1386	**13 November. Chaucer Mainprise for Simon Manning.**
1386	**4, 14 December. Chaucer permanently leaves Controllership.**
1387	3 May. Astronomical reference in *Knight's Tale*.
1387	**18 June. Last time Philippa Chaucer collects her annuity.**
1387	**5 July. Chaucer goes to Calais with William Beauchamp.**
1387	**1 August. Chaucer as Justice *Ad Inquirendum* in Dartford.**
1387	25 December. Astronomical reference in *Franklin's Tale*.
1388–92	*Chaucer writes* General Prologue *and earlier of the* Canterbury Tales.
1388	15 March. Astronomical reference in *Merchant's Tale*.
1388	**1 May. Chaucer transfers annuities to John Scalby.**
1388	3 May. Astronomical reference in *Knight's Tale*.
1388	5 May. Astronomical reference in *Knight's Tale*.
1388	13 May. Astronomical reference in *Squire's Tale*.
1388–99	**Chaucer as Mainprise for Matilda Nemeg.**
1388–99	**Actions against Chaucer to recover debt .**
1389	16 April. Astronomical reference in *Parson's Prologue*.
1389	**12 July. Chaucer named Clerk of the Works.**
1389	**15 July. Chaucer no longer listed as Justice of Peace.**

1390	**12 March. Chaucer becomes Commissioner of Walls between Woolwich and Greenwich.**
1390	**12 July. Chaucer given additional duties as Clerk of the Works.**
1390	**3 September. Chaucer robbed at 'le Fowle Ok'**
1390–97	**Chaucer shares duties Forester of Petherton, Somerset**
1391	**17 June. Chaucer ceases to be Clerk of the Works.**
1392–95	*Chaucer writes most of the* Canterbury Tales.
1392	26 April. Astrological reference in *Nun's Priest's Tale.*
1392	3 May. Astrological reference in *Nun's Priest's Tale.*
1392	**28 July to 3 August. Chaucer borrows 2 marks for a week.**
1392	**31 December. Date of the 'Radix Chaucer' in Peterhouse 75.1.**
1393	March. Conjectured date of writing *Astrolabe.*
1393	**4 May. Chaucer as witness at Woolwich.**
1393	June. Conjectured date of writing *Equatorie.*
1394	**28 February. Richard renews Chaucer's Exchequer annuity.**
1394	18 April. Astronomical reference in *Man of Law's Prologue.*
1394	15 May. Nominal date for revision of *Prologue* to *Legend of Good Women* (*G* Version).
1394	5 June. Hypermnestra's twentieth anniversary, gloomy horoscope.
1394	**7 June. Death of Anne of Bohemia.**
1395–96	**Chaucer as witness and attorney at Combe.**
1395–96	**Chaucer receives gifts from Henry, Earl of Derby.**
1396–1400	*Chaucer writes latest of the* Canterbury Tales, *including* Nun's Priest's Tale.
1397	**30 September. Sheriff of Kent has failed to find goods to distrain or to attach Chaucer in person; debt transferred to Sheriffs of London and Middlesex.**
1397–1400	**Chaucer becomes sole Forester of Petherton Park, Somerset.**
1398	**4 May. Royal protection for Chaucer against suits .**
1398	**30 September. Sheriffs of London and Middlesex have failed to collect debt from Chaucer; transferred to 'desperate debts'.**
1399	**Henry IV awards Chaucer Exchequer annuity.**
1399	**24 December. Chaucer signs lease on house in Westminster.**
1400	**25 October. Death of Chaucer.**

WORKS CITED

Barron, C.M.
    1971   'The Quarrel of Richard II with London 1392–97', in F.R.H.
                DuBoulay and C.M. Barron (eds.), *The Reign of Richard II: Essays in
                Honour of May McKisack* (London: Athlone Press): 173-201.
Bell, S.G.
    1988   'Medieval Women Book Owners: Arbiters of Lay Piety and Ambas-
                sadors of Culture', in M. Erler and M. Kowaleski (eds.), *Women and
                Power in the Middle Ages* (Athens, GA: University of Georgia Press):
                149-87.
Benson, L.D. (ed.)
    1987   *The Riverside Chaucer* (Boston: Houghton Mifflin).
Brown, R.A., and H.M. Colvin
    1963   'The King's Houses 1066-1485', in Colvin 1963: II, 949-50.
Carey, H.M
    1992   *Courting Disaster: Astrology at the English Court and University in the
                Later Middle Ages* (London: Macmillan).
Catto, J., and L. Mooney (eds.)
    1998   *The Chronicle of John Somer, OFM* (London: Royal Historical Society,
                Camden Society, 5th series 10, *Chronology, Conquest and Conflict in
                Mediaeval England,* Camden Miscellany 34: 197-285.
Colvin, H.M. (ed.)
    1963   *The History of the King's Works* (3 vols.; London: HMSO).
Crow, M.M., and C.C. Olson (eds.)
    1966   *Chaucer Life-Records* (Oxford: Oxford University Press).
Curry, W.C.
    1960   *Chaucer and the Mediaeval Sciences* (London: George Allen & Unwin,
                rev. edn).
Deanesley, M.
    1922   *The Lollard Bible and Other Medieval Biblical Versions* (Cambridge:
                Cambridge University Press).
Dugdale, Sir W.
    1675–76   *The Baronage of England* (3 vols. in 1; London: Roper).
Eade, J.C.
    1984   *The Forgotten Sky: A Guide to Astrology in English Literature* (Oxford:
                Clarendon Press).
Eisner, S. (ed.)
    1980   *The Kalendarium of Nicholas of Lynn* (Athens, GA: University of
                Georgia Press).
Forbes, E.G.
    1975   *Greenwich Observatory: The Royal Observatory at Greenwich and Herst-
                monceux, 1675–1975. I. Origins and Early History (1675–1835)* (3 vols.;
                London: Taylor & Francis).

Given-Wilson, C.
  1986   *The Royal Household and the King's Affinity: Service, Politics and Finance in England 1360–1413* (New Haven: Yale University Press).
Hobhouse, C.
  1939   *Oxford As It Was and As It Is Today* (London: Batsford).
Howse, D.
  1980   *Greenwich Time and The Discovery of the Longitude* (Oxford: Oxford University Press).
James, M.R.
  1900–1904   *The Western Manuscripts in the Library of Trinity College, Cambridge* (4 vols.; Cambridge: Cambridge University Press).
Kay, R.
  1994   *Dante's Christian Astrology* (Philadelphia: University of Pennsylvania Press).
Krása, J.
  1971   *Die Handschriften König Wenzels IV* (Prague: Odeon).
Manly, J.M.
  1896   'On the Date and Interpretation of Chaucer's *Complaint of Mars*', *Harvard Studies and Notes* 5: 107-26.
Mitchell, S.
  1965   *Medieval Manuscript Painting* (New York: Viking).
Mooney, L.R. (ed.)
  1998   *The Kalendarium of John Somer* (Athens, GA: University of Georgia Press).
Nicolas, H. (ed.)
  1834–37   *Proceedings and Ordinances of the Privy Council* (7 vols.; London: Record Commission).
North, J.D.
  1969   '"Kalenderes enlumyned ben they": Some Astronomical Themes in Chaucer', *Review of English Studies* NS 20: 129-54, 257-83, 418-44.
  1977   'The Alfonsine Tables in England', in Y. Maeyama and W. Saltzer (eds.), *Prismata; naturwissenschaftsgeschichtliche Studien* (Festschrift Willy Hartner; Hildesheim: Georg Olms): 269-301.
  1986   *Horoscopes and History* (London: Warburg Institute).
  1988   *Chaucer's Universe* (Oxford: Clarendon Press).
O'Connor, J.J.
  1956   'The Astronomical Dating of Chaucer's *Troilus and Criseyde*', *Journal of English and Germanic Philology* 55: 556-62.
Pace, G.B., and A. David (eds.)
  1982   *A Variorum Edition of the Works of Geoffrey Chaucer. V. The Minor Poems, Part 1* (gen. ed. P. Ruggiers; Norman, OK: University of Oklahoma Press).
Page, W. (ed.)
  1932   *The Victoria History of the County of Kent* (3 vols.; London: Constable & St Catherine Press).
Palgrave, F. (ed.)
  1836   *The Ancient Kalendars and Inventories of the Treasury of His Majesty's Exchequer* (3 vols.; London: Eyre & Spottiswoode).

Pearsall, D.
1992   *The Life of Geoffrey Chaucer: A Critical Biography* (Oxford: Basil Black-
            well).
Price, D.J.
1955   *The Equatorie of the Planetis* (Cambridge: Cambridge University
            Press).
Rickert, M.
1965   *Painting in Britain: The Middle Ages* (Harmondsworth: Penguin
            Books, 2nd edn).
Robinson, P. (ed.)
1988   *Catalogue of Dated and Dateable Manuscripts c. 737–1600 in Cambridge
            Libraries* (Cambridge: Brewer).
Root, R.K., and H.N. Russell
1924   'A Planetary Date for Chaucer's *Troilus*', *PMLA* 39: 48-63.
Skeat, W.W. (ed.)
1894–97   *The Complete Works of Geoffrey Chaucer* (7 vols.; Oxford: Clarendon
            Press).
Smyser, H.M.
1970   'A View of Chaucer's Astronomy', *Speculum* 45: 359-73.
Steele, A.
1941   *Richard II* (Cambridge: Cambridge University Press).
Stow, G.B. (ed.)
1977   *Historia Vitae et Regni Ricardi Secundi* (Philadelphia: University of
            Pennsylvania Press).
Streatfield, T., and L.B. Larking
1886   *Hundred of Blackheath: Part I of Hasted's History of Kent* (rev. H.H.
            Drake; London: Mitchell & Hughes).
Thompson, E.M. (ed.)
1904   *Chronicon Adae de Usk, AD 1377–1421* (London: Henry Frowde, 2nd
            edn).
Tout, T.F.
1967   *Chapters in the Administrative History of Mediaeval England* (4 vols.;
            Manchester: Manchester University Press).
Van Dorsten, J.A.
1960   'The Leyden "Lydgate Manuscript"', *Scriptorium* 14: 315-25.
Wood, C.
1970   *Chaucer and the Country of the Stars: Poetic Uses of Astrological Imagery*
            (Princeton: Princeton University Press).

The Use of Caxton Texts and Paper Stocks in Manuscripts of the *Canterbury Tales*

Daniel W. Mosser

While the technologies of book production in England were indisputably transformed by Caxton's introduction of the printing press into England in the last quarter of the fifteenth century, the replacement of the scribe and the manuscript codex was neither immediate nor absolute, and for some time the relative value—in esthetic and 'prestige' terms—of each method's product was not a settled issue. Indeed, it was some time before the printing press achieved the kind of market dominance we have up to now taken for granted. Only some six hundred years later is that *status quo* at all threatened.

This paper examines two intersections of the scribal and print cultures. While it is obvious that printers would employ manuscripts as copy texts, the converse necessarily strikes us as a less obvious practice. Appropriately, Norman Blake has had occasion to address this issue in 'Manuscript to Print,' his contribution to *Book Production and Publishing in Britain, 1375–1475* (Griffiths and Pearsall 1989). My focus here, however, is narrower—dealing only with manuscripts containing some or all of the *Canterbury Tales*— and in some respects more detailed than Blake's study. The second part of the essay examines instances of shared materials: manuscripts of the *Canterbury Tales* that employ identical and/or similar paper stocks to those found in editions of Caxton.

I

Curt Bühler, writing in 1940, observed that

> in the early days of printing manuscript copies were occasionally
> made from printed books. Apparently these were specially written
> for the purpose of presentation to some distinguished individual
> and were generally noteworthy works in the various national
> languages (1940b: 65).

This description does not accord well with the examples I will cite
here, as few if any of these manuscripts would have been suitable
as 'presentation' copies. For most it is rather the case that not-so-
well-off individuals substituted personal labor to produce a text
that was otherwise unaffordable, or to extract a portion of a much
larger printed text. This is the situation that Norman Blake
describes:

> It may seem strange to modern readers that people would make
> manuscript copies of printed books, since it might easily be
> thought that the invention of printing would put an immediate
> end to copying. A little reflection will suggest how improbable this
> is. Even in modern times, before the invention of the copying
> machine, a student at university, for example, who wanted a copy
> of an article had the option of buying the journal or copying out
> the article in full or in part...As students often did not want the
> whole text, copying represented the quickest and cheapest method
> to use. The same would apply in the fifteenth century to all classes
> of reader. If you wanted a copy of a book, then you could have a
> copy made for you if you could not acquire a printed text. In the
> days when the book-trade was not so well developed throughout
> the country, it may well have been simpler and cheaper to have
> your own copy written out (1989: 412).

In an address to the Grolier Club in 1952 Bühler suggested that
the practice of copying a manuscript from a printed book was,
after all, not so extraordinary:

> Numerous formal, carefully written volumes are recorded—some-
> times inscribed on vellum and often handsomely decorated—which
> are nothing more than copies of books printed in the last half of
> the fifteenth century. There are a great many more such manu-
> scripts extant than we have been led to believe; a hasty survey shows
> that *at least* a score of such manuscripts copied from Caxton

editions are preserved in the great English and American research libraries (1952: 12).[1]

Some years later A.S.G. Edwards asserted in his introduction to the facsimile edition of MS Pepys 2006 that 'The practice of copying from printed editions back into manuscript was common during the late fifteenth and early sixteenth centuries' (1985: xxix). Thus, what was once regarded as exceptional is now increasingly viewed as commonplace.

As Blake observes (1989: 417), it is not always easy to determine whether a manuscript is copied from a printed edition or from a shared ancestor, as exemplified by the relationship between Caxton's first edition of the *Canterbury Tales* (Cx^1; *STC* 5082) and Trinity College Cambridge MS R.3.15 (Tc^2). The relationship of the two texts is extremely close, with the manuscript's text apparently subordinate to that of the Caxton. However, while both texts follow the *b* ordering, something happened to the Tc^2 copy text that required the scribe to turn to an Ra^2 exemplar[2] for the latter two-thirds of the *Clerk's Tale*. In Tc^2 the *Pardoner's Tale* follows the *Clerk's Tale*, and the *Physician's Tale* follows the *Second Nun's Tale*, with the *Canon's Yeoman's Tale* missing entirely. For the *Physician's Tale*, the *Shipman's Tale*, and the *Prioress's Prologue* the scribe again required an alternative exemplar, one that apparently lacked the *Prioress's Tale* and *Thopas*. Clearly the copy text was damaged, but whether that exemplar was a manuscript or a copy of Cx^1 is probably impossible to say.[3]

Peter Robinson and Elizabeth Solopova's transcriptions of the *Wife of Bath's Prologue* (Robinson 1996) and my own transcriptions of the *Cook's Prologue* and *Tale* (unpublished) allow for convenient collation of those texts from Cx^1 and Tc^2. Tc^2 lacks lines 27 and 28 of the *Cook's Prologue*, which means that Cx^1 could not have been copied from it. The two differ otherwise in the *Cook's*

1.   Hindman (1977: 102-103) quotes Bühler as saying here that 'in American and English libraries alone there are at least 100 manuscript copies from Caxton imprints'. The list in Blake (1989: 419-25) numbers fewer than 40, and not all of these are considered certain.

2.   I.e. the text of Manly and Rickert's subgroup consisting of Bodleian MSS Rawlinson poet. 149 (Ra^2) and Hatton donat 1 (Ht).

3.   Owen (1991: 85-87) clearly believes that the manuscript uses the Cx^1 exemplar, which has suffered serious damage.

Prologue only in spelling and abbreviations. In the *Cook's Tale* both omit I.4404 and add a spurious line before I.4403: 'Where he his vnthriftynees sore aboughte.' This variant is shared by no other witnesses. Their disagreements in the *Tale* are trivial. In the *Wife of Bath's Prologue* in Fragment III, Tc^2 has a spurious line in place of 46, shared with a large number of ab^* manuscripts: 'I wille hym not forsake nathynge at all.' At 72 Cx^1 has the reading found in *b* manuscripts, *Cast*, while Tc^2 deletes that reading and adds *Cache*. Tc^2 also diverges from the Cx^1 text in sharing the transposition of 433 and 434 with the rest of the *b* manuscripts. Both Cx^1 and Tc^2 place line 510 between lines 536-37. As Peter Robinson's stemmata for the *Wife of Bath's Prologue* (Robinson 1997: figs. 2-4) illustrate, the relationship is extremely close throughout this text as well.

The probability is even greater that Trinity College Cambridge MS R.3.19 (Tc^3) derives its text of the *Monk's Prologue* and *Tale*—the only *Canterbury Tales* material in the manuscript—from a copy of Cx^1.[4] The *Prologue* commences on f.170v with a spurious line in place of VII.1967: '[w]Orshipfull and dyscrete that here p[re]sent be.' The following line is also slightly modified to adjust for the text's context as an extract, cut loose from the narrative frame of the *Canterbury Tales*: 'I wyll yow tell a tale two or thre.' Over the remaining 28 lines of the *Prologue* there is no compelling evidence to associate Tc^3 specifically with Cx^1, though its readings are in the main those of the *b* group. These lines, combined with the first two stanzas of the *Monk's Tale*, constitute the 'proem' in Tc^3. Extracts from Lydgate's *Fall of Princes* follow, and it is not until f.179 that the *Monk's Tale* resumes with 'The Tragedy of Sampson.'[5] In the *Monk's Tale* the number of readings unique to Cx^1-Tc^2-Tc^3 accumulate persuasively (at VII.2048, 2053, 2054, 2059-60, 2067, 2070, 2077, 2107, 2165, 2253, 2342, 2515 and 2574). The Tc^2 reading at VII.2226—combining 2226 and 2227—argues

4.   See Fletcher (1987: xviii). Blake's census incorrectly construes Manly and Rickert's account of Tc^3 in stating that it contains 'part of the General Prologue' of the *Canterbury Tales* 'and all of the Monk's Tale'; it is, rather, the *Monk's Prologue* and *Monk's Tale* that are extracted (Blake 1989: 419; cf. Manly and Rickert 1940: I, 533).

5.   For a detailed account of the nature of the Chaucer-Lydgate compilation in Tc^3 see Dixon (1995: 184-94).

against that manuscript as the source for **Tc**³. The observation in Manly and Rickert (1940: I, 353) that 'in B 3297 [VII.2107] the misreading of "Cakus" (**Cx**¹) as "Calrus" seems due to the fact that the *k* in **Cx**¹ looks much like *lr*'is perhaps the strongest evidence for preferring **Cx**¹ as the copy text rather than its exemplar.

Cx¹ also exerted a belated influence on another manuscript of the *Canterbury Tales*, Bodleian Library MS Laud Misc. 739 (**Ld**²). Although **Ld**² is interesting because it may have employed another surviving manuscript as its copy text—British Library Royal MS 18.C.ii (**Ry**²)—it is also worth noting here that it contains corrections in a sixteenth-century hand that appear to be motivated by comparison with a copy of the printed edition (Manly and Rickert 1940, I, 319). A similar phenomenon occurred in Cambridge University Library MS Gg.4.27 (**Gg**). Manly and Rickert (1940: I, 178) connects the 55 leaves added at the end of the manuscript, that supply the text contained on missing leaves written in an early seventeenth-century hand, with 'the 1598 edition [i.e. Speght], but supplemented from Caxton's second edition and other sources'. Of this material, however, only the 'Retractions' is likely to derive from **Cx**² (*STC* 5083).[6]

Chetham's Library MS Mun. A.4.104 (**Ct**; *olim* Chetham's Library MS 6709), a collection of saints' lives, was copied between 1485 and 1490 by William Cotson, a canon from Dunstable (the name and range of dates are provided by the colophons on ff.173 [1490], 198v [1486], 267v [1485]).[7] Cotson employed two Caxton

6.   Parkes and Beadle (1979–80: III, 6); Caldwell (1953: 299 n. 44) states: 'The Retraction, which is on fol. 29v of Gga [the added leaves with missing passages], is not found in any edition between Pynson's (1526) and Urry's (1721). Gga omits I, 1081-83, and *Wherfore* of I, 1084; from that point it shares all variants of Cx² and nowhere agrees with any edition or other manuscript against Cx².'

7.   Manly and Rickert (1940: I, 87) states that 'No William Cotson has thus far been found, of Dunstaple or any other place.' McGregor's inventory of Bedfordshire Wills (McGregor 1979: 62, No. 47) includes that of 'Jn Worelich, Potton [n.d.] pr. 20 March 1503/4 (Latin),' in which he provides 'For the keeping of an anniversary to be raised annually from his tenement in Horselow situated between the tenement of Wm. Clais on the north and the tenement of Wm. Cotes on the south.' There were other members of the Cotes family in Potton, Bedfordshire, and it seems a reasonable inference that William Cotson could be 'Wm. Cotes' son'.

editions as copy texts: **Cx²** for the *Second Nun's Tale* and the *Prioress's Tale*; and *STC* 17023 for its text of Lydgate's *Lyf of Our Lady* (Blake 1992; Klinefelter 1952).

A pair of 'miscellany' manuscripts that contain extracts from the *Canterbury Tales*—Huntington Library MS HM 144 (**Hn**) and Oxford, Trinity College MS 29 (**To²**)—copied by the same scribe, an Augustinian canon in Bisham Montague, Berkshire (Harris 1983: 31), make use of Caxton editions of authors other than Chaucer. Both manuscripts extract portions of Caxton's edition of the *Polychronicon* (*STC* 13438, dated 'after 2 July 1482'), incorporating them along with extracts from other works into what is characterized by Kate Harris as 'sometimes a bizarre compilation' (Harris 1983: 31). Curt Bühler argues that the seven stanzas of Lydgate's *Horse, Sheep and Goose* (*IMEV* 1629) that are unique to **Hn** and the printed editions were copied into **Hn** from Caxton's first edition (*STC* 17019 [1476]; Bühler 1940a; see also Dutschke 1989: I, 200). Dutschke (1989: I, 200) suggests further that the text of Cato's *Disticha* (the *Parvus Catho* and *Magnus Catho*) in **Hn**, posited by previous editors as a 'sister' to the Caxton edition, 'may instead have been copied from the Caxton edition' (*STC* 4850 [1477]).[8]

The remaining candidate for this catalogue of *Canterbury Tales* manuscripts that make use of Caxton editions as copy texts is MS Pepys 2006 (**Pp**). The Pepys volume combines two manuscripts in one binding. The structure of the book is a complicated one, which I deal with elsewhere (Mosser forthcoming), and it is remarkable textually in that it contains in the second section some texts that also occur in the first section, all by Chaucer: *Complaint of Mars, Complaint of Venus, An ABC,* and *Fortune.* Both texts of *An ABC* are severely truncated, ending at line 59, and both are followed by the same spurious line. The first section of the manuscript is probably too early to have been influenced by printed texts, but Brusendorff believes

> That the sources [for the texts in the second part of the manu-
> script] were a number of independent booklets...indicated by

---

8.   Kuriyagawa (1974: 2), citing Max Förster's stemma, collates **Hn** as 'the sister manuscript to Caxton's text'. Dutschke suggests the alternative analysis: that **Hn** might be a copy of the Caxton edition. This example is not included in Blake's census.

their textual connection with a set of small printed booklets, issued by Caxton and containing works by Chaucer, Lydgate, and others (1925: 195).

He refers to a parallel collection of Caxton editions that were bound together—as a *sammelband*—formerly in the collection of Bishop John Moore, and conveyed to Cambridge University Library by George I.[9] Brusendorff states that

> All these items [contained in the Moore volume] (except Scogan's *tretyse*, III.2) are paralleled in Pepys I-II in closely agreeing texts, and accordingly we may safely assume the existence of a set of MS. booklets as the sources of Pepys-Caxton (1925: 196).

Edwards (1985: xxix) suggests an alternative possibility: that texts in the second part of Pepys might derive from a lost printed source, 'whether Caxton or Caxton derived', a speculation echoed in Blake (1989: 420). Pepys remains a tantalizing puzzle in many respects; however, despite the closeness of many of the texts in both the first and second parts of the manuscript to editions of Caxton, no 'smoking gun' has surfaced to link either part to a print ancestor.

9. See Needham (1986: 18-19): 'Perhaps the greatest of all Caxton-related volumes was the one acquired in the late seventeenth or early eighteenth century by John Moore, bishop of Ely. In 1715, by the benefaction of George I, the volume was presented with the rest of Moore's library to Cambridge University. This volume contained eight verse quarto tracts printed by Caxton in 1477, including texts of Chaucer and Lydgate, all but one of which are (with the exception of a few fragments) unique. An entire chapter of Caxton's printing history was preserved within this pair of covers. In the nineteenth century, for reasons no longer easily ascertainable, the volume was broken up, and each title bound separately. This is not precisely comparable with book-breaking by a dealer, for these copies will always remain at Cambridge, and the history of their former association and single provenance will not be lost. But still, their integrity—and whatever evidence resided in their earlier binding—has been lost.' The volume included: Lydgate, *Stans puer ad mensam* [?1476], *STC* 17030; Cato, *Disticha*[2] [1477], *STC* 4850; Lydgate, *Churl and Bird* [1477], *STC* 17008; Lydgate, *Horse, Sheep, and Goose*[2] [1477], *STC* 17018; Lydgate, *Temple of Glass* [1477], *STC* 17032; Chaucer, *Temple of Brass* (etc.) [1477], *STC* 5091; *Book of Courtesy* [1477], *STC* 3303; Chaucer, *Anelida and Arcite* (etc.) [1477], *STC* 5090. See also Duff (1905: 41) and Brusendorff (1925: 195 n. 3).

II

While much of the preceding essentially follows material contained in Blake's 'Manuscript to Print' essay, constituting a narrowing of focus and a deepening of the examination, the discussion of paper stocks that follows is for the most part new and derives from my work on the manuscripts and pre-1500 editions of the *Canterbury Tales*.[10] Again, the first correspondences noted are between **Cx¹** and manuscripts of the *Canterbury Tales*.

In Manly and Rickert's description of MS Cod. Bodmer 48 (**Ph²**; *olim* Phillipps 8136) it is stated that there are

> At least six [watermarks], but the writing is so crowded that they cannot be clearly distinguished. Three of them seem to be shields with initials and on top a fleur-de-lys or a crozier (1940: I, 421).

In fact, the watermarks are readily discernible, and among them are two shields: an *armoire* with a fleur-de-lis ascendant, closest to Briquet 1886 ('Ecu au nom de Lile', dated 1471 [with variants to 1480]), and a similar mark, but with a crozier ascendant, closest to Briquet 1885 (also an 'Ecu au nom de Lile', dated 1469 [with variants to 1473]). Briquet 1886 is extremely close to, if not identical with, a paper stock used by Caxton in his first edition of the *Canterbury Tales*. Stevenson assigns the whole family of these marks 'to the late 1460s and the 1470s' and traces them to a mill 'at the village of Lisle-en-Ricault.'[11]

Another paper stock from **Cx¹**, marked by a pair of unicorns *passant*, appears in the section of British Library MS Sloane 1009 (**Sl³**) that contains the text titled in the manuscript 'Rubrica De

10. *A Descriptive Catalogue of the Manuscripts and Pre-1500 Editions of the Canterbury Tales*, a work in progress. Some of this material has appeared in preliminary form in Mosser (1996); most of those descriptions will appear, corrected and revised, in the *Canterbury Tales* Project's edition of the *General Prologue*, along with several descriptions of manuscripts not included in Mosser (1996).

11. See Allan Stevenson's discussion of this mark in the introduction to the Briquet Jubilee edition (Briquet *23-*25). A mark similar to Briquet 1885 also occurs in MS Bodley 221, a copy of Hoccleve's *Regiment of Princes*, copied in a hand very similar to that of **Ph²**, but in a markedly different dialect. (I am grateful to John Thompson for bringing this manuscript to my attention.)

vita & honestate Clericor[um]' (ff.49-57). The Caxton and Sl^3 paper stocks are identical, with both twins appearing in the Sloane manuscript (cf. Briquet 10024). This same paper stock also appears in British Library MS Royal 17.D.xv (Ry^1, ff.302-10), a section of the manuscript copied by the 'Hammond Scribe.'[12] Ry^1 and Sl^3 share yet another paper stock, also a unicorn, near Briquet 9997 (1477–78). I have found remnant examples of this or a very similar watermark in Caxton's *Chronicles of England* (*STC* 9991, dated 10 June 1480) in the gathering signed *c.*

Oxford, Trinity College MS 29 (the 'new' Chaucer manuscript, containing extracts from *Melibee* and the *Parson's Tale* first identified by Kate Harris), shares another paper stock with Cx^1, the crozier described by Briquet as a 'Crosse à laquelle pend un huchet' (Briquet 5803, dated 1475). Allan Stevenson describes this as:

> Species common in the *Archives de la Meuse* at Bar-le-duc. Appears as running-mark towards end of Chaucer, *Canterbury Tales* [Caxton 1478] and helps to date this very important first edition (Briquet *69).

The mark appears only on the first folio of the Trinity manuscript. Also in this manuscript is another shield, of Piccard's species 'Lilie' type III and Briquet's 'Armoires Trois fleurs de lis,' that closely resembles another paper stock in Cx^1, but the relationship of the mark to the chainlines differs. It may, however, represent a different state of the mark, perhaps resewn on the mold, or it may constitute what Paul Needham has labeled a 'multi-geminate' mark.[13]

A similar relationship exists between the Gothic **Y**-with-trefoil mark[14] that occurs in Caxton's edition of his translation of Le

---

12. The 'Hammond Scribe,' so-called because of Eleanor Hammond's pioneering work on this prolific scribe, produced at least 14 manuscripts in the second half of the fifteenth century. For additional detail, see Hammond (1905, 1929); Doyle (1959, 1983); Green (1978); Mooney (1993, 1996; and forthcoming).

13. In a paper delivered at The First International Conference on the History, Function and Study of Watermarks, 10–13 October 1996, Roanoke, Virginia. 'Multi-geminate' refers to the hypothesized use of more than two pairs of molds (mutiple pairs) in the production of some paper stocks.

14. Similar to Briquet 9184. A type of this mark, found in Caxton's

Fevre's *History of Jason* (*STC* 15383 [1477]) and a watermark found in **To**^{2}. *STC* 9991 (*The Chronicles of England*) provides an even closer analogue, which may be from the same mold as the **To**^{2} mark; the structures and chainlines correspond very closely, with the tail of the **Y** being slightly more vertical in the Caxton paper. A structurally similar, though not identical mark, also occurs on one folio (f.65) of **Tc**^{2}. In their discussion of the watermarks in **Tc**^{2} Manly and Rickert cite three references to Sotheby's *Principia Typographica*, III, plates Q^{A-C}, nos. 15, 50, and 59 (Manly and Rickert 1940: I, 527). No. 50 is the **Y** mark commented on previously. No. 15 is a bull's head/ 'Tête de boeuf' surmounted by cross, 'several varieties' of which Sotheby records as occurring in Cato's *Disticha* (Sotheby 1858: III, 85); a very similar, though not identical mark does appear in the 1477 edition (*STC* 4850). Another manuscript of the *Canterbury Tales*, Bodleian MS Rawlinson C.86 (**Ra**^{4}), contains another example of this bull's-head paper stock.[15] No. 59 is an 'Anneau' (ring) surmounted by a six-pointed star, which certainly occurs in *STC* 4850 (*Disticha*, 1477) and *STC* 24873-74 (*Golden Legend*, 20 November 1483). The 'Anneau' mark in **Tc**^{2}, however, is a ring surmounted by a crown, and so Manly and Rickert are wrong in their identification of the **Tc**^{3} paper stock with that of Caxton. **Ra**^{4} has several other marks that I suspect are the same or very close to Caxton paper stocks. In addition to the bull's-head paper stock previously mentioned are at least three 'Main'/hand marks. One of these has a detached quatrefoil element and is bisected by a chain line, with attendant chains 2.7 to 3 cm apart. A nearly identical mark is found in the

manuscript translation of Ovid's *Metamorphoses*, dated 22 April 1482 (Magdalene College, Cambridge), is reproduced by beta-radiography in the Briquet 'Jubilee' edition. Stevenson there states that this paper was 'Made at Troyes in Champagne about 1481' (Briquet, commentary to Pl. *B4). The paper stock in the Ovid is actually different—'Median' size—as is the stock that appears in Caxton's *Confessio Amantis* (2 September 1483, *STC* 12142); the paper stock in *Churl & Bird* ([1476]; *STC* 17009), and *Cordiale des iv dernières choses* ([c. 1475]; Duff 108: printed at Bruges) is 'Chancery' size (Paul Needham, private communication).

15. The marks are the same size, the chainline spacing is identical, but my sketch shows a slightly different structure for the ears as compared with a reproduction (using transmitted light) of the Trinity manuscript's mark.

edition of the *Cordiale* Caxton printed in England, dated 24 March 1479 (*STC* 5758).

In his introduction to the facsimile edition of Trinity College, Cambridge MS R.3.19 (**Tc³**) Fletcher states that 'the seated pope found in quire *t* is Briquet 7546-50, France, 1451–84, and used by Caxton' (Fletcher 1987: xxiv). Comparison of the Fletcher beta-radiograph to the paper stock in the Pierpont Morgan Library's copy of Caxton's *History of Jason* (*STC* 15383 [1477]; PML 672/ChL^f1758) confirms the identity of these paper stocks.

Several watermarks will require more detailed comparison when opportunity allows. In addition to the hand watermarks in **Ra⁴**, there are also several hand watermarks in **Hn** that may be the same as those found in Caxton's editions of the *Cordiale* (*STC* 5758) and *Reynard the Fox* (*STC* 20919; [1482]). Two scissors watermarks in **Hn** (similar to Briquet 3728 [1481]) and Huntington Library MS HM 140 (**Ph⁴** [*olim* Phillipps MS 8299]; similar in structure to Briquet 3754 [1456]) are also temptingly like those which appear in the *Golden Legend* and *Renard the Fox*.

British Library MS Egerton 2864 (**En³**) uses six paperstocks, including a dragon ('Basilic') mark that occurs only on f.79. A structurally very similar mark appears in the last item printed by Caxton—the *Ars Moriendi* [1491]—and the first item printed by Wynkyn de Worde three years later, the second edition of the *Golden Legend* (*STC* 24875; Duff 1905: 410). The **En³** mark and the Caxton paper stock are by no means identical—especially the configuration of the tails—but many other elements correspond very closely and so they may derive from the same mill within a reasonably short period of time.

Finally, there is at least a similarity between a mark that occurs in Rylands English MS 113 (**Ma**)—'Armoires Deux Pals' (near Briquet 2064, dated 1464)[16]—and one of similar morphology (recorded as no. 8 in Sotheby 1858: III, 85) in Caxton's editions of Cato's *Disticha*, and Guillaume de Deguilleville's *Pilgrimage of the Soul* (6 June 1483, *STC* 6473-74). Although Sotheby does not clearly distinguish among the Cato editions (*STC* 4851 [1476], *STC* 4850 [1477], *STC* 4852 [1483] or *STC* 4853 [1484]), the mark

---

16. The 'Armoires Deux Pals' mark also occurs in varying states in British Library *Canterbury Tales* MSS Additional 5140 (**Ad¹**), Harley 2251 (**Hl²**) and Royal 17.D.xv (**Ry¹**).

certainly occurs in *STC* 4853, as well as in the *Pilgrimage*. The mark
in **Ma** (and the other *Canterbury Tales* manuscripts listed in n. 16
above) has two *pales* (vertical bars), while the Caxton mark has
fesses (horizontal bars). What the relationship—if any—between
these similar watermarks might be constitutes another area for
further investigation.

I suspect that, as a more accurate record accumulates, we will
find other material correspondences between English manuscripts
of the late fifteenth century and editions produced by Caxton,
Pynson and de Worde.

III

Of what value, then, are these connections—textual and material—between Caxton printed editions and manuscripts of the
Canterbury Tales? The most obvious value of both kinds of evidence is that those correspondences that are certain provide us
with a *terminus post quem* for the undated manuscripts when they
are correlated with those Caxton editions for which dating is far
more certain. Thus **Tc**^{3} would have to have been produced after
the 1477 date assigned to Caxton's *History of Jason* (with which it
shares a paper stock), which is roughly in accord as well with the
1476–77 date hypothesized for the first edition of the *Canterbury
Tales* (with which it shares text). Similarly, those other manuscripts that share paper stocks with Caxton editions—**Ph**^{2}, **To**^{2},
Tc^2 (although the paper stocks in **Tc**^{2} are not, *pace* Manly and
Rickert, identical to those in Caxton editions), **Ry**^{1}, **Sl**^{3}—can be
assigned to relatively constrained dates of production, say 1475–
90 (for **To**^{2}, however, see below).

Manly and Rickert (1940: I, 421) assigned a date for **Ph**^{2} of
'1450–70'. Given the dates of all of the watermarks in the manuscript (see my description in Mosser 1996), it is probable that the
1470 date would mark the earliest rather than the latest date
possible for its production. Since **En**^{3} (dated by Manly and Rickert
'1460-80') shares the sun / 'Lettres assemblées' mark with **Ph**^{2},
and, perhaps less certainly on the basis of the similarity of the
dragon watermark with that in Caxton-de Worde editions, it
would also appear to fall into the latter part of Manly and
Rickert's range of dates, say 1475–80.

The watermarks in $\mathbf{To^2}$, taken in conjunction with the use of Caxtons as copy texts, point to $\mathbf{Hn}$ and $\mathbf{To^2}$'s having been completed after '2 July 1482' (the date of Caxton's issue of the Trevisa edition). If, as Harris suggests (Harris 1983: 32-33), the Trinity Oxford scribe used Wynkyn de Worde's *Informacion for pylgrymes vnto the holy londe* (*STC* 14081), the date for the copying of that section of the manuscript would fall after 1500. It is probable that the scribe produced his compilation over a period of time, and the age of the paper when it was actually put to use is an open question. It should be remembered that the crozier watermark occurs only on the outer sheet of the first gathering.

One very intriguing area of speculation remains. While the appearance of Caxton paper stocks in the majority of manuscripts catalogued above is no doubt only coincidental, there is one group of manuscripts for which the correspondence of texts and material may amount to something more than coincidence. Linne Mooney identifies the hand of Scribe C in $\mathbf{Tc^3}$ as the scribe of Oxford, St John's College MS 266, a copy of Lydgate's *Siege of Thebes* (Mooney 1993; see also Fletcher 1987: xxvi-xxviii). This manuscript is bound together with *STC* 5083 (Caxton's second edition of the *Canterbury Tales*), *STC* 5094 (Caxton's [1483] edition of *Troilus and Criseyde*) and *STC* 17957 (Caxton's [1482–83] edition of the *Quattuor Sermones*.[17] The Lydgate manuscript served as copy text for Wynkyn de Worde's edition (c. 1500, *STC* 17031; see Bone 1931–32: 286-95). The paper stock in St John's MS 266 is the same throughout, a 'Chien'/dog, virtually identical with Briquet 3624 (1476), which Briquet associates with an 'imp. de Caxton 1480', citing Sotheby (1858) 'Qb. n°s 28^a and 29.' Sotheby no. 28^a (a dog with head facing backwards) occurs in Caxton's *Pilgrimage of the Soul, Life of Our Lady* (*STC* 17024 [1483]), and in one of the texts bound together with St John's 266, *Troilus and Criseyde*. Sotheby cites no. 29 as being one of the marks in the *Chronicles of England* (it is not in the copies I have seen), but he does not mention that it is one of the marks in $\mathbf{Cx^1}$ (*STC* 5082), where it occurs infrequently. The St John's watermark, however, while of the same type, is not identical to the one that occurs in copies of $\mathbf{Cx^1}$,

---

17. See Needham (1986: 73) for details of this 'tract volume'. The St John's shelfmark for the printed texts is b.2.21.

but it may well be that of a Caxton paper stock that I have not yet seen.

Mooney (1993) details other textual connections between Tc^3 and de Worde editions (echoing Bone 1931–32), and notes that one of the owners of Tc^3, Roger Thorney, was a patron of de Worde, who was acknowledged as such by the printer at the end of his *De Proprietatibus Rerum* and in the opening of the *Polychronicon* (see Bone 1931–32: 295-304). Mooney goes on to suggest that, together with the connections suggested by Tc^3 and the St John's Lydgate manuscript, the scope and method of production of other manuscripts associated with the Hammond Scribe may suggest a very close connection with the printing shop of Caxton and, subsequently, de Worde. The evidence of shared material— that is paper—might help further this suggestion, and there are other paper stocks in Hammond Scribe manuscripts (those that do not contain *Canterbury Tales*) that are close to and may well be the same as those used by Caxton. There are, then, a number of areas that might reward further investigation, and a number of paper stocks that will require more detailed and precise comparison.

WORKS CITED

Blake, N.F.

    1989   'Manuscript to Print', in J. Griffiths and D. Pearsall (eds.), *Book Production and Publishing in Britain 1375–1475* (Cambridge: Cambridge University Press): 403-32.

    1992   'MS Chetham 6709 and Some Manuscript Copies of Caxton Prints', in C. Blank (ed.), *Language and Civilisation: A Concerted Profusion of Essays and Studies in Honour of Otto Hietsch* (Frankfurt-am-Main: Peter Lang): 239-54.

Bone, G.

    1931–32   'Extant Manuscripts Printed from by W. de Worde, with Notes on the Owner, Roger Thorney' *The Library*, 4th series 12: 284-306.

Brusendorff, A.

    1925   *The Chaucer Tradition* (Oxford: Clarendon Press).

Bühler, C.F.

    1940a   'Lydgates's *Horse, Sheep and Goose* and Huntington MS HM 144', *Modern Language Notes* 55: 563-69.

    1940b   'An Unusual Fifteenth-Century Manuscript', *La Bibliofilia* 42: 65-71.

    1941   'A Note on Stanza 24 of Lydgate's *The Churl and Bird*', *Journal of English and Germanic Philology* 40: 562-63.

1952   *Fifteenth Century Books and the Twentieth Century: An Address by Curt F.*
                Bühler, and a Catalogue of an Exhibition of Fifteenth Century Books held at
                the Grolier Club, April 15–June 1, 1952 (New York: The Grolier Club).

Caldwell, R.A.
1943   'Joseph Holland, Collector and Antiquary', *Modern Philology* 40: 295-
                301.

Dixon, L.J.
1995   'The "Canterbury Tales" Miscellanies: A Contextual Study of the
                Manuscripts Anthologizing Individual Canterbury Tales' (PhD dis-
                sertation, University of Delaware, Newark).

Doyle, A.I.
1959   'An Unrecognized Piece of *Piers the Ploughman's Creed* and Other
                Work by its Scribe', *Speculum* 34: 429.

1983   'English Books In and Out of Court from Edward III to Henry VII',
                in V.J. Scattergood and J.W. Sherbourne (eds.), *English Court Culture*
                in the Later Middle Ages (London: Gerald Duckworth): 163-87.

Duff, E.G.
1905   *William Caxton* (Chicago:The Caxton Club).

Dutschke, C.W.
1989   *Guide to Medieval and Renaissance Manuscripts in the Huntington*
                Library (2 vols.; San Marino: Huntington Library).

Edwards, A.S.G. (introd.)
1985   *Manuscript Pepys 2006* (Norman, OK: Pilgrim Books).

Fletcher, B.Y. (introd.)
1987   *MS Trinity R.3.19* (Norman, OK: Pilgrim Books).

Green, R.F.
1978   'Notes on Some Manuscripts of Hoccleve's *Regiment of Prices*', *British*
                Library Journal 4: 39-41.

Hammond, E.P.
1905   'Two British Museum Manuscripts (Harley 2251 and Additional
                34360): A Contribution to the Biography of John Lydgate', *Anglia:*
                Zeitschrift für Englische Philologie 28: 1-28.

1908   *Chaucer: A Bibliographical Manual* (London: Macmillan).
1929   'A Scribe of Chaucer', *Modern Philology* 27: 27-33.

Harris, K.
1983   'John Gower's *Confessio Amantis*: The Virtues of Bad Texts', in
                D. Pearsall (ed.), *Manuscripts and Readers in Fifteenth-Century England:*
                The Literary Implications of Manuscript Study: Essays from the 1981
                Conference at the University of York (Cambridge: Brewer): 27-40.

1998   'Unnoticed Extracts from Chaucer and Hoccleve: Huntington HM
                144,Trinity College, Oxford, D 19 and the *Canterbury Tales*', *Studies*
                in the Age of Chaucer 20: 167-99.

Hindman, S.
1977   'Cross-Fertilization: Experiments in Mixing the Media', in S. Hind-
                man and J.D. Farquhar (eds.), *Pen to Press: Illustrated Manuscripts and*
                Printed Books in the First Century of Printing (College Park, MD:
                University of Maryland): 101-56.

Klinefelter, R.A.
'Lydgate's "Life of Our Lady" and the Chetham MS 6709', *Publications of the Bibliographical Society of America* 46: 396-97.

Kuriyagawa, F. (ed.)
1974 *Parvus Cato, Magnus Cato, Translated by Benet Burgh, edited from William Caxton's First Edition, ca. 1477* (Tokyo: Seijo, 1974).

Manly, J.M., and E. Rickert (eds.)
1940 *The Text of the Canterbury Tales: Studied on the Basis of All Known Manuscripts* (8 vols.; Chicago: University of Chicago Press).

McGregor, M.
1979 *Bedfordshire Wills Proved in the Prerogative Court of Canterbury 1383–1548* (Bedford: Publications of the Bedfordshire Historical Record Society, 58).

Mooney, L.R.
1993 'A Middle English Text on the Seven Liberal Arts', *Speculum* 68: 1027-52.
1996 'More Manuscripts Written by a Chaucer Scribe', *Chaucer Review* 30: 401-407.
forthcoming 'The Booklets of Trinity College, Cambridge MSS R.3.19 and R.3.21', in A. Minnis (ed.), *Papers of the 1996 York Manuscripts Conference, in Honour of Professor Derek Pearsall*.

Mosser, D.W.
1996 *'Witness Descriptions'*, in Robinson 1996.
forthcoming 'Corrective Notes on the Structures and Paper Stocks of Four MSS Containing Extracts from Chaucer's *Canterbury Tales*', *Studies in Bibliography* 52.

Needham, P.
1986 *The Printer and the Pardoner: An Unrecorded Indulgence Printed by William Caxton for the Hospital of St. Mary of Rounceval, Charing Cross* (Washington: Library of Congress).

Owen, C.A. Jr.
1991 *The Manuscripts of the Canterbury Tales* (Cambridge: Brewer).

Parkes, M.B., and R. Beadle (introds.)
1979–80 *The Poetical Works of Geoffrey Chaucer: A Facsimile of Cambridge University Library MS Gg.4.27* (3 vols.; Norman, OK: Pilgrim Books): III, 1-67.

Piccard, G.
1983 *Wasserzeichen Lilie: Die Wasserzeichen Piccard im Haupstaatsarchiv Stuttgart, Findbuch XIII* (Stuttgart: Kohlhammer).

Robinson, P. (ed.)
1996 *The Wife of Bath's Prologue on CD-ROM* (Cambridge: Cambridge University Press).

Robinson, P.
1997 'A Stemmatic Analysis of the Fifteenth-century Witnesses to the Wife of Bath's Prologue', in N. Blake and P. Robinson (eds.), *The Canterbury Tales Project Occasional Papers II* (London: Office for Humanities Communication): 69-132.

Sotheby, S.L.

1858   *Principia Typographicai* (3 vols.; London). (Vol. 3, 'Paper-Marks: Books from the Press of William Caxton, England's First Printer', is available online at:
http://128.173.125.124:591/DBs/Gravell/sotheby/sotheby.html.)

The Weak Declension of the Adjective and its Importance in Chaucerian Metre*

Derek Pearsall

The weak, or definite, form of the Middle English adjective goes back to Anglo-Saxon and beyond, and is used only when the adjective immediately precedes the noun that it qualifies. It is used in two principal situations in Chaucer's verse: when the adjective is preceded by what might be called a 'defining word', such as the definite article, a demonstrative adjective, a possessive adjective, or a noun in the genitive case; and secondly, in vocative phrases.[1] The use of the weak adjective was archaic in Chaucer's time, though it is difficult to be precise about the degree to which it was moribund, since the evidence of scribal spelling is so inconclusive and the evidence of metre, especially in non-Chaucerian verse, so difficult to interpret. The weak form of the adjective

*   This paper is offered to Norman Blake as the tribute of an old friend, and also as an acknowledgment, in so far as I am capable of making it, of the importance of the work he has done on Chaucer's language and text. I am very grateful to my Harvard colleague Dan Donoghue for his careful reading of this piece; he has saved me from many errors.

1.   Examples: *the olde wyf* (*CT* III.1046); *this olde wyf* (*CT* III.1000); *his olde wyf* (*CT* III.1086); *Epicurus owene sone* (*CT* I.336); *Sire olde lecchour* (*CT* III.242), *Goode lief* (*CT*, III.431). My description of the weak declension draws on the account of Chaucer's Language and Versification provided by Norman Davis for *The Riverside Chaucer* (Benson 1987: xxxv). See also Skeat (1894–97: VI, lxx), Ten Brink (1901: 157-60), Schipper (1910: 151-70), Eliason (1972: 30-32), Jordan (1974: 142-43), Burnley (1983: 13-15), Smith (1995: 76-77). Attention will be paid in due course to the character of the edited text in the citations from Benson (1987) and its relation to the principal manuscript witnesses.

appears only in reduced form as *-e* in Chaucer's verse, and is indistinguishable in form, therefore, from the inflexional *-e* of the strong plural adjective (e.g. *smale foweles*, *CT* I.9), or the inflexional *-e* occasionally used with singular adjectives after prepositions (e.g. *of alle charitee*, *CT* I.452).

The purpose of this essay is to test some of the assumptions commonly made about Chaucer's metre and the metre of his successors by examining a particular feature of his linguistic and metrical practice, namely the 'building block' consisting, in its simplest form, of monosyllabic adjective with unelided weak inflexion followed by noun with stress on the first syllable.[2] The point of examining this building block is that it is unambiguous in its metrical structure: there can be no doubt that the inflexional *-e* has syllabic value, that is, is sounded as an unstressed syllable in the metre of the line. In other metrical situations within the line, inflexional *-e*, whether in plural nouns, or in the plural of adjectives used predicatively, or in verbal endings, or in other situations, is capable of ambiguity, and may be read as unsounded because of the possible presence of stress-reversal or hiatus at the caesura.[3] The inflexional *-e* of the weak adjective cannot possibly occur at the caesura, or in other such metrical situations, and its loss will therefore be impossible to explain in terms of 'broken-backed' or 'Lydgate' lines, such as do genuinely occur in Chaucer from time to time for particular rhetorical purposes (Pearsall 1991).

2.   Common among these adjectives in the examples that follow are: *al, best, fair, first, foul, fressh, glad, good, gret, heigh (hy), hool, hoot, ilk, leef, leest, moost, next, old, right, sad, sharp, sik, smal, swich, which, worst, wys, yong*; and, among adjectives of French origin, *blew, fals, fiers, gay*. Both Samuels (1972) and Burnley (1982) recognize the diagnostic value of the weak declension of the adjective, but they work with a wider range of examples and from the point of view exclusively of grammar and spelling, with metre deliberately set aside; the valuable study by Minkova (1990) pays close attention to the prosodic rules that operate with weak adjective plus noun.

3.   Chaucer's flexibility in this respect has encouraged a degree of metrical libertinism in his readers (e.g. Southworth 1947 and 1954; answered by Donaldson 1948; the debate summarized by Mustanoja 1968: 65-67; Southworth's views restated by Robinson 1971; answered by Samuels 1972), or a milder form of *laissez-faire* (e.g. Elliott 1974: 22-29) which may need severer regulation.

The simplest form of the building block, as it has been described in the previous paragraph, that is, monosyllabic adjective with unelided weak inflexion followed by noun with stress on the first syllable, is the form evidenced in all the phrases quoted in n. 1 above. For the purposes of unequivocal demonstration, all the phrases quoted are in the singular, since in the plural the weak form of the adjective in *-e* falls in with and becomes indistinguishable from the strong plural of the adjective in *-e*. But both weak and strong plurals of prenominal monosyllabic adjectives can equally form the first element of the building block, as can prenominal monosyllabic adjectives in the singular with inflexional *-e* following a preposition (the latter is rare). For the purposes of a historical examination, it is also important to take account of those forms of the building block in which the adjective of the first element is an originally dissyllabic adjective with unstressed second syllable in *-e*. Whether in weak or strong declensions, singular or plural forms, though particularly in the singular, the second syllable of such adjectives was occasionally treated by later scribes as an inflexional *-e* and, as a consequence, and to the detriment of metre, dropped.[4]

It will be clear that the building block I am talking about can take other forms, for instance, dissyllabic adjective plus noun, or adjective with final *-e* elided before a noun beginning with a vowel or *h*. But I am not interested in these forms, only in those that are vulnerable to scribal corruption by omission of final *-e* and that can therefore provide unambiguous evidence of the understanding or misunderstanding of Chaucer's metrical practice on the part of scribes and Chaucerian imitators.

The first conclusion to be drawn from an examination of over 3000 lines of Chaucer's verse in the *General Prologue*, the *Wife of Bath's Prologue* and *Tale* and the *Clerk's Prologue* and *Tale* (up to IV.1176), taken arbitrarily as examples of Chaucer's mature and representative writing in both pentameter couplet and rhyme royal, is that Chaucer's metrical practice, in this particular linguistic context, is strikingly precise and consistent, though not inflexible. There are 83 examples of the simple form (Form A) of the building block (e.g. *the yonge sonne*, I.7), including forms with *this*

---

4.   Examples of such adjectives are: *clene, dere, drye, ferne, fewe, grene, lasse, newe, softe, stierne, sweete, trewe,* and (from French) *chaste, queynte, riche*.

ilke and *thilke* (always singular) which are inevitably weak (e.g. *this ilke Monk*, I.175). There are a further 19 examples of the form with *owene* (e.g. *his owene cost*, I.213), which is also always weak, because of the necessary presence of the possessive adjective before *owene*, but which is distinguished here as a separate category (Form B), in the interests of the longer-term historical examination, because later scribal loss of final *-e* could be compensated for by the syllabization of the medial *-e-*. There are also, as variant forms of the simple building block (combined as Form C), 12 examples with weak plurals of monosyllabic adjectives in *-e* (e.g. *the yonge girles*, I.664) and 25 examples with strong plurals of monosyllabic adjectives in *-e* (e.g. *smale foweles*, I.9).[5] The grammar of these forms is completely consistent: in each of the 139 cases cited, the final *-e* of the weak adjective (or of the strong plural) is entirely in conformity with the traditional grammatical rules, and in each case it is present and in all but two cases, both strong plurals (IV.634, 739, where presumably the final *-e* of *whiche* makes a light extra syllable), it functions as a metrical syllable. There are no situations, except one which needs to be brought up later as an emendation (I.8), where this final *-e* is required and is not present.

Monosyllabic adjectives before nouns in the singular with stress on the first syllable very rarely add *-e* in situations other than those described above. In the 3284 lines scanned, there are only two cases of a strong nominative in *-e* (*hye God*, III.60, 206, beside *the hye God*, III.1173, 1178; IV.821): this may be a fossilized phrase (cf.

5.   The evidence, according to the categories listed, is in the following lines: (Form A) *CT* I.7, 59, 64, 175 (*ilke*), 182, 252, 354, 394, 424, 429, 476, 533, 721, 831, III.18, 21, 35, 42, 177, 235, 242, 291, 296, 297, 331, 357, 363, 365, 431, 460, 505, 608, 651, 656, 660, 708, 762, 763, 800, 865, 955, 993, 1000, 1005, 1010, 1046, 1052, 1072, 1076, 1086, 1094, 1125, 1166, 1171, 1173, 1178, 1231, IV.49, 77, 197, 210, 222, 273, 278, 302, 372, 557, 567, 590, 705, 745, 777, 779, 807, 821, 852, 877, 892, 904 (*olde*), 913, 948 (*thilke*), 966, 1045; (Form B) I.213, 336, 611, 663, 804, III.68, 233, 280, 421, 449, 487, 819, 964, 1091, IV.143, 504, 652, 881, 889; (Form C, weak plural of monosyllabic adjective) I.664, III.121, 187, 225 (these two are a special case of the weak plural following a pronoun used attributively), 835, 857, 953, 1004, IV.13, 1081, 1084, 1093; (strong plural of monosyllabic adjective) I.9, 53, 90, 146, 175, 213, 234, 245, 346, 534, III.197, 221, 323, 326, 642, 687, 870, 1216, IV.339, 584, 634, 739, 1002, 1140, 1157.

Burnley 1982: 175-76), as is suggested by the frequent presence of the phrase in the normal weak form and also after a preposition in *for hye Goddes sake*, IV.135. There are six cases where the adjective has final *-e* after a preposition (*of alle charitee*, I.452; *in alle gentillesse*, IV.593, the one with *hye* just quoted, and the three with *seinte*, I.120, 509; III.604, discussed below) and one in a quasi-adverbial phrase (IV.442).[6] The three instances where Chaucer seems to allow *oure/youre* as dissyllables (III.595, 1042, 1091)— alongside a vast preponderance of instances, in both oblique and plural forms, where they are monosyllabic—should be emended (Ralph Hanna in Benson 1987: 1126) or scanned otherwise. These scattered exceptions, or apparent exceptions, all of which are susceptible of particular explanations, contrast with the systematic regularity with which the zero form of the singular monosyllabic adjective is used in strong positions before nouns with accent on the second syllable (*a yong Squier*, I.79; *a gay bracer*, I.111; *a gay daggere*, I.113; *a fair forheed*, I.154; *a good pitaunce*, I.224), even after prepositions (*in swich licour*, I.3; *of greet desport*, I.137; *of smal coral*, I.158), and even in weak positions (Ten Brink 1901: 157-58) before such nouns (*hire old richesse*, III.1118; *hire heigh bountee*, III.1160; *hire heigh lynage*, IV.991; but cf. *hire grete estaat*, IV.925, where the *-e* of the weak inflexion is elided).

Another form of the building block is that in which the first element is an originally dissyllabic adjective with unstressed second syllable in *-e* (e.g. *his sweete breeth*, I.5; *the newe world*, I.176; *a clene sheep*, I.504).[7] These forms are important in those cases where the unstressed second syllable came later to be thought of

6.   Chaucer's lack of interest in the use of final *-e* with prenominal monosyllabic singular adjectives after prepositions is suggested by forms such as *and of greet strengthe*, I.84; *and in good poynt*, I.200; *But of greet norissyng*, I.437; *and with glad cheere*, IV.782; where the metrical accent can be shifted back to the preposition because of the presence of the preceding conjunction. The insertion of *ful* is another common way of avoiding stress-clash, e.g., *upon a ful good stot*, I.615; *with ful sad face*, IV.552.

7.   The evidence is in the following lines: (weak singular) I.5, 176, 682, III.335, 385, 447, 510 (these two are 'naturalized' French forms), 804, 819, 1087, IV.120, 141, 394, 805, 838, 841, 1056; (weak plural) III.559; (strong singular) I.504, 531, 549, III.320, 435, 516, 522, 1221, IV.146, 942, 1005; (strong singular after preposition) III.459, 861, IV.340, 465; (strong plural) I.14, 607, 639, IV.223.

as an inflexional weak *-e* and dropped. In other words, they are not particularly informative in relation to Chaucer's metrical practice, since the final *-e* will always be present and always constitute a metrical syllable, whether the adjective is weak or strong, singular or plural, but they are important for understanding the practice of later scribes and Chaucerian imitators. In the count of such forms given below, those that contain adjectives such as *large, lige, more, nyce, rude, rype, same, straunge,* where the spelling with *-e* was preserved into later English as a means of indicating the pronunciation of a previous vowel or consonant (Jordan 1974: 245), are omitted, since the final *-e* could always remain capable of carrying syllabic value and playing its part in the building block. Such forms of the building block are therefore not of discriminatory value in relation to scribal practice.

So far, Benson (1987) has provided the evidence for Chaucer's grammatical and metrical usage. It is time now to check the edited text against the two principal (indeed, almost the sole) witnesses that went to its making, the Hengwrt (**Hg**) and Ellesmere (**El**) manuscripts (Ruggiers 1979). The evidence derived from this examination demonstrates the extraordinary fidelity of this early scribe, in his two manuscripts of the *Canterbury Tales,* to Chaucer's textual intentions, as those intentions can be recovered with some degree of certainty from examination of the 'building block'. There are only 14 instances where **Hg** and **El** have, singly (**Hg** 8, **El** 11) or in agreement (**HgEl** 7), in the context of the building block, different readings from those adopted in Benson (1987). Two of these are indifferent variants in **El** that do not affect the structure of the building block (*faire*] **El** *yonge,* I.234; *dere*] **El** *goode,* IV.1056); two are variant versions in **El** (III.18, 121) of lines where the variation destroys the building block but was not motivated by misunderstanding of it; and one is a variant, common to **HgEl**, of a line (III.197) that looks to be the product of fussy emendation in Benson (1987). Of the nine remaining variants, six are common to **HgEl**: three involve straightforward misunderstanding of the simple building block (*good* in vocative *goode lief,* III.431; *which* in *the whiche vice,* III.955; *glad* in *hire glade chiere,* IV.1045), and there are further such misunderstandings in **El** (*that* for *thilke* in *of thilke tonne,* III.177, and *which* in *the whiche daunce,* III.993). There is one case in **Hg**—such is the fidelity of the scribe and such the precision that Chaucer asks of him—where final *-e* is added improperly to a weak adjective before a noun with accent on the second syllable (*hye* for *heigh/hy* in *hire heigh bountee*, III.1160). Another such case, left unemended in Benson (1987), where both **HgEl** read, 'correctly' but incorrectly, *heighe*, in *hire heighe bountee* (IV.418), should be emended. The other three variants common to **HgEl** are capable of explanation in terms of competing constraints upon the scribe. They all have to do with Chaucer's apparent use of *seinte*, within the building block, as an inflected adjective (on the model of French) after a preposition: *by Seinte Loy*, I.120; *unto Seinte Poules*, I.509; *of seinte Venus seel*, III.604. In each case, the scribe of **HgEl** seems to understand the adjective as the normally uninflected appositional noun. The crux is a familiar one, and has been much discussed, but the conclusions of Donaldson (1949) concerning the adjectival use of *seinte* have been generally accepted and agree entirely with the evidence of the building block.

Apart from these cases, there are others where Benson (1987) accepts the readings of **HgEl** but where those readings need examining in the light of the evidence provided by the building block. In I.8, *half*, in *his half cours*, which is the reading of both **HgEl**, clearly needs emendation to *halve*, an adjectival form with weak inflexion and voicing of medial consonant which is found, in the plural, elsewhere in Chaucer (*halve goddes, Troilus*, IV.1545). Skeat and other earlier editors, including F.N. Robinson in the 1933 and 1957 editions that preceded Benson (1987), were happy to emend thus, and Donaldson (1974: 98-99) suggested that 'scribes may have tended to think of the word as an uninflected noun' (like *seint*, above); but an awed respect for the manuscripts and a fear of textual litigation have made more recent editors excessively cautious. At I.850, **HgEl** read *this goode man*, in accordance with the rules for the building block, even though the *-e* of *goode* is metrically superfluous; one suspects that Chaucer's intention was to use the compound noun *goodman*, as in *CT* VI.361, where Benson (1987) does indeed emend **HgEl** *goode* to *good*.[8]

---

8.   Chaucer's practice elsewhere is to have the *-e* of the weak singular in *goode man* pronounced (*CT* III.1768; IV.1897; VII.29, 33, 107), though there is some question about the pronunciation of the weak plural in *-e* in *goode*

Finally, though not strictly the business of this essay (since it is not an example of the weak declension), *a wys wyf,* in III.231, is metrically impossible, and unemendable from its present form: it should possibly be emended to *a wys womman,* with accent on the second syllable of the noun, as in III.209.

It will be evident that the analysis of the building block has a valuable function in providing precise information to assist the editor in determining the relative authenticity of minor variants of grammar and spelling. It has another valuable function in providing an index to the general reliability of a manuscript in its record of such features, and of course if the analysis were extended to include all relevant lines of Chaucer's verse it would perform this function in a much more than merely suggestive manner. In Hengwrt, for instance, the 'accuracy quotient' for Forms A, B and C, based on the 3284 lines of the analysis, and calculated as the percentage of correct forms in relation to the relevant total of forms (the relevant total of forms being that remaining after the removal from the full count of 140 lines, including *halve,* I.8, of those lines where the forms are not present because of reconstruction or other large-scale variation), is 97.1 per cent, or 95.6 per cent if the stricter count is observed that includes as 'errors' those forms of the building block where *-e* is retained in accordance with correct grammar but not in accordance with Chaucer's metrical practice (I.850; III.1160). The corresponding figures for Ellesmere are 95.6 per cent and 94.8 per cent respectively. Such precise figures are specious, of course, being drawn from such a small sample, but they are not misleading if they are understood to be significant in a strictly comparative way.

British Library MS Harley 7334, another very early manuscript, is well known for the meticulousness of its care with language and metre, and also for the occasional fussiness with which it tidies up perceived irregularities in Chaucer. With this building block, as might be expected, the scribe appears a paragon. Discounting those lines where the building block, for unrelated reasons, does not appear as in **HgEl** (I.175, 831; III.121, 197, 608, 708, 870, 1072), there are only five errors in the representation of Forms A,

---

men (III.835; IV.2416; VII.3402; but cf. VI.377, 904; VII.3440, 3445). Only those occurrences that appear in **HgEl** are cited.

B and C (I.804; III.18; IV.273, 948, 1002); in all but one of those cases (IV.1002) the metre is corrected by compensation elsewhere in the line. Elsewhere, Harley has correct forms where both **HgEl** are in error (I.8; III.431, 955; IV.1045) and, according to the simple count based on Forms A, B and C, has an accuracy quotient of 96 per cent. Harley also makes some extraordinarily intelligent deductions concerning the author's intentions in variant forms of the building block: *seynte* in I.509 (though not elsewhere); *heigh* in *hire heigh bounte*, IV.418, where both **HgEl** have *heighe* as the 'correct' but incorrect form of the weak adjective before a noun with accent on the second syllable; *gret* in *hir gret estate*, IV.925, where the scribe makes the 'correction' even though in this case it is not necessary, since the *-e* is elided and metre not affected; and *such* for *swiche* in IV.739, where the scribe recognizes that the final *-e* is hypermetrical (but misses the similar case in IV.634) and removes it, even though grammatically it must stand. Editors clearly have to be careful with such a busybody of a scribe, but his feeling for Chaucer's metrical practice is not to be ignored.

Second-generation manuscripts of the *Canterbury Tales* show increasing signs of strain, as scribes struggle to pay attention to grammatical forms that are increasingly strange to them. An exception has to be made here for Cambridge University Library MS Gg.4.27 (c. 1420–30), always an aberrant manuscript (Parkes and Beadle 1979–80), which shows an extraordinary degree of accuracy in the representation of adjectival *-e* within the building block. Exact comparison with other manuscripts is not easy to make, given the many lines not present in this much-mutilated manuscript and given too the many occasions where the destruction of the building block is the accidental result of a grosser error (e.g. *false*] **Gg** *om.*, III.800; *grete*] **Gg** *om.*, III.865; *whiche*] **Gg** *om.*, III.993). There is also the **Gg** habit of spelling *straunge* as *strong* (I.464; III.1161), which introduces the possibility of error into a normally stable form of the building block. Nevertheless, the accuracy quotient, based on the number of errors (I.464; III.221, 297, 763, 1161; IV.584, 1045) in the 116 lines which are present and where the building block survives or is newly vulnerable, is still high, at 94 per cent.

With other second-generation manuscripts, available for study, along with **Hg**, **El** and Harley 7334, in the Six-Text prints of

Furnivall (1868–79), the processes of erosion begin to be more evident. In Corpus Christi College, Oxford, MS 198, there are six errors (I.8; III.221, 763; IV.49, 197, 1045) in the 134 lines where the building block survives in analysable form, plus a further two in which substantive error of other kinds introduces the possibility of error in the representation of the weak adjective (*trewe*] Cp. *good*, III.320, *straunge*] Cp. *strong*, III.1161). The score here is 94 per cent. There are also elsewhere the beginnings of those scatterings of final *-e* in inappropriate places (e.g. *olde*, III.281) or in places where the use of final *-e* had been deliberately inhibited in the earlier witnesses in order to display metre correctly (e.g. *olde*, III.1118; *heye*, IV.468; *sadde*, IV.552).

In British Library MS Lansdowne 851 and Petworth House, Sussex, MS 7, the building blocks that Chaucer had constructed, like sea-walls to protect his verse from the erosions of 'miswriting' and 'mismetring' (*Troilus*, V.1795-96), are crumbling. In Lansdowne there are 31 errors in 133 relevant lines (76.7%), including instances now with loss of *-e* in the prenominal form of the dissyllabic adjective (*trew*, I.531; *new*, IV.394, 942), but not including the many cases where *owene* is reduced to *owen*. The decline in the capacity to recognize metrically significant final *-e* carries with it the freedom that scribes perceive they have to scatter unnecessary or ungrammatical instances of *-e* around like confetti (*broune*, I.109; *gaie*, I.111, 113; *smale*, I.158; *goode*, I.200; *fatte*, I.206, etc.). In Petworth, beside a few happy guesses (*halfe*, I.8; *seynte*, I.120), there are 36 errors in 131 lines (score 72.5%), with particular carnage wrought among the forms with *ilke* (III.18, 177, 297, 651, 1076, 1166; IV.197, 278, 557, 807, 877) and adjectives in *-st* (I.831; III.505, 608, 1052; IV.49, 745, 966). There are striking differences, not for the first or only time, between the rate of success in the *General Prologue* and in the other two tales, which one may attribute to decline in the scribe's attentiveness rather than change in the exemplar.

The processes of decay, which were to leave Chaucer's verse with only the rude sweetness of a Scotch tune, could be traced thus in melancholy detail, but the story can be brought to an abrupt close with the figures for Thynne's edition of *Chaucer's Works* (1532). Here there are 39 errors in 135 relevant lines (71.1%), an accuracy quotient which would have been much lower were it not that Thynne was a comparatively careful editor and somehow recognized *ilke* and *thilke*, which he almost never mistakes, as desirable archaisms; *owene*, meanwhile, is frequently reduced to *own*, and there is the usual proliferation of otiose final *-e*.

The *Canterbury Tales* survive in good early manuscripts, based on copies of high quality and worked upon by careful scribes with an attentive eye to Chaucer's grammar, spelling and metre. The situation is unusual, and the editor's task simple. With *Troilus and Criseyde* the situation is different. Only second-generation manuscripts survive and, quite apart from the contentious question of their accuracy in representing Chaucer's larger textual intention, or intentions, there is already much for the editor to do in reconstructing the minor but metrically significant detail of Chaucer's grammar and spelling. In a sample of 3284 lines taken from *Troilus* (Book IV and Book V, lines 1-1667, making 3284, allowing for the loss of 84 lines in the copy-text manuscript at IV.491-532; V.1233-74), there are, in Benson (1987), 93 examples of Form A of the building block, including 14 of *ilke/thilke* (singular), 23 of Form B, mostly spelt *owen*, but also *owne* and *owene*, and 32 of Form C, including 6 with *ilke/thilke* (plural).[9] Of the total of 148 examples of the simpler forms of the building block, a total remarkably consistent with that (140) for the same number of lines in the *Canterbury Tales*, 29 are mistranscribed in Corpus Christi College, Cambridge MS 61 (see Parkes and Salter [1978], which is chosen as the copy-text in Benson [1987] and also in the

9.   (Form A) IV.8, 26* (*ferthe*), 43, 47, 104, 127, 229*, 239, 308*, 354, 452, 458, 541, 659 (*swifte*), 663*, 666*, 752, 926, 1116*, 1161, 1240, 1292, 1425, 1429, 1461, 1532, 1567, 1595, 1598, 1660, V.75, 184*, 219, 232*, 240*, 244, 307, 342, 424, 476, 477, 493*, 507, 567, 572*, 642, 648, 653*, 655, 680, 681, 683*, 685, 708, 717, 842, 904, 909, 1016, 1022 (*faire, brighte*), 1038, 1103 (*nynthe*), 1126, 1136, 1205 (*thridde, ferthe, fifte, sexte*), 1317, 1392*, 1412 (*faire, fresshe*), 1454*, 1475, 1486, 1521*, 1539*, 1653; (with *ilke/thilke*) IV.26*, 317*, 747, 773, 1070*, 1236, 1534*, 1551, 1656*, V.869*, 956*, 1103*, 1187*, 1513; (Form B) IV.405, 1089, 1311, 1449, 1450, 1552, 1640, V.49, 63, 162, 218, 340, 467, 521, 588, 669, 865, 1280, 1315, 1344, 1390, 1401, 1421; (Form C) IV.40, 129, 247, 248, 402*, 636, 659 (*false*), 661, 814, 930, 968, 1384*, 1545, 1658, V.362, 379, 552, 768, 790, 848, 915, 1047, 1459, 1478, 1481, 1562; (with *ilke/thilke*) IV.370, 715, 1005, 1049, 1148, V.1311. In those marked with *, final *-e* is not present in the Corpus MS.

more comprehensive critical edition of Windeatt [1984]). The accuracy quotient is 80.4 per cent, there being particular problems with *ilke/thilke* and *righte*. The scribe of this sumptuous manuscript was evidently already careless of or out of touch with essential elements in the structure of Chaucer's verse, elements furthermore that are unambiguously prescribed by the metrical form of the building block. For if it be argued that the reasoning here is circular, in that the forms chosen as the basis of the analysis are, in part, those reconstructed by editors from the evidence of the majority of forms in the manuscripts, then it would have to be reiterated that the linguistic and metrical structure of the form is fixed: there is rarely an alternative to the scansion that requires the presence of sounded final *-e* (the two exceptions are *my good word*, V.1081; and *youre good word*, V.1622; where there may be an effect of compounding, as in *good man* above). The two major modern editions agree in every detail in emending the 29 errors in the Corpus manuscript. They could have gone further without fear, for instance in regularizing all forms of *owen/owene/owne* as *owene* on the basis of good Chaucerian practice overwhelmingly evidenced in **HgEl**. Corpus is particularly bad among these second-generation manuscripts of *Troilus* in its insensitivity to final *-e* (Samuels 1983: 32): other manuscripts, however, are considered to be inferior in quality in respect of substantives.

It is possible to hint at some ways in which this investigation might be carried forward into a consideration of the metre of Chaucer's successors. The accepted view, which I do not believe to be mistaken, is that declining understanding of the metrical significance of final *-e* and the loss of final *-e* in poor scribal copies caused confusion among his followers and led to a breakdown in the pentameter (see the summary in Pearsall 1970: 58-63). There is no doubt that this did happen, but one wonders whether it happened as quickly and universally as is sometimes assumed. Hoccleve presumably had access to good early copies of Chaucer and he writes perfect syllabic pentameter. Lydgate, in his prime during the same years as Hoccleve, is assumed to have been denied this access or to have misunderstood everything that Hoccleve understood perfectly clearly and to have erected Chaucerian variants of the pentameter, like the 'headless' line and the 'Lydgate' line, which Chaucer used very occasionally for special

rhetorical effect, into fixed forms. I begin to wonder whether this
is entirely fair. It is a view based on imperfect evidence, for,
though there are texts of Lydgate in plenty, there are very few
proper editions. An examination of 140 lines (III.1667-806) from
the *Life of Our Lady* (Lauritis *et al.* 1961), shows nine examples of
Form A (1668, 1675, 1687, 1711, 1717, 1734, 1761, 1764, 1765)
and two of Form C (1752, 1759). There are a further four examples of Form C (*smalle* 1708; *alle*, 1728, 1733 and 1784) which are
not recognized by the editors, but which can be argued for from
the evidence of their copy-text (Durham University Library MS
Cosin V.ii.16, ff.66-68), where all are spelt with barred -*ll*. Some
editors of fifteenth-century texts print this as -*lle*, but most ignore
the bar as merely otiose. There is a case to be made that editors
should use their discretion in the author's favour and interpret as
-*lle* when normal grammar and metre so require. There are also
six instances where the edited text needs to be corrected from the
copy-text (*highe* 1800) or where emendation is needed (*smale*
1682; *yonge* 1683; *alle* 1745; *graye* 1763; *highe* 1785) in order to
restore regular forms of the building block that no poet, not even
Lydgate, could have failed to recognize. In each case the emendation restores a regular pentameter. There are still some awk-
ward lines among the 140, but it is clearer what Lydgate is trying
to do.

   There are some conclusions to be drawn from this brief investigation, sketchy as it is. Comparatively little of a systematic nature
has been done on the details of Chaucer's grammatical and
metrical practice, and the views of critics (including mine) have
tended to be based on broad subjective assumptions. Metre has
been regarded by some as a matter of intuition: a 'good reader'
will recognize when final -*e* is to be sounded and when not. There
is of course an element of the intuitive about scansion, some
room for creative disagreement, and one can understand why linguistic scholars such as Burnley (1982) and Samuels (1983) have
preferred to base their investigations on graphemic rather than
metrical evidence. But at the basis of metre there are the fundamental building blocks which follow fixed rules of linguistic and
metrical construction: they offer a much securer foundation for
the analysis of metre than the whole line, where *ad hoc* scansions
can almost always be engineered to support a particular metrical

theory. Anglo-Saxon alliterative metre was not understood until the metre of phrasal groupings was worked out; the understanding of Middle English alliterative metre has been revolutionized by the discovery of fixed patterns of stress-distribution in the b-line (Duggan 1986). Chaucerian metre and the metre of his successors needs the same systematic attention to the fixed elements in its structure.

WORKS CITED

Benson, L.D. (ed.)
 1987   *The Riverside Chaucer* (Boston: Houghton Mifflin).
Burnley, J.D.
 1982   'Inflexion in Chaucer's Adjectives', *Neuphilologische Mitteilungen* 83: 169-77.
 1983   *A Guide to Chaucer's Language* (London: Macmillan).
Donaldson, E.T.
 1948   'Chaucer's Final -e', *PMLA* 63: 1101-24.
 1949   'Middle English *Seint, Seinte*', *Studia Neophilologica* 21: 122-30.
 1974   'The Manuscripts of Chaucer's Works and their Use', in D.S. Brewer (ed.), *Geoffrey Chaucer: Writers and their Backgrounds* (London: Bell): 85-108.
Duggan, H.N.
 1986   'Alliterative Patterning as a Basis for Emendation in Middle English Alliterative Poetry', *Studies in the Age of Chaucer* 8: 73-105.
Eliason, N.
 1972   *The Language of Chaucer's Poetry* (Copenhagen: Rosenkilde & Bagger).
Elliott, R.W.V.
 1974   *Chaucer's English* (London: Deutsch).
Furnivall, F.J. (ed.)
 1868–79   *The Corpus MS of Chaucer's Canterbury Tales*, Chaucer Society, 1st series 5, 11, 18, 34, 41, 53, 67; *The Petworth MS of Chaucer's Canterbury Tales*, Chaucer Society, 1st series 6, 12, 19, 35, 42, 54, 68; *The Lansdowne MS of Chaucer's Canterbury Tales*, Chaucer Society, 1st series 7, 13, 20, 36, 43, 55, 69 (London: Trübner).
 1885   *The Harleian MS 7334 of Chaucer's Canterbury Tales* (Chaucer Society, 1st series 73; London: Trübner).
Jordan, R.
 1974   *Handbook of Middle English Grammar* (trans. R. Cook; The Hague: Mouton, rev. edn).
Lauritis, J., *et al.* (eds.)
 1961   *A Critical Edition of John Lydgate's* 'Life of Our Lady' (Pittsburgh: Duquesne Studies).

Minkova, D.
  1990   'Adjectival Inflexion Relics and Speech Rhythm in Late Middle and
                Early Modern English', in S. Adamson *et al.* (eds.), *Current Issues in
                Linguistic Theory* 65 (Amsterdam: Benjamins): 313-36.
Mustanoja, T.F.
  1968   'Chaucer's Prosody', in B. Rowland (ed.), *Companion to Chaucer
                Studies* (Oxford: Oxford University Press): 58-84.
Parkes, M.B., and R. Beadle (introds.)
  1979–80   *Geoffrey Chaucer: Poetical Works: A Facsimile of Cambridge University
                Library MS Gg.4.27* (3 vols.; Norman, OK: Pilgrim Books).
Parkes, M.B., and E. Salter (introds.)
  1978   *Troilus and Criseyde: A Facsimile of Corpus Christi College Cambridge MS
                61* (Cambridge: Brewer).
Pearsall, D.
  1970   *John Lydgate* (London: Routledge & Kegan Paul).
  1991   'Chaucer's Metre: The Evidence of the Manuscripts', in T.W.
                Machan (ed.), *Medieval Literature: Texts and Interpretation* (Bing-
                hampton, NY: Center for Medieval and Early Renaissance Studies):
                11-57.
Robinson, I.
  1971   *Chaucer's Prosody: A Study of the Middle English Verse Tradition* (Cam-
                bridge: Cambridge University Press).
Ruggiers, P.G. (ed.)
  1979   *Geoffrey Chaucer: The Canterbury Tales. A Facsimile of the Hengwrt Manu-
                script, with Variants from the Ellesmere Manuscript* (Norman, OK: Uni-
                versity of Oklahoma Press).
Samuels, M.L.
  1972   'Chaucerian Final -e', *Notes and Queries* 217: 445-48.
  1983   'Chaucer's Spelling', in D. Gray and E.G. Stanley (eds.), *Middle
                English Studies Presented to Norman Davis* (Oxford: Oxford University
                Press): 17-37.
Schipper, J.
  1910   *A History of English Versification* (Oxford: Clarendon Press).
Skeat, W.W. (ed.)
  1894–97   *The Complete Works of Geoffrey Chaucer* (7 vols.; Oxford: Clarendon
                Press).
Smith, J.J.
  1995   'The Language of the Ellesmere Manuscript', in M. Stevens and
                D. Woodward (eds.), *The Ellesmere Chaucer: Essays in Interpretation*
                (San Marino: Huntington Library).
Southworth, J.G.
  1947   'Chaucer's Final -e in Rhyme', *PMLA* 62: 910-35.
  1954   *Verses of Cadence: An Introduction to the Prosody of Chaucer and his
                Followers* (Oxford: Oxford University Press).

Ten Brink, B.
  1901   *The Language and Metre of Chaucer* (rev. F. Kluge; trans. M.B. Smith; London: Macmillan, 2nd edn).
Windeatt, B.A. (ed.)
  1984   *Geoffrey Chaucer, Troilus and Criseyde: A New Edition of 'The Book of Troilus'* (London: Longman).

Can we Trust the Hengwrt Manuscript?

Peter Robinson

A survey of Norman Blake's publications over the 35 years of his academic career suggests a rather neat division between the Caxton Norman and the Chaucer Norman. Up to 1979 he published some 26 articles and six books on aspects of Caxton; since 1979 he has published on aspects of Chaucer around 15 articles, two books, and edited (with the author of this article) the two volumes of the *Canterbury Tales* Project *Occasional Papers*. Of course, this schematization into a career of two halves is too neat. It ignores (among other matters) the work Norman has done on Old English and Old Norse. It ignores, too, the continuing thread of interest in the history of English which runs through all his work. He wrote about Chaucer before 1979 and he has continued to work on Caxton since that date.

However, simplifications are sometimes useful, and the choice of 1979 as the date marking this hypothetical division is not fortuitous. In that year Norman published his article 'The Relationship between the Hengwrt and the Ellesmere Manuscripts of the *Canterbury Tales*' (1979). This sounded the keynotes for his later work on the *Tales*. In it he focused on the differences between the Hengwrt and Ellesmere manuscripts and the implications of these for editors. The article is notable, too, for its uncompromising insistence that understanding of the complex tradition of the *Tales* can be obtained only by exploration of the whole tradition, not just by study of these two manuscripts, and certainly not by simply accepting the judgments of earlier editors and scholars. All must be tested anew. Through a series of later articles, through his edition of the *Tales* based on the Hengwrt manuscript (1980), through his book the *Textual Tradition of the Canterbury Tales* (1985), and latterly through his collaboration with the *Canterbury Tales* Project, he has continued this exploration.

Simplifications can sometimes be useful as an intellectual short-hand for complex arguments. But they can also be simply wrong. Through all these publications Norman has advocated the primacy of the Hengwrt manuscript as the single most authoritative source for any edition of the *Tales*. His position has been reduced by other scholars to the crude formula 'if it is not in Hengwrt it cannot be by Chaucer'.[1] Ralph Hanna defines this 'hard Hengwrtism' (1989: 65) as the belief that Hengwrt gives 'an absolutely accurate record of Chaucer's text in all particulars'. It not only accepts exclusively Hengwrt readings but also its ordering of the tales as 'thoroughly reliable'. It claims that Hengwrt is the oldest manuscript and was the very first copy made direct from Chaucer's own holograph, and that all later manuscripts are derived either from Hengwrt or this holograph.

So put, this is an extreme testament of faith in the efficacy of this one manuscript. If all these claims were true, all an editor of Chaucer would ever need to do would be just to reproduce the Hengwrt manuscript. One could see this as a 'reification' of this one text on a grand scale (Hanna 1995: 239-40) and an egregious instance of the sort of 'best-text' editing so roundly condemned by A.E. Housman as being 'in the same spirit of gloomy resignation with which a man lies down on a stretcher when he has broken both his legs'.[2] It is as if people find it pleasant to come across a scholar who appears to hold a view one can so easily attack—so pleasant, in fact, that they ignore the inconvenient fact that Norman does not actually hold this view.[3] Norman's position

1. For example, this sentence from Helen Cooper's essay in the volume devoted to the Ellesmere Chaucer: 'N.F. Blake's argument, repeated in his contribution to this volume—that any portion of text that does not appear in Hengwrt cannot be authentic—has not received general acceptance.' As the quotation below from his essay shows, this is not what he says (Blake 1995: 212; cf. Cooper 1995: 259).

2. From Housman's Preface to his 1905 edition of Juvenal, reprinted in Ricks (1988: 399-400).

3. To be fair to the scholars who have ascribed this view ('if it isn't in Hengwrt it cannot be genuine') to Norman, he has several times in the

is more complex than the crude characterization of 'hard Hengwrtism' has it. He explains it carefully in his essay in the *Ellesmere
Chaucer*:

> I have always made it clear that I regard the order of tales in
> Hengwrt as scribal and not Chaucerian; the Hengwrt order simply
> represents the first attempt to put the tales left by Chaucer into
> some kind of order. The Hengwrt order has no more validity than
> any other; the important question is the relationship among the
> orderings in various manuscripts.
>
> The question of the text also needs a different emphasis. If
> Hengwrt is the earliest manuscript and contains a good—and
> perhaps the best—text, one then starts from the presumption that
> what is not in Hengwrt needs justification it it is to be accepted as
> Chaucerian. Arguments to this effect may well be made success-
> fully, but until they are we have to be skeptical of claims that any
> additional passages or alternative readings are Chaucerian. To
> claim authenticity for readings or passages simply on the basis that
> they have always been accepted as Chaucerian, or that they agree
> with a scholar's subjective idea of what is Chaucer's, is simply not
> good enough (1995: 212).

It is clear from this statement that Blake's position on Hengwrt
is not just a flat assertion: it is a hypothesis and a challenge. The
hypothesis is this: If scholars agree that Hengwrt offers the best
text (and this view has not been seriously challenged since Manly
and Rickert 1940 established the precedence of the Hengwrt text;
it is accepted for example, albeit grudgingly, by Hanna in his essay
in the *Ellesmere Chaucer* [1995]), then we should presume that
Hengwrt is the nearest we have to an autograph manuscript. It
follows that what is in Hengwrt is a priori likely to be by Chaucer,
and that what is not in Hengwrt requires justification. It is difficult
to see a flaw in this logic. The challenge is this: Prove or disprove
the hypothesis. Norman explicitly accepts that counter-arguments
might be successful ('Arguments to this effect may well be made
successfully...'). Indeed, his edition of the *Canterbury Tales*, while
avowedly based on Hengwrt, also prints passages found in other

course of his writing on Hengwrt made assertions which could be seen as
consistent with this, if taken out of context (for example, this remark from a
long footnote in Blake 1979: 14: 'I believe that [the *Canon's Yeoman's Tale*] is
spurious because it is not in Hengwrt...'; but this same footnote is careful to
present other arguments).

manuscripts, opening the possibility that these passages (including the whole *Canon's Yeoman's Prologue* and *Tale*) might actually be part of the *Tales*, even though they are not in Hengwrt.

In the last sentence of the passage quoted above Norman lays down a condition: argument on these matters cannot be based simply on what has always been 'accepted'. That a particular tale order has appeared in almost every modern edition, or a particular reading has been quoted over and over by scholars and students, or a particular passage has shaped modern perceptions of Chaucer's attitude to women, is no argument at all. To discover the earliest forms of the text we have to return to the manuscripts themselves. Only then can we begin to make judgments on what might or might not be 'Chaucerian', in the sense of likely to have been present in Chaucer's own manuscript of the *Tales*. In his own essays and books over the last two decades Norman has attempted exactly this, most fully in his *Textual Tradition of the Canterbury Tales* (1985).

This is a demanding prescription. It means, for example, that a scholar should check the manuscript authority for any reading before quoting it. This is far from easy. Even if one has the full corpus of variants in Manly and Rickert (1940) to hand, it is very difficult to determine from these exactly what reading is in any given manuscript. Nor is this knowledge (even if one can get it) very useful in itself: it may be significant that a particular group of 5 manuscripts has one reading, while 50 others have another reading; or it may not. Given this absence of tools, it is very hard to prove or disprove any hypothesis, or even to know whether it is meaningful at all.

It was the perception that we lacked these tools which led to the inception of the *Canterbury Tales* Project. This project aims to transcribe all the manuscripts of the *Tales* into electronic form, to use computer tools to collate the transcriptions, and then to analyse the record of agreements and disagreements with the aid of further computer methods. At the least, this would give scholars the ability to discover what manuscript says what. It might go further and, by uncovering the relations between the manuscripts, allow us to reconstruct the early history of the text and its copying. The relevance of this to the work Norman had been doing led to a meeting in June 1992 between Norman and myself (who in the early 1990s had begun the work which preceded the project). At this meeting we both saw the potential this approach had to advance work on the *Tales*, especially to frame and test hypotheses about the early history of the tradition. We agreed to cooperate, to seek ways to carry on this work, and thus the *Canterbury Tales* Project was born.

Five years have passed since then. The Project has won useful (though never sufficient) funding, and under Norman's wise leadership has grown to include some dozen scholars in five different countries. Two volumes of Project *Occasional Papers* have been published, edited by Norman and myself, and a CD-ROM of *The Wife of Bath's Prologue* (Blake and Robinson 1993; Robinson 1996; Blake and Robinson 1997). This CD-ROM presents all 58 fifteenth-century witnesses to this part of the *Tales* in transcription, collation and image, together with fully-lemmatized spelling databases, manuscript descriptions and much else. The CD-ROM and the articles in the second *Occasional Papers* on the textual tradition of the *Wife of Bath's Prologue* represent, as it were, the first steps towards the Project's overarching aim: to discover the earliest stages of the history of the text and so arrive at a well-grounded base for editing the *Tales*.

In addition to these publications, preparation of the next Project CD-ROM, that of the *General Prologue* (to be edited by Elizabeth Solopova) is nearly complete, and we are well advanced on another four CD-ROMs, representing different selections of text and manuscripts. Already we have gathered sufficient materials and tools to begin to answer the problems posed in Norman's work. One may express these problems in terms of the following four questions:

1. Does Hengwrt have the best text?
2. Does Hengwrt include all the *Tales* and the whole text of the *Tales*?
3. Does Hengwrt have the best tale order?
4. Does Hengwrt have the best spelling?

From our work the answer to the first question, so far as the *Wife of Bath's Prologue* is concerned, is unequivocally yes. Stemmatic analysis of 58 witnesses suggested that some 12 of the 58 belonged to what we have come to call the *O* group witnesses.[4] These *O* witnesses are distinguished from all the other fifteenth-century witnesses in two respects:

1. They contain few or none of the readings characteristic of any of the seven groups of witnesses (labelled *a* through *f*, with **Cx²**) to which most other witnesses belong and which show evidence of significant scribal revision.

2. They contain some of the 27 readings which seem to have been present in *O* (as we call the ancestor of the whole tradition), in witnesses close to *O*, but not usually in witnesses belonging to the seven groups referred to above.

Close scrutiny of these 27 readings suggests that their authorial character is a 'compendium of just what scribes found difficult in Chaucer's poetic' (Robinson 1997: 102). Accordingly, these readings are peculiarly liable to alteration during scribal copying, hence their absence from the seven groups characterized by scribal revision. Hence, too, their presence in the *O* witnesses is evidence of the proximity of these witnesses to *O* itself. An example of these readings is the compression of this phrase from line 36 of the *Wife of Bath's Prologue* in Hengwrt (and other *O* witnesses):

> he hadde wyues many oon

widely replaced in other manuscripts by:

> he hadde wyues mo than oon

(for examples, see Robinson 1997: 102). Among the 12 or so *O* witnesses for this part of the *Tales* (see n. 4 below), Hengwrt has outstandingly the best text—a text so good that an editor needs to correct only some two or three minor slips. In his 1980 edition Norman makes only two emendations in the text of the *Prologue*, and our work suggests that this is a just conservatism.

However, while Hengwrt might have the best text for the *Wife of Bath's Prologue*, this does not of itself mean that in other parts of

---

4. The exact number of *O* manuscripts is imprecise, as several manuscripts (among them Ellesmere) appear to use an *O* exemplar for part of the text and some other exemplar for other parts. Ellesmere, for example, uses an *E* exemplar up to around line 400 and an *O* exemplar from that point.

the *Tales* other manuscripts might not have better texts. This is particularly likely if it is established that separate parts of the *Tales* have separate textual histories. Many scholars (notably Manly and Rickert; also Benson) have claimed that the *Tales* were issued in parts in Chaucer's lifetime, a position vigorously opposed by Norman (Manly and Rickert 1940: II, 489; cf. Blake 1985: 51-54, 188-90). Part publication would render it unlikely that any one text would have the best text of the whole *Tales*. At the time of writing the Project's stemmatic analysis of the *Wife of Bath's Prologue* is complete, and that for the *General Prologue* is well advanced. While there are differences between the stemmatic relationships of the witnesses for these two parts of the *Tales*, they are not such as to require that these two parts of the *Tales* have separate textual histories.[5] These two parts of the *Tales* are widely separated in the manuscripts, the *General Prologue* being always at the beginning of the first fragment and the *Wife of Bath's Prologue* and *Tale* always at the beginning of a later fragment, placed somewhere in the middle of the whole. If these two distinct segments of the *Tales* have the same textual history, then it is likely that no part of the *Tales* has a separate textual history from the rest.

This does not mean that no part of the *Tales* was ever published distinct from the rest in Chaucer's lifetime. One cannot prove a negative, and the reference to the Wife of Bath in the *Envoy to Bukton* may be taken as implying that Bukton at least knew her *Prologue*, which is consistent with publication of this section during Chaucer's lifetime. However, this separate publication (if it did happen) appears to have left no trace in the manuscript tradition.[6] Accordingly, if Hengwrt has the best text of the *Wife of Bath's*

5.   This analysis will be published either in Solopova's forthcoming edition of the *General Prologue* or in the next volume of the *Canterbury Tales* Project *Occasional Papers*. It appears that the differences in the textual histories are due partly to a switch of exemplars between the two parts in individual manuscripts, and partly to the likelihood that the ancestors of some of the fundamental groups defined in Manly and Rickert (1940) and Robinson (1997) were considerably closer to *O* in the *General Prologue* than they are in the *Wife of Bath's Prologue*.

6.   As well as the apparent identity of the textual history of these two parts of the *Tales*, no early manuscript represents anything but a full text of the whole *Tales*. We have no early manuscript containing just the *Wife of*

Prologue (as it clearly has) and of the *General Prologue* (though here the Ellesmere text is extremely close to the Hengwrt text, as is not the case in the first half of the *Wife of Bath's Prologue*), then it is likely that Hengwrt has the best text throughout the *Tales*.

Of course, Hengwrt can only have the best text where it has a text at all. This brings us to the second question: Does Hengwrt include all the *Tales* and the whole text of the *Tales*? It is notorious that other manuscripts have many lines, and even whole links and tales, which are not present in Hengwrt. Norman summarizes these in pages 193-200 of his the *Textual Tradition of the Canterbury Tales* (1985). By including these 'extra passages' in his edition, though only in an appendix, he leaves open the possibility that at least some of them might have been written by Chaucer and might have been intended to be part of the *Tales*. However, as he points out, the primacy of the Hengwrt text where we have it means that scholars must explain, for each case, why the passage is absent from Hengwrt and why it should be included in the *Tales*. We cannot simply presume that a particular line, passage or tale is by Chaucer just because it is found in a particular manuscript (but not Hengwrt), is included in most editions, and has been well-loved by generations of readers.

This question is related to the issue of possible revisions of the *Tales*. It is argued that the presence of much extra material in Ellesmere and its absence in Henwgrt, alongside other differences, suggests that Hengwrt is a 'first edition' and Ellesmere a 'second edition' of the *Tales*, and that Chaucer was responsible for both (Fisher 1988).[7] Our investigations of the *Wife of Bath's Prologue*, now confirmed by our work on the *General Prologue*, suggest that there is no evidence that Chaucer ever issued a line-by-line, word-by-word revision of the *Tales*. If there had been such a revision, then we would expect to see two competing sets of *O*

Bath's Prologue or just the *General Prologue*, and the stemmatic analyses show no evidence that any such manuscript ever existed.

7.   Benson also argues for two 'lifetime' editions of the *Tales*, but suggests a different relationship between them. According to his account, there may have been an earlier version lacking the tales of the Manciple and the Parson, while the later version (represented by the Ellesmere order and contents) was Chaucer's 'final' version. He suggests that Hengwrt represents a scribal attempt to reorder the *Tales* after they had become disordered in the exemplar (1981: 100-101, 106).

variants in distinct sets of manuscripts. Each set of *O* variants
would have the same authorial character as was noted above, and
each would be differently distributed across the manuscripts.
Instead, both in the *Wife of Bath's Prologue* and in the *General Prologue* we see only one group of *O* variants, and in each of these
sections we find this one group of variants in broadly the same
manuscripts (throughout **Hg, Ch, Ad**[1] and **En**[3]), and in parts of
others. If there had been such a revision, the most likely place to
find it would have been in manuscripts descended from what we
call the *α* exemplar. Analysis of the *Wife of Bath's Prologue* suggests
the existence of this early and now lost exemplar (Robinson 1997:
103-104). This appears to have been the ancestor of the *ab* groups
of manuscripts, of parts (at least) of Ellesmere, and to have been
closely related to the manuscript used by Caxton in preparing his
second edition. However, so far as we have been able to judge
from the study of manuscripts close to *α* (the *ab* manuscripts,
Caxton's second edition and the second half of the *Wife of Bath's
Prologue* in Ellesmere) where both Hengwrt and *α* have the same
lines they seem to have had virtually the same text.[8] There is
certainly nothing like the word-by-word variation between competing and authorial variants that one finds in, for example, the
opening lines of the *Legend of Good Women*.[9]

However, Hengwrt and *α* do not appear to have had the same
lines and only the same lines. In the *Wife of Bath's Prologue, α*
appears to have had some 26 lines in five different passages, the
so-called 'added passages.'[10] The authorial character of these lines
and their presence in a witness apparently so close to Chaucer's
original are strong arguments that Chaucer did indeed write them
and at some time include them in the text of the *Wife of Bath's
Prologue*. The overall effect of several of these passages is to
coarsen the Wife's character, ascribing a crude, violent and

8. Thus Solopova's conclusion regarding the 'added passages' and these
two exemplars: 'The presence or absence of these passages could have been
their main or even their only distinction' (1997b: 142).

9. In her analysis of possible authorial variants in the *Wife of Bath's
Prologue*, Solopova suggests that the readings *experiment/experience* in line 1
and *for sothe/for sithe* in line 46 might be authorial (1997a: 138-39). Cf.
Robinson 1997: 129-30 n. 21.

10. In the Project's numbering these passages appear after lines 44, 574,
589, 604 and 694.

promiscuous sexuality to her which cannot be paralleled outside these passages. I have suggested elsewhere that Chaucer wrote these passages when he intended the Wife to tell what is now the *Shipman's Tale*. Scholars have long presumed, on internal evidence, that Chaucer originally had this tale told by the Wife, and that tale's rude sexuality would be appropriate to the character of the Wife created by these passages. It seems that he later decided to give the Wife the tale she now has, stressing social mastery rather than sexual domination, and accordingly deleted these passages as inappropriate to the new and more subtle characterization he now intended (Robinson 1997: 125-26).

It appears from this that O, the exemplar of both Hengwrt and α, was Chaucer's working copy. He marked these passages for deletion in this working copy. Most early copies (including Hengwrt) respected these marks for deletion and did not include the passages. However, at least one early copy, α, did not respect these marks and included the passages. The treatment of other passages might have been different: Chaucer might have marked lines for deletion which Hengwrt (wrongly) included and other early copies (rightly) excluded (the presence of lines 253-54 of the *General Prologue* in Hengwrt, and their absence from α, might be due to this). In other cases, lines may be absent from Hengwrt through simple miscopying, and their appearance in α and other early copies is then good evidence of their authenticity. The couplet appearing after line 638 of the *General Prologue* in Ellesmere, apparently missing through eyeskip in Hengwrt, seems an instance of this (Blake 1985: 193).

This analysis does not suggest that Chaucer issued two versions of the *Tales*. Rather, these apparent authorial variations are due to different scribes reacting in different ways to what they saw in O, Chaucer's working copy. One might explain in the same way other instances of variation involving whole lines, passages and larger units of text, such as the presence or absence of the *Man of Law's Epilogue* and of the *Canon's Yeoman's Prologue* and *Tale*, the uncertainties surrounding the 'Host stanza', the 'modern instances' and the 'Adam stanza', and the different versions of the *Nun's Priest's Prologue*.

These uncertainties suggest that in some places, at least, O was somewhat disordered and ambiguous—exactly as one would expect from an author's working draft of an unfinished work. In some cases, Hengwrt might have interpreted *O* correctly (as apparently in the omission of the so-called 'added passages' in the *Wife of Bath's Prologue*); in other cases we might reasonably prefer the version found in other witnesses. As Norman suggests, each case must be examined separately, on its own merits and on the base of close analysis of what is actually in the tradition.

This picture of the state of *O* as apparently rather disordered might influence our answer to the third question posed above: Does Hengwrt have the best tale order? Attention focuses here on the sequence *Squire's Tale/Merchant's Tale/Franklin's Tale* found in Hengwrt. It is clear that the scribe first received these tales without any links. However, he expected links to arrive and so copied the tales in this order and left spaces between the tales for the links. Later, linking passages did arrive and the scribe copied the links into the spaces he had left between the Squire and Merchant and between the Merchant and Franklin: this is the clear evidence of the spacing and different inks in the manuscript.

In Ellesmere these three tales appear in the order Merchant/ Squire/Franklin—that is, reversing the order of the Squire and Merchant. Furthermore, in Ellesmere the passage linking the Merchant and Squire (here called Link 17, following the *Canterbury Tales* numeration devised by Norman) is nearly identical to the passage linking the Merchant and Franklin in Hengwrt, and the passage linking the Squire and Franklin in Ellesmere (Link 20) is nearly identical to the passage linking the Squire and Merchant in Hengwrt. One may put this as follows:

Hengwrt: Squire—Link 20—Merchant—Link 17—Franklin
Ellesmere: Merchant—Link 17—Squire—Link 20—Franklin.

The question as to which of these orders is correct—that is, whether the order should be Squire/Merchant as Hengwrt has it, or Merchant/Squire as in Ellesmere—might be resolved by scrutiny of the text of the links. The matter has been studied recently by Larry Benson and Helen Cooper, and I here summarize their arguments (Benson 1981; Cooper 1995). The third line of Link 20 (*CT* V.673) in Hengwrt, linking the Squire and Merchant, reads thus:

Quod the Marchant considerynge thy youthe...

The same line in Ellesmere, linking the Squire and Franklin, reads:

Quod the Frankeleyn considerynge thy youthe...

Here, the Hengwrt text is one syllable short of a regular pentameter, while in Ellesmere it is regular. In line 696 Hengwrt again reads *Marchant* where Ellesmere has *Frankeleyn*, and again Hengwrt is one syllable short and Ellesmere is regular. In line V.699 Ellesmere is again regular:

That knowe I wel sire quod the Frankeleyn,

while this time Hengwrt has one syllable too many:

That knowe I wel sire quod the Marchant certeyn.

As Benson observes, it can hardly be chance that three times within a few lines Hengwrt is less regular than Ellesmere by one syllable, and that in each case the one syllable is the difference between the disyllable *Marchant* and the trisyllable *Frankeleyn*.

Benson and Cooper point to similar anomalies in the text of Link 17. The opening lines of the link (*CT* V.1-3) read very easily in Ellesmere, where they introduce the Squire:

Squier com neer if it youre will be
And sey somwhat of loue for certes ye
Konnen ther on as much as any man...

However, they read very awkwardly in Hengwrt, where they introduce the Franklin:

Sire Frankeleyn com neer if it youre will be
And sey vs a tale for certes ye
Konnen ther on as much as any man...

Not only is the first line now metrically clumsy, but the *ther on* in the third line has no referent.

From this Benson and Cooper argue that the Ellesmere version of the links is original and Chaucerian and the Hengwrt version the result of scribal tinkering, and thus that the Ellesmere order Merchant/Squire/Franklin for these three tales is correct, and not the Hengwrt order. To these arguments our work on the *Wife of Bath's Prologue* provides strong further support. The metrical difficulties in the Hengwrt version of the links appear the more anomalous in view of Solopova's demonstration that (despite common opinion) Hengwrt usually has a significantly more regular metre than Ellesmere (1997a). Most of all, the Ellesmere order appears to have been the order of α, the very early exemplar we think was copied (like Hengwrt itself) direct from Chaucer's working draft of the *Tales*. We find this order in the *a* manuscripts and (most striking of all) in Caxton's second edition, which introduces this order rather than that found in his first edition, presumably on the model of the 'better' manuscript he used in preparing this second edition, a manuscript which appears to have been very close to α. Locating this order in α places it very close to *O* itself.

This has far-reaching conclusions. If α has the correct order here, and Hengwrt the incorrect order, what does this tell us of the relative precedence of the α and Hengwrt copies? Once the tales and links had got into the wrong order, as they are in Hengwrt, it is very hard to see how any fifteenth-century scribe or editor could have put them back in the right order. This suggests that the α exemplar was copied from *O* while the papers in *O* containing the sequence Merchant-Link 17—Squire—Link 20—Franklin were in the correct order. However, these papers in *O* then became disordered, and Hengwrt was copied from them while they were in this disordered state.

The evidence of Hengwrt itself allows us to go beyond this. It is clear, as I noted above, that the Hengwrt scribe received the three tales without the links. He knew that there were links, and so left spaces for them as he copied the tales. But, without the links, he did not know the correct order of the tales and so copied them in the wrong order. When the links did arrive he would have seen that he had copied the tales in the wrong order. The solution seemed simple: just adjust the links slightly, for example substituting *Marchant* for *Frankeleyn* in Link 20, and similarly in Link 17, so that the links are now made to join the tales as copied. Thus, the amendment of the links is the direct result of the confusion in the Hengwrt copying.

There is a further consequence to this: the same 'incorrect' order of these three tales, and the sequence Squire—Link 20—Merchant, found in Hengwrt, is also found in many other manuscripts (essentially, those labelled type *d* by Manly/Rickert and Benson). Many of these manuscripts use exactly the same altered Links 17 and 20 as does Hengwrt. I suggested above that these links were altered as a direct result of the Hengwrt scribe's error in copying these three tales in the wrong order. Yet it is not possible that the manuscripts of type *d* are copies from Hengwrt itself, for there are far too many differences between these manuscripts and Hengwrt for this to be the case. But if they are not copies of Hengwrt, how do they come to have the same erroneous order, and links, as Hengwrt?

The only possible explanation is that the text of the links was not altered just in Hengwrt. It was altered, probably by the scribe's supervisor, in the exemplar, that is, in *O* itself. The three tales were then placed in the exemplar in the same order as they are copied in Hengwrt, with the now-altered text of the links connecting them. This newly reshuffled *O*, then, in turn became the exemplar not only of the type *d* copies but also of Manly and Rickert's *c* group and the additional group I label *f*. In the case of the sequence Squire—Link 20—Merchant, almost all the manuscripts of the *c*, *d* and *f* groups—over 20 manuscripts in all—inherit the same order and the same links as Hengwrt from this reordered and altered *O*.[11] This explanation is very close to the theory Norman offers of the 'developing copy text'. It is only common

11. The disposition of the various forms of these links and tales in the manuscripts are conveniently summarized in the charts (made by Robert Campbell) in Manly and Rickert (1940: II, 494-95; see also III, 480-81 and IV, 484-85). Six manuscripts have Link 17 introducing the Franklin (**Hg, Ht, Ii, Mm, Pl** and **Pw**; of these **Mm** and **Pw** are *c* group manuscripts, and **Ii** is usually *b* but shows clear evidence of contamination). Of these six, only three (**Hg, Ht** and **Ii**) place the link after the Merchant and before the Franklin (**Mm** and **Pw** have it between the Clerk and Franklin, and **Pl** is uncertain). A considerably larger number of manuscripts have the Hengwrt order of Squire—Link 20—Merchant: Manly and Rickert name 21 including **Hg**. These are **Dl, En², Fi, Gl, Ha², Mg, Mm, Nl, Pw, Py, Ra³, Sl¹, Tc¹**, all of which are in Manly and Rickert's *c/d* constant groups; **Bw, Ld², Ln, Ry²**, all in the *f* group of Robinson 1997; and the anomalous **Hg, Ht, Ii** and **Ra²**. Two other *c/d* manuscripts, **Lc** and **Ph³**, also apparently had this arrangement. The inheritance of this part of the **Hg** arrangement, but not of the other part of the **Hg** arrangement, by the *c/d* and *f* groups suggests that yet further disordering took place in the manuscripts before the ancestors of *c/d* and *f* were copied.

sense, as Norman puts it, that *O* hardly remained stable: sections might be lost, added, reordered, and texts altered. This appears to be what happened with *O* in the section under discussion.

The explanation offered in the last paragraph has several consequences. Looked at one way, it diminishes the authority of Hengwrt. It suggests that at least one copy, what we call the α exemplar, was made from *O* before Hengwrt itself was copied. Further, this α exemplar was made at a time when the pile of papers and fragments constituting *O* was in better order than when Hengwrt was copied. One might reasonably argue from this that the α order, found in Ellesmere and other manuscripts, represents Chaucer's conception.

However, looked at another way, this explanation greatly increases the authority of Hengwrt. If a scribal editor altered the text of the links in *O* as the direct result of the Hengwrt scribe's having copied these three tales in the wrong order, as I have argued above, then Hengwrt must be a direct copy of *O* itself. In our assessment of the *Wife of Bath's Prologue* and of the *General Prologue* we argue that Hengwrt is a direct copy of *O* on rather circumstantial evidence—in essence, the excellence of the text. This explanation adds a further layer of probability to this argument.

This position—that Hengwrt has the best text, where it has a text, but may not have the best order—is close to the 'soft Hengwrtism' described by Hanna. The fourth question takes this further. If we trust the text of Hengwrt where it has a text (as its status as the only extant direct copy of Chaucer's own working copy of the *Tales* suggests we should), should we not also trust the spelling? The spelling of the Hengwrt/Ellesmere scribe has been closely studied by several scholars in the last two decades (Samuels 1983a; Samuels 1983b; Smith 1985; Benson 1992; Smith 1995). Their conclusions are identical: the Hengwrt/Ellesmere scribe was an extremely thorough and skilled 'translator' of the various spellings found in his exemplar into a single spelling system in his own copies. This can be seen clearly in this scribe's stint in Trinity Gower (MS R.3.2), where comparison with the other scribes, and with the spelling of Hengwrt and Ellesmere, shows that he had his own precisely articulated spelling system, and that he was able to impose that system on an exemplar with a very different system of spelling.

Just how consistent the spelling system of the Hengwrt/Elles-mere scribe is, and how different it is from that of other scribes, can now be evaluated yet more exactly through two new and pow-erful tools available to us. The first tool is the complete Okoyama concordance to Norman's edition of the Hengwrt manuscript (Blake *et al.* 1994). This presents in marvellously compact and usable form every instance of every distinct spelling in Hengwrt. The second tool is the spelling databases for all the manuscripts of the *Tales* being prepared as part of the work of the *Canterbury Tales* Project. These go further than the Okoyama concordance in preserving all instances of abbreviation in the manuscripts, in distinguishing homographs, in sorting all spellings by headword and grammatical function, and in providing information for all the extant manuscripts, not just for Hengwrt. To date only the spelling databases for the *Wife of Bath's Prologue* have been pub-lished; that for the *General Prologue* is now complete and will be published during 1998 (Robinson 1996; Solopova forthcoming). Preliminary analysis of these, concentrating on the spellings in Hengwrt and in the *Wife of Bath's Prologue* and the *General Prologue* alone, confirms the extraordinary consistency of this scribe's spell-ing system. For example, from the Okoyama concordance of Hengwrt we find the following instances where the scribe had common alternatives available to him but consistently uses one and only one spelling:

> *mayde* 58 instances, never *maid, maide, mayd* etc. (*WBP/GP*: c. 100 *maid-*, 160 *mayd-*)
>
> *hoost* 47 instances, never *host*; but *hostilry/hostiler* etc., 13 instances, never *hoostilrye/hoostiler* (*WBP/GP*: c. 35 *host-*, 46 *hoost-*)
>
> *wight* 140 instances, never *wyght* (*WBP/GP*: c. 140 with *wy-*, 400 with *wi-*)
>
> *word* 149 instances, never *worde* (*WBP/GP*: c. 225 with *word*, 250 with *worde*)
>
> *propre/proprely* 32 instances, never *proper* (*WBP/GP*: c. 110 with *propre*, 45 with *proper*)

Most remarkable is a group of common words in which Hengwrt/ Ellesmere share spellings with -*oo*-, which are found almost nowhere else:

dooth: This occurs as the spelling of the 3rd singular present indicative ten times in *GP/WBP* in **Hg** and **El**; apart from in these two manuscripts it occurs only some six times in *GP* and *WBP* across five different manuscripts, out of a total of some three hundred instances of this part of the verb in the manuscripts of these tales.

namoore: This is the invariable spelling of the Hengwrt/Ellesmere scribe throughout Hengwrt, occurring six times in *WBP* and *GP* (and 88 times throughout Hengwrt); it is used by no other manuscript in these parts of the *Tales*, in some 150 occurrences of the adverb. The line 'He slepte namoore, than dooth a nyghtyngale' (*CT*, I.98) is found with this spelling in no manuscript written by any other scribe.

moore: This spelling is found 25 times in *GP* and *WBP* in Hengwrt and Ellesmere but in no other manuscript at all in *WBP* (from some 450 occurrences of the adverb) and five times only in two manuscripts in *GP* (these are **Ld²** and **Ch**, known from other evidence to be close to **Hg**).

These, and many more instances, reinforce the impression of a careful, almost pedantic, consistency in this scribe's application of a single spelling system.[12] However, as one might expect, there are indeed inconsistencies, and these new tools enable them to be revealed and carefully analysed. At the beginning of our analysis we expected that these inconsistencies of spelling might have arisen from the different exemplars used by the scribe. In my stemmatic analysis of the witnesses of the *Wife of Bath's Prologue* (Robinson 1997) I suggested that three different exemplars underlie the copies of the *Wife of Bath's Prologue* in the Hengwrt and Ellesmere manuscripts. I argued that Hengwrt is copied throughout from *O*, Chaucer's own working copy of the *Tales*, whereas Ellesmere is copied from a group *e* exemplar (itself descended from an *e/f* exemplar, and closely related to the exemplar used by **Gg** and **Ha⁴**) up to around line 400, from which point it is copied from the *α* exemplar.[13] In view of the ideas of

12. This consistency in distinctive spellings across Hengwrt and Ellesmere is a further argument against the hypothesis, advanced by Vance Ramsey, that the two manuscripts were written by different scribes (Doyle and Parkes 1978; Ramsey 1982; Samuels 1983b; Ramsey 1986; Doyle 1995).

13. At the time of writing stemmatic analysis of the textual tradition of the *General Prologue* had not settled the affiliations of Hengwrt and Ellesmere in this section of the *Tales*. It seems likely that Hengwrt is once more a copy of

'mischsprachen' and 'relict' forms developed by Benskin, Laing and Samuels in relation to scribes copying from exemplars with different spelling systems, it seemed probable that one would find differences in the spelling in these three sections of text, differences which would be attibutable to the three separate exemplars (Benskin and Laing 1981; Samuels 1983b). Close analysis of these 'relict' forms might in turn reveal something of the exemplars themselves. One might expect traces of Chaucer's own spelling and punctuation to survive in the copy in Hengwrt, but to be lost in the copy in Ellesmere, especially since the first half of the *Wife of Bath's Prologue* in Ellesmere was copied from an exemplar at least two copies removed from Chaucer's own copy whereas Hengwrt may be copied direct from *O* itself.

However, study of these ranges of text of the *Wife of Bath's Prologue* in Hengwrt and Ellesmere showed something rather different. Far from there being distinct shifts in spelling matching the shifts of exemplar, there seemed to be virtually no shifts of spelling at all, or none which easily confirm this hypothesis. This can be seen most clearly in the first and second halves of the *Wife of Bath's Prologue* in Ellesmere. My analysis focused on *that* used pleonastically (in constructions such as *whan that*) and on spellings with *-uer-*, *-ver-* in *euere*, *euery* and so on. Throughout both Ellesmere and Hengwrt the scribe uses both abbreviated and unabbreviated spellings of these: þ† and *that*, u̇/v̇ and *uer/ver*. In the terms of Benskin, Laing and Samuels, all these spellings were in the scribe's 'active repertoire', and it seemed likely that the scribe might have been influenced in his choice of one or other spelling by the different exemplars used in the two halves of the *Wife of Bath's Prologue* in Ellesmere. What I found may be summarized as follows:

0-400	þ†: 4 *that*: 17	u̇/v̇: 13 *uer/ver*: 20
400-end	þ†: 14 *that*:13	u̇/v̇: 18 *uer/ver*: 23
totals:	þ†: 18 *that*: 30	u̇/v̇: 31 *uer/ver*: 43

O. Ellesmere is at least as close to Hengwrt throughout the *General Prologue* as it is in the second half of the *Wife of Bath's Prologue* (the 'added passages' aside). However, it may be a copy of *a* once more, with *a* here being very near Hengwrt. Other key manuscripts (notably Christchurch and perhaps Laud Misc. 739) may be copies of Hengwrt itself, or descended independently from manuscripts very close to Hengwrt.

These figures suggest a preference for the uncontracted form of pleonastic *that* in the first half of the *Wife of Bath's Prologue* in Ellesmere; in the second half the two forms are evenly distributed. Taken on their own, they might be used to support a hypothesis that the exemplar in this first half used the form *that* and this has left its mark in the copy. However, compare the figures for these forms for the same divisions of text in Hengwrt:

0-400	þᵗ: 12 *that*: 22	u̇/v̇: 9 *uer/ver*: 23
400-end	þᵗ: 12 *that*: 13	u̇/v̇: 11 *uer/ver*: 27
totals:	þᵗ: 30 *that*: 35	u̇/v̇: 20 *uer/ver*: 50

And compare too the figures for these forms for the whole of the *General Prologue* in these two manuscripts:

Ellesmere	þᵗ: 17 *that*: 11	u̇/v̇: 17 *uer/ver*: 49
Hengwrt	þᵗ: 24 *that*: 4	u̇/v̇: 15 *uer/ver*: 54

In the context of these figures the shift in treatment of þᵗ/*that* between the two halves of Ellesmere seems less decisive. In the *General Prologue*, Hengwrt shows an even more marked preference for contracted *that* forms than the preference for uncontracted *that* in Ellesmere in the *Wife of Bath's Prologue*: 24 þᵗ for 4 *that*. Yet in the *Wife of Bath's Prologue* Hengwrt reverses this preference, having more uncontracted *that* forms than contracted. Should we presume a change of exemplar here, too, to account for this one spelling shift? Note, too, that in Ellesmere the proportion of contracted and uncontracted *uer/ver* spellings works in reverse between the *General Prologue* and the *Wife of Bath's Prologue*, from a preponderance of uncontracted forms in the former to nearer equality in the latter.

The easiest explanation of these inconsistencies is that they are simply inconsistencies. The scribe's spelling system is so strongly marked that it is immune to influence from the exemplar, and indeed from anywhere else: it is inconsistent in its own way, just as it is consistent in its own way.[14] Further evidence for this may be found in tabulating the points where the two manuscripts agree in

14. It follows that inferences drawn from these inconsistencies about 'relict' forms, or about shifts in the scribe's practice, may be misleading, as Benson (1992: 73) comments of Samuels' arguments ('we can never be sure whose relicts we are dealing with').

having exactly the same spelling of these forms at points where they have the same word. This may be summarized as follows:

		instances	agreements	disagreements	
GP	þᵗ/that	27	20	7	74%
WBP 0-400	þᵗ/*that*	19	12	7	63%
WBP 400-end	þᵗ/*that*	23	16	7	70%
GP	u̇,v̇/*uer, ver*	66	50	16	75%
WBP 0-400	u̇,v̇/*uer, ver*	30	23	7	77%
WBP 400-end	u̇,v̇/*uer, ver*	38	27	11	71%

Where the two manuscripts have a preference of around 70/30 for one form over another, as is broadly so in these instances, if the choice of form at any one point is simple chance, then the two will tend to agree and disagree in about the same 70/30 proportion.[15] That is exactly what happens here. It is as if the scribe simply does not 'see' what is in the exemplar, but is driven as by a slightly faulty internal clock to be regular in some ways, irregular in others.[16]

It follows from all this that both the remarkable consistency and the occasional inconsistency are properties of the spelling system of this scribe. The spelling system is very much his own. Accordingly, it could be quite distinct from that of Chaucer. However, it is also possible that it could be the same as Chaucer's—that the scribe learnt this spelling system from Chaucer and is applying it. Indeed, there is some evidence for this. Elizabeth Solopova has remarked that the punctuation system used by this scribe differs

15. In simple terms, if the preference for one form over another were 50/50 then the two might agree around 50% of the time. As the preference rises, so will the rate of agreement, to the point where one form is preferred all the time and the two so agree 100% of the time.

16. Although the concordance and database tools provide access to all the spellings, I have chosen (like Samuels, Smith and Benson) to focus on just a few spellings. This selective and impressionistic method might skew analysis. Computer-assisted tools which will allow meaningful comparision of the whole range of spellings in different witnesses, to deliver useful statistical measures of likeness and consistency, may here provide real assistance. Cladistic and database tools have helped stemmatic analysis; spelling analyis might be similarly advantaged.

markedly from that found in other manuscripts (1996). She has suggested that this scribe's punctuation is rhetorical and poetic, and so likely to have originated with Chaucer himself. If the scribe learnt to punctuate from Chaucer, he might also have learnt to spell from Chaucer.

Samuels and Benson have also compared the spelling system of Hengwrt and Ellesmere with what can be deduced about Chaucer's own spelling (Samuels 1983a; Benson 1992). Their findings are not encouraging. They point out several particulars (spellings of the past of *se*; forms of adverb *yet*; and a few others) in which Chaucer's spelling appears to have been different from that of this scribe.[17] Evidence of the unreliability of this scribe's spelling as a guide to Chaucer's may also be found in the scribe's handling of metre, and especially of final and medial *e*. From a study of the metre of the early manuscripts of the *Wife of Bath's Prologue* Solopova concluded that the scribe was insensitive to metre (1997a). While this might encourage trust in the scribe, as less likely to try to 'improve' the metre, the scribe might well have inserted or removed an *e* where his spelling system—and not Chaucer's metre—demanded it. This appears to have been very often the case. In many instances of medial *-uer-/-ver-* in words like *euery, euere* (and *Auerill* in the first line of Hengwrt) the medial *-e-* can have no metrical value: it may be *svarabhakti*, orthographic or merely conventional, but not metrical.

This article asks: 'Can we trust Hengwrt?' The answer is: 'Yes, in parts.' It has the best text, where it has a text, but it may not have all the text which Chaucer wrote, nor have it all in the best order, nor spell the text as Chaucer spelt it. However, the excellence of the text and the even more problematic spelling and metre of other manuscripts confirm that Hengwrt is the best choice for a base text for an edition, as Manly and Rickert, the *Variorum* editors and Norman himself have all insisted. How far we must depart from Hengwrt, on the basis of what is in other manuscripts and our sense of Chaucer's metre, is likely to be the centre of

17. Thus, Samuels (1983a) and Benson (1992). However, Samuels and Benson differ in their identification of 'Chaucerian' spellings not present in Hengwrt and Ellesmere and in their conclusions. Samuels sees *Equatorie of the Planetis* as Chaucer's autograph whereas Benson (following Partridge 1992) denies this.

future scholarly debate about the text of the *Tales*. We are still learning to trust Hengwrt; now we have to learn how to distrust it wisely.

WORKS CITED

Benskin, M., and M. Laing
    1981   'Translations and *Mischsprachen* in Middle English Manuscripts', in M. Benskin and M.L. Samuels (eds.), *So Meny People Longages and Tonges: Philological Essays in Scots and Mediaeval English Presented to Angus McIntosh* (Edinburgh: Benskin & Samuels): 55-106.

Benson, L.D.
    1981   'The Order of *The Canterbury Tales*', *Studies in the Age of Chaucer* 3: 77-120.
    1992   'Chaucer's Spelling Reconsidered', *English Manuscript Studies 1100–1700* 3: 1-28.

Blake, N.F.
    1979   'The Relationship between the Hengwrt and Ellesmere Manuscripts of the *Canterbury Tales*', *Essays and Studies* NS 32: 1-18.
    1985   *The Textual Tradition of the Canterbury Tales* (London: Arnold).
    1995   'The Ellesmere Text in the Light of the Hengwrt Manuscript', in Stevens and Woodward 1995: 205-24.

Blake, N.F. (ed.)
    1980   *The Canterbury Tales by Geoffrey Chaucer, edited from the Hengwrt Manuscript* (London: Arnold).

Blake, N.F., *et al.*
    1994   *A New Concordance to The Canterbury Tales based on Blake's Text edited from the Hengwrt Manuscript* (Okayama: University Education Press).

Blake, N.F., and P.M.W. Robinson (eds.)
    1993   *The Canterbury Tales Project Occasional Papers* 1 (Oxford: Office for Humanities Communication).
    1997   *The Canterbury Tales Project Occasional Papers* 2 (London: Office for Humanities Communication).

Cooper, H.
    1995   'The Order of the Tales in the Ellesmere Manuscript', in Stevens and Woodward 1995: 245-62.

Doyle, A.I.
    1995   'The Copyist of the Ellesmere *Canterbury Tales*', in Stevens and Woodward 1995: 49-67.

Doyle, A.I., and M.B. Parkes
    1978   'The Production of Copies of the *Canterbury Tales* and *Confessio Amantis* in the early Fifteenth Century', in M.B. Parkes and A.G. Watson (eds.), *Medieval Scribes, Manuscripts and Libraries: Essays Presented to N.R. Ker* (London: Scolar Press): 163-210.

Fisher, J.H.
 1988   'Animadversions on the Text of Chaucer', *Speculum* 63: 779-93.
Hanna, R.W.
 1989   'The Hengwrt Manuscript and the Canon of *The Canterbury Tales*',
             English Manuscript Studies 1100–1700, 1: 64-84.
 1995   '(The) Editing of (the) Ellesmere Text', in Stevens and Woodward
             1995: 225-44.
Manly, J.M., and E. Rickert (eds.)
 1940   *The Text of The Canterbury Tales: Studied on the Basis of All Known
             Manuscripts* (8 vols.; Chicago: Chicago University Press).
Partridge, S.
 1992   'The Vocabulary of *The Equatorie of the Planetis* and the Question of
             Authorship', *English Manuscript Studies 1100–1700* 3: 29-37.
Ramsey, R.V.
 1982   'The Hengwrt and Ellesmere Manuscripts of the *Canterbury Tales*:
             Different Scribes', *Studies in Bibliography* 35: 133-54.
 1986   'Paleography and Scribes of Shared Training', *Studies in the Age of
             Chaucer* 8: 107-44.
Ricks, C. (ed.)
 1988   *A.E. Housman: Collected Poems and Selected Prose* (Harmondsworth:
             Penguin).
Robinson, P.M.W.
 1997   'A Stemmatic Analysis of the Fifteenth-Century Witnesses to The
             Wife of Bath's Prologue', in Blake and Robinson 1997: 69-132.
Robinson, P.M.W. (ed.)
 1996   *The Wife of Bath's Prologue on CD-ROM* (Cambridge: Cambridge
             University Press, The *Canterbury Tales* Project).
Samuels, M.L.
 1983a   'Chaucer's Spelling', in D. Gray and E.G. Stanley (eds.), *Middle Eng-
             lish Studies Presented to Norman Davis* (Oxford: Oxford University
             Press: 17-37.
 1983a   'The Scribe of the Hengwrt and Ellesmere Manuscripts of *The
             Canterbury Tales*', *Studies in the Age of Chaucer* 5: 49-65.
Smith, J.J.
 1985   *Studies in the Language of some Manuscripts of Gower's Confessio Amantis*
             (PhD thesis, Glasgow: University of Glasgow).
 1995   'The Language of the Ellesmere Manuscript', in Stevens and Wood-
             ward 1995: 69-86.
Solopova, E.
 1996   'The Survival of Chaucer's Punctuation in the Early Manuscripts of
             The Canterbury Tales' (unpublished paper given at the York
             Conference on Medieval Manuscripts).
 1997a   'Chaucer's Metre and Scribal Editing in the Early Manuscripts of
             The Canterbury Tales', in Blake and Robinson 1997: 143-64.
 1997b   'The Problem of Authorial Variants in The Wife of Bath's Pro-
             logue', in Blake and Robinson 1997: 133-42.

Solopova, E. (ed.)
    forthcoming *The General Prologue of The Canterbury Tales: An Electronic Edition*
        (Cambridge: Cambridge University Press).
Stevens, M., and D. Woodward (eds.)
    1995   *The Ellesmere Chaucer: Essays in Interpretation* (San Marino: Hunting-
        ton Library).

Personality and Styles of Affect in the *Canterbury Tales*

Irma Taavitsainen

> Personality: 1. *Psychol.* the sum total of all the behavioural and mental characteristics by means of which an individual is recognized as being unique 2. the distinctive character of a person that makes him socially attractive 3. a well-known person in a certain field, such as entertainment 4. a remarkable person (*Collins English Dictionary* 1993).

Introduction

It would be unusual to have expressions of personality in the sense of a unique individual in Middle English literature, just as it is unusual to have expressions of personal authority in moral or religious matters (Blake 1977: 104).[1] Fictional characters are rather instances of more general principles of the medieval world

1.   Chaucer's pilgrims in the *Canterbury Tales* are sketched according to literary or allegorical models, or they rely on the scientific doctrines of the day combined with contemporary common knowledge of features that signify status or character. Such codes were accessible to his audience but are lost for today's readers without further study. In the *General Prologue* the pilgrims are grouped according to the medieval hierarchy of social ranks and the descriptions are modelled on estates literature (Mann 1973). The Canterbury portraits have been studied from various angles, e.g., from literary, psychological, sociological, feminist and historicizing viewpoints, including a trend that deals with the characters as real, fully developed personalities. There is a rich scholarly literature (see Benson 1987 and recent bibliographies); criticism against the portraits representing both types and individuals has been advocated, e.g., by Morgan (1977).

order imposed on the microcosm of man by astrological influ- ences, physiognomical details, the ages of man, and various other grids (see, e.g., Burrow 1986). Against this background the essential questions are to what degree the characters represent social stereotypes, to what degree they stand for medieval ideals of personality in their behavioural patterns and mental traits, and how their personalities are mediated to us in their use of language. In this essay I attempt to combine recent research in pragmatics with linguistic stylistics in an approach which, according to Norman Blake, 'should be exploited much more than is currently the case' (1990: 103).

Definition of Personal Affect

I shall attempt to give an answer to the above questions by looking at the realization of personal affect, that is, how speakers' subjective emotions, feelings, moods and attitudes are embedded in language use. My aim is to find out how personal affect features connected with different characters reflect their personalities. People's behaviour in everyday life is in different ways conditioned by, and intertwined with, personal affect. Communicative styles show various degrees and foci of involvement according to the foregrounded locus of interest (Caffi and Janney 1994b).[2] Personal affect is a component of participant relations and finds outlets in various forms; thus it gives us a picture of the person's behavioural patterns and mental characteristics. It may exhibit more permanent qualities of emotion, with a long-term realization, for example, love, fondness, sadness or dislike, or more transient and volatile states of mind like anger, or dislike erupting into telling someone off. These outbursts of emotion can be called surge features. The basic realization system is like amplification on a stereo set; it can be turned on or off, and the volume can be adjusted (Martin 1992: 533). Personal affect seems to be a good tool for defining genre styles (Taavitsainen 1993 and 1995a), and

2. Traditionally three kinds of involvement have been established: speaker-centered ego-involvement, hearer-centered and content-centered involvement (Chafe 1985). This basic division has been developed in a number of studies, e.g., in more detailed descriptions of personal affect. See Caffi and Janney (1994a).

perhaps it can be extended to describing personalities as well.
Besides positive and negative affect (Biber and Finegan 1989),
other qualities can be distinguished, and I shall test whether they
are applicable to character description in the *Canterbury Tales*.
Social groups differ from one another in the degree to which
high or low involvement is viewed as necessary or valuable, and
ideals of personhood vary accordingly (Besnier 1994: 287).

Linguistic Features of Personal Affect

According to my earlier studies, outbursts of emotion in surge
features of personal affect include exclamations, swearing and
pragmatic particles. The speaker's or narrator's mental afflictions
or temporary states of mind find linguistic outlets in these features. Surge is a salient quality of personal affect in early modern
fiction, and interaction is another. The dichotomy between 'self'
and 'other' is expressed in a reference system of personal pronouns, questions and answers, comments and responses; speech
sequences with turn-taking are basic components of this system.
Indexical features of proximity also manifest involvement and
personal affect. These features bring the events to the immediate
experience of the reader by indicating that the action is simulta-
neous with the narration and that the things referred to are close
at hand. In addition, special elements like modal auxiliaries help
to build up the fictional world and act as space-building devices
(Taavitsainen 1997a). Linguistic features that encode personal
affect are mostly found in direct-speech quotations that imitate
natural speech, but fictional language may condense the contents
of a speech act so that one feature may stand for the whole speech
act and typify it (Fludernik 1993: 423-29). Suspense and reader
involvement are also created by linguistic features of personal
affect, and they have important textual functions in fiction
(Taavitsainen 1995b and 1998).

Personal Affect and Character Descriptions

It has been noted that oaths are a good index to the piety of
characters in the *Canterbury Tales*, and swearing provides another
index; the medieval period is a religious age, and blasphemous
abuses of religious language are revealing (Hughes 1991: 63;

Taavitsainen 1997b). The emotions expressed in swearing range from anger to surprise and incredulity, but swearing is not always linked to a surge of emotions, as these expressions are tied to character descriptions so that people swear from habit as well, and some do not swear at all. The characters that swear do so both in their own person and in their tales (see Elliott 1974: 240-84 and Hughes 1991: 62-89). Interjections are tied to genres, and a straightforward correlation between the character who narrates and the genre that unfolds is obvious: the Knight tells a courtly story, the Prioress a saint's legend, the Wife of Bath a kind of romance, the Miller a fabliau, etc.; interjections in them follow generic patterns established more widely in contemporary literature (Taavitsainen 1995a and 1997c). In Chaucer's works members of the nobility use high style, whereas the language of the lowest classes is rude. The division into courtly language versus *cherles termes* reflects a literary convention, but at the same time it refers to both actual social class and social ideals (Burnley 1983: 182-83). In Chaucer, Langland and Caxton words suggest the characters of people who speak them: words of abuse and low register indicate that their moral character is wicked, evil, angry or vulgar. This vocabulary acts as a contrast to the more elevated speech of the good characters (Blake 1977: 159).

Layers of Character Description

I have selected the Knight, the Prioress, the Wife of Bath and the Miller for closer scrutiny here. They provide counterpoints in this fictional world, they have distinctive character traits, and their social positions are explicit. The *Canterbury Tales* contains several layers, and my analysis tries to take this into account:

1. I shall first look at the character description in the *General Prologue*. The scope of introduction varies, but most of the portraits contain details of the physical appearance and speech habits of the pilgrims.

2. The frame story provides links between the tales and gives us snapshots of interaction between the characters, and their behavioural patterns come out. Differences are great when measured, for example, on a scale of politeness versus impoliteness (see Sell 1985). The report is

given by an eye-witness, the narrator pilgrim. He observes what is said and what happens. An eye-witness's position enhances the truthfulness of the story. The frame story is mostly told in the prologues of the tales, but the character's motivation for telling the story and other background facts may be included. In these parts it is mostly the narrator that has the floor, and the speeches display his or her language.

3.   The tales are told by the pilgrims; they are the narrators, and their personal comments may be revealing. The characters' speeches or indirect speeches quoting the actual words of the speakers are also significant, as they are tied to the genres. The final invocations indicate the teller's religious sensibilities, and thus in a religious age reveal his or her character (Hughes 1991: 67).

The Knight

1. The *General Prologue* outlines a portrait of an ideal knight, with attributes that give a stereotypical characterization. His speech habits are in accordance with this.

2. The frame story gives us an instance of the Knight's behaviour in reaction to the result of the lottery for sharing the turns:

> He seyde, 'Syn *I* shal bigynne the game,
> *What, welcome* be the cut, *a Goddes name!*
> *Now lat us ryde,* and *herkneth* what *I* seye' (I.853-55).

The reaction *what* conveys surprise, or gives him time to make up his mind. The following word, *welcome* shows his mental disposition, his readiness to take the challenge and collaborate for the common goal. Mild Christian swearing enforces the speech act of agreement. The concluding line contains the proximal deictic adverb *now*, and a performative *lat us ryde* calls for collaboration from the other parties and sets the scene. The imperative forms are addressed to the fictional characters but they also serve as an invitation to the reader/listener to stay in the company and participate in the journey. Thus they act as reader-involvement devices. This speech is condensed and typified in the sense that it contains the whole code of idealized behaviour of the knightly class.

3. The *Knight's Tale* deals with the upper classes, in accordance with the narrator's social position. The story has the traditional setting and the beginning calls for generic expectations: *Whilom, as olde stories tellen us* (I.859). The characters are noblemen, and the repertoire of surge features includes the following interjections: *allas, o/oo, lo/loo, a, weylawey* and *fy*. Swearing is also found, but in a refined form, as the characters swear by invocations, with proper names of classical gods in the vocative, collocated with the interjection *o* according to the Latinate model. Oaths are both pagan and Christian:

> *This worthy* duc answerde anon agayn,
> And seyde, '*This* is a short conclusioun
> …
> *Ye shul be deed, by myghty Mars the rede!*' (I.1742-47).

> *As fiers as leon* pulled out his swerd,
> And seyde thus: '*By God that sit above*' (I.1598-99).

There seems to be a pattern. An oath by the pagan god of war and cruel planet, Mars, enforces the proclamation of death, an extreme speech act: the proximal pronoun *this* underlines the deictic centre, the modal verb *shall* expresses the speaker's determination to bring the action about (Kerkhof 1982: 173-74), and the oath provides the climax. In contrast, Christian imagery is used in a speech accompanied by a brisk knightly action of pulling out a sword, which is emphasized by a simile. This usage is well in accordance with the portrait depicted in the *General Prologue*.

Mostly personal affect features describe the depth of emotions:

> *So greet* wepyng *was ther noon, certayn,*
> Whan *Ector* was ybroght, *al fressh* yslayn,
> To Troye. *Allas, the pitee that was ther* (I.2831-33).

The intensity of pity and grief is emphasized by the allusion, and the exclamatory sentence enhances the emotive tone of compassion. The interjection *allas* expresses the narrator's stance, but often it typifies the emotional state of grief more generally. For example, in the following the proximal deictic pronoun *this* serves to bring the events close, and *lo* focuses the audience's attention on this particular word:

> *Lo, alle thise* folk *so* caught were in hir las,
> Til they *for wo ful ofte seyde 'allas!'* (I.1951-52).

Intensified feelings may also be conveyed with strings of personal
affect features like direct questions, imperative forms, mild swearing, and exclamatory sentences. The strongest example is found
in a contemplation on love and the transitory nature of human
life. The repetition of *now* focuses the contrast and brings it to the
present moment, and, although third-person pronouns normally
have a distancing effect, here the combination of elements working in opposite directions is extremely effective. *Allas* is repeated
several times with elliptical sentences explaining the cause of grief
and sorrow:

> Allas, the wo! Allas, the peynes stronge,
> That I for yow have suffred, and so longe!
> Allas, the deeth! Allas, myn Emelye!
> Allas, departynge of oure compaignye!
> Allas, myn hertes queene! Allas, my wyf,
> Myn hertes lady, endere of my lyf!
> What is this world? What asketh men to have?
> Now with his love, now in his colde grave
> Allone, withouten any compaignye.
> Fare wel, my sweete foo, myn Emelye! (I.2771-80).

In such passages the speeches form long monologues so that
the contemplative mood takes over and the plot level becomes
distanced. Thus they serve as descriptive pauses (cf. Toolan 1988:
55-56). The style is emotional, and a wide repertoire of personal
affect features is used to convey the heightened feelings of love
and compassion; yet the emphasis is more on permanent features
of affect than transitory surge. The key verb here is *suffer*, depict-
ing a private state of mind; the other sentences are either exclamatory without a verb, or generic questions about the purpose of
life. In these contemplative passages the 'volume' of emotion is
'turned on' and the emotions overwhelm the speaker's mind; the
reader is engaged to feel compassion, pose the same questions
and find the same answers. The elevated style of the story is
mainly created by personal affect features, and is well in accordance with the chivalric code and ideals of courtly culture. The
final line of the tale expresses a pious wish: *And God save al this
faire compaignye! Amen* (I.3108).

The Prioress

1. The portrait of the Prioress contains subtle irony. She is described according to the conventions of courtly love, her bias to secular matters is shown by various details (see below), and in her speech the greatest oath is *by Seinte Loy* (I.120).

2. Her role in the overall frame story is minor, and the *Prologue* to her tale shows no interaction. Instead, she indulges in a prayer with frequent exclamations and invocations to the Virgin Mary according to the Latinate model, in a conscious attempt to build up an elevated state of mind. Thus the high style focuses on self-presentation of her own person, and is in accordance with the ironical mode of the portrait.

3. An analysis of the features of personal affect in the legend reveals a repertoire well in accordance with the genre, but taken to the extreme. Adjectives, descriptive nouns and images have emotive connotations from opposite ends of the scale: *foule, hateful, cursed, the serpent Sathanas, waspes nest* versus *blisful, deere, swetnesse, tendre, the white Lamb celestial, this gemme of chastite, this emeraude, the ruby bright*, etc. The Prioress combines extreme sentimentality with violent xenophobia (Hughes 1991: 79). Solemn invocations, both positive and negative, are frequent:

> *O martir, sowded to virginitee* (VII.579).
> *O cursed folk of Herodes al newe,*
> *What may youre yvel entente yow availle?* (VII.574-75).

Allas is a sigh of grief that gives a summary of the emotional contents of the story after a vocative that reveals the agent of the atrocious deed: *O Hebrayk peple, allas!* (VII.560). *Lo* foregounds the climax and points out the moral of the legend, according to sermon conventions. The vocative and the direct address to God underline the heightened feelings:

> *O grete God, that parfournest thy laude*
> *By mouth of innocentz, lo, heere thy myght!* (VII.607-608).

The last stanza of the legend uses the vocative to reveal the name of the Saint, its only instance: *O yonge Hugh of Lyncoln* (VII.684). The vocative is used frequently. The emphasis is not so much on the development of the plot or dramatizing the events (cf. the *Second Nun's Tale*) as on the narrator's dominant rhetoric, and the focus is on her affected diction. The end is a pious appeal to the

Saint to pray *for us, we synful folk unstable* (VII.687), and the very
end extends the appeal to the Virgin Mary, linking it with the
invocations of the *Prioress's Prologue*: *For reverence of his mooder
Marie. Amen* (VII.690).

The Wife of Bath

1. The *General Prologue* describes the Wife of Bath as an independent, rich, jolly and oversexed middle-class woman in the wool
trade (Blake 1982: 47). She is easily angered and her physiognomical characterizations include: *Boold was hir face, and fair, and reed
of hewe* (I.458). She was also *gat-tothed* (I.468).[3]

2. The *Prologue* to her tale has two parts. The first is a mock-
sermon, a blasphemous abuse of a religious genre, thus comparable to swearing and indicative of the speaker's character. The *Wife
of Bath's Prologue* is conducted as a monologue, except for a short
episode with the Pardoner in the middle. Yet the presence of the
audience is strong, as she addresses her speech to the listeners,
and their responses are reflected in it. The result is a dialogue,
with only the turns of the dominating side recorded; no verbal
responses of the listeners' reactions are given, but they are left for
the reader's imagination (see below). The forms of address that
the Wife of Bath uses are either plain *lordynges* (III.4), or more
polite *lordynges, by youre leve* (III.112), or appeals with manipulative
additions, for example, *Lordynges, right thus, as ye have understonde*
(III.379), or admonitions with the verb in the imperative form
and *lo* for emphasis: *Herkne eek, lo, which a sharp word for the nones*
(III.14). Direct questions are posed, and the dichotomy between
the narrator and the audience is maintained by further appeals
and admonitions. The truthfulness is enhanced by pleas, such as
Now wol I seye yow sooth, by Seint Thomas (III.666). Together, the
above-mentioned features contribute to a style that is extremely
involved:

> *Wher can ye seye, in any manere age,*
> *That hye God defended mariage*
> *By expres word? I pray yow, telleth me.*

3.   Her personality as a reflection of physiognomical features and her
astrological chart has received a great deal of attention (see, e.g., Curry
1960).

Or where comanded he virginitee?
I woot as wel as ye, it is no drede... (III.59-63).

Her argumentative technique is persuasive. The grounds are
given with the cognitive verb and various factual statements; the
reasoning is then posed in direct questions with modal expressions, *why sholde...*; direct questions involve the listeners: *But that I
axe, why that the fifthe man / Was noon housbonde to the Samaritan?*
(III.21-22). They demand an answer, which is left for the listeners
to give. Such questions hand the reasoning process over to the
audience. Thus the whole argumentation is interactive and the listeners are forced to take part in it. Several statements start in a
parallcl way—*But wel I woot, expres, withoute lye* (III.27), *Eek wel I
woot* (III.30)—which gives the speech a rhetorical structure, builds
up the argument, and persuades the listener/reader to agree. The
narrator uses surge features of affect like swearing and exclamations such as *a Goddes half* (III.50) or *God yeve me sorwe!*
(III.151). Reactions to the audience's non-verbal responses
include demands for counter-examples like *Telle me also* (III.115),
and questions such as *say ye no?* (III.123). These follow-up questions and pleas are extremely persuasive, and the whole mechanism of reader involvement is aggressive.

An explicit dialogue is inserted in the middle of the *Wife of
Bath's Prologue* as first-hand evidence of the reactions of the audience. The Pardoner's speech expresses incredulity and surprise
first: '*Now, dame,*' quod he, '*by God and by Seint John!*' (III.164); but
he soon reverts to perhaps exaggerated politeness that shows his
attitude and desire to keep a distance: '*Dame, I wolde praye yow, if
youre wyl it were*' (III.184).

In the autobiography that follows, involvement is created by
different means. A great part of the story is told in direct speech
as a debate between the Wife and her husbands. The interaction
is conducted with the first and the second person singular *I, thou*;
ye addresses the audience; and a generic *we* includes all wives
(III.282, 283, etc.) Addresses to the audience form a sequence
with parallel beginnings: *But yet I praye to al this compaignye*
(III.189), *Now, sire, now wol I telle forth my tale* (III.193), *Now herk-
neth hou I baar me proprely* (III.224). Likewise, within the debate the
accusations addressed to the husband are similar in form: *Thou
seist to me* (III.248), *Thou seyst* (III.254, 257, etc.), *But tel me this:*

why...? (III.308), etc. Such addresses are extremely frequent, and regardless of whom they are originally intended for they appeal to the listener. They are powerful involvement features and contribute to the volume of personal affect and the aggressive tone of the Wife's *Prologue*. Some lines show cumulative lists of affect features to express outbursts of anger, for example, *Wy, taak it al! Lo, have it every deel!* (III.445) and *Lat go. Farewel! The devel go therwith!* (III.476). Self-disclosure is the main strategy, and it is used as a means of increasing intimacy between the narrator and her audience; such revelations indicate that intimacy is desired in the relationship (Gallois 1994: 308). Active participation in negotiating the meaning is required of both the speaker and the interlocutor—hence the involvement of all participants in the process of construing linguistic and interactive meaning, which is an involvement strategy with persuasive power (Besnier 1994: 288).

3. The tale that unfolds is a romance. Its surge features are fairly few and in accordance with the generic conventions. The personality of the narrator is depicted more vividly in the *Wife of Bath's Prologue*, though it has been noted that the two belong together so that the message of an abuse of power is present in both and they form a single unit (see Blake 1982: 52). The tale ends in a blasphemous curse to all those who will not be governed by their wives: *And olde and angry nygardes of dispence, / God sende hem soone verray pestilence!* (III.1263-64).

The Miller
1. The *General Prologue* gives physiognomical details of the Miller: *Ful byg he was of brawn, and eek of bones... short-sholdred, brood, a thikke knarre* (I.546-49); he has *a werte* on his nose and his *nosethirles blake were and wyde*...and his *mouth as greet was as a greet forneys* (I.555-59). They are important details that, according to medieval physiognomies, signify arrogance.[4] The Miller was *a janglere and a goliardeys, / And that was moost of synne and harlotries* (I.560-61),

---

4. The interpretations give him a shameless, talkative, lecherous and quarrelsome character (see Benson 1987: 820), but, according to John Metham, 'Nosethyrlys the qwyche be wyde, thei sygnyfye strenght and myrth off hert' (Craig 1916: 135). The combination may have served to set the audience's expectations.

which sets the audience's expectations to hearing something of that kind.

2. In the frame story the Miller's arrogance is combined with drunkenness. Surge features include swearing in a rude way: *By armes, and by blood and bones* (I.3125) and *By Goddes soule* (I.3132). He gets his will by threatening to go away, which is a strong persuasive speech act.

3. The *Miller's Tale* is a fabliau of *lewed dronken harlotrye* that fulfills the promise given in the *General Prologue*. It is perhaps the most canonical example of the genre in English literature (see Hines 1993). This is an essentially humorous genre, and the comic effects are built on character types and unexpected turns of the plot. Personal affect features achieve different functions here: interjections mark turning points in the plot and guide audience reactions. Instead of describing emotive states of mind they depict stereotypical reactions to situations. The reversal of the courtly romance is explicit in the portraits of Alison and Absolon, and it reaches the level of linguistic details, for example, in adjectives and interjections. In Alison's speech it is a mock-protestation, a stereotypical reaction. No trace of the emotional loading of the contemplative monologue of the *Knight's Tale* is present; the pace is quick, enhancing the contrast:

> *'Why, lat be!'* quod she. *'Lat be, Nicholas,*
> *Or I wol crie 'out, harrow' and 'allas'!* (I.3285-86).

Fabliaux and jest books belong to carnivalistic literature as they mock society with their own laws of justice and reverse hierarchies. The linguistic means of achieving this effect are mainly personal affect features removed from their original context and used in a new way. Ironical use is explicit: *Lo* is taken from sermons and *allas* from romances, but in fabliaux they gain comical connotations; for example, the narrator makes a pronouncement with biblical certainty: *Lo, which a greet thyng is affeccioun!* (I.3611). Another salient use of personal affect features is found in cumulative strings of short components (cf. above) with quick pace and emphasis on the action, such as *what!* and *how!* with names and other interjections. They contribute to the overall effect and bring important overtones to the passages in which they occur (Blake 1992), for example, *What, how! What do ye, maister Nicholay?* (I.3437) and *What! Nicholay! What, how! What, looke adoun! / Awak,*

and thenk on Cristes passioun! (I.3477-78). The climax in the plot of
the misplaced kiss is marked by similar devices. The fulfilment of
the carpenter's punishment is described by exclamations: *Up stirte
hire Alison and Nicholay, / And criden 'Out' and 'Harrow' in the strete*
(I.3824-25). This is the stereotypical use of interjections and the
set pattern of behaviour in fabliaux (Taavitsainen 1995a). The
public verbs *crie* and *say* provide another contrast to the emphasis
on private states of mind such as *suffer* in the *Knight's Tale*. The
plot of the Second Flood is a carnivalistic reversal of the biblical
story, and thus blasphemous, which again is indicative of the
genre and the narrator's personality. The last line echoes the
Knight's Tale, but the tone is different: *This tale is doon, and God
save al the rowte!* (I.3854).

Qualities of Personal Affect and Reader Involvement

The different qualities of personal affect identified here fit in well
with the earlier definitions of personal affect. They provide an
efficient means of reader involvement. Emotional communication
is realized in surge features like interjections, oaths and swearing.
This quality of affect is prominent in the monologues of the
Knight's Tale and in the *Prioress's Prologue*. In the *Knight's Tale* the
mood is contemplative, and the story is meant to provide an aes-
thetically elevating experience for the audience, as the reader is
supposed to share the feelings evoked. The Prioress indulges in
a prayer and her tale is a saint's life, which genre aims at edifica-
tion and entertainment. Here, too, the reader is supposed to
empathize with the emotions, and the entertaining function is not
really present. The *Wife of Bath's Prologue* shows a totally different
mechanism of involvement. It is highly interactive, persuasive,
even aggressive, and the emotive communication becomes a
dynamic process of negotiation between text participants.[5] Interaction is a salient quality of emotive communication, which consists of intentional, strategic signalling of affective information in
order to influence partners' interpretations of situations and

---

5.   The distinction between emotive and emotional use of language (for
a discussion of the terms see Caffi and Janney 1994b) corresponds well with
the main qualities of personal affect in early literature, i.e., surge and interaction.

reach the desired goal. It has no automatic or necessary relation to 'real' inner affective states, but is related to self-presentation as an inherently strategic, persuasive, interactional and other-directed strategy (Caffi and Janney 1994b: 328-29). The Wife of Bath's self-presentation both in the sermon and in the autobiography is characterized by an interactive focus. It is in striking contrast to the spontaneous, unintentional revealing or bursting out of emotion in the *Knight's Tale* or the *Prioress's Prologue*. In the *Miller's Tale* reader involvement is again totally different. Personal affect features are removed from their original meaning and used in a carnivalistic way in a condensed and typified form as signals to the audience. Readers are guided through the story, and are asked to pay attention to certain points, enjoy the apprehensions and sudden turning points of the plot and laugh at the characters. The Miller is in charge and controls the reader's reactions, and he is extremely skilful in doing so.

Personality, Affect and Humour

In this essay I set out to see whether personal affect features play a role in defining personalities in the *Canterbury Tales*. The answer is affirmative. Fictional characters exist in interaction with other fictional characters, and show a repertoire of behavioural patterns and mental states. The pilgrims' personalities are sketched as instances of medieval ideals or types, and the personalities are formulated through their use of language.

The techniques of description vary: each character is depicted by different means. The *General Prologue* sets readers' expectations: the Knight is an ideal type and his speech of agreement reinforces the ideal image, his readiness to act for the common goal. His tale exhibits deep emotions as he pauses to contemplate in the romantic mood. The Prioress concentrates on her own feelings and exhibits them in an elevated way. Personal affect features of surge are essential in her portrait. She focuses on the upheaval of her own emotional state, in the same way as her refined table manners or the upgraded term of address she uses of herself are ironical (see Burnley 1983: 141-42). Irony is often based on a particular word or phrase, and it may be very subtle; in her invocations the Latinate interjection *o* provides the key.

Parody can be defined as the emotional counterpoint of a tragical
theme, and laughter is often created through exaggeration. The
Wife of Bath's Prologue is a satirical anti-feminist tract, a parody of
sermon style with aggressive manipulation of the audience. The
Wife of Bath is presented to us as a dominant, bullying personality. Her self-presentation is aimed at manipulating the audience,
and the repertoire of personal affect features is interpersonal.
Here, in spite of the monologue form, interaction is prominent;
both what she tells her audience about her life and how she tells it
are important. She interacts both with the fictional audience and
the actual readership. Carnivalism in the Bakhtinian sense means
a special kind of parody (Morson 1981: 89), and this is evident in
the *Miller's Tale*. The emotions depicted seriously in tragic literature are reduced to stereotypical reactions to situations in fabliaux. The reduction of meaning is perhaps best seen in personal
affect features like interjections. The story the Miller tells is in
accordance with his social position, and the 'quitting' of the
Knight's Tale reaches the level of personal affect features. The
repertoire of personalities and their tales in the *Canterbury Tales*
is wide, including reverse pairs, depicted with irony and satire
through various styles of affect: *loveris up and doun... Thise noble
wyves and thise loveris eke... the Seintes Legende* (II.53-61).

WORKS CITED

Benson, L.D. (ed.)
    1987   *The Riverside Chaucer* (Boston: Houghton Mifflin).
Besnier, N.
    1994   'Involvement in Linguistic Practice: An Ethnographic Appraisal', in
                    Caffi and Janney 1994a: 279-99.
Biber, D., and E. Finegan
    1989   'Styles of Stance in English: Lexical and Grammatical Marking of
                    Evidentiality and Affect', *Text* 9.1: 93-124.
Blake, N.F.
    1977   *The English Language in Medieval Literature* (London: Dent).
    1982   'The Wife of Bath and her Tale', *Leeds Studies in English* NS 23: 42-
                    55.
    1990   *An Introduction to the Language of Literature* (London: Macmillan).
    1992   '*Why* and *What* in Shakespeare', in T. Takamiya and R. Beadle
                    (eds.), *Chaucer to Shakespeare: Essays in Honour of Shinsuke Ando* (Cam-
                    bridge: Brewer): 179-93.

Burnley, D.
1983   *A Guide to Chaucer's Language* (London: Macmillan; reissued 1989 as *The Language of Chaucer*).

Burrow, J.A.
1986   *The Ages of Man: A Study in Medieval Writing and Thought* (Oxford: Clarendon Press).

Caffi, C., and R.W. Janney (eds.)
1994a   *Involvement in Language*: Special issue of *Journal of Pragmatics* 22.

Caffi, C., and R.W. Janney
1994b   'Toward a Pragmatics of Emotive Communication', in Caffi and Janney 1994a: 325-73.

Chafe, W.
1985   'Linguistic Differences Produced by Differences between Speaking and Writing', in D.R. Olson *et al.* (eds.), *Literacy, Language and Learning: The Nature and Consequences of Reading and Writing* (Cambridge: Cambridge University Press): 105-23.

1986   *Collins Dictionary of the English Language* (London: Collins, 2nd edn).

Craig, H. (ed.)
1916   *The Works of John Metham* (EETS, 132; London: Oxford University Press).

Curry, W.C.
1960   *Chaucer and Mediaeval Sciences* (London: George Allen & Unwin, rev. edn).

Elliott, R.W.V.
1974   *Chaucer's English* (London: Deutsch).

Fludernik, M.
1993   *The Fictions of Languages and the Language of Fiction* (London: Routledge).

Gallois, C.
1994   'Group Membership, Social Rules, and Power: A Social-Psychological Perspective on Emotional Communication', in Caffi and Janney 1994a: 301-24.

Hines, J.
1993   *The Fabliau in English* (London: Longman).

Hughes, G.
1991   *Swearing: A Social History of Foul Language, Oaths and Profanity in English* (Oxford: Basil Blackwell).

Kerkhof, J.
1982   *Studies in the Language of Geoffrey Chaucer* (Leiden: E.J. Brill, 2nd edn).

Mann, J.
1973   *Chaucer and Medieval Estates Satire* (Cambridge: Cambridge University Press).

Martin, J.R.
1992   *English Text: System and Structure* (Amsterdam: Benjamins).

Morgan, G.
1977   'The Universality of the Portraits in the General Prologue to the
            Canterbury Tales', *English Studies* 58: 481-93.
Morson, G.S. (ed.)
1981   *Bakhtin: Essays and Dialogues on His Works* (Chicago: University of
            Chicago Press).
Oizumi, A. (ed.), programmed by K. Miki
1991–92   *A Complete Concordance to the Works of Geoffrey Chaucer* (10 vols.;
            Hildesheim: Olms-Weidmann).

Sell, R.D.
1985   'Politeness in Chaucer: Suggestion towards a Methodology for
            Pragmatic Stylistics', *Studia Neophilologica* 57: 175-85.
Taavitsainen, I.
1993   'Genre/Subgenre Styles in Late Middle English?', in M. Rissanen *et*
            al. (eds.), *Early English in the Computer Age* (Berlin: Mouton de
            Gruyter): 171-200.
1995a   'Narrative Patterns of Affect in Four Genres of the *Canterbury Tales'*,
            Chaucer Review 30: 82-101.
1995b   'Interjections in Early Modern English: From Imitations of Spoken
            to Conventions of Written Language', in A.H. Jucker (ed.),
            Historical Pragmatics (Amsterdam: Benjamins): 419-45.
1997a   'Genre Conventions: Personal Affect in Fiction and Non-Fiction in
            Early Modern English', in M. Rissanen *et al.* (eds.), *English in Tran-*
            sition: Corpus-Based Studies in Linguistic Variation and Genre Styles
            (Berlin: Mouton de Gruyter): 185-266.
1997b   'By Saint Tanne: Pious Oaths or Swearing in Late Middle English',
            in R. Hickey and S. Puppel (eds.), *Language History and Linguistic*
            Modelling: Festschrift for Jacek Fisiak on his Sixtieth Birthday (Berlin:
            Mouton de Gruyter): 815-26.
1997c   'Exclamations in Late Middle English', in J. Fisiak (ed.), *Studies in*
            Middle English Linguistics (Berlin: Mouton de Gruyter): 573-607.
1998   'Emphatic Language and Romantic Prose: Changing Functions of
            Interjections in a Sociocultural Perspective', in M. Fludernik (ed.),
            Linguistic Theory and Practice in Current Literary Scholarship: Special
            issue of *European Journal of English Studies* 2.
Toolan, M.
1988   *Narrative: A Critical Linguistic Introduction* (London: Routledge).

Part II

Non-Chaucerian Writing

Wynkyn de Worde and Misogyny in Print

Julia Boffey

Among the bibliographical mysteries in the books associated with Wynkyn de Worde is the record of a certain *Ragmannes Rolle*, the fragmentary final leaf of which was apparently noted in a sale catalogue of 1825, but has since disappeared.[1] The printer's envoy, which was the only portion of the book recorded by nineteenth-century bibliographers, directs it thus:

> Go lytyl rolle where thou arte bought or solde
> Amonge fayre women behaue the manerly:
> Without rewarde of any fee or golde,
> Say as it is touchynge trouthe hardely (Hazlitt 1876–1903: I, 350)

and its details suggest that the text must be identical to that of a verse game-kit, designed for female contestants, which survives in two related fifteenth-century Chaucerian anthologies: Oxford, Bodleian Library MSS Fairfax 16 and Bodley 638.[2] Spoken of as a roll, although neither its manuscript nor printed forms preserves it thus, the poem consists of a number of stanzas which are to be randomly awarded to the 'fayre women' in its audience and range

---

1. Not listed in *STC*, but noted by Hazlitt (1876–1903: I, 350, and Hazlitt 1867: 495). Hazlitt's dating of the poem to before 1533, on the grounds that 'ragman rolls' are referred to in Heywood's *mery play betwene the pardoner and the frere* (*STC* 13299), printed in that year, is unconvincing. See also Utley (1944: 201-202).

2. (*S*)*IMEV* 2251, beginning 'My ladyes and my maistresses echone'; see Norton-Smith (1979) and Robinson (1982); edited from MS Fairfax 16 by Hazlitt (1864–66: I, 68-78). Traces of printer's ink in MS Bodley 638 have been taken as evidence that this must have served as the copytext for de Worde's edition: see Moore (1992: 16).

from the laudatory to the gross: 'your colour fressh, your percyng eyen gray'; 'your shrunkyn lyppis and your g[?r]owndyn teth'.[3] Like the *christmasse carolles* (*STC* 5204) or the *demaundes joyous* (*STC* 6573) which de Worde printed, this text presumably served essentially convivial ends, and was marketed as a social diversion to be enjoyed in mixed company. Its laboured jesting with a range of pro- and anti-feminist positions locates it in a long line of satires which may have originated in a misogynist clerical *milieu* but soon circulated beyond this, with provocation that can only be guessed at, to a wider and less select audience.

The patterns of manuscript and printed transmission which *Ragmannes Rolle* seems to reflect in its fragmentary way, as well as something of its appeal and flavour, are duplicated in another of de Worde's books, *The payne and sorowe of euyll maryage* (*STC* 19119, assigned to c. 1530), about which rather more is known. Addressed to a 'litel childe', this text, conventionally ascribed on no very compelling grounds to John Lydgate, offers the wisdom of authority garnered by a first-person narrator who has narrowly escaped 'the yok and bonde of mariage'. It purveys some of the traditional anti-feminist jibes inherited from a Latin tradition which comprehended Theophrastus's *Liber Aureolus de Nuptiis* and Jerome's treatise against Jovinian, and which infiltrated vernacular works like *Le Roman de la Rose* and the *Wife of Bath's Prologue*.[4] Like *Ragmannes Rolle*, it was produced in manuscript as well as printed form, notably in a Chaucerian anthology, Oxford, Bodleian Library MS Digby 181, which is textually related to MSS Fairfax 16 and Bodley 638 and has been associated with them in a so-called 'Oxford group' of the witnesses of Chaucer's minor poems.[5] Outside this context it is preserved variously in London, British Library MS Harley 2251; in Rome, English College MS A.347 (a manuscript sometimes inaccurately cited under the shelfmark 1306); and in Cambridge University Library MS Ff.1.6, the

3.   For fuller discussion see Långfors (1920). The text is considered, along with another fortune poem which appears in the same two manuscripts, in Hammond (1925).

4.   Edited in Wright (1841: 295-99) and MacCracken (1934: no. 17, 456-60). For the wider tradition see Blamires (1992).

5.   Described in Root (1914: 9-10), d'Evelyn (1935: 60-61), Mosser (1988 and 1990).

so-called Findern Anthology.[6] While the patterns in which material of this kind has survived testify to both manuscript and
printed circulation, the transference from one form to another
appears in England to have taken place relatively slowly: such
texts are notably absent, for example, from the output of William
Caxton's press. The crucial role of Wynkyn de Worde in their cul-
tivation as a printed commodity, and his motives and procedures
in making them available in this new form, will be the subjects of
this discussion.[7]

The *payne and sorowe of euyll maryage*, which owes a good deal to
the literary concern with gender issues stimulated in England by
Chaucer, is in essence a reformulation of a long-established text
which circulated in both Latin and Anglo-Norman. The Latin
versions, of which at least 55 manuscripts survive, were copied and
recopied from the thirteenth to the fifteenth centuries, and could
have come the way of the author of the fifteenth-century English
redaction though a number of routes.[8] For example, the Latin
text in London, British Library MS Cotton Vespasian E.xii appears
to have been the work of a fifteenth-century scribe associated with
the University of Oxford, and the manuscript bears the signature
of John Russell, Bishop of Lincoln, with the date 1482. The earlier
fifteenth-century copy in Cambridge, Trinity College MS R.3.20,
headed 'quedam disputacio in consilio nubendi' and 'A counseyle
howe to beo wedded', was made by the London scribe John
Shirley between Lydgate's *Mumming at London* (*IMEV* 1928) and a
series of French courtly balades. Of the Anglo-Norman texts, one
was copied in London, British Library MS Harley 2253, along with
some anti-matrimonial and anti-feminist works such as 'Le blasme
des fames'.[9] Interest in such texts is anticipated in the earlier
anthology which is now Bodleian Library MS Digby 86, and

    6.   Described respectively in Hammond (1905), Klinefelter (1953),
Robbins (1955), and Beadle and Owen (1977).
    7.   The differing scopes of Caxton's and de Worde's interests are made
clear in Blake (1965, 1971 and 1972).
    8.   Rigg (1986); also edited in Wright (1841: 77-85), with the title 'Golias
de conjuge non ducenda'. For a full list of the manuscripts of the Latin see
Rigg (1986: 13-22; 1992: 236).
    9.   Ker (1965).

includes along with 'Le blasme des fames' a text on 'La bonte des femmes' and a version of 'Ragemon le Bon'.[10]

Some sense of the appeal which an English version of the *payne and sorowe of euyll maryage* offered to fifteenth-century readers may be gleaned from the different manuscript contexts in which it survives. Digby 181 is primarily a Chaucerian collection, containing *Troilus and Criseyde, The Parliament of Fowls* and *Anelida and Arcite*.[11] Together with these are poems in Chaucerian mode— Lydgate's *Complaint of the Black Knight* and Hoccleve's *Letter of Cupid*—with *Peter Idley's Instructions* and a unique verse list of *Examples against Women*, which has been attributed to Lydgate.[12] The *payne and sorowe*, sandwiched between the *Letter of Cupid* and *Examples against Women*, is part of a sequence of items which pursue the questions raised by the *querelle de la rose* and are addressed in Hoccleve's translation of Christine de Pizan's verse contribution to it.[13] In the Findern manuscript, where the text is the work of one of the many scribes who copied only one item into this complex and essentially accretive collection, its surroundings include love lyrics, short poems on topical and moral themes, and Lydgate's 'Wicked Tongue'.[14]

The writings of Lydgate are the focus of Harley 2251, a manuscript copied by a London-based scribe, apparently from exemplars in the hand of John Shirley, but the *payne and sorowe* nonetheless keeps company there with other anti-feminist poems: a series of extracts from the *Fall of Princes* which preserve a humorous pro-feminist commentary by Shirley, a short poem on 'wommans trechery' with the refrain 'Be ware therfor the blynde ete

10. Tschann and Parkes (1996: items 29, 36, 56). On the circulation of some of this material see Fiero *et al.* (1989).

11. Mosser's proposed collation suggests that the shorter poems (ff.1-53) need not have been conceived as part of the same volume as *Troilus*, which is copied by a different scribe on a distinct paperstock.

12. *IMEV* 3744, beginning 'To Adam and Eve Crist gave the soueraig[n]te'; see MacCracken (1934: No.13, 442-45).

13. Christine's *Epistre de Cupide* and Hoccleve's translation are both edited in Erler and Fenster (1990).

14. The construction of the manuscript does not allow for generalization about possible intended themes: see Beadle and Owen (1977) and Harris (1983). 'Wicked Tongue', beginning 'Considre wele with euery circumstance' and with the refrain 'A wykked tunge wil alwey deme amys', is *IMEV* 653.

many a flye',[15] and a stanza enumerating 'Four things which cause a man to fall from reason' (a list which, of course, includes women).[16] The incorporation of the *payne and sorowe* in a collection of this kind gives some support to arguments for Lydgate's authorship, and indeed the Rome manuscript (whose text of the poem was not known to either of its early editors, Wright or MacCracken) is essentially a Lydgate anthology, drawing together the *Life of Our Lady* and a number of Lydgate's shorter poems with the *Master of Game* and a few anonymous texts. Although its interests are broad, encompassing topical poems and works of moral exhortation,[17] this volume also contains some anti-feminist poems whose grouping recalls the contents of the other manuscripts in which the *payne and sorowe* found a home: 'The blynde eteth many a flye', 'Four things that make a man fall from reason' (both in Harley 2251) and 'Wicked Tongue' (in Harley 2251 and Cambridge University Library Ff.1.6).

In manuscript copies the forms of most of these poems seem to have been eminently pliable: they were open to abbreviation, extension or reformulation to suit exigencies of space, of scribal proclivity, or simply of taste, in the manner of certain topical satires and following the ample precedent of the Latin textual tradition of *De Coniuge Non Ducenda*.[18] The *payne and sorowe* survives differently in all four of its manuscripts, and its relationship to the other anti-feminist poems with which it apparently circulated, and their forms in turn, underwent serial changes. The version in Digby 181, for instance, lacks the opening stanza of address to a 'lytell chylde'[19] and omits another stanza, detailing

15. *IMEV* 1944, beginning 'Loke wel aboute ye that lovers be'.

16. *IMEV* 4230, beginning 'Worship wymmen wyne and vnweldy age'.

17. 'Henry VI's Triumphal Entry into London', *IMEV* 3799; 'A Song Made of the Duke of Burgundy', *IMEV* 3682; 'The Siege of Calais', *IMEV* 1497; and *Parvus* and *Magnus Cato*, *IMEV* 3955, 854.

18. For some comparable cases see Boffey (1993, especially n. 15). Rigg (1986) writes in some detail on the different versions of the Latin and the role of textual and memorial contamination in the circulation of this work.

19. It is claimed in Renoir and Benson (1980: 2132) that the introductory stanza occurs only in de Worde's print, and that it comes from Cambridge, University Library MS Dd.4.54, f.229b. This misunderstanding seems to stem from a conflation of two *IMEV* entries: 3250, an entry for 'Take hede before þat you be not lore', in the Cambridge University Library manuscript, and a

the tribulations of husbands, which begins 'The husband euer abideth in travaile' (MacCracken 1934: No. 17, 456-60). The Rome manuscript has the opening stanza and this one, but lacks a further later stanza on women's spiritual hypocrisy (which is present in Digby), beginning 'Of ther nature they gretly hem delite'. The opening stanza of address is present in Cambridge University Library MS Ff.1.6, but this version breaks off altogether part-way through the problematical stanza on husbands' tribulations, as if the exemplar might have presented some kind of crux at this point in the text.[20] And in Harley 2251 the *payne and sorowe* is copied immediately after 'The blynde etith many a flye', signalled as a new item only by a large initial letter and conveying the impression that it is some kind of extension of this other piece. Only six stanzas are copied here, beginning part-way into the poem, including the problematical stanza on husbands' tribulations, but then merging indistinguishably into the stanza on 'Four things that make a man fall from reason' (see MacCracken 1934: No. 17, 456-60). Further confirmation of the flexibility of this material is demonstrated in a short poem in Cambridge, Trinity College MS R.3.19,[21] which begins with the stanza missing in the Rome manuscript ('Of theyre nature they gretly theym delyte') and in its three other apparently unique stanzas cites once the refrain 'Beware alwey the blynde eteth many a fly', and in another the variation 'I pray god kepe the fly out of my dyssh'.[22]

De Worde's printed edition is fuller than any of the surviving manuscript copies of the text. It includes the prefatory stanza of address ('Take hede and lerne, thou lytell chylde...') and the stanza on husbands' tribulations ('The husband euer abideth in travaile...'). Like all the other witnesses except Digby 181, it omits the stanza on women's hypocrisy ('Of ther nature they gretly hem delite'), but at this point, before ending with a concluding stanza

preceding cross-reference (without separate entry number, although with a direction to 919) to the first line of the introductory *payne and sorowe* stanza.

20. The text ends at the foot of f.156 at the end of the third line of this stanza.

21. *IMEV* 2661; see Fletcher (1987: f.156v).

22. The more familiar poem with this refrain, *IMEV* 1944, beginning 'Looke well about ye that louers be', also appears in this manuscript, on f. 207r-v.

which it shares with Digby 181 and the Rome manuscript, it inserts five unique stanzas.[23] It is not easy to make any sense of the relationship of the printed text to the manuscript versions. The common presence of the prefatory stanza would seem to relate the print to the the texts of the Rome and Findern manuscripts, but the Findern text is too truncated to allow for extensive collation, and there are some variants—quite apart from the added stanzas—which suggest that the Rome manuscript cannot have been the precise copy-text. De Worde may simply have taken his copy from a lost witness which happened to contain a fuller version of the poem than any of the others which have survived.

There is, however, a further possibility which may account for the extra length of de Worde's text. It is printed as a small quarto volume of four leaves (Ai-Aiv). Sig. Ai[r] is taken up with a title and woodcut and sig. Aiv[v] with one of de Worde's versions of Caxton's printer's device—a common format for the short works of this kind that he printed. If the text of the *payne and sorowe* which came his way had followed even the longest of the surviving manuscript witnesses (Rome or Digby 181), it would have ended, laid out as it is with four stanzas to each page, on sig. Aiii[v], and even with the insertion of the printers' device would have left one or other side of sig. Aiv blank. With flexible texts of this sort the provision of some extra stanzas would not have been taxing work; the accumulation of compelling reasons for not taking a wife, or of instances of the general odiousness of women, cannot have required great originality, and the apparent continuing circulation of the Latin and/or Anglo-Norman text which seems to be the original source of the *payne and sorowe* may have made the work of extension still easier.[24] In general terms the English version with its variant stanzas seems to be based on a very loose translation of either the Latin or the Anglo-Norman. In occasional details the various versions seem to share a common closer debt to the Latin, but there is no way of demonstrating that any were executed in complete ignorance of the Anglo-Norman

23. MacCracken (1934: No. 17, 456-60), unaccountably prints only the first four of these in his textual notes to the poem. All the added stanzas are present in Wright (1841).

24. Utley (1944: 135-37), suggests that these stanzas may have been an addition, possibly translated by William Copland.

text.[25] While both the Anglo-Norman and the Latin versions have a tripartite structure in which the advice of each of three counsellors is canvassed in turn, the English dispenses with this, and proffers the words of only 'Peter, called the Corbelio'; equally, while both the Latin and the Anglo-Norman return at the end to the narrator's predicament and his undertaking not to marry, the English turns the advice to readers and audience without any reference to the narrator's decision about his own intentions. Additions seem to creep in from elsewhere—as, for example, a stanza which decries women's desire for public display at 'grete gaderynges', particularly performances of plays, as if recalling in very specific terms the activities of the Wife of Bath.[26] The most that can be said of the stanzas added in de Worde's printed edition is that they are roughly analogous to portions of the Latin text and may have been supplied by someone who knew this.

Textual enhancement of this kind is not unusual in de Worde's books, a number of which contain introductions or interpolations, usually anonymous but occasionally supplied by individuals such as Robert Copland, who seems to have been retained by de Worde in some capacity. Occasionally these serve specific purposes of dedication or acknowledgment, as in the 'prohemium' to *bartholomaeus de proprietatibus rerum* (*STC* 1536) which names de Worde, the mercer Roger Thorney at whose 'prayer and desyre' the book was printed, and John Tate, papermaker. Sometimes they offer a commentary on the nature of the text printed, like the verse epilogue to the *noble and amerous auncyent hystory of Troylus and Cresyde* (*STC* 5095), which reviles Criseyde as an example of women's faithlessness,[27] or the moralizing stanzas by Robert Copland in William Walter's translation of Boccaccio's story of *Guystarde and Sygysmonde* (*STC* 3183.5).[28] Some small extension of

25. Rigg (1986: 103-104), supplies an appendix on the English translation, based on consultation of MacCracken's edition, and notes that the English is 'a muddle: it follows the Latin fairly closely in the Introduction, and in part of the Peter section, but after that picks up only one or two details from the Latin'. Towards the end of the translation are some clues that the Anglo-Norman version may have been used, 'but as the exact correspondence with the Latin breaks down near this point it is hard to be sure'.

26. *CT* III.558.

27. See Benson and Rollman (1981).

28. See Erler (1993: 149-59).

the *payne and sorowe* would not have been a difficult commission.

Works dealing with the nature or, more often, the supposed wiles of women seem to have been actively sought out by de Worde and promoted in what might be thought of as his 'list' as a particular area of interest and market appeal. Some of the translators who regularly supplied him with copy ventured into this field, with Henry Watson offering the *gospelles of dystaues* (*STC* 12091)[29] and Copland apparently supplying the *complaynte of them that ben to late maryed* (*STC* 5728) and a *complaynt of them that be to soone maryed* (*STC* 5729), both of which have verse epilogues which contain his name in acrostics.[30] An anonymous translator provided the *fyftene Ioyes of maryage* (*STC* 15257.5), writing in the prologue how 'of late I was desyred / Out of the [f]renche to drawe a lytell boke / Of .xv. Ioyes...' (sig. Aii[r]).[31] The ready availability of continental printed editions of texts such as these must have been part of their appeal for de Worde and his translators, as well as a testimony to their market success. Printed editions of *Les quinze joies de mariage* were produced in Lyons between 1480 and 1490 and in Paris by Jean Trepperel before 1499.[32] Mansion printed *Les Evangiles des Quenouilles* at Bruges c. 1475.[33] A printed *Complainte de trop tost marie* was in circulation, as was a matching *Complainte de trop tard marie,* the latter evidently the work of Pierre Gringore, whose name in an acrostic at the end probably prompted Copland's similar flourish.[34] Even in the case of books printed by de Worde with no explanatory prologue it is sometimes possible to trace a printed continental source. His *interlocucyon with an argument betwyxt man and woman whiche of them could proue to*

29. 'at the request of some my welbeloued I.H.W. haue translated this treatyse yat conteyneth the texte of the gospelles of dystaues...' sig. y[r]; Watson also translated the *shyppe of fooles* (*STC* 3547), the *chirche of the euyll men and women* (*STC* 1966), *Valentine and Orson* (*STC* 24571.3) and the *hystorye of Olyuer of castylle* (*STC* 18808).

30. Erler 1993: 43-8.

31. Erler (1993: 110) dismisses the attribution of this translation to Copland.

32. See Rychner (1963) and Jannet (1857).

33. Bornstein 1978.

34. For editions of the first (also printed as the *Complainte du nouveau marie*) see Brunet (1860–78: II, 198); for the second see Brunet (1860–78: II, 1755-56) and Oulmont (1911: 43).

be most excellent (*STC* 14109) appears to have a French source, some variant of the *debat de lhome et de la femme*, by Guillaume Alexis, which was printed in Lyons, Paris and elsewhere from c. 1490 onwards.[35]

Most of these translations, like the *payne and sorowe* itself, and like *Ragmannes Rolle*, lay claim to at least some degree of sophistication: a few are presented as debates, and most encapsulate their provocation in the comparatively polite stanza forms of rhyme royal or ballade. But alongside these de Worde seems not to have neglected texts of a cruder kind: gossips' poems and wives' tales, as represented by his printing of *a lytell propre ieste. Called cryste crosse me spede a.b.c. How ye good gosyps made a royall feest* (*STC* 14546.5), or indeed of Skelton's *tunning of Elinor Rumming* (*STC* 22611.5). *Cryste crosse me spede*, of which only the first and last leaves survive,[36] tells how 'A grete company of gossyps gadred on a route / Went to besyege an ale hous rounde aboute', with the comic substitution of distaffs, buckets and gallon pots for the instruments and weapons of a siege. It does not survive in manuscript but it has manuscript analogues among poems like 'The Ten Wives' Tales' and two separate versions of 'Gossips' Meetings', as well as more generally among fifteenth-century burlesques like the *Tournament of Tottenham*.[37]

Texts of this kind, like the earliest copies of the *payne and sorowe* itself, owe their preservation in large part to the fact of their inclusion in manuscript anthologies—environments which gave some kind of physical security to short poems which may otherwise have circulated, for convivial or occasional ends, without the

35. *STC* suggests this as the source, presumably on the authority of Piaget and Picot (1896–1908: I, 121-55), where de Worde's text ('un petit poeme anglais qui paraissait calqué sur celui d'Alexis') is also edited.

36. Details, and the text on the two surviving leaves, are reproduced in Ames (1810–19: II, 367-68); the single surviving copy is listed in *STC* as 'Hofmann & Freeman Ltd'.

37. 'The Ten Wives' Tales', *IMEV* 1852, survives in Aberystwyth, National Library of Wales MS Porkington 10; one 'Gossips' Meeting, *SIMEV* 2358.5, is in British Library Cotton Vitellius D.ix and Cotton Titus A.xxvi (both originally parts of the same manuscript); the other, *IMEV* 1362, survives in Oxford, Bodleian Library MS Eng. poet. e.1 and in Oxford, Balliol College 354. For discussion of the genre and of these poems see Robbins (1969); Bennett (1991); and Hanna (1996).

necessity for written copies.[38] These anthologies range from the-matically conceived and formally produced collections such as MS Digby 181 to the more heterogeneous miscellanies which often provided an environment for anti-feminist material of a more popular kind. 'The Ten Wives' Tales', for example, survives in Aberystwyth, National Library of Wales MS Porkington 10, seem-ingly a household miscellany produced somewhere near the Welsh borders.[39] Its contents include a romance (*Sir Gawain and the Carl of Carlisle*), saints' lives in prose and verse, some exemplary stories, and a number of medical, astronomical and meteorologi-cal notes. It has religious lyrics and carols, some of which (such as the *Boar's Head Carol*) would have been suitable for convivial pur-poses, and light-hearted parodies of favourite contemporary secu-lar lyric forms. Among the many practical contents are instruc-tions for journeys, for the rearing of children, for the health of hawks, and for domestic tasks like carving, dyeing fabric, and maintaining trees and plants. One of the 'Gossips' Meeting' poems (*IMEV* 1362) survives in a repertory of carols (MS Bodley eng. poet. e.1), and the other in a now dismembered volume of miscellaneous content.[40]

The London provenances of some of the manuscripts which include this material suggest that de Worde would have had ready access to copy for his printed ventures. Harley 2251 and probably also the Rome manuscript of the *payne and sorowe* were London productions.[41] Among de Worde's contacts were men like the London mercer Roger Thorney, who is known to have owned both manuscripts and printed books, and who appears to have

38. Rigg (1986) postulates a degree of oral transmission for *De Coniuge non Ducenda*.

39. See most recently Huws (1996).

40. For brief descriptions of all of these see Greene (1977: 320-21, 317-18, 297). *IMEV* 1362 is also to be found in the commonplace book of the London grocer Richard Hill (now Oxford, Balliol College MS 354), although possibly, like some of the other contents of that collection, it was copied from a printed edition.

41. For the *milieu* of the 'Multon scribe' of Harley 2251 see most recently Kekewich *et al.* (1995: 107-12). The contents and at least one of the hands of the Rome MS suggest connections with London anthologies such as Cam-bridge, Trinity College R.3.19 and R.3.21.

instigated or underwritten some printing projects.[42] While the contents of some London manuscript anthologies might have indicated to de Worde a market demand for short verse texts of particular kinds, however, his own decision as a printer was to make these texts available as separable commodities—small, cheap, independent booklets or pamphlets—rather than as components of larger collections.

One striking innovation which was part of the commodification of texts such as these was the enhancement of their appeal by means of the provision of woodcuts, or of variously deployed factotum figures and line ornaments. Though these are arranged simply and sometimes match only approximately the writings they accompany, they add to the texts an attraction which is lacking in any of the surviving manuscript copies. The title-page of the *payne and sorowe* has a woodcut of a marriage ceremony, apparently originally cut for use in in the *Example of vertu* (*STC* 12946) but put to service thereafter in other contexts which included, besides the *payne and sorowe*, de Worde's edition of the *Fyftene joyes of maryage*.[43] *Cryste crosse me spede* is enhanced more economically still by the insertion of three factotum figures and some lozenge ornaments on the first page. The all-purpose destination of the figures is suggested by the fact that the scrolls above two of them remain blank, and they can indeed be spotted in other books printed by de Worde.[44]

42. Thorney owned at least part of Trinity MS R.3.21, as well as manuscripts of Chaucer's *Troilus*, Lydgate's *Siege of Thebes*, and a copy of Caxton's printed edition of *Godfrey of Boulogne* (see Bone 1931–32). His name also appears in the Huntington Library copy of the *boke of Justices of peas* printed by de Worde in 1515 (*STC* 14864.5).

43. Hodnett (1973: No.1264).

44. The central figure appears in one of the factotum cuts in the *knyght of the swanne* (*STC* 7571), where the scroll identifies her as 'Clarysse'; again in *The dystruccyon of Iherusalem* (*STC* 14518) as 'the quene'; and in the *noble history of king Ponthus* (*STC* 20107) as 'Sydoyne'. For reproductions (simply the instances which have come to my attention—there are doubtless more) and further discussion of the use of factotum figures see Driver (1986 and 1996). The right-hand female figure on the title-page of *cryste crosse*, like other of de Worde's factotums, appears to be based on cuts employed by Vérard—in this instance one of the female figures who appears in *Le Jardin de Plaisance* of 1501 (Driver 1996: fig. 21). The left-hand figure serves as

Innovations such as these, like de Worde's readiness to look for translations to provide new material for his press and like his pragmatic adaptability in the matter of filling available space by the easiest means to hand, are perhaps to be interpreted as evidence of the business acumen which is often all he is credited with. Equally, though, they might be seen to represent his willingness to experiment with the printing of genres and forms which had hitherto apparently been overlooked, if not consciously rejected. From the first decade of the sixteenth century, after his move to Fleet Street from Westminster, de Worde seems to have put some energy into developing a line of short 'mery jests' in which the subcategory of humorous misogynist material played an important role. The evidence of surviving books suggests that this material had been ignored by Caxton and that de Worde's initiative in developing it was to set a precedent of some importance for his contemporaries and successors.[45]

Octavian's daughter in the *Chronicles of England* and perhaps in a later cut appears on the title page of Copland's edition of *Jyl of breyntfords testament* (see Erler 1993: 165).

45. For some comparable productions, cf. the *boke of the mayde Emlyn that had v husbandz* (*STC* 7680.5), printed by Pynson ?1510 and Skot c. 1525, and the *mery jest of an old fool with a young wife* (*STC* 14520.5), Treveris 1530? William Copland seems to have been an energetic successor to de Worde in this area, probably because of his special access to Robert Copland's own translations: see, for example, his editions of *Jyl of breyntfords testament* (*STC* 5730, 5731) and the *seuen sorowes that women haue when theyr husbandes be deade* (*STC* 5734).

WORKS CITED

Ames, J. (ed.)
    1810–19   *Thomas Frognall Dibdin: Typographical Antiquities* (4 vols.; London: Miller).

Beadle, R., and A.E.B. Owen (introds.)
    1977   *The Findern Manuscript* (London: Scolar Press).

Bennett, J.M.
    1991   'Misogyny, Popular Culture and Women's Work', *History Workshop Journal* 31: 166-88.

Benson, C.D., and D. Rollman
    1981   'Wynkyn de Worde and the Ending of Chaucer's *Troilus and Criseyde*', *Modern Philology* 78: 275-79.

Benson, L.D. (ed.)
    1987   *The Riverside Chaucer* (Boston: Houghton Mifflin).

Blake N.F.
    1965   'Caxton's Choice of Texts', *Anglia* 83: 289-307.
    1971   'Wynkyn de Worde: The Early Years', *Gutenberg Jahrbuch*: 62-69.
    1972   'Wynkyn de Worde: The Later Years', *Gutenberg Jahrbuch*: 128-38.

Blamires, A. (ed.)
    1992   *Woman Defamed and Woman Defended: An Anthology of Medieval Texts* (Oxford: Oxford University Press).

Boffey, J.
    1993   '*The Treatise of a Galaunt* in Manuscript and Print', *Library*, 6th series 15: 175-86.

Bone, G.
    1931–32   'Extant Manuscripts Printed from by W. de Worde, with Notes on the Owner, Roger Thorney', *Library*, 4th series, 12: 284-306.

Bornstein, D. (introd.)
    1978   *Distaves and Dames: Renaissance Treatises for and about Women* (New York: Delmar).

Brunet, J.-C.
    1860–78   *Manuel du libraire et d'amateur de livres* (8 vols.; Paris: Firmin-Didot).

Driver, M.W.
    1986   'Illustration in Early English Books: Methods and Problems', *Books at Brown* 33: 1-57.
    1996   'The Illustrated De Worde: An Overview', *Studies in Iconography* 17: 349-403.

Erler, M.C. (ed.)
    1993   *Robert Copland: Poems* (Toronto: Toronto University Press).

Erler, M.C., and T. Fenster (eds.)
    1990   *Poems of Cupid, God of Love* (Leiden: E.J. Brill).

d'Evelyn, C. (ed.)
    1935   *Peter Idley's Instructions to his Son* (Boston: Modern Language Association).

Fiero, G.K., *et al.* (eds. and trans.)
    1989   *Three Medieval Views of Women* (New Haven: Yale University Press).

Fletcher, B.Y. (introd.)
1987   *Manuscript Trinity R.3.19: A Facsimile* (Norman, OK: Pilgrim Books).
Greene, R.L. (ed.)
1977   *The Early English Carols* (Oxford: Clarendon Press, 2nd edn).
Hammond, E.P.
1905   'Two British Museum Manuscripts: A Contribution to the Bibliography of John Lydgate', *Anglia* 28: 1-28.
1925   '*The Chance of the Dice*', *Englische Studien* 59: 1-16.
Hanna, R.
1996   'Brewing Trouble: On Literature and History—and Alewives', in B.A. Hanawalt and D. Wallace (eds.), *Bodies and Disciplines: Intersections of Literature and History in Fifteenth-Century England* (Minneapolis: Minnesota University Press): 1-17.
Harris, K.
1983   'The Origins and Make-Up of Cambridge University Library MS Ff.1.6', *Transactions of the Cambridge Bibliographical Society* 8: 299-333.
Hazlitt, W.C. (ed.)
1864–66   *Remains of the Early Popular Poetry of England* (4 vols.; London: Smith).
1867   *Handbook to the Popular, Poetical and Dramatic Literature of Great Britain* (London: Smith).
1876–1903   *Collections and Notes* (6 vols.; London: Reeves & Turner).
Hodnett, E.
1973   *English Woodcuts 1480–1535* (Oxford: Oxford University Press, 2nd edn).
Huws, D.
1996   'MS Porkington 10 and its Scribes', in J. Fellows *et al.* (eds.), *Romance Reading on the Book: Essays on Medieval Narrative presented to Maldwyn Mills* (Cardiff: University of Wales Press): 188-207.
Jannet, P. (ed.)
1857   *Les quinze joyes de mariage* (Paris: Bibliothèque Elzevirienne, 2nd edn).
Kekewich, M.L., *et al.*
1995   *The Politics of Fifteenth Century England: John Vale's Book* (Stroud: Sutton).
Ker, N.R. (introd.)
1965   *Facsimile of British Museum MS Harley 2253* (EETS, 255; London: Oxford University Press).
Klinefelter, R.A.
1953   'A Newly Discovered Fifteenth-Century English Manuscript', *Modern Language Quarterly* 14: 3-6.
Långfors, A.
1920   *Un jeu de société du moyen âge: Ragemon le Bon, inspirateur d'un sermon en vers* (Helsinki: Annales Academia Scientiarum Fennicae).
MacCracken, H.N. (ed.)
1911, 1934 *The Minor Poems of John Lydgate* (EETS ES, 107 and OS 192; London: Oxford University Press).

Moore, J.K.
1992   *Primary Materials Relating to Copy and Print in English Books of the Sixteenth and Seventeenth Centuries* (Oxford: Oxford Bibliographical Society).

Mosser, D.W.
1988   'A New Collation for Bodleian MS Digby 181', *Proceedings of the Bibliographical Society of America* 82: 604-11.
1990   'The Scribe of the Chaucer Manuscripts Rylands English 113 and Bodleian Digby 181', *Manuscripta* 34: 129-47.

Norton-Smith, J. (introd.)
1979   *Bodleian MS Fairfax 16* (London: Scolar Press).

Oulmont, C.
1911   *Pierre Gringore* (Paris: Champion).

Piaget, A., and E. Picot (eds.)
1896 1908   *Oeuvres poetiques de Guillaume Alexis* (3 vols.; Paris: Société des anciens textes français).

Renoir, A., and C.D. Benson
1980   'John Lydgate', in A.E. Hartung (gen. ed.), *A Manual of the Writings in Middle English 1050–1500*, VI (Hamden, CT: Connecticut Academy of Arts and Sciences).

Rigg, A.G.
1986   *Gawain on Marriage: The Textual Tradition of the 'De Coniuge Non Ducenda' with Critical Edition and Translation* (Toronto: Pontifical Institute of Medieval Studies).
1992   *A History of Anglo-Latin Literature, 1066–1422* (Cambridge: Cambridge University Press).

Robbins, R.H.
1955   'A Middle English Diatribe against Philip of Burgundy', *Neophilologus* 39: 131-46.
1969   'John Crophill's Ale-Pots', *Review of English Studies* NS 20: 182-89.

Robinson, P.R. (introd.)
1982   *MS Bodley 638: A Facsimile* (Norman, OK: Pilgrim Books).

Root, R.K.
1914   *The Manuscripts of Chaucer's Troilus* (London: Chaucer Society, 1st series 98).

Rychner, J. (ed.)
1963   *Les xv. joies de mariage* (Geneva: Librairie Droz).

Tschann, J., and M.B. Parkes (introds.)
1996   *Facsimile of Oxford, Bodleian Library MS Digby 86* (EETS SS, 16; Oxford: Oxford University Press).

Utley, F.L.
1944   *The Crooked Rib: An Analytical Index to the Argument about Woman in English and Scots Literature to the End of the Year 1568* (Columbus: Ohio State University Press).

Wright, T. (ed.)
1841   *The Latin Poems Commonly Attributed to Walter Mapes* (London: Camden Society, 1st series 16).

An Eighteenth-Century Edition of Hoccleve*

John Burrow

In 1796 George Mason published the first printed book devoted to works of Thomas Hoccleve: *Poems by Thomas Hoccleve, Never Before Printed: Selected from a MS. in the Possession of George Mason. With a Preface, Notes, and Glossary* (London: Printed by C. Roworth, for Leigh and Sotheby, York Street, Covent Garden. MDCCXCVI).[1] George Mason, according to the *Dictionary of National Biography*, was born in 1735, studied at Oxford, and was called to the bar from the Inner Temple.

> Having inherited ample means, including the estate of Porters, in the parish of Shenley, Hertfordshire, and another property at Havering, Essex, he was enabled to fully gratify his taste for letters and landscape-gardening (*DNB* 36, 419).

He collected old books and published a number of works, including, in addition to the *Hoccleve*, a treatise on garden design and a corrective supplement to Johnson's Dictionary. He died in 1806.

---

* I am indebted to Colin Burrow, Ian Doyle, Tony Edwards and Pat Rogers for help with this essay, which I am happy to dedicate to a scholar to whom I owe more general debts.

1. Neither the *Regiment of Princes* nor the *Series* was printed until the nineteenth century. The only Hoccleve texts to appear in print before 1796 were four of the pieces classified as minor poems in the Early English Text Society editions (Furnivall 1892; Gollancz 1925). These were the *Complaint of the Virgin* (Furnivall no. I), printed in Caxton's *Pylgremage of the Sowle* (1483), and three poems included by William Thynne in his *Workes of Geffray Chaucer* (1532) and thence in subsequent Chaucers: Furnivall nos. V and VI and the *Letter of Cupid* (Gollancz no. VIII).

In March 1785, at a sale of manuscripts formerly owned by Anthony Askew, Mason purchased a copy of Hoccleve's shorter poems—the manuscript now in the Huntington Library, California, and catalogued there as MS HM 111 (Dutschke 1989: 144-47). Most of the earlier history of this copy is obscure. As Mason himself observed in the Advertisement to his edition, arms on the binding show that it was once in the possession of Prince Henry (1594–1612), son of James I; and this was evidently the copy used by Richard James (1592–1638) for his editing of Hoccleve's poem against Oldcastle.[2] But in the following century it was apparently unknown even to learned antiquaries such as Thomas Tanner and Thomas Warton—men who were otherwise acquainted with the poet's *Regiment of Princes, Series,* and *Letter of Cupid* from manuscript copies in Oxford and London.[3]

The manuscript contains 18 poems, all of which were later printed by F.J. Furnivall, numbered by him I to XVIII (Furnivall 1892). Mason gives an account of all these in his Preface (pp. 10-17), but he selected only six to print. In his order, these are: *La Male Regle* (Furnivall no. III), *Balade and Chanson to Henry Somer* (Furnivall no. XIII), *Balade by the Court of Good Company to Henry Somer* (Furnivall no. XVII), *Balade to King Henry V* (Furnivall no. XV), *Balade to Master John Carpenter* (Furnivall no. XVI), and

2.   The James edition was not printed at the time. It survives in two manuscript copies (Burrow 1994: 21 n. 84). It so happens that three of the four minor poems printed before 1796 do occur in Mason's manuscript (Furnivall nos. I, V, VI); but neither Caxton nor Thynne used that copy.

3.   Tanner did however find, in what he calls 'Baleus MS Glynn', a reference to what is evidently the *Male Regle* (a poem now known, apart from one fragment, only in HM 111): '*De suis prodigalitatibus,* lib. I. "O pretiosum et incomparabilem"' (Tanner 1748: 557). Following Tyrwhitt (see his letter in the Appendix here), Mason made the identification, adding 'where the poem itself existed, Tanner could give no intimation' (p. 9). Tanner's source was a copy of John Bale's *Catalogus,* Part I (1557), containing manuscript notes added by Bale in the last years of his life. This copy was formerly in the possession of William Glynne and is now in the British Library: see Beal (1980: I.i, 59). Bale may or may not have known the *Male Regle* from HM 111 itself. The fuller form of his note, adding 'Thesaurum', may be found in Thomas Hearne's edition of Johannis de Trokelowe, *Annales Edvardi II* (Oxford, 1729: 287). Tanner's transcription of the Bale notes occupies ff.101-103 and 166-67 of British Library MS Additional 6261 (the Hoccleve note on f. 101v).

Balade to the Duke of York (Furnivall no. IX).[4] The selection
excludes the four poems concerned with the Virgin Mary and also
the long anti-Lollard piece addressed to Oldcastle. Mason
explains that he has preferred those pieces which display the 'circumstances of Hoccleve's private life': 'Private anecdotes in the
least degree characteristical are always amusing; and when they
bring us acquainted with peculiar habits and manners after the
intervention of centuries, can hardly fail of interesting readers of
curiosity' (Preface, pp. 4-5).

Furnivall made only passing references to Mason's book, whose
contents he lists incorrectly in his Forewords (p. xlii), and it has
been little noticed since. Yet the *Dictionary of National Biography* is
entirely justified in calling it a 'very creditable performance'.
Mason much admired Thomas Tyrwhitt as a scholar 'whose
accuracy in researches of this kind needs not be expatiated upon'
(Preface, p. 9). He learned a great deal from Tyrwhitt's edition of
the *Canterbury Tales* (1775–78); and shortly after purchasing his
manuscript he lent it to Tyrwhitt for a first inspection.[5] Mason's
own little quarto deserves to be recognized as a worthy satellite to
his master's great edition, most especially for its treatment of
Hoccleve's language and metre.

In the short account of Hoccleve himself with which Mason
opens his Preface, he refers chiefly to what were then the standard biographical sources: John Bale, *Scriptorum Illustrium Maioris
Brytannie: Catalogus* (1557–59); John Pits, *Relationum Historicarum
de Rebus Anglicis Tomus Primus* (1619); and especially Thomas
Tanner's *Bibliotheca Britannico-Hibernica* (1748).[6] In common with
all these authorities, he notes that Hoccleve was Chaucer's disciple; and he follows Tanner in observing that he 'studied the law
at *Chester's Inn*, and was a writer to the *Privy Seal* for twenty years'.[7]

---

4.   The order is Mason's. I cite poems according to the EETS numbering,
for convenience of reference.

5.   Tyrwhitt rapidly made a number of interesting observations, which he
reported to Mason in the letter reproduced here in the Appendix.

6.   The entries on Hoccleve are found in Bale (1557–59: I, 537); Pits
(1619: 587); and Tanner (1748: 557). The last is much the fullest.

7.   Mason wrongly ascribes this to Pits (p. 2). Tanner found the reference
to Chester Inn in *Regiment of Princes* 5. His observation that Hoccleve 'scriptor
erat per XX annos ad officium custodis privati sigilli pertinens' must derive
from *Regiment* 804 (where line 805, however, adds a further four years).

Like Tanner, too, he dissociates himself (pp. 4, 12) from the
opinion of Bale, already doubted by Pits, that Hoccleve was a
Wycliffite.[8] He also refers to Tanner's statement that the poet
celebrated his patron Humphrey Duke of Gloucester 'in carmin-
ibus mirifice'; but he says he does not know any evidence for this
opinion, proving that he had not seen the *Dialogue with a Friend*—
probably because there were no complete copies of the *Series* in
London.[9] On the other hand, his privileged access to MS HM 111
allowed him to contribute new suggestions about the poet's life
and circle. He was the first to propose a date for Hoccleve's birth
(pp. 1 and 35 n.). This date, 1370, which is no more than three or
four years too late, he derived from his assignment of the *Male
Regle* to the end of 1406 or early 1407 (p. 55 n.), itself an estimate
very close to the mark.[10] Mason was less fortunate in adopting
from Tanner the date 1454 as the likely time of Hoccleve's death
(pp. 3-4, 77 n., 79 n.). This estimate depended upon identifying
'Prince Edward' in the York poem (Furnivall no. IX) as the future
Edward IV, born in 1442—an error which Furnivall perpetuated
in the EETS edition.[11]

The poems in his manuscript also enabled Mason to throw new
light on Hoccleve's life in the Privy Seal and the people with
whom he had dealings. Mason's zeal in these matters appears
in his correspondence with the antiquarian Samuel Pegge the
younger (1733–1800).[12] Thus, they exchange information about
Chester Inn, and about the topography of the passage in the *Male
Regle* describing how Hoccleve walked to the 'brigge' and took a
boat 'hoom to the priuee seel' (Nichols 1817–58: IV, 564-66).
They also discuss the 'Court of Good Company', on behalf of

8.   See also Tyrwhitt's letter in the Appendix here.

9.   In a footnote (on p. 18), Mason refers to the *Tale of Jonathas* in a
British Library copy, Royal 17. D. vi; but this contains only *Jereslaus, Learn to
Die*, and *Jonathas*.

10. Hoccleve was probably born in 1367 or 1366, and the *Male Regle* probably written between Michaelmas 1405 and March 1406 (Burrow 1994: 2, 15).

11. Furnivall 1892: xxvii. Mason followed Tyrwhitt's letter. The correct
identification is with the Duke of York killed at Agincourt (Schulz: 1937).
Hoccleve is now held to have died in 1426 (Burrow 1994: 29).

12. Pegge is that 'judicious author of the *Curialia*' whose help Mason
acknowledges (p. 26). Extracts from the Mason-Pegge correspondence are
printed in Nichols (1817–58: IV, 561-70).

which Hoccleve sent a balade (Furnivall no. XVII) to the Chancellor of the Exchequer, Sir Henry Somer.[13] Editing the other poem addressed to Somer, when he was Undertreasurer (Furnivall no. XIII), Mason observes that Somer 'was made a Baron of the Exchequer, Nov. 8th, 1408', and dates the poem to the end of 1407—a conclusion which Furnivall adopts, without acknowledgment.[14] Mason was further successful in identifying 'my lord the Fourneval', to whom *Male Regle* is addressed, as Thomas Nevill, who became Treasurer in 1405, and also the 'Meistre Robert Chichele' who commissioned Furnivall no. XVIII as the twice Lord Mayor of London of that name.[15] He suggests that the two joint petitioners of Furnivall no. XV are to be looked for among the three Privy Seal clerks named in Furnivall no. XIII (p. 71 n.); but he is doubtful—rightly, I think—whether the 'Prentys and Arondel' referred to in *Male Regle* 321 also belonged to the same office.[16]

It will be evident that Mason made some real progress in elucidating Hoccleve's 'private anecdotes'; but his major contributions lie in the treatment of the six texts he chose to publish. He was particularly fortunate in that his manuscript (assigned by him to about the middle of the fifteenth century, p. 10) was in fact one of those now recognized as having been copied by the poet himself (Schulz 1937). He cannot be faulted, therefore, for the infrequency of his substantive emendations. In all 688 lines there are

13. Mason presents his conclusions in a note to the poem (p. 66): 'This *Company* seems to have been formed of members of the *Middle Temple*. The *Temple* is mentioned in the poem; and *Chestre's Inn* (where Hoccleve studied the law) appears to have then belonged to the *Middle Temple*. Though the editor can throw very little light upon the particular custom of the feast here treated of; yet he gives the piece to the public, as a singular curiosity in its way.'

14. Mason 1796: 59 n.; Furnivall 1892: 59. A more likely date is 1408 (Burrow 1994: 16).

15. Mason 1796: 55 n. and 16 n. Both identifications had been discussed with Pegge. In a note on 'maistre Carpenter' (Furnivall no. XVI, 1), Mason correctly refers to the London town clerk John Carpenter, but mistakenly identifies him with a later bishop of Winchester.

16. Mason 1796: 49 n.: 'Whether these two gentlemen belonged to the Privy Seal, or not, seems doubtful: had they been in the same department with Hoccleve, they would most likely have been mentioned in the next poem [i.e. Furnivall no. XIII].'

only two, both marked by italics. He adds '*an*' before 'hawe' in *Male Regle* 380, noting that the word is 'wanted for the metre' and comparing Furnivall no. XVIII, 20; and at Furnivall no. XVI, 23 he adds '*hem*' after 'betwixt', noting that the word is 'clearly required both for sense and metre'. Both emendations are surely correct, and Furnivall follows.[17] Furnivall's only other emendation in the six poems is incorrect, and would have been avoided if he had consulted his predecessor. At Furnivall no. XIII, 18, Mason follows the manuscript: 'Yee wole us helpe, and been our suppoaill.' Furnivall emends the last word to 'suppo[rt]aille'; but Mason's footnote refers to his Glossary, where the entry reads: 'Support. L[ydgate] has the same word in his *Storie of Thebes*; but Dr. Morell in his common place book (which is now in the editor's possession) has unaccountably copied Lydgate's word, as if it was *supportayle*. With a slight variation of orthography *suppowail* is in Hardynge's, and in Wyntown's chronicles.' Here the modern dictionaries fully vindicate Mason against Morell and Furnivall: *MED* s.v. *suppowaille*; *OED* s.v. *suppowell*. Mason also has the advantage at Furnivall no. III, 265, where Hoccleve writes a mark of punctuation like an S on its side between 'A' and 'nay', a reading better represented by Mason's 'Ah nay' than by the EETS 'As nay'.

However, Mason's text does have a dozen substantive misreadings not shared by Furnivall (though two are corrected in the Errata). These affect mostly small words, for example, 'In' for MS 'At' (Furnivall no. III, 162); 'the' for 'this' and for 'Tho' (XIII, 14, III, 225); 'And' for 'My' (III, 114). At III, 442 he reads MS 'Shameth' as 'Shunneth', and for once goes badly astray at III, 258, printing 'So thus hem all saved his providence' for Hoccleve's 'Lo thus hem all*e* saued his prudence.' In the matter of orthography, Mason claims in his Preface to have 'scrupulously adhered to the practice of the Ms.' (p. 24); but he is not entirely successful in this. Occasional words are slightly modernized in spelling, for example, 'shall' for 'shal', 'thou' for 'thow', 'discretion' for 'discrecion', and Hoccleve's regular 'con-' becomes 'com-' in words such as 'conpleyne' and 'conpellith'. His most frequent divergences, however, affect final -*e*. This is omitted on eight

---

17 Mason also makes two other smaller corrections, both followed by Furnivall: 'deceyvours' for MS 'deceyuous' (Furnivall no. III, 227) and 'sonne' for 'senne' (Furnivall no. XIII, 6).

occasions where the poet wrote it out, and on eight occasions *-e* is added where none is called for; but Mason, like Furnivall, had most difficulty with those places where Hoccleve indicates *-e* by either a bar through final *-ll* or a flourish on final *-r*. I find 17 places where he expands correctly, but on some 52 occasions he fails to do so.

Such errors in the treatment of final *-e* would be expected to result in lines lacking the requisite 10 or 11 syllables. Remarkably, however, not one of the lines with unexpanded final *-e* is in that way unmetrical.[18] Indeed, Mason's edition is much superior to Furnivall's in its respect for the importance of syllable-count in Hoccleve's verse. The section on versification in his Preface (pp. 25-26) refers the reader to Tyrwhitt's analysis of Chaucer's metre. Thus, Tyrwhitt wrote:

> the correctness and harmony of an English verse depends entirely upon its being composed of a certain number of syllables, and its having the accents of those syllables properly placed. In order therefore to form any judgement of the Versification of Chaucer, it is necessary that we should know the syllabical value (if I may use the expression) of his words, and the accentual value of his syllables, as they were commonly pronounced (1775–78: IV, 88).[19]

In his Preface, accordingly, Mason offers some notes on 'syllabical values', observing that the endings *-es*, *-en* and *-ed* normally make a syllable, as does medial *-e*; that endings such as *-ioun* are normally disyllabic; and that final *-ie* can be monosyllabic in words such as 'verifie'. He ends by saying that '*particular* distinctions of pronunciation will be pointed out by marks'—a promise fully honoured in the texts themselves.

18. Of the 52 cases, 28 occur in eliding position, and 18 in rhyme where the extra unstressed syllable is metrically optional. Four are compensated for elsewhere in the line, as in Furnivall no. III, 258 quoted above. The remaining cases are Furnivall no. III, 191, where omission of *-e* in 'alle' actually gives an easier decasyllabic reading, and Furnivall no. XVI, 1, where Mason has 'See heer my maistr' Carpenter, I yow preye.' The apostrophe here indicates awareness that with disyllabic 'maistre' the line has 12 syllables—an unmetrical result produced, in fact, by the poet substituting 'Carpenter' for an erased name with only two syllables.

19. See Mason's note to Furnivall no. III, 219: '*Contrarie*] This seems to be an instance of what Mr Tyrwhitt has remarked in Chaucer; that two quick syllables sometimes make but one in metre.'

Tyrwhitt objected to 'innovations in orthography' (1775–78: IV, 95), but Mason employs four diacritic marks to guide the reader. One of these, an acute accent, generally indicates stress-placement in Hoccleve's words 'as they were commonly pronounced', though on occasion it stretches a point in the interests of iambic rhythm, as when an accent is placed over the second syllable of 'only' (Furnivall no. III, 83). The remaining three marks all indicate 'syllabical values'. A broad circumflex acts as a 'mark of contraction', indicating that 'outrageously', for instance, has not five but four syllables in *Male Regle* 109. An apostrophe is used to mark elision or syncope in doubtful cases, most often where a possibly syllabic consonant is concerned, as in 'So is my spirit simple' and sore agast' (Furnivall no. III, 424).[20] The most frequent of these marks, however, is a short sloping 'equals' sign. This is used in all but rhyming positions to indicate syllabic final -*e*, with such consistency that its absence (except in rhyme) can safely be taken as a mark of elision. The opening lines of *Male Regle* will illustrate its use:

> O Precious tresor incomparable,
> O ground and roo=te of prosperitee,
> O excellent riches=se commendable
> Aboven al=le that in eer=the be,
> Who may sustee=ne thyn adversitee?
> What wight may him avante of worldly welthe,
> But if he fully stand in grace of thee,
> Eerthely god, piler of lyf, thow helthe?

Syllabic -*e* is here marked, not only in words such as 'richesse' in non-eliding position, but also in 'roote'. This indicates Mason's awareness that elision may not occur across the midline break. Absence of the mark in 'avante' and 'grace' indicates elision. Mason very rarely goes wrong in such marking, and further evidence of his care for 'syllabical values' is provided by his footnotes to the texts. Thus, on *Male Regle* 37, 'Whan I was weel, cowde I considere it? Nay', he notes: '*Considere it* pronounced *considrit*';

---

20. In accordance with Hoccleve's usage elsewhere, Mason alters MS 'the ordre' to 'thordre' at Furnivall no. IX, 50, observing 'metre requires the contraction; and, that being the case, the Ms. authorises this mode of junction by many similar ones'. Similarly, at III, 308 he alters MS 'to endure' to 'tendure'.

and on the line 'That it me reveth many a sleep and nap'
(Furnivall no. XVI, 21), he notes: '*Many a...*makes but two syllables; as is always the case in Milton, and frequently in Spenser.'[21]
All in all, readers of Mason's *Hoccleve* were given no excuse for not
appreciating the old poet's care for metrical correctness.

Mason's Preface also devotes short sections to language and
orthography. The former (pp. 17-22) notes the similarity of
Hoccleve's language to Chaucer's, and goes on to discuss the
pronominal forms *hem* and *hir*, the variation between *-es* and *-s* in
plural nouns, and the verb endings *-en* and *-eth* and *-ith*.[22] The one
syntactic observation, on Hoccleve's frequent omission of *to*
before infinitives, is repeated in several footnotes. The editor's
punctuation of the texts does not reproduce Hoccleve's virgules,
but shows a generally firm grasp of syntactic structure.[23] Footnotes
occasionally comment on syntactic irregularities (on *Male Regle*
237, '*Shee* has no proper antecedent'); but the infrequency of
such criticisms suggests that this eighteenth-century reader found
little to trouble him in the articulation of Hoccleve's sentences—
which is indeed generally very correct, certainly by comparison
with the syntax of his contemporary, John Lydgate.

The main business of the footnotes, however, is with the expli-
cation of the meaning of words and phrases; and in this they are
supported by a very substantial Glossary, extending to twenty-eight
pages and containing 439 entries. Introducing the Glossary in his
Preface (pp. 22-24), Mason takes justifiable pride in its fullness:
'In a volume of so little bulk, as the present is, there can be no
excuse for sparing any pains in composing the *glossary*, which may
tend to render it more useful.' He explains that he has taken care

21. Other notes refer to rhyme and stanza form. On Furnivall no. XIII,
28, Mason observes that 'Hoccleve was exacter in his rimes than even most
modern poets.'

22. Pegge argued that Hoccleve's language showed him to be of Northern
extraction. Mason in his edition wisely reserved judgment on the point
(pp. 13 and 35-36).

23. He mispunctuates *Male Regle* 270-72 (failing for once to see that
'to' must be understood) and Furnivall no. XVII, 13-14. The latter passage
puzzled Mason, as he confessed to Pegge, and his note in the edition is
desperate. The correct sense of an undoubtedly difficult place is given by
Seymour: 'but we note you do not bid us be unreasonable' (Seymour 1981:
112).

to refer each use to the line in which it occurs: 'This method of making a glossary serve in some respect as a verbal index to the work itself, is a considerable help to all those, who are disposed to be studiers of language.' However, he excludes (p. 23) all those words 'whose old signification is properly given in Johnson's Dictionary—which, with all its faults, should be in every reader's hands, till the public is provided with a better'.[24]

The Glossary itself is headed with an explanation of references and abbreviations—in effect, a list of most authorities consulted and cited. Mason names Caxton, Chaucer, Gower, Lydgate, Mandeville, 'Pierce Ploughman's Visions' and Spenser, and lists seven early printed books, together with six eighteenth-century editions of medieval texts and three works of reference.[25] Of all these, 'Tyrwhitt's Glossary to Chaucer' is by far the most important, being cited in 219 of the 439 entries. Lydgate comes next, with 85 citations, followed by the Wycliffite New Testament (28 entries), Mannyng's translation of Langtoft's *Chronicle* (17 entries), Mandeville (16 entries), and *Dives and Pauper* (12 entries). Consultation of these and other authorities allowed Mason to produce a glossary remarkable not only for its fullness but also for the accuracy of its definitions. Real mistakes are few, the worst being the gloss 'family' for 'femel' in *Male Regle* 138. More pardonable is Mason's failure to understand the metaphor in *Male Regle* 31: 'Nat sholde his lym han cleved to my gore.' In the poet's system of orthography 'lym' must have a long vowel and is certainly 'lime'; but Mason takes it to represent 'limb', in the sense 'active minister' or 'instrument'. In this case, no later editor or lexicographer has succeeded in improving upon him.[26] Mason's correspondence

24. Mason's low opinion of Dr Johnson appears from an extraordinary excursus in his Glossary. Glossing the word 'skill', he takes occasion to introduce a mock epitaph on Johnson (pp. 106-107) attacking, among other things, his 'pedantic verbosity', political bigotry, failure as a poet, and incompetence as a critic.

25. The early printed books are: the *Moral Proverbs* of Rivers (Caxton, 1478), Tiptoft's *Of Friendship* (Caxton, 1481), the *Boke of St. Albans* (1486), *Dives and Pauper* (Pynson, 1493), *Promptorium Parvulorum* (Pynson, 1499), Hilton's *Scale of Perfection* (Notary, 1507) and Fabyan's *Chronicle* (1516).

26. The EETS edition (Furnivall 1892) passes over the word; Hammond follows Mason (Hammond 1927: 402); and Seymour glosses 'limb, arm'

with Pegge shows him struggling with another difficult word, 'owter' in the line 'Be thow an owter of my nycetee' (Furnivall no. IX, 17).[27] They also discuss (Nichols 1817–58: IV, 568) the problem of 'lagh', in the passage where Hoccleve urges Henry Somer to 'paie your lagh' for the Court of Good Company (Furnivall no. XVII, 33). Pegge understood the word as '*Arrears, i.e.* of his annual quota', relating it to a Saxon 'laf' meaning 'residue'; but Mason referred it to the word 'law' and glossed it 'just share' in the edition. Mason's interpretation is supported by *MED*, which records 'lagh' as occurring only here and glosses it 'share of payment, contribution'.[28]

At the time when Mason published his book Hoccleve's verse was almost unknown outside antiquarian circles.[29] Mason's own interests were themselves largely antiquarian, but he also paid some regard to the quality of the writing. Appreciation of Hoccleve's verse technique appears both in his editorial diacritics and also in his comment on the rhymes: 'exacter...than even most modern poets'. In the Preface, he devotes a section to 'poetical merit' (pp. 6-9). Here he cites the testimony of William Browne of Tavistock (d. 1643/45?), an earlier admirer of Hoccleve, who modernized the *Tale of Jonathas* in his *Shepherd's Pipe*.[30] Browne's own 'easy vein of harmonious poetry', Mason observes, qualified him to praise Hoccleve as one who 'did

(Seymour 1981: 146). *MED* wrongly cites the passage under *lim* n.(1), sense 2(c) 'hand'. Cf. *Regiment of Princes* 4571.

27. 'He [Mason] would have preferred *display*, but can bring nothing to the purpose to confirm such interpretation. He therefore adopts *completion*, and relies on the old French verb *outrer*, which Carpentier interprets by *achever*' (Nichols 1817–58: IV, 569). 'Display' was in fact nearer the mark: the poem is to display Hoccleve's foolishness. *MED* cites only this passage (*outer(e* n.) for sense (a) a publisher.

28. *MED lagh* n. *OED* (*Law* sb²) records only the Hoccleve and two later Scottish examples. *MED* compares Old Icelandic 'lag', 'market price'.

29. The only substantial piece available in print was the *Letter of Cupid*, found in collected editions of Chaucer from Thynne's until Urry's in 1721. Speght and his successors ascribed it to Hoccleve. George Sewell published an interesting modern rendering of that poem in 1718 (Fenster and Erler 1990).

30. Browne owned manuscript copies of the *Series, Regiment* and *Letter of Cupid,* and projected an edition of the poet's works: see Edwards (1997: 441-49).

quench his thirst / Deeply, as did ever one, / In the Muses' Helicon' (p. 6). Elsewhere, in a footnote to *Male Regle* 31-32, the editor remarks: 'Lines like these might well occasion W. Browne to say of Hoccleve, in the beginning of the seventeenth century, "There are few such swaines as he / Now adayes for harmonie."' Mason also addresses himself, however, to some rather dismissive comments made by Thomas Warton in his *History of English Poetry*. Warton had objected to Hoccleve's version of the *Gesta Romanorum* story of Jonathas on the grounds that he failed to embellish it. Mason, who had read *Jonathas* in the British Museum copy (see n. 9 above), responds: 'Hoccleve indeed adheres closely to the substance of the story, yet embellishes it in various places by judicious insertions of his own, and of which there are no traces at all in his original' (Preface p. 7). He also cites Warton's description of Hoccleve as 'a feeble writer' who exhibits 'coldness of genius' and a total lack of 'invention and fancy'.[31] He denies the first two charges, but admits the last—as well he might, if by 'invention and fancy' is understood the ability to create imaginary worlds. Yet he goes on to remark that Warton had not seen most of the poems in his manuscript: 'Now had some of these, especially some of the present selection, been seen by Mr. Warton, the editor really thinks, that this discerning critic would have perceived more originality in Hoccleve, than he deemed him possest of, and consequently have held him in a somewhat higher degree of estimation' (p. 9). Here perhaps, in employing what was then the quite recently adopted critical term 'originality', Mason had in mind the distinctiveness of Hoccleve's poetic voice (*OED* sense 3). His sense of that voice may be suggested by a comment on the poet's 'embellishments' in the *Jonathas*: 'In some of them there is a strain of pleasantry similar to that of Prior.' The comparison with Matthew Prior (d. 1721) is suggestive. Prior—another 'correct' poet, albeit in the Augustan mode—speaks of himself in a vein of humorous self-depreciation which can sometimes recall Hoccleve.[32]

31. Warton 1774–81: II, 38. The discussion of *Jonathas* is in the dissertation on the *Gesta Romanorum*: III, lvi-lvii.

32. Mason 1796: 7-8. He refers again to Prior in a footnote to Furnivall no. III, 165-66, citing a parallel from his *Solomon*. Dr Johnson's criticisms of Prior are much like Warton's of Hoccleve: 'If Prior's poetry be generally

George Mason was lucky in the acquisition of MS HM 111, as it now is. In his Advertisement he invites fellow scholars to inform him of other copies of its contents; but none have come to light since, and even if they did, they could hardly present a challenge to what is in fact, though Mason did not know it, the poet's own transcript. Yet he deserves all credit for adhering closely in his text to that manuscript, and also for his achievements in scanning, glossing and annotating six previously unstudied Middle English poems. Indeed, so far as those poems are concerned, it cannot be said that today, 200 years later, we know or understand much more than he already did.

APPENDIX

Mason lent his Hoccleve manuscript, very shortly after purchasing it on 7 March 1785, to Thomas Tyrwhitt. Tyrwhitt drew up a table of contents, sent to Mason along with a letter dated 4 April 1785. Mason fixed both to the inside front cover of the manuscript, adding a short comment of his own. Tyrwhitt's letter and Mason's comment are here reproduced, with the kind permission of the Huntington Library.

Welbeck Street 4 April 1785

Dear Sir,
   As a small return for your favour in lending me this MS. I have indeavoured to save you the trouble of making a *Table of contents* to it.
   I have also numbered the leaves, which I hold every possessor of a MS bound to do, if he means that it shall be useful.
   I suspect that the 5 leaves, which are now placed between fol. 2 & fol. 8, originally preceeded fol. 1. They contain the latter part of a *Compleynte* of the Virgin, of which the first part was probably contained in a leaf which is lost. That leaf, with these 5, & the 2 first leaves of the Balade to Oldcastel, would make exactly a sheet. The reason for transposing these leaves seems to have been, that the book might not appear evidently defective at the beginning.
   The Balade to Oldcastel is not mentioned, I believe, by any of our bibliographers. It is the more curious as Hoccleve has been generally represented as a favourer of the new opinions. He is here most furiously

considered his praise will be that of correctness and industry, rather than of compass of comprehension or activity of fancy. He never made any effort of invention' (Hall 1905: II, 207).

orthodox, though in what he says about *the real presence* fol. 8. he does not speak directly to the point. There is a good list of books, fol. 10. which he advises Oldcastel to read instead of the bible.

La male regle de T.H. fol. 16.b. I take to be what is mentioned by Tanner, from Bale MS. Glynn. as entitled, *De suis prodigalitatibus*. lib. I. I know not that it is extant any where else. It appears from fol. 25.b. to have been written while Lord Fourneval was Treasurer. I find Johannis Talbot, Dominus de Furnival, was *first* summoned to Parl^t 11 H.4. & to many subsequent Parl^ts in that reign & the next.

The Balade to the Duke of York, fol. 32b. shows that Hoccleve lived to a very advanced age. Prince Edward (afterwards Edward 4th) was not born till about 1442. If we suppose him 6 years old (& he could not be much less to be under the tuition of Maister Picard) this poem was written in 1448. He says, fol. 33.b. that he was almost blind, but too proud to wear spectacles.

The poem, fol. 37.b. to Monsr Johan (afterwards Duke of Bedford) & that fol. 39.b. to the Prince (afterwards Henry 5) were both sent with the book of the *Regimen of Princes* & are added at the end of that book in MS. Reg. 17 D XVIII.

Of the other poems in your volume you are (for aught I know) the only possessor. I congratulate you upon so invaluable a treasure. I am always, dear sir,

> Your very faithful
> humble serv^t T. Tyrwhitt

This letter contains much satisfactory information. Yet on one circumstance it deviates a little from the point. The Lord Furnival who was Treasurer was not a Talbot but his predecessor in the title, Thomas Nevil. They both held it jure uxoris. GM

WORKS CITED

Bale, J.
  1557–59   *Scriptorum Illustrium Maioris Brytannie: Catalogus* (2 vols.; Basle: Oporinus).
Beal, P.
  1980–93   *Index of English Literary Manuscripts* (4 vols.; London: Mansell).
Burrow, J.A.
  1994   *Thomas Hoccleve* (Aldershot: Variorum).
Dutschke, C.W.
  1989   *Guide to Medieval and Renaissance Manuscripts in the Huntington Library* (2 vols.; San Marino: Huntington Library).

Edwards, A.S.G.
    1997   'Medieval Manuscripts Owned by William Browne of Tavistock
                (1590/1?–1643/5?)', in J.P. Carley and C.G.C. Tite (eds.), *Books and
                Collectors 1200–1700: Essays Presented to Andrew Watson* (London: The
                British Library): 441-49.
Fenster, T.S., and M.C. Erler (eds.)
    1990   *Poems of Cupid, God of Love* (Leiden: E.J. Brill).
Furnivall, F.J. (ed.)
    1892   *Hoccleve's Works: I. Minor Poems in the Phillipps MS. 8151 (Cheltenham)
                and the Durham MS. III. 9* (EETS ES, 61; London: Kegan Paul,
                Trench, Trübner).
Gollancz, I (ed.)
    1925   *Hoccleve's Works: II. Minor Poems from the Ashburnham MS. Addit. 133*
                (EETS ES 73; London: Oxford University Press).
Hall, G.B. (ed.)
    1905   *Lives of the English Poets by Samuel Johnson* (3 vols.; Oxford: Clarendon
                Press).
Hammond, E.P. (ed.)
    1927   *English Verse between Chaucer and Surrey* (Durham, NC: Duke Univer-
                sity Press).
Mason, G. (ed.)
    1796   *Poems by Thomas Hoccleve...* (London: Leigh & Sotheby).
Nichols, J.
    1817–58   *Illustrations of the Literary History of the Eighteenth Century* (8 vols.;
                London: Nichols, Son & Bentley).
Pits, J.
    1619   *Relationum Historicarum de Rebus Anglicis Tomus Primus* (Paris: Thierry
                & Cramoisy).
Schulz, H.C.
    1937   'Thomas Hoccleve, Scribe', *Speculum* 12: 71-81.
Seymour, M.C. (ed.)
    1981   *Selections from Hoccleve* (Oxford: Clarendon Press).
Tanner, T.
    1748   *Bibliotheca Britannico-Hibernica* (London: Bowyer).
Tyrwhitt, T.
    1775–78   *The Canterbury Tales of Chaucer* (5 vols.; London: Payne).
Warton, T.
    1774–81   *The History of English Poetry* (3 vols.; London: Dodsley).

Editing and Ideology: Stephen Batman and the *Book of Privy Counselling*

A.S.G. Edwards

That a variety of editorial presuppositions, conscious and uncon-
scious, can inform the edited text is hardly news. The existence of
various forms of assumption about the nature of the universe has
often impinged upon the editorial process in relation to Middle
English texts, as has been seen in discussions of the work of such
nineteenth- and early twentieth-century positivist editors and the-
orists like Walter Skeat, Henry Bradshaw and R.K. Root (on whom
see Edwards 1984 and Hanna 1984). And we see narrower his-
toricist assumptions in the activities of a modern editor like Israel
Gollancz, in his editing of the fourteenth-century *Winner and
Waster*, whereby the text is emended to help to make the poem
accord with his view of it as a historical allegory—'An Alliterative
Poem on Social and Economic Problems in England in the Year
1352', as his subtitle has it (see Trigg 1986).

Such assumptions draw on a tradition of interpositions between
received text and edited text that we can broadly locate within
forms of ideological assumption. Most obviously such assumptions
involve issues of faith. In the case of medieval English texts such
assumptions can go back to actual manuscript traditions, most
obviously in the various Wycliffite modifications or additions to
received 'orthodox' vernacular works in prose and verse, like the
Pore Caitif (see Brady 1989) or the adaptations of Rolle's prose
Psalter and the *Mirror of St Edmund* (see Hudson 1988: 424-25) as
well as Latin ones, like the *Polychronicon* (see Talbert 1942).

Such doctrinal preoccupations with earlier literature continued
in England into the sixteenth century, particularly after the

Henrician reformation and the Elizabethan settlement, and are evidenced both by the reprinting of Lollard works (see Hudson 1983) and such curious strategies as the Protestant use of the fiercely (Catholic) orthodox *Piers Plowman* in both manuscript and printed forms to further the cause of the reformers (see Jansen 1989; King 1982: 319-57). In Scotland in the mid-sixteenth century religious reform led to the 'correcting' of medieval poems, including some by Dunbar and Henryson deemed too exuberant in their piety for Caledonian temper (see MacDonald 1983).

One aspect of these political and ideological preoccupations with such literature is the scholarly activities with which the Elizabethan church became involved immediately after Elizabeth's succession, whereby earlier works of history and other medieval manuscripts were scrutinized to provide justification for the contemporary reforms of the English church. A crucial figure here is, of course, Elizabeth's first Archbishop, Matthew Parker (1504–75), who developed the programme of research that focused this preoccupation, one in which he was himself actively engaged (see Greg 1935–36; Wright 1949–53).

Parker's household also included scholars who can be associated with his own interest in medieval manuscripts, notably his secretary, John Joscelyn, a distinguished early Anglo-Saxon scholar (on whom see Adams 1917: 17-21). A less definable figure was Stephen Batman (d. 1584), a cleric who appears to have been employed within his household in some way.[1] Batman was, like Parker, a collector of medieval manuscripts (see Brockhurst 1947; McKitterick and Beadle 1992: 88; and Parkes 1997) and early printed books.[2] His own collecting seems to have had a distinct focus on Middle English texts, primarily but not exclusively of a

---

1.   Dr Parkes, in his study of Batman's manuscripts, notes (p. 126) that there is no evidence that he was Parker's domestic chaplain as has sometimes been asserted. I am greatly indebted to Dr Parkes for permitting me to see his study in advance of publication.

2.   Dr Parkes's study does not include printed books owned by Batman. I know of the following: (i) Corpus Christi College, Cambridge SP 311 (Vegetius, *De Re Militari*, 1535, on which see Page 1993: 18 and Pl. 23); (ii) Trinity College, Cambridge Herman Schedel, *Nürnberg Chronicle* (1493); (iii) *Polychronicon* (de Worde, 1495), sold by H.P. Kraus, List 203, part 1, 1983.

devotional cast. A number of the manuscripts he possessed were prose religious texts, including Trinity College, Cambridge B.1.38 and B.2.7 (both Wycliffe Bible commentaries), Trinity B.14.15 ('þe doctrine of þe hart'), Trinity B.14.19 (*The Chastising of God's Children* and other works), Bodleian Library Bodley 480 (*The Pricking of Love*), and Magdalene College, Cambridge Pepys 2498 (a large collection of devotional texts in both prose and verse), which he annotated with some frequency. He also owned a famous copy of Chaucer's *Troilus and Criseyde* (Corpus Christi College Cambridge MS 61) and a manuscript of *Piers Plowman* (Bodleian Library MS Digby 171). The range of his interest in Middle English texts is further attested in the work for which he is probably best known to posterity, his edition of Trevisa's translation of Bartholomaeus Anglicus, *Batman vppon Bartholome*, published by Thomas East in 1582.

Batman was not simply a collector. He was also no mean artist, adding illustrations to some of the manuscripts he owned or copied.[3] He sometimes also composed verses to accompany texts.[4] His interests extended beyond just collecting to transcriptions of other manuscripts.[5] One collection he prepared is now Harvard University, Houghton Library MS f Eng 1015, a late sixteenth-century miscellaneous collection of 127 leaves, copied throughout by him in a variety of scripts, and containing medieval and post-medieval works in both verse and prose in English.[6] It includes, on ff.114v-124, a previously unrecorded copy of the *Book of Privy Counselling*.[7] The work is headed 'The trw Coppy of An Anciant Wretten Epist=/le tituled The Epistle of priuat counsaile / of Olde tyme the yere neither Autor sertainly / knowen.' The

---

3.   Including his copy of *Piers Plowman*, Bodleian MS Digby 171, f.2 and in the Harvard manuscript, including one (f.124) immediately following the *Book of Privy Counselling*.

4.   Some are printed in Zettersten (1976: xii, xiv).

5.   Another collection in his hand is Bodleian Library MS Douce 363; for a brief description see Sylvester (1959: 278-79).

6.   The manuscript is not noted in Voigts (1985); it also includes a previously unrecorded version of stanza 4 of the B version of the 'Earth upon Earth' verses (*IMEV* 704 and 3985) on f.127v. I am indebted to Dr Richard Beadle for drawing my attention to the Harvard manuscript.

7.   The most recent listing of manuscripts of the *Book of Privy Counselling* records nine copies; see Lagorio and Sargent (1993: 3429 [26]).

text itself is headed 'The pystle of pryuate cownsell / As yt was written after the olde Englyshe & noted by S.B.'[8]

The *Book of Privy Counselling* is a devotional treatise in Middle English prose, written by the author of another, longer mystical work, *The Cloud of Unknowing*.[9] With one exception all the surviving manuscripts of the *Book* collocate it with the *Cloud*. This exception is of immediate interest because it is possible to identify it as the manuscript from which Batman copied his text into the Harvard manuscript. Cambridge University Library MS Ii.vi.31 is a parchment manuscript of 64 leaves; it contains only the *Book of Privy Counselling*.[10] A note on the verso of the front (unnumbered) flyleaf in a late-sixteenth-century hand reads: 'William dunly is my m^r given vnto hym by / Stephen Batman.' A number of marginal notes which correspond to those in the Harvard manuscript have been added to the text in Batman's hand, as well as a number that do not appear in his transcript.

This seems to have been the only Middle English religious prose text Batman transcribed. His motives for undertaking it and for inserting the annotations that he added both to his Harvard copy and to the Cambridge manuscript merit some examination.

Batman's treatment of the text of the *Book of Privy Counselling* has two main aspects: his transcription of the text and the notes he added to it that constitute its apparatus. The transcription itself seems remarkably accurate in its preservation of the substantive readings of Cambridge; he even replicates the positioning of the paraph marks that constitute its main form of punctuation. He does change orthography and introduce contractions, but this is the extent of his purposive changes to the text. It was evidently Batman's concern to present his text faithfully.[11]

---

8.   On Batman's habit of using his initials in manuscripts he owned see Parkes and Salter (1978: 12).

9.   For a summary see Lagorio and Sargent (1993: 3072-73). The standard edition is Hodgson (1957); parenthetical line references are to this edition.

10.   The manuscript is described in Hodgson (1957: xiii).

11.   One distinctive feature of the text is its ending. The standard edition concludes 'and also a soule is maad sekir (I mene in þe tyme of þis doynge) þat it schal not moch erre' (172/16-18). The Cambridge manuscript ends: 'And therfore goo forthe wth mekenes & feruent desyre yn thys werke, the whyche begynnyth yn thys lyfe: and neuer shal haue ende yn the lyfe

Batman writes the main text in a well-formed and quite legible cursive secretary hand, but with Latin quotations, and some titles in a larger and heavier display script; there are also a number of marginal notes copied in a larger secretary hand.[12] The notes in the Harvard manuscript seem to have been systematically organized. They are numbered in two consecutive sequences, 1-58 (with two numbered '35') and 1-13 (with two numbered '8'); a number of brief notes are not included in either sequence. There is a general correspondence between the first sequence of these notes and those added to the Cambridge manuscript, although a few from Harvard do not appear in Cambridge.[13] There seems virtually no correspondence between the second series of numbers in Harvard and the annotations in Cambridge. In Harvard the level of annotation drops off markedly after f.116v, the end of the first numbered sequence of notes. The notes in the Cambridge manuscript are not numbered, but indicated sometimes by underlining the text, sometimes by asterisks, sometimes by pointing hands. They extend throughout the manuscript and offer a far greater density of annotation than in Harvard.[14]

These notes raise rather more complex issues than Batman's actual transcription. Most generally they can be located in the religious controversies of the latter half of the sixteenth century, controversies to which Batman can be linked through his association with Parker. That Batman should interest himself in the

euerlastyng To the whyche I beseche almyghty iesu to brynge all those the whych he hath bowght w^t hys precyous blode Amen.' This is not the only manuscript to add this additional passage: it also appears in Bodleian Douce 262, f.153, Bodley 576, f.138v and Cambridge University Library Ff.vi.41, f.28. It does not appear in British Library MSS Harley 674 or 2373, Cambridge University Library Kk.vi.26, St Hugh's Charterhouse (Sussex) Parkminster D.176 or Trinity College, Dublin 122, f.102. (I am much indebted to Professor John Scattergood for help with this last.)

12. For a helpful discussion of the various scripts Batman employed and his annotational practices see McLoughlin (1994).

13. These are nos. 4, 24, 35 (bis), 37, 38, 40, 44, 53, 55, 57, 58.

14. These notes appear on ff.1, 1v, 2, 2v, 3, 3v, 4, 4v, 5, 5v, 6, 6v, 7, 7v, 8v, 9, 9v, 10, 10v, 11, 11v, 12, 12v, 13, 14, 14v, 15, 15v, 16, 16v, 18v, 19, 19v, 20, 21, 21v, 22, 22v, 23, 23v, 24, 24v, 25, 25v, 26v, 27, 28, 28v, 29, 29v, 31v, 32, 32v, 33, 34v, 35, 36, 38v, 39, 39v, 40v, 41, 41v, 42v, 43, 43v, 44, 44v, 46, 47, 48, 48v, 49, 49v, 52, 52v, 53, 54, 56, 57, 58, 58v, 59, 59v, 62, 62v, 63, 64.

study of Catholic religious texts is unsurprising, given the political agendas that clearly informed Parker's own collecting and study of earlier historical and religious works (see further McLoughlin 1994; Wright 1949–53). But his treatment of the *Book of Privy Counselling*, both in terms of his annotations to his exemplar and the text that is presented in his own transcription, afford a rare opportunity to assess the relationship between an Elizabethan Anglican of reformist temper and a medieval, mystical Catholic work. What are Batman's motives here? Is he concerned with the scholarly elucidation of the text for a contemporary audience? Or is he engaged in some more polemic undertaking? To what degree does ideology affect editing in its basic aspects of annotation and commentary?

Where Batman's annotations correspond in both copies, that is, in the early parts of both manuscripts, they vary greatly in length and in preoccupation.[15] Some are simply glosses, either of Middle English words ('wood is madd' **C**, f.8v; **H**, f.115v) or biblical citations. Others offer glosses or commentaries on the theological implications of the text, particularly with justification by faith, as where he notes 'Dismaye the not y^t the Grace of God iz not sufficient for the: for it sufficeth all y^t are believing' (**C**, f.1v, **H**, f.114v) opposite a passage he has underlined: 'thynke not before what thow shall doo after bot forsake as well goode thowghtys as euyll thowghtys' (135/13-14). This concern recurs. He notes elsewhere: 'the deth of Christ is the purgation of sinne, to beleue not only y^t he died but y^t his deth is oure Iustification for wee being Iustified by faith are at peace with god through jesu Christ our Lord' (**C**, f.43v, **H**, f.121); here he endorses an assertion in the text: 'þei scholen fynde goostly fode of deuocion inowȝ, soffisaunt & aboundyng to þe helþe & sauyng of here soules, þof al þei comen neuer ferþer inwardes in þis liif' (160/1-3).

Other passages seem to offer some form of oblique commentary on the Elizabethan religious situation. He observes in a note on a passage on the limitations of meditation (140/2-6): 'How vnequal mans Iudgement is in the wisdom of God in his worde which is the cause of so mani errours and sectes in the which ye godly

---

15. In what follows the manuscripts are cited parenthetically by the sigils **C** (= Cambridge) and **H** (= Harvard). I have not noted minor variations between the two copies, generally following the versions in **H**.

minded are greatly hindered' (**C**, f.9; **H**, f.115v). Only occasionally is there any sharper polemical edge to his comments. At one point opposite a passage exhorting 'and therefor hold the before in the fyrst poynte of thy spirit whiche is thy beyng and goo not backe for noo maner of thyng seme it neuer soo good nor soo holy the thyng that thi wittes wolde lede the vnto' (140/6-9; **C**, f.9; **H**, f.115v) he comments: 'A good note against golden Copes and painted Idolls'; at another, opposite a passage which he has underlined which speaks of 'the passyon only of Christ' (142/17; **C**, f.13; **H**, f.116), he adds the comment 'Against all papisticall mediation.' But at least as often there is a degree of expository sympathy with the argument of the original, as in the following note, opposite another underlined passage concerned with instruction of the unlearned and those who believe themselves to be learned (137/22-25): 'The autor glorieth not in his knowledge for y^t he confessith it to be vnperfit notwithstanding he beeway-leth those whose curiusnesse is such haueng but slender knowl-edge booste of there vnderstandeng' (**C**, f.5; **H**, f.115). At other points he seems to draw on his wider awareness of Middle English religious texts as in his suggestion as the author of this work: 'I take the autor of this Copy to be Richard hampole hermet' (**H**, f.118v), an attribution which, while incorrect, reflects Batman's knowledge of vernacular devotional traditions.[16]

This last note does not appear in the Cambridge manuscript. But, in general, where the notes become peculiar to one manu-script or the other this expository sympathy seems to be sustained. In another of the notes unique to Harvard, commenting on a reference to 'þi nakyd blinde beyng þe whiche is þi God' (147/11-12), Batman observes: 'It semeth by the autor yt this naked being so often spoke of iz the cleare thinckeng of the mynd in the bodye, by the which the body for the tyme iz in a maruelus heauenly imagination which he sayth to be his God as it is in deede' (**H**, f.117v). Similarly, in Cambridge, it is the elucidation of the meaning of the work that seems his main concern. Com-menting on a passage discussing the necessity to keep 'alle þe commaundementes & þe counselle, as well of þe Olde Testament as of þe Newe' (146/7-8), he notes 'not y^t ther is any poure of keepeng with oute a keper: the body is kept for a tyme by the lyfe.

16. The Rolle attribution is not mentioned in Allen (1927).

But the wisdom of the sowle is kept for God and therfore called
an euerlasting wisdom by the which the body is made companion
of the soule and the soule with God' (**C**, f.19v). In other respects
his comments in Cambridge offer opinions that seem likely to
be doctrinally unexceptionable to Anglicans and Catholics alike,
as in this comment near the end of the work on the need to
'wiþouten cesyng lene to the nakid felyng of þi-self' (171/16), on
which he observes: 'there is no gretur reioyceng to a Christian
minde then when beinge weried with sinne he haue the desire of
vertwe because the continuance thereof is the entrance to felicite'
(f.62v).

   In this regard it may be worth noting how markedly unpolem-
ical or explicitly anti-Catholic most of his annotation is. His final
annotation is positively approbatory. In its concluding sentence
the *Book* speaks of a soul that is 'maad sekir...þat it schal not
moche erre' (172/17-18). Batman writes: 'a good note a cannot
those faine a perfect purite in this lyfe' (**C**, f.64). It is not clear
whether he has specific persons in mind here, but occasionally
elsewhere it is possible to discern a degree of political special
pleading though that is not very marked. In commenting on a
warning against spiritual presumption (150/20ff) he observes: 'to
presume of the mercy of God breedes contempt of reformation'
(**C**, f.28v). What may seem slightly more surprising is that the later
annotations in the Cambridge manuscript occasionally reflect
some explicit concerns with the state of the clergy. In commenting on the criteria for those to 'be admittyd to prelacye' (163/3ff)
he offers two pointed observations about the contemporary situation of the clergy: 'y^t this weake in right execution the prelaci
sholde bee more exceptid which wolde bee a cause alle of more
learned for the decaye of lerneng is the want of preferment' (**C**,
f.48v); 'phasitions surgeons players and lauiers haue dayli
prefermentes in larged. Bisshops preachars parsons and Curattes
have dayly their leuenges deminished' (**C**, f.48v). These comments seem to be made with sufficient feeling to lead one to suppose that they may reflect upon Batman's own clerical situation
and his view that learning was undervalued, perhaps after Parker's
death in 1575.

   Batman's annotations suggest in general, though, more an
explanatory than a polemical concern. Kate McLoughlin writes

felicitously in another context of Batman's 'positive assimilation of the text, of a wish to educe and utilize its wisdom' (McLoughlin 1994: 533). The same impulses seem to underly his annotations to the *Book of Privy Counselling*. There seems to be a degree of scholarly detachment that enables him to stand apart from doctrinaire reflexes and response with a considerable degree of sympathy to the actual concerns of the work itself.

Several factors are striking in Batman's engagement with this text. One is his fidelity in his own transcription to a Catholic original. His was not the only post-medieval attempt to reconcile Middle English religious texts with current religious orthodoxy. In the early seventeenth century, for example, the Catholic exile Augustine Baker produced a modernized version of the *Book of Privy Counselling* along with other such versions of Middle English devotional texts (see Salvin and Cressy 1993). And a little later there occurs a reworking of the much longer Middle English prose translation of Deguileville's *Pilgrimage of the Life of Man*, rewritten to bring it into closer conformity to Anglican theology.[17] But these solutions to the tension between received text and current theological disposition, involving as they do rewriting and attendant modifications, make Batman's resolute preservation of the text itself even more striking. His response to the text takes place entirely outside it and is expressed largely through his attempts at elucidation by annotation which testify to a range of impulses: the expository, the scholarly and the theological.

There is also the question of the markedly variant degrees of annotation in his original and his transcript. As I have noted, the level drops off discernibly in the Harvard copy after the opening leaves, while Batman continued unflaggingly to comment on the

17. This version, ascribed to one Walter Parker, in 1645, is extant in several seventeenth-century manuscripts, notably Magdalene College Cambridge MS Pepys 2258; for a description see James (1923: 82-84). The colophon to another copy, in Cambridge University Library MS Ff.6.30, f.124, describes it as 'written according to ye first copy. The Originall being in St Johns Coll. in Oxford & thither given by Will. Laud, Archbp. of Canterbury. Who had it of Will. Baspoole who, before he gaue to ye Archbp the Originall, did copy it out. By which it was verbatim writtin by Walter Parker 1645. & from thence transcribed by G.G. 1649. and from thence by W.A. 1655.' An edition is in progress by K.M. Walls for the Renaissance English Text Society.

Cambridge manuscript throughout. The Harvard copy has, moreover, been clearly ruled to accommodate annotation, which makes its abandoning, given the manifest existence of additional material, even more perplexing No obvious reason suggests itself for his disinclination to transfer the bulk of his notes into his transcript. One might, however, speculate that one possible motive was ideological. As I have noted, Batman clearly had a sustained interest in such devotional texts. The preparation of a careful transcript, with various hierarchies of script and numbered notes (something he does not seem to have attempted with any of the other manuscripts he owned) might be viewed as a preliminary to possible publication. The abandoning of annotation in the Harvard manuscript might be linked to the abandoning of any such plan. Perhaps like John Stow, another more famous antiquary and another associate of Parker's, he came to feel the risk of too great an interest in Catholic texts,[18] especially given the degree of sympathy he seems able to muster for the arguments presented in the *Book*. What we may see ultimately is a conflict between the ideology of the editor, other compelling institutional ideologies, and the ideology of the text itself, a range of conflicts which led the editor to choose, for whatever personal or political reasons, to remain silent.

18. Among the other texts Batman transcribed was a version of George Cavendish's *Life of Wolsey*, a Catholic account of Wolsey's life and notably of Henry's divorce from Katherine of Aragon, preserved in another of his collections (Bodleian MS Douce 363, ff.48-93).

WORKS CITED

Adams, E.N.
    1917   *Old English Scholarship in England from 1566–1800* (New Haven: Yale
                   University Press).
Allen, H.E.
    1927   *Writings Ascribed to Richard Rolle, Hermit of Hampole* (New York:
                   Modern Language Association).
Brady, Sr M.T.
    1989   'Lollard Interpolations and Omissions in Manuscripts of *The Pore
                   Caitif*, in M. Sargent (ed.), *De Cella in Seculum* (Cambridge:
                   Brewer): 183-203.

Brockhurst, Elizabeth
1947   *The Life and Works of Stephen Batman* (MA thesis, London: University
               of London).
Edwards, A.S.G.
1984   'Walter W. Skeat', in Ruggiers 1984: 207-30.
Greg, W.W
1935–36   'Books and Bookmen in the Correspondence of Archbishop
               Parker', *Library*, 4th series 16: 243-79.
Hanna, R.
1984   'R.K. Root', in Ruggiers 1984: 191-206.
Hodgson, P. (ed.)
1957   *The Cloud of Unknowing and The Book of Privy Counselling* (EETS, 218;
               London: Oxford University Press; rev. edn).
Hudson, A.
1983   '"No newe thynge": The Printing of Medieval Texts in the Early
               Tudor Period', in D. Gray and E.G. Stanley (eds.), *Middle English
               Studies Presented to Norman Davis* (Oxford: Clarendon Press): 153-74.
1988   *The Premature Reformation: Wycliffite Texts and Lollard History* (Oxford:
               Clarendon Press).
James, M.R.
1923   *A Descriptive Catalogue of the Library of Samuel Pepys*. III. *Medieval
               Manuscripts* (London: Sidgwick & Jackson).
Jansen, S.L.
1989   'Politics, Protest, and a New *Piers Plowman* Fragment: The Voice of
               the Past in Tudor England', *Review of English Studies* NS 40: 93-99.
King, J.N.
1982   *English Reformation Literature* (Princeton: Princeton University
               Press).
Lagorio, V., and M.G. Sargent
1993   'English Mystical Writings', in A.E. Hartung (gen. ed.), *A Manual of
               the Writings in Middle English 1050–1500*, IX (New Haven: Connecti-
               cut Academy of Arts, Sciences and Letters).
MacDonald, A.A.
1983   'Poetry, Politics and Reformation Censorship in Sixteenth-Century
               Scotland', *English Studies* 64: 410-21.
McKitterick, R., and R. Beadle
1992   *Catalogue of the Pepys Library at Magdalene College, Cambridge*. V. *Manu-
               scripts: Part i: Medieval* (Cambridge: Boydell and Brewer).
McLoughlin, K.
1994   'Magdalene College MS Pepys 2498 and Stephen Batman's Reading
               Practices', *Transactions of the Cambridge Bibliographical Society* 10: 525-
               34.
Page, R.I.
1993   *Matthew Parker and his Books* (Kalamazoo: Medieval Institute Publica-
               tions).

Parkes, M.
1997   'Stephen Batman's Manuscripts', in M. Kanno *et al.* (eds.), *Medieval Heritage: Essays in Honour of Tadahiro Ikegami* (Tokyo: Yushodo Press): 125-56.
Parkes, M., and E. Salter
1978   *Geoffrey Chaucer, Troilus and Criseyde: A Facsimile of Corpus Christi College Cambridge MS 61* (Cambridge: Brewer).
Ruggiers, P. (ed.)
1984   *Editing Chaucer: The Great Tradition* (Norman, OK: Pilgrim Books).
Salvin, Fr P., and Fr S. Cressy
1933   *The Life of Augustine Baker* (London: Burnes & Oates).
Sylvester, R.S. (ed.)
1959   *The Life and Death of Cardinal Wolsey* (EETS, 243; London: Oxford University Press).
Talbert, E.W.
1942   'A Lollard Chronicle of the Papacy', *Journal of English and Germanic Philology* 41: 163-93.
Trigg, S.
1986   'Israel Gollancz's "Wynnere and Wastoure": Political Satire or Editorial Politics?', in G. Kratzmann and J. Simpson (eds.), *Medieval English Religious and Ethical Literature: Essays in Honour of G.H. Russell* (Cambridge: Boydell & Brewer): 115-27.
Voigts, L.E.
1985   'A Handlist of Middle English in Harvard Manuscripts', *Harvard Library Bulletin* 33: 1-96.
Wright, C.E.
1949–53   'The Dispersal of the Monastic Libraries and the Beginnings of Anglo Saxon Studies. Matthew Parker: a Preliminary Study', *Transactions of the Cambridge Bibliographical Society* 1: 208-37.
Zettersten, A. (ed.)
1976   *The English Text of the Ancrene Riwle Edited from Magdalene College, Cambridge MS. Pepys 2498* (EETS, 274; London: Oxford University Press).

Notes toward a Future History of Middle English Literature: Two Copies of Richard Rolle's *Form of Living*

Ralph Hanna III

Writing histories of medieval literatures has proved particularly difficult in the past for two reasons. First, the survivals are undoubtedly fragmentary and discontinuous, thereby disrupting any possible smooth single narrative of developments. Second, medieval literary production occurred in a situation of 'pre-national literature', in a context in which the single canon presumed by traditional literary history did not exist. This model relies upon assumptions about literary production and literary publics which are profoundly anachronistic when applied to the Middle Ages. As a model it is much more relevant to the culture of early printing with its fixed centers of mechanized book production, its standardized texts, and its relatively homogeneous mass audience. And established literary history hitherto has relied upon generic categories reified in the last century or so on the basis of source study but generally foreign to the discernible literary categories preferred by medieval writers and readers, excluding Chaucer.

Indeed, Chaucer's modern canonical centrality in many ways badly skews approaches to Middle English literature.[1] Our

---

1. See Hanna (1996a: 267-79 [nn. at 322-26], and 1996b). I implicitly suggest that integration of Chaucer with other literary traditions is impossible, that we should expect to (re)construct a fragmented and polyvocal narrative of vernacular literary culture, in n. 15 below. One might also note the nearly utter absence of my central subject, Richard Rolle, from the canon of

modern enthusiasm for the Chaucerian imagination marginalizes many of the texts I will treat here. Just as neocolonialist critics argue that forming the nation is an act of forgetting, medievalists need to recognize that the construction of the national literary canon c. 1580 was a similarly 'forgetful' act. In forming the canon, critics like Puttenham and Sidney suppressed the variousness of medieval literature in favor of Chaucer, perhaps especially the Chaucer of *Troilus and Criseyde*. Yet it is simultaneously indisputable that our recovery of a historical sense of vernacular written culture in the Middle Ages depends heavily on rediscovering the connection of more minute works with what one is conditioned to admire as 'canonical Middle English literature'.

To evade the problems the categories developed in modern study have created, one needs to return to the most abundant available evidence for medieval literature, the surviving books on which modern critical editions are based. Through interpreting these material objects, it is possible to create a literary history appropriate to that manuscript culture from which they come. In this essay I want to outline how I believe the construction of such a historical narrative might proceed.[2] I will discuss the literary-historical evidence provided by an arbitrarily chosen pair of books. They are among the more than one hundred manuscripts which transmit the English works of a single medieval author and happen to have ended up near at hand for my scrutiny. My examples, two manuscripts in the Henry E. Huntington Library, San Marino, HM 127 and HM 502, contain copies of the vernacular epistle of instruction *The Form of Living*, written by the hermit/mystic Richard Rolle, who died in 1349.[3]

print-book culture until the later nineteenth century (only a scrap, used as a prologue to William Flete's *Remedies*, appeared in an early print).

2.   Compare the earlier essays, Hanna (1996a: 35-47, 63-82 [nn. at 287-90, 291-96]; and 1996b), where I implicitly developed this model, while leaving it at the periphery of a discussion devoted to more local issues. And see a preliminary version of this argument in Hanna (1996a: 7-12).

3.   I ignore other Rolle texts in Huntington collections: *The Commandment* in HM 148, together with a copy of Rolle's vernacular prose Psalter, the text plus Peter Lombard's commentary; a fragment of the English Psalter prologue in a manuscript of Lollard Bible excerpts, HM 501 (four plus earlier quires of this book are now Tokyo, Keio University Library MS 170X9.6;

This text is especially interesting in terms of information available about original date, purpose and audience. Rolle himself was born in Thornton Dale (North Yorkshire) shortly after 1300; he went to Oxford for some years under the patronage of Thomas de Neville, a younger son of the baronial family Neville of Raby. At age 18 he abandoned Oxford, returned briefly to his family to create himself a hermit, and was initially patronized by John Dalton, constable of Pickering Castle, very near his birthplace. After some wanderings about North Yorkshire (and possibly sojourns at the Sorbonne), he eventually settled near the house of Cistercian nuns at Hampole (West Yorkshire), where he died. He wrote voluminously, in the main on the contemplative life, both in English and Latin, the vernacular works apparently only at the very end of his life.[4]

The work I survey represents a literary output in origin both geographically limited and gender-specific, one composed for a known and limited female audience. *Form* has written into the text an address to 'Margaret'. The rubric in the northern collection of epistles, Cambridge University Library MS Dd.v.64, further specifies 'forma uiuendi scripta...ad Margaretam anchoritam suam dilectam discipulam', and that of Longleat House, Marquis of Bath MS 29, adds additional information, 'Tractatus...ad Margaretam de Kyrkby Reclusam.'[5]

Moreover, other vernacular works of Rolle have similar histories. Dd.v.64 also identifies the recipients of the other two epistles, *The Commandment* ('tractatus...scriptus cuidam sorori de Hampole') and *Ego Dormio* ('tractatus...scriptus cuidam moniali de 3edyngham', that is, Yedingham, North Yorkshire, a house located near both Thornton Dale and Pickering).[6] Medieval tradition also

see Quaritch catalogue 1036 [1984], 90, item 120); and a Rolle lyric in EL 34 B 7.

4.   The standard biographical account has been Allen (1927: 430-526), now heavily revised in Watson (1991: 31-53, 273-94). For Neville, see Emden (1957–59: II, 1351 [and, for a skeletal discussion of Rolle, III, 1586–87]).

5.   The standard text is now Ogilvie-Thomson (1988); for the Margaret reference and the **Dd** and Longleat rubrics (cf. also the rubric at the end of the Rolle materials in Longleat, with its reference to 'Margaretam Reclusam de Kyrkby'), see Ogilvie-Thomson (1988: 25, 894; xxxvii; xxiv, xxxvi, lii-liii; and xxv, respectively).

6.   For the rubrics, see Ogilvie-Thomson (1988: lxxix, lxvi). But Ogilvie-

identifies Margaret Kirkby as the recipient of Rolle's English Psalter. A poem affixed as a prologue to the copy of the work in Bodleian Library MS Laud Misc. 286, states that Rolle wrote the work at Margaret's request and that his holograph remained at Hampole.[7] Whatever the truth of this statement, the prose prologue to the Psalter describes the use of the work in terms that would be appropriate to a text for a devout woman literate only in the vernacular:

> In þis werk I seke no strange Inglis, bot lightest and comunest and swilke þat is mast like vnto þe Latyn, so þat þai þat knawes noght Latyn, be þe Inglis may cum tille many Latyn wordes (Allen 1931: 7, 91-94).

A few details of the life of 'Margareta de Kyrkby', apparently Rolle's favorite disciple, are known.[8] Records in the registers of the Archbishops of York indicate that her surname was 'la Boteler', and Allen wished to associate her with a Butler family from Skelbroke in the parish of South Kirkby (West Yorkshire). She became a nun at nearby Hampole about 1343 and in 1348 entered the ancoritic life, first in a cell at East Layton and later (after 1356) at Ainderby, both isolated North Yorkshire locales. She eventually retired to Hampole (probably long after Rolle's death).

To this point I have remained firmly within the confines of traditional Middle English literary history. I have laid out the basic facts of origin and relationship which underlie *The Form of Living*; in doing so I assume the work (or author) as an isolated production. Traditional literary history might add a little more detail, but well within this narrative of isolation. For example, the author/work might be embedded in some larger genre-based narrative; there Rolle would fall somewhere between *Ancrene Riwle* and Walter Hilton. Or the historian might mention some ideas central

---

Thomson (lxvi-lxviii) queries the Yedingham ascription for *Ego Dormio* and argues on the basis of the Longleat rubrics, which bracket the Rolle materials in this manuscript, that all its contents were at least revised to be included in a package for Margaret Kirkby.

7.   *IMEV* 3576, partially printed in Allen (1927: 174).

8.   The materials were discovered by the great student of English ancoritism Rotha Mary Clay (Clay 1914: 139, 142-43); Allen (1927: 502-13) remains the standard treatment, but see most recently Warren (1985: 212-13).

to (and uniquely individuating) Rolle's idea of an appropriate 'living'.

In the remainder of my essay I will contrast this history with another, one I hope more respectful of a medieval context, for the narrative I have just provided profoundly misrepresents the way in which we know Rolle in medieval literary culture. Both *Form* and the prose Psalter were immensely popular works in the fifteenth century. The close to 50 surviving copies of the first and 40 of the second place them among the dozen or so most often reproduced Middle English prose texts. And the diffusion of excerpted and interpolated versions further testifies to their cultural centrality.[9] The redesigning of these works to appeal to new audiences is a strong sign of their status as important cultural models. We do not (and cannot) know Margaret Kirkby's book(s) or its/their use; we know only the surviving copies. In what form do personalized occasional works, which I think typify medieval author-original audience situations (see Hanna 1996b: 66-68), enter general literary circulation? How does that circulation resituate them? And what does such resiting reveal of discrete literary communities, however defined? In the following pages I use these two copies of *Form* as exemplary in proposing a methodology to address such issues.

The Manuscripts[10]

Examining the manuscripts immediately indicates two ways in which reading Rolle's *Form* in the Middle Ages differed profoundly from our experience with a modern edition. Both volumes are miscellanies, where *Form* appears intermixed with other contents—in neither case with any other work associable with Rolle. Indeed, author-oriented selections are exceedingly unusual. Both Allen, who presents Dd.v.64, and Ogilvie-Thomson, basing her text on Longleat 29, follow presentations we feel *should* have been

---

9. I mention one *Form* excerpt, known in three manuscript copies as well as early prints, but ignored by Ogilvie-Thomson, in n. 1 above. On interpolations in the psalter see Everett (1922) and the further specifications in Hudson (1988: 25-27, 259-64).

10. For professional descriptions see Dutschke (1989: I, 158-61 [for HM 127], 237-39 [for HM 502]).

familiar in the Middle Ages, when Rolle should have been honored as an Author (as we honor him). But in the medieval tradition of transmission such authorial anthologies are quite aberrant. Only a very few manuscripts, almost exclusively representatives of Ogilvie-Thomson's *alpha* tradition (of which more below), ever seem consciously to have grouped even Rolle's epistles as a self-contained unit.[11]

Secondly, like all manuscript miscellanies, these books reflect non-preplanned, non-continuous modes of book production. The contents of these books have been derived from different sources, perhaps reflecting happenstance acquisition. In these cases the text has been subjected to processes of serendipitous contextualization.

HM 127 is a book in fairly standard late medieval quarto format (its dimensions are about 265 mm × 190 mm). The text is copied in an anglicana of the first quarter or third of the fifteenth century. The collation is 1^{8+1} (+1, the tabula for *Fervor Amoris*) $2\text{-}4^8$ (f.33, the end of a fascicle) $5\text{-}7^8\ 8^6$ (-6). There are regular catchwords at quire ends within continuous texts (thus, none at f.33v). Virtually all signatures have been pared at binding: the exception, in rubricator's red, occurs on f.18, probably a bit of the expected *c*.

The contents are:

1.   ff.1-32 (quires 1-4): *Fervor Amoris* (*IPMEP* 362), with filler (a), ff.32-33v; the colophon for the main text, 'Tractatus de quatuor gradubus [sic] amoris', follows the filler items on f.33v.
2.   ff.34-50v (quires 5, 6, and head of 7): Rolle's *Form* (*IPMEP* 351), followed by filler (b), ff.51-52v, extended into
3.   ff.53-62v (most of quire 7 and quire 8): *Benjamin Minor* (*IPMEP* 4), followed by filler (c), f.62v.

11. Outside the five central *alpha* copies (see below), only a few books transmit even two of the epistles, in the overwhelming majority of instances as widely separated items (e.g. Cambridge, Trinity College MS O.1.29), in separately produced parts of the book (e.g. Dublin, Trinity College MS 155 [C.5.7]), in excerpted forms (e.g. British Library MS Additional 37790), or as accidental intrusions (e.g. British Library MS Arundel 507). Quite atypical is a presentation like Tokyo, Toshiyuki Takamiya MS 66, with *Ego Dormio* and *Commandment* consecutively at ff.25-33.

The fillers include:

(a)   at the end of text 1: a series of prayers, mostly Latin, but an English one to a guardian angel (*IPMEP* 40; see the Appendix below) and an English meditation on the sorrows of the Virgin (*IPMEP* 323);

(b)   at the end of text 2: *IMEV* 611, a passion lyric, in double column; and Becket's Latin devotion on the joys of the Virgin with Latin lyric and prayers, followed by a translated rubric (see Appendix) and lyric, *IMEV* 465;

(c)   at the end of text 3: *IMEV* 3459 on the works of mercy (two stanzas in double column) and a Latin note 'Septem dona spiritus sancti', a brief septenary alining gift (from Isa. 11.2-3), the associated remedial virtue, and the deadly sin it battles.

HM 502 is a pocket-sized book (dimensions about 145 mm × 105 mm), the whole copied in probably a single textura (with considerable variation in size and style) of the first half of the fifteenth century. The book was produced as two fascicles (catchwords fail only at f.34) with a full set of consecutive signatures *a-m*, small notations not in the text hand, probably added to facilitate binding. The collation is 1^{12} (-4, -9), $2\text{-}3^{8}$ [lost quire *d*] 4^{8} [f.34, the end of a fascicle] $5\text{-}11^{8}$.

The contents are:

1.   ff.1-26v: Thomas Wimbledon's sermon 'Redde racionem' (atelous; *IPMEP* 560); the conclusion, along with the head of the next item, appeared in the lost quire *d*.

2.   ff.27-34: Rolle's *Form* (*IPMEP* 351), even before the loss of quire *d* an excerpt, only the first 385 lines, less than half the text. The work expires in mid-sentence, and f.34v was originally blank, now with an added draft letter (s. xv/xvi) and verses, *IMEV* 1151 etc.

3.   ff.35-60v: *þe Lyfe of Soule* (*IPMEP* 243).

4.   ff.60v-74: two large excerpts from an unpublished translation of St Edmund Rich's *Speculum Ecclesie*, these materials corresponding to the version printed Horstman (1895–96: I, 241-45, 254-58) (*IPMEP* 706).

5.   ff.74-87: the Wycliffite exposition of the *Pater Noster* (*IPMEP* 604).

6.   ff.87-90v: an unedited instructional text, beginning 'Pryde
      wraþþe & envie ben synnes of þe fend' (atelous; Jolliffe
      1974: F.21). The work discusses, in turn, the seven sins,
      things that God loves (the remedial virtues), and, follow-
      ing a textual division with space for a decorative capital,
      the five bodily and five spiritual wits, the seven virtues
      (cardinal and theological), the seven bodily and seven
      spiritual works of mercy, the three 'goods' (of grace,
      nature and fortune).[12]

The Texts

A substantial step in explaining the books, which to this point I
have examined only as physical objects, is to connect them with a
historical context. Initially one can identify, as specifically as
possible, the patterns of transmission underlying the text presented and the mode by which each copy received Rolle's *Form*.
This procedure requires editorial thought.

The text transmitted depends, to a degree not at this stage
ascertainable, on the materials available to the producers of the
manuscript under discussion. To identify these materials one
must analyze the readings provided by the manuscript, identify
some of them as erroneous, and compare them with the errors of
other extant copies. Only error is historicizable; persistent agreement in errors indicates that two or several manuscripts have
relied upon a shared source copy (or archetype), and such a
shared source implies some physical relationship in historical
time between the producers of different books.

Thus the currently fashionable attack on editing texts incapaci-
tates itself. It can have no serious interest in Middle English literary history (nor, I would think, in history at large). An initial ges-
ture at historicization requires, at the least, an effort at recreating

---

12. The text is identical with Cambridge University Library MS Nn.iv.12,
ff.7v-11 (which is complete); Oxford, Bodleian Library MS Lyell 29, ff.99v-
102, and Manchester, John Rylands Library MS Eng. 85, ff.9-13, are identical
with the first half (Rylands incomplete). For the last topic, cf. the treatment
in the *Book of Vices and Virtues* (Francis 1942: 75-79); this portion of 'Pride
wrath and envy' occurs as the separate extract Jolliffe 1974, I.19.

the archetype of all surviving copies,[13] from which deviation of individual copies may be measured and connections between copies ascertained.

The *Form* in HM 127 clearly descends from the **Dd** branch of Ogilvie-Thomson's bifid stemma. This editor notes, among very commonly attested agreements in error, certain ones (corresponding in part to the stemma in Ogilvie-Thomson 1988: lxi, predicated only on agreements in omissions) which imply a tightly connected group of manuscripts (see Ogilvie-Thomson 1988: lx-lxi). This may be represented through two alternate notations:

$$< [\ (\textbf{PF}) \ (\textbf{Ld} \ \{\textbf{HT}^2\} \ ) \ ] \ \textbf{B}^2 >$$

or the more historically explicit

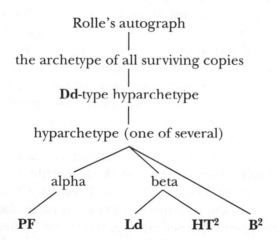

Rolle's autograph
|
the archetype of all surviving copies
|
Dd-type hyparchetype
|
hyparchetype (one of several)

alpha   beta

PF   Ld   HT²   B²

HM 127 is Ogilvie-Thomson's **H**, and

P = Cambridge, Magdalene College MS Pepys 2125

F = Beeleigh Abbey nr. Maldon (Essex), the Foyle MS

Ld = Oxford, Bodleian Library MS Laud Misc. 210

T² = Cambridge, Trinity College MS B.15.17, where the same lyric follows as in **H**[14]

B² = Oxford, Bodleian Library MS Bodley 938

13. Which may, of course, not be identical at any particular point with an authorial text.

14. There is a third copy, in an unrelated book. In Hanna (1987: 422-23) I argued that congruence of contents may often imply related textual

Given the persistence of these relationships and the similarity in contents, the grouping of HM 127 with the single copy T^2 probably speaks to the two books' reliance on identical source material. (It probably further indicates the limits of this exemplar; the next English text in HM 127, *IMEV* 465, is unique, and although no fascicle boundary occurs, the HM 127 team probably broke off their copying here before acquiring the next major text from a different source.)

Trinity B.15.17, copied around 1400, displays two features unusual in the transmission of *Form*. Here Rolle's work occupies nearly all of an unsigned two-quire booklet (ff.131-47) in double-column format added by the scribe to his major work in the codex, a copy of *Piers Plowman* B (presented in a single text column). This separateness of production is telling, for *Form* both is and is not joined with *Piers* in the manuscript. In certain respects this accords with general features of Rolle transmission; although *Form* was a culturally central text in the fifteenth century, transmission of the work occurred almost exclusively apart from any texts which we would consider canonical in the twentieth century. Even though the two works are not absolutely joined in terms of production detail, Trinity B.15.17 remains one of the very few exceptions to this challenge to modern notions, that textual canons cohere.[15]

Coupled with this feature is a second unusual aspect of Trinity B.15.17, that it is a metropolitan book. The scribe writes London English of a type resembling such well-known Chaucer manuscripts as Hengwrt and Ellesmere; indeed, his hand also resembles that of the Hengwrt-Ellesmere scribe, Doyle and Parkes's scribe B. Not only is the other text of the volume one securely canonical in our century, but the book itself suggests connections with the very center of what we take to be canonical medieval literary

histories; the argument here recurs, as it will in my discussions of *Þe Lyfe of Soule*, *Fervor Amoris*, and *Benjamin Minor* below. Cf. the Rouses' alarming exposé of classicists' failing to heed this tendency with Ciceronian texts (Rouse and Rouse 1991: 61-98).

15. The other exceptions can be described in this brief footnote: New York, Morgan Library MS M 818, from South Lincolnshire, has the alliterative *Susannah* and *Form* in one fascicle, *Piers Plowman* A in a second; Longleat 29, an Anglo-Irish book, contains, in the same fascicle, along with extensive Rolle, Chaucer's *Parson's Tale*. For a professional description of Trinity B.15.17 see Kane and Donaldson (1975: 14-15).

production (as opposed to the overwhelming majority of *Form* manuscripts, like HM 502 certainly provincial). The archetype shared with HM 127 implies that we should consider carefully whether this book belongs within a London ambit as well.

Ogilvie-Thomson designates the copy of *Form* in HM 502 H^2. Because it is a partial text (only lines 186-385 survive), she makes no effort to analyze or to collate it in full. But its readings, where they agree with other copies, do appear in her collation (Ogilvie-Thomson 1988: xcv-xcvi). These suggest very close relations with those manuscripts she designates *alpha*, a peculiar recension related to Longleat 29 (the other half of the stemma from **Dd**) and transmitted in

> **R** = Oxford, Bodleian Library MS Rawlinson A 389
> **G** = Paris, Bibliothèque de Ste. Geneviève MS 3390
> **S** = the Simeon MS (London, British Library MS Additional 22283)
> **V** = the Vernon MS (Oxford, Bodleian Library MS Eng. poet. a.1)[16]
> **W** = London, Westminster School MS 3
> **T** = Cambridge, Trinity College MS B.14.38

The evidence for such a genetic placement is extensive. Ogilvie-Thomson cites H^2 nearly 120 times in her collations; of about 100 agreements with limited numbers of texts H^2 shares errors with *alpha* copies on just over 60 occasions. And among individual *alpha* copies HM 502 shows closest relations with the pair **VS**, with each of which it shares about a dozen unique wrong readings.

This evidence should be qualified in a couple of ways, however. First, HM 502 fails to transmit a very great many distinctive *alpha* readings. Second, the *alpha* readings in the text are far from consistently distributed: they tend to appear in clumps, then cease for a while. This suggests that the HM 502 *Form* is a conflate, apparently, given the profusion of *alpha* readings, one derived from an archetype like that available to **VS** but with readings from a second source overriding these in many instances. It is very difficult to pin down the source of these less deviant readings, but HM 502 does agree 15 times in error with TCD 155, more than with any other text.[17]

16. On Vernon and Simeon see Doyle (1987); I describe Rawlinson A 389 and Ste. Geneviève in Hanna (1988: 211-12).

17. The next most prominent agreements are with Bodley 110 (**B**,

This recension of *Form* has long been recognized and discussed as deviant. All copies ultimately depend upon editorial procedures undertaken in producing Rawlinson A 389. This book was almost certainly copied in Lichfield (where it belonged to the cathedral canons from at least the second half of the fifteenth century). Rawlinson probably depends, at but a single remove, upon Yorkshire sources; Lichfield lay on one of the great medieval roads joining York and Worcester (see Hanna 1995: 296). And, in the main, use of this archetype was confined to this West Midland area; Vernon and Simeon, even if copied by a North Worcestershire scribe, have close connections with Lichfield, and Ste. Geneviève 3390 is a Warwickshire book. In contrast to the metropolitan centrality of HM 127, we might associate HM 502 with a specific provincial environment.

Manuscript Context and Provenance

One can more narrowly specify the historical context to be assigned the two copies of *Form* by considering the miscellaneous quality of the books which transmit them. One residue of the New Criticism, a tendency to study single texts as isolated entities, is debilitating, and to understand Rolle's *Form* as a literary-historical object one must work across the totality of the manuscripts. Such an investigation should oscillate between two poles: on the one hand, one must discover the textual affinities of other works which appear with Rolle, to ascertain whether copies of *Form* were transmitted to the surviving books already contextualized, in the company of other works; on the other, one should address the contextualization in the instant volumes and offer generalizations about the ideologies embedded in the books and the services to which Rolle was appropriated in the course of his textual life.

Examining HM 127 in these terms reveals the book to be a remarkably miscellaneous production. The producers of the volume appear to have acquired three main texts from diverse sources, in each case with pendant minor items forming part of the archetypal supply. Other than their shape, none of the three archetypes appears to have had any common textual affinities or

10 times), Pepys 2125 (**P**, 8 times), the Foyle manuscript (**F**) and British Library MS Arundel 507 (**Ar**, 7 times each).

history, although their juxtaposition places *Form* within a context one might describe as weighted toward 'practical contemplation/meditation'.[18]

The first text of HM 127, *Fervor Amoris*, has a universal form of address, to both sexes and all classes. Moreover, like several other popular instructional books (e.g. *Pore Caitif*), it is Rolle-derived; Chapter B both refers to and cites materials on three degrees of love from *Form* and *Ego Dormio*.[19] Although her evidentiary sample might be queried, Margaret Connolly demonstrates the existence of a transmissional group {[**CaT**] **Ht**}, with **H**^{2} perhaps rather distantly related, where this copy is **Ht**, and

> **Ca** = Cambridge University Library MS Additional 6686, part 2, text copied in the dialect of Lincolnshire[20]
> **T** = Cambridge, Trinity College MS B.15.42
> **H**^{2} = London, British Library MS Harley 2409, text copied in the dialect of Essex

The relationship of HM 127 and Additional 6686 should remind one of that between HM 127 and Trinity B.15.17. In both cases HM 127 shares with another book multiple contents from a narrowly delimited archetype. In Additional 6686 all materials in common with HM 127 appear in a separate production unit (pp. 235-74), and a substantial portion of that unit—in addition to *Fervor amoris*, everything up to a change of hands at p. 270, the guardian angel prayer, additional Latin prayers, and the sorrows of the virgin—is common to both copies.

This thorough congruence proves Additional 6686 the closest textual relative of HM 127, even though in the stemma Additional appears a twin of Trinity B.15.42. HM 127, through carelessness in copying which produces in the manuscript a layer of erroneous readings in addition to those inherited from copy shared with related books, must, in a stemmatic representation, appear

18. The two related books I now discuss have one text in common, but not one shared with HM 127, 'The Short Charter of Christ' (*IMEV* 4184).

19. See Connolly (1993: xiv-xv, for audience; xvi-xvii for use of Rolle [and 104-105, notes to B, 16-41, 64-81]). On the manuscript relations see xxvii-xxxi; and on the language of copies, xlii.

20. A professional description appears in Sargent (1992: lxxiv-lxxvi [and cxlviii-cliii for plates]); for the language see *LALME*, III, 382-83, LP 508 (coordinates 506/362).

uniquely deviant in origin. It remains unclear how this small packet of material became joined to the remainder of the Additional codex, a copy of Nicholas Love's *Mirror of the Blessed Life of Jesus Christ*, prepared in anticipation of an armigerous owner and written in a Northamptonshire dialect identical with that of the Mount Grace (OCart, North Yorkshire) copy of the *Mirror*, Cambridge University Library MS Additional 6578.[21]

Phyllis Hodgson (Hodgson 1955: xx-xxi) identifies the *Benjamin Minor* of HM 127 (**C**) with a small subfamily, part of her group B. This group has the form { **F** (**CR**) }, where

> **F** = Cambridge University Library MS Ff.vi.33, in the dialect of Middlesex, in the hand of William Darker, monk of Sheen (OCart)
> **R** = Cambridge (Mass.), Harvard University Library MS Richardson 22, where the same lyric follows[22]

One might note the connection of both books with London and with generally contemplative issues. Not only was Darker a member of a metropolitan house, his Ff.vi.33 transmits, in the main, materials concerned with Carthusian rules and culture (a potential connection with Additional 6686). And the primary text of Richardson 22, which it shares with British Library MS Cotton Titus C.xix, is a translation of the pseudo-Augustinian *Soliloquies*; this South-East Midland text was prepared for a group of women, presumably inclaustrated and committed to the contemplative life (see Sturges 1985).

HM 502 again shows itself to be a book with strong regional

---

21. See *LALME*, III, 383, LP 9340 (coordinates 453/234). *LALME* places the third portion of the manuscript (pp. 275-361), with Walter Hilton's *Scala*, in Nottinghamshire (see *LALME*, I, 66). In this context Harley 2409 is probably only distantly relevant. The single hand responsible for the book represents an absorptive copyist; he appears to have carried over intact the archetypal language of each individual work he transmitted—in turn, forms of Essex (ff.1-51, *Fervor amoris*), Lincolnshire (ff.52-69v, William Flete), Nottinghamshire (ff.70-75, Catherine of Siena), and West Yorkshire (see *LALME*, I, 112). The last, limited to the lyric printed in Horstman (1895–96: II, 455-56), perhaps represents his usual language; before 1482 the book passed from one Yorkshire nun, Maud Wade, prioress of Swyne, to another, Joan Hyltoft of Nun Cotham.

22. I describe Ff.vi.33 in Hanna (1987: 435); for its scribe see Hodgson (1955: xivn) and Doyle (1990: 14 and 19 n. 75). For a contents list of Richardson 22, see Voigts (1985: 56-60 [with plate]).

affiliations. These point, as does the scribe's *Form*, to a locale in the West Midlands, perhaps more narrowly Worcestershire or Warwickshire. Þe *Lyfe of Soule* is a pure western text, only known elsewhere in two local copies: Laud Misc. 210 (associated Doyle 1953: II, 39-40 with Strensham, Worcestershire, and, if so, perhaps with the family of royal servants, the Russells);[23] and British Library MS Arundel 286, localized near Coventry. In both books the text follows the Middle English *Twelve Profits of Tribulation* (*IPMEP* 143, cf. Jolliffe 1974: J.3).[24] Þe *Lyfe of Soule* is an instructional tract, which, in a longish way, presents many of the same topics as 'Pride wrath and envy' later in HM 502.[25]

As I indicated in Hanna (1988), the HM 502 version of the *Mirror of St Edmund*, another basic instructional text, is related to at least one Warwickshire manuscript, Oxford, Bodleian Library MS Bodley 416. And Knight's study of manuscript relations of Wimbledon's sermon (Knight 1967: 27-31), a contemplation of Last Judgment which frequently appears with instructional materials, reveals two genetic groups, with a possible pair related to one of these.[26] The unclassified manuscripts include, along with HM 502 (Knight's **Hu**), at least two further copies which can be assigned to the West Midlands: Oxford, University College MS 97

23. The language is various, six scribes having participated in the book, but two write the forms of Warwickshire and two those of Worcestershire (one Cambridgeshire and one Lincolnshire). I have elsewhere (Hanna 1988: 207-11) described Sidney Sussex 74 (as also Hudson 1983: I, 70-72), Bodley 938, Arundel 286, Laud 210, and Bodley 416.

24. See Moon (1978: xvi) on dialectal similarities of all three copies; and Barratt (1983: 36), for the dialect of Arundel.

25. Instructional topics in Þe *Lyfe of Soule* include the creed (Moon 1978: 18, 6ff.), the New Testament commandments as including the Decalogue (28, 13ff.), the seven deadly sins (38, 10ff.), the corporal works of mercy (41, 6ff.), the remedial virtues as expressions of love (? only six of the conventional set, 44, 19ff.).

26. Knight's edition is incomplete, based on only 13 of the manuscripts; see *IPMEP* 560 for a full listing. Among the relevant copies Knight missed is TCD 155, a composite book. The Wimbledon here was copied by a North Worcester scribe, *LALME*, III, 563, LP 7810 (coordinates 385/236); the *Form*, potentially related to that of HM 502, appears in an originally different manuscript copied in East Central Staffordshire dialect (*LALME*, III, 456, LP 215 [coordinates 418/327]), a placement suggestive in the light of the *alpha* tradition of *Form*.

(**U**; see Doyle 1981 for connections with Pirton, Worcestershire around 1400 and with Lichfield and South Staffordshire around 1460); and Cambridge, Sidney Sussex College MS 74 (**S**, in a Warwickshire dialect).[27] As the positioning of these works in HM 502 indicates, reliance on Worcester/Warwick texts and archetypes is a property of both fascicles and unifies the production of the whole volume.

Only the last two texts in the manuscript, neither ever the subject of editorial scrutiny, resist localization. Both—a tract on the basic prayer, the Pater Noster, and the economical general instruction of 'Pride wrath and envy'—belong to a virtually anonymous class of medieval religious productions, works presenting basic parochial instruction. Substantial further study is necessary to untangle textual relations here, but one should note that British Library MS Harley 2398 and Cambridge, Trinity College MS B.14.38, have both Wimbledon and the Pater Noster tract (neither Wimbledon copy related to that in HM 502 but Trinity also an *alpha* copy of *Form*), and that Rylands Eng. 85 and Cambridge University Library MS Nn.iv.12 include versions both of 'Pride wrath and envy' and the Pater Noster (in separate fascicles in Rylands), while Bodley 938 has both *Form* (more closely related to the copy of HM 127, however) and Pater Noster.

The Audience and its Interests

The preceding pages should indicate one methodology for investigating medieval literary works and returning them to some literary community. On this occasion space limitations prevent my offering in equal detail 'the proof of the pudding', what I describe above as 'the ideologies embedded in the books and the services to which Rolle was appropriated'. But as a provisional conclusion I present some fragmentary gestures in this regard, in the main concentrating upon HM 502.

First, however, one should notice that both books are audience-specific and, to an extent, replicate the original situation of Rolle's epistles, for each codex contains signs that it was constructed for a woman reader (given the 'bespoke trade' context

27. Knight's two further unrelated manuscripts are **Ra** = British Library MS Royal 18.A.xvii and **C** = Cambridge, Corpus Christi College MS 357.

from which both emanate, a known woman reader). A Latin prayer in HM 127, f.32v, contains a feminine form (Dutschke 1989: I, 160). And as Moon noted (Moon 1978: x-xi), the version of *Þe Lyfe of Soule* in HM 502 has been rhetorically recast into the traditional form of female instruction, a priest addressing a devout woman; the participants in the dialogue here, uniquely, are 'fader' and 'suster'.

Whatever the reflection of Rolle's relations to Margaret Kirkby, such an overtly gendered audience is unusual in the transmission history. One need only contrast HM 148, which looks as if it was copied for a male community, probably in North Yorkshire (and perhaps specifically Mount Grace Charterhouse, as Keiser [1981: 309-10] argues). This contrast suggests one typology worth investigating in future studies—the gendering of textual reception.

In this regard one feature common to a variety of HM 502 texts deserves notice. Textual editors typically deprecate partial and rewritten texts, for those flagrantly misrepresent the goal of editorial endeavors, the recuperation of author or archetype. But one can perceive such medieval behaviors in another light, as generative and helpful. Excerption indicates care and forethought, the desire for utterly efficient instruction. HM 502 frequently testifies to such ends: not only did the book's compiler revise the dialogue and rename its participants, he also carefully edited the text (Moon 1978: xvi-xviii). And similar practices inform the *Speculum Ecclesie* translation and probably the incomplete copy of Rolle's *Form* here. Rather than some 'dumbing down', one should associate this behavior with a quite precise (although arguably patriarchal) sense of the audience needs to be served by the book. Certainly, the bent of HM 502 contents, toward parochial instruction as traditionally construed, implies a goal of clarity within (a limited) comprehensiveness.

The recoverable provenance of HM 502 raises a second typology worth protracted study. I have already indicated the quite persistent reliance of the book's producer on South-West Midland archetypes, especially those circulating in Worcestershire and Warwickshire. The scribe's dialect confirms such a placement; he writes in the forms of North Central Warwickshire.[28] And the book contains a good many marks of early sixteenth-century use,

28. See *LALME*, III, 519-20, LP 4675 (coordinates 420/281).

if not ownership. Most extensively, ff.53v-54 record John Baker, John Fuller and Edmund Baker, and John Baker's hand appears at a number of other points. *LALME* identifies him, on evidence uncited (and not, so far as I can see in the book), as coming from Solihull, Warwickshire.

Such information would place HM 502 within a vital and long- (if only vaguely) noted provincial cultural community centered on the dioceses of Worcester and Hereford. This vernacular center had developed initially out of post-Conquest resistance to Normanization; HM 502 represents but one example (of many) of the ongoing life of these provincial communities in the early fifteenth century. Substantial further investigation will be required to sort the various levels of this regional literature and the interplays between them, which involve such diverse later fourteenth-century enterprises as the earliest translations of scientific and informational prose, alliterative poetry, and the religious prose so well attested in books related to HM 502 which I have studied here.

APPENDIX

Middle English Prose Texts in San Marino, Huntington Library MS 127

In a prior listing of the prose texts in HM 127 (Hanna 1984: 12), I described *Fervor Amoris* according to the best evidence available at the time. The appearance of Connolly's edition, although uncertainly, suggests that I erred in treating a concluding prayer as an actual portion of the text, rather than a pendant to it. On this basis the presentation in this *IMEP* fascicle should be emended:

First, provide the following explicit for HM 127 [1], *Fervor Amoris* (I present these items according to the format rules of *IMEP*, not those of editorial transcription):

> f. 32
> ...felinge in preier and in holi meditacions oþerwise þan y can schewe goode broþer or suster preie þan for me whiche be þe techinge of almiȝti god haue write to þe þes fewe wordes in helpinge of þi soule ardeat in nobis domini feruor amoris.

Then, add a new second item to the description (while renumbering *Form of Living* as item [3]):

[2]
f. 32

A goode curteis angel ordeined to my gouernaille i knowe wel myn feblenes and myn vnkunning wel also y woot þat strengþe haue y noon to do godis seruice but onliche of his ʒifte and of oure besi wepinge kunninge þat y haue comiþ noþinge of me but what god wole sende me be ʒowre goode techinge now goode gracious...
f. 32v

...gladliche wolde y worsche ʒow as myʒte þe to ʒowre likinge þerfore god to worsche for ʒow ʒow also in him aftir holi techinge i þanke him with þis holi preier pater noster &c. et ne nos inducas in temptacionem set libera nos a malo.

A prayer to one's guardian angel (*IPMEP* 40), previously printed *Yorkshire Writers*, II, 105.
Other texts: *IPMEP* lists four copies (and miscites the shelfmark of this manuscript).

In addition, I ignored one bit of English prose of a sort later *IMEP* fascicles have routinely included, an extended English rubric. Add this item to the description (*Benjamin Minor* now should be renumbered as HM 127 [5]):

[4]
f. 52

Hit is yfounde and ywrite þat oure lady apered to seint thomas of caunterbury [the name later lined] and badde him and tauʒt him to worschipe here for þe seuene ioyes durable and euerelastinge þat sche haæ now in heuene as wel as he deede [-ede *later, in margin*] now for þe five temporal ioyes þat sche [*corrected later from* he] hadde on erþe þe which beþ passed and þese beþ þe seuene þat folweþ.

An English rubric to introduce the following verse, *IMEV* 465, quoted in full above (previously printed Brown [1939: 59]). The rubric reproduces in highly abbreviated form the materials of the corresponding Latin on fol. 51rv, just as *IMEV* 465 translates the Latin lyric, 'Gaude flore virginali' which that rubric introduces. Since the Middle English poem appears nowhere else, this is probably a unique text.

WORKS CITED

Allen, H.E.
1927   *Writings Ascribed to Richard Rolle Hermit of Hampole and Materials for his Biography* (New York: Modern Language Association).

Allen, H.E. (ed.)
1931   *English Writings of Richard Rolle Hermit of Hampole* (Oxford: Claren-
                don Press).
Barratt, A. (ed.)
1983   *The Book of Tribulation* (Middle English Texts, 15; Heidelberg:
                Winter).
Brown, C. (ed.)
1939   *Religious Lyrics of the XVth Century* (Oxford: Clarendon Press).
Clay, R.M.
1914   *Hermits and Anchorites of Medieval England* (London: Methuen).
Conolly, M. (ed.)
1993   *Contemplations of the Dread and Love of God* (EETS, 303; Oxford:
                Oxford UniversityPress).
Doyle, A.I.
1953   'A Survey of the Origins and Circulation of Theological Writings in
                English in the 14th, 15th, and Early 16th Centuries, with Special
                Consideration of the Part of the Clergy Therein' (2 vols.; PhD
                thesis, Cambridge: University of Cambridge).
1981   'University College, Oxford, MS 97 and its Relationship to the
                Simeon Manuscript (British Library Add. 22283)', in M. Benskin
                and M.L. Samuels (eds.), *So meny people longages and tonges* (Edin-
                burgh: Benskin & Samuels): 265-82.
1990   'Book Production by the Monastic Orders in England (c. 1375-
                1530): Assessing the Evidence', in L.L. Brownrigg (ed.), *Medieval
                Book Production: Assessing the Evidence* (Los Altos Hills: Anderson-
                Lovelace): 1-19.
Doyle, A. I. (introd.)
1987   *The Vernon Manuscript: A Facsimile of Bodleian Library, Oxford, MS.
                Eng. poet. a.1* (Cambridge: Brewer).
Doyle, A. I., and M.B. Parkes
1978   'The Production of Copies of the *Canterbury Tales* and the *Confessio
                Amantis* in the Early Fifteenth Century', in M.B. Parkes and A.G.
                Watson (eds.), *Medieval Scribes, Manuscripts, and Libraries: Essays
                Presented to N. R. Ker* (London: Scolar Press): 163-210.
Dutschke, C.W.
1989   *Guide to Medieval and Renaissance Manuscripts in the Huntington
                Library* (2 vols.; San Marino: Huntington Library).
Emden, A.B.
1957–59   *A Biographical Register of the University of Oxford to AD 1500* (3 vols.;
                Oxford: Clarendon Press).
Everett, D.
1922, 1923   'The Middle English Prose Psalter of Richard Rolle of Hampole',
                Modern Language Review 17: 217-27, 337-50; 18: 381-93.
Francis, W.N. (ed.)
1942   *The Book of Vices and Virtues* (EETS, 217; London: Oxford University
                Press).

Hanna, R.

1984   *The Index of Middle English Prose, Handlist I: A Handlist of Manuscripts Containing Middle English Prose in the Henry E. Huntington Library* (Cambridge: Brewer).

1987   'The Middle English *Vitae Patrum* Collection', *Mediaeval Studies* 49: 411-42.

1988   'The Origins and Production of Westminster School MS. 3', *Studies in Bibliography* 41: 197-218.

1995   'With an O (Yorks.) or an I (Salop.)? The Middle English Lyrics of British Library Additional 45896', *Studies in Bibliography* 48: 290-97.

1996a   *Pursuing History: Middle English Manuscripts and Their Texts* (Stanford: Stanford University Press).

1996b   'Miscellaneity and Vernacularity: Conditions of Literary Production in Late Medieval England', in S.G. Nichols and S. Wenzel (eds.), *The Whole Book: Cultural Perspectives on the Medieval Miscellany* (Ann Arbor: University of Michigan Press): 37-51.

Hodgson, P. (ed.)

1955   *Deonise Hid Diuinite and Other Treatises on Contemplative Prayer Related to The Cloud of Unknowing* (EETS, 231; London: Oxford University Press).

Horstman, C. (ed.)

1895–96 *Yorkshire Writers* (2 vols.; London: Swan Sonnenschein).

Hudson, A.

1983   *English Wycliffite Sermons*, I (Oxford: Clarendon Press).

1988   *The Premature Reformation: Wycliffite Texts and Lollard History* (Oxford: Clarendon Press).

Jolliffe, P.S.

1974   *A Check-List of Middle English Prose Writings of Spiritual Guidance* (Toronto: Pontifical Institute).

Kane, G., and E.T. Donaldson (eds.)

1975   *William Langland: Piers Plowman: The B Version* (London: Athlone Press).

Keiser, G.R.

1981   '"Þe Holy Boke Gratia Dei"', *Viator* 12: 289-317.

Knight, I.K. (ed.)

1967   *Wimbledon's Sermon 'Redde Rationem Villicationis Tue'* (Pittsburgh: Duquesne University Press).

Moon, H.M. (ed.)

1978   *Þe Lyfe of Soule: An Edition with Commentary* (Salzburg: Institut für englische Sprache und Literatur).

Ogilvie-Thomson, S.J. (ed.)

1988   *Richard Rolle: Prose and Verse* (EETS, 293; Oxford: Oxford University Press).

Rouse, M.A., and R.H. Rouse

1991   *Authentic Witnesses: Approaches to Medieval Texts and Manuscripts* (Notre Dame: University of Notre Dame Press).

Sargent, M.G. (ed.)
1992   *Nicholas Love: Mirror of the Blessed Life of Jesus Christ* (New York: Garland).
Sturges, R.S.
1985   'A Middle English Version of the Pseudo-Augustinian *Soliloquies*', *Manuscripta* 29: 73-9.
Voigts, L.E.
1985   'A Handlist of Middle English in Harvard Manuscripts', *Harvard Library Bulletin* 33.1: 1-96.
Warren, A.K.
1985   *Anchorites and their Patrons in Medieval England* (Berkeley: University of California Press).
Watson, N.
1991   *Richard Rolle and the Invention of Authority* (Cambridge: Cambridge University Press).

'Deprece Your Prysoun':
Sir Gawain and the Encircling Narrative

David Mills

Circular diction—concluding a work with an echo of its opening line or lines—can be regarded, as Judith Davidoff has argued, as an extension of the long-established structure of the framing fiction, and at least 15 Middle English narrative poems employ this device. Davidoff goes on to suggest that the technique was so commonly employed that 'when a contemporary audience first perceived that a poem was both alliterative and also was opening with a framing fiction, its members were very likely to entertain the possibility that the work would have circular diction' (1988: 189-91).

The *Gawain*-poet's predilection for such formal circularity in his works is well known, but to him that circular structure became more than a mechanical device of entry and closure. In all four poems attributed to him he invests poetic form with thematic significance. In *Purity*, the one poem which does not use circular diction, the text takes on the same qualities of outward manifestation as the body or the rich vessels, as sign of grace or corruption:

> Clannesse who-so kyndly cowthe comende…
> Fayre formes myght he fynde in forthering his speche,
> And in the contraré kark and combraunce huge (1, 3-4).[1]

In *Patience* the final echo of the first line returns us triumphantly to the opening proposition, the poem itself having been presented as an exercise in patient obedience by a servant to his lord. And *Pearl*, with its complex interlinking, enacts in its structural

---

1. Quotations are from Anderson (1996).

circularity the physical and symbolic Pearl of the vision.

When, therefore, the poet turned his skills to a romance narrative, in *Sir Gawain and the Green Knight*, it is not surprising to find him employing his favoured 'encircling' device to thematic effect and endowing the form with thematic significance, stressing the repetitive cycles of history. In Sheila Fisher's words: 'The poem alerts us to the connections between beginnings and ends through the cyclical emphases of its narrative and specifically through the articulations of historical betrayal and of the loss of a civilization that frame the romance' (1988: 129). Critics have also noted the poet's concern with confined spaces in his narrative, and have recognized the analogy between those confined physical spaces and the spatial divisions within the poem itself. At least one has interpreted the pentangle as a sign of the poem, and others have suggested a link between the art and artifice of the courtly world and the self-evident art and artifice of the narrative.[2] These are perceptive and valuable points, to which in this paper I wish to add a further suggestion—that the encircling structure signals the narrator's determination to coerce reader, hero and narrative.[3] Both reader and hero are confined within a narrative against the propositions of which they constantly, and to some degree successfully, struggle.

Encircling the Narrative

Catherine Batt's statement that

> the [poem's] opening stanzas' brief résumé of historical events stresses humankind's impulse to mark off fixed boundaries, to create particular areas of control, whether in terms of geographical or rhetorical space' (1992: 122)[4]

2. For a useful summary of some recent criticism see Blanch and Wasserman (1992–93).

3. 'Narrator' here signifies a device by which the story is told. I would agree with A.C. Spearing that the narrator is not a consistently realized 'person' but a means to 'a pervasive heightening of the general characteristics of the narrating process in Middle English romance—dramatic immediacy, emotional identification, wholehearted commitment to a fictive reality shared by story and audience' (1997: 45).

4. For a contrary, critical view see Nuttall (1992: 214): 'The curious "Trojan" induction of *Sir Gawain and the Green Knight* can indeed look like an

first suggested to me that the opening two stanzas of *Sir Gawain* enact the narrator's authority over the narrative. Although the first stanza is primarily an account of historical beginnings, the foundation of the nations of Europe, including Britain, the poem actually begins with an ending which suggests the arbitrariness of the boundary set:

> Sithen the sege and the assaut was sesed at Troye (1)

The line predicates a continuum from preceding, undescribed events which, the allusive comment implies, the reader is expected to know. A defence is broken and the following lines make explicit the consequences. The destruction of Troy liberates its heroes, who scatter to found the nations of Europe. As Piero Boitani reminds us, this is a past 'which is mythological and fantastic for us but was historical for the readers of the time' (1982: 61). The disembodied voice in which it is transmitted reads, as John M. Ganim aptly puts it, 'as if the narrator were a primeval epic poet speaking out of the collective memory of his race',[5] authoritatively and unchallengeably. But the epic allusion and historical continuation are not sustained. Instead, these 'historical' events generate the marvels that provide the subjects for writers of popular romance. Before the end of stanza 1, terms of subjective response (*wonder* 16, *blysse and blunder* 18) appear, heralding the group of 'marvel' words in stanza 2—*ferlyes* 23, *aunter* 27, *selly* 28, *an outtrage awenture* 29, and *wonderes* 29.

Simultaneously, the narrator emerges from behind his disembodied historical voice and admits that the information that he has at his disposal comes not as objective historical fact but through a process of transmission (*I wot* 24, *as I haf herde telle* 26, *as I in toun herde* 31). He now locates his present chosen narrative among these competing stories and the miscellany of 'historical' material which they transmit. Here romance and chronicle become interchangeable, most obviously at the end of the poem, which states that the marvel the poet narrates is now recorded in both *the best boke of romaunce* (2521) and *the Brutus bokes* (2523).

almost barbarous prefix to an otherwise masterly narrative fiction.'

5.   See Ganim (1983: 62). Ganim's analysis establishes the transition from the absolute of history in stanza 1 to the relative of fiction in stanza 2 on which I build here.

That historicity claimed for the narrative heightens its *wonder* for the mundane present, and is perhaps sustained in what Ad Putter calls '*Gawain*'s paradoxical blend of the verisimilar and the marvellous' throughout the poem (Putter 1996: 47). Moreover, the oral form in which the narrator claims to have received the poem is construed as further authentication. His account origi- nates fictively in Gawain's 'original' report to the court on his return (2493-504), which must encompass Bercilak's accounts of the hunts (1626-28, 1950-51). The paradoxical phrase *the bok as I herde say* (690) blurs the distinction between the written and oral records as transmitters of material.[6] Finally, the narrator can appeal to the allegedly material evidence preserved in the ritual objects which also validate the story—the axe which was hung up above the door 'ther alle men for mervayl mught on hit loke' (479), and the green girdle, which becomes a formal badge of honour 'for the sake of that segge...evermore after' (2518-20). The concluding, non-scribal addition, 'Hony soyt qui mal pence', indicates that at least one subsequent reader recognized a conti- nuity from the girdle to the contemporary Order of the Garter.

But the narrator has chosen this story not because it has histori- cal significance:

> Forthi an aunter in erde I attle to schawe,
> That a selly in sight summe men hit holden,
> And an outtrage awenture of Arthures wonderes (27-29).

His selective principle is the degree of dislocation from the nor- mative experience of the contemporary reader. He leads that reader to this selection by what appears an inevitable and logical process (*Forthi*), although the selection is personal and arbitrary. His opening summary suggests that the choice results from wide knowledge and informed judgment. The narrator has examined the range of material available and offers *an outtrage awenture*, a romance of unusually amazing marvels.[7]

Having justified his choice of subject and his authoritative

----

6. This claim develops the suggestion, made in Burrow (1965: 173), that the poem presents the adventure as 'a characteristic episode in the history of a country where such adventures are not at all uncommon'.

7. *MED* **outrage** adj (a) extravagant, excessive, immoderate; bibulous; (b) proud, exalted; also, boastful.

position, the narrator comments on the form of his narrative, which reflects that of his fictive source:

As hit is stad and stoken
In stori stif and stronge,
With lel letteres loken,
In londe so has ben longe (33-36).

The matter (*stori*) and the form (*letteres*) are invested with physical, concrete properties. *hit* (33) has as its antecedent the *laye* (30) heard in town, which is now fixed in shape and expression; *stad*, from *steden*, suggests something firmly established (*MED* 4[a]), and also brought to a halt (*MED* 2[a]), while *stoken* means literally 'nailed down' (*steken, MED*). The *stori stif and stronge* evokes a bastion, while the words in which the *laye* is transmitted are personified as men bound together in a bond of loyalty (*lel*); *loken* may be taken with *letteres* as a continuation of *lel*, intensifying the sense of bonding, but may also be taken with *stori*, suggesting that the words confine and contain the narrative. The lines stress fixedness and stability, but also defensiveness, a narrative under siege, barricaded against a range of competing material and forms such as have already been invoked.

Nevertheless, those contending narratives cannot be totally excluded. They are carried into the poem by the 'Trojan Horse', the Lady of the castle, who has read other stories of Gawain (1223-36, 1297-1301) and of chivalric romance in general (1508-27) which she urges upon him. And her husband Bercilak brings other, darker narratives, of Arthur and the Round Table, which challenge the narrator's confident claim that

Ay was Arthur the hendest, as I haf herde telle (26).

Bercilak knows another story, of

The duches doghter of Tyntagelle, that dere Vter after
Hade Arthur upon, that athel is nowthe (2465-66).

Historical present and the narrative meet in the adverb *nowthe*; Arthur is noble both 'at this time' and 'in this story'. These intrusions heighten our awareness that the narrator is wilfully excluding such stories and substituting a different version of Arthurian 'history'. Yet, as Sheila Fisher says: 'The end of the Arthurian legend in the collapse of the Round Table accounts for the beginning of this poem, for its motivation, its selected and selective emphases, and its design' (1988: 129).

Encircling the Reader

The opening account of origins comprehends the nationalist story of the origins of Britain itself. In locking his narrative into this national context the poet establishes a solidarity between narrator and reader. There is from the start, as noted above, an implicit collusion with the reader in the references to Troy and Aeneas and to the nations and their eponymous founders; the implied reader is imagined as recognizing these passing allusions. When the poem describes the foundation of Britain, the references become more proprietorial—*this Bretayn* (20), *this folde* (23), *here* (25). The narrator proudly sets Britain uniquely apart because of its marvellous past (*mo ferlyes...then in any other* [23-24]). He mediates to the reader that distant unfamiliar national past of *outtrage awenture* because he and the reader both are heirs to that same past. He bonds his readership even more specifically by locating the source of his narrative *in toun* (31). As with the past, our narrator is a mediator, a reporter coming from the supposedly familiar town. His implied reader is both of and apart from that urban community, an ambivalent position which accounts for what Jill Mann terms the 'overlay of knightly and mercantile values' in the poem, manifested in its recurrent imagery of bargain and exchange (1986: 314). That urban context may lend a further implication to the emphasis on the marvellous, and perhaps also to the suggestion of limited attention-span:

> If ye wyl lysten this laye bot on littel quile,
> I schal telle hit astit...(30-31; see also 1996–97).

The narrator also appeals to a cultural heritage shared with his readership, which is represented by the allegedly traditional story and also by the alliterative form in which it is told:

> In londe so has ben longe (36).

By emphasizing the alliterative line as the distinctively British form of narrative, he further validates his claim for popular and unbroken oral transmission and implicitly rejects the alternative, rhymed syllabic verse in the French tradition.

The narrator thus constructs the reader as a fiction within the poem and brings him or her under his narrative control. V.Y Haines makes the important distinction between the 'narrative audience' constructed by the poem and 'the authorial audience', what I term the 'actual' reader, to whom the poem is addressed (1982: esp. Chapters 2 and 3). The 'actual' reader is not so constrained and imports into the poem expectations deriving from external reading and practical experience. Even at the start of the poem, that reader, if alert, is conscious of the attempts to coerce and to exclude. Not all the founders' names have been identified; Ticius, eponymous founder of Tuscany (11), exists only here. No other narrative combining the Beheading and Temptation narratives is known, despite the claim of its wide currency (28, 31).

The reader is coerced in much the same way when the pentangle is introduced:

> and Englych hit callen
> Overal as I here, the endeles knot (629-30).

Overal as I here (630) again draws the reader into a fictive national community of shared knowledge amd shared language, but the supposedly current phrase *the endeles knot* is recorded nowhere else in Middle English. Similarly the claim that

> Gawan was for gode knawen, and, as golde pured (633)

cannot be substantiated. It is generally recognized that Gawain's reputation in England was not of the good, pure knight but of a smooth-talking and treacherous individual (see Whiting 1947). The fictive reader is constrained by the narrator to accept these claims on the authority of their general currency, but the 'actual' reader inevitably will regard them with scepticism.[8]

Tantalizingly, the 'actual' reader is provided with alternative representatives within the poem. One obvious surrogate is the commonsense court, who reject the whole idea of absurd quests, preferring an image of settled feudalism and estate-management (674-83). Their 'contemporary' voice of normative experience is complemented by that of the Lady who, again standing for the 'actual' reader within the text, introduces the Gawain familiar

---

8. Matthews (1994: 308) claims that 'both Gawain and reader are subject to the workings of a plot in two different senses [of that word]'.

from the narratives that she or he carries as counter-texts in his or her mind. In her words and in Bercilak's final comments we recognize the pressure from those stories that the strongly buttressed and highly selective narrative seeks to keep at bay. The result is a curious duality in which the reader occupies two roles, within and outside the poem, identifying with the 'narratorial' Gawain as the hero while acknowledging the alternative narratives which his antagonists introduce.

Encircling the Hero

Perhaps the most puzzling aspect of the poem is the choice of Gawain as hero. As noted above, his roles in other romances do not suggest that he is qualified for this adventure. The narrator takes a strangely oblique view of him:

> Now thenk wel, Sir Gawan,
> For wothe that thou ne wonde,
> This aventure for to frayn,
> That thou has tan on honde (487-90).

This address to the hero endows him with the potential for independent action, as if at any moment he may decide to give up and walk out of the story, and suggests that the narrator's control is not absolute nor the outcome predetermined. The Green Knight reiterates the uncertainty:

> Loke, Gawan, thou be graythe to go as thou hettes (448)

and emphasizes Gawain's promise (*layte als lelly* 449, *as thou has hette* 450, *I charge the* 451), concluding:

> Forthi me for to fynde, if thou fraystes, fayles thou never.
> Therfore com, other recreaunt be calde the behoves (455-56).

The conditional *if* suggests that Gawain might not come; *other* suggests an available alternative, to be instantly foreclosed. Narrator and challenger are united in their uncertainty about Gawain's willingness to see the adventure through.

The events of the first fitt explain that uncertainty. The true action can begin only when the challenge is accepted, and we wait for a long time for that beginning; only at lines 341-42 does Gawain come forward. This delay comically frustrates our expectations. In romance some knight is always ready to accept the challenge, and conversely a challenge selects its champion. When a damsel comes into court with a sword in Malory, the king and all the knights take up the challenge, but the sword selects Balin; and when Gareth has spent a year at court he somehow knows that the quest presented by Lyonet belongs to him (Vinaver 1954: 44-71, 212-73). But in this narrative no-one comes forward, and anti-climax results. Potentially the story ends before it has begun. Only when Arthur, in anger and desperation, has taken up the axe does Gawain, reluctantly and from a sense of family and social duty, at the last minute accept the challenge. The Green Knight's delight (390-91) seems double-edged. It suggests the challenger's intention that Gawain should be the participant and therefore that the test is uniquely his, as would be usual. But it also signals the narrator's relief, as well as the Green Knight's, that the narrative can now proceed.

The court's apparent terror at the first appearance of the Green Knight has already extracted a nervous reassurance from the narrator that they are, surely, not going to abandon their traditional role, as if he too is beginning to have doubts and is trying to infer motives:

> I deme hit not al for doute,
> Bot sum for cortaysye (246-47).

But he offers no excuse for their reluctance to accept the challenge. Their commonsensical views as Gawain departs seem to explain their attitude and make us doubt Gawain's parting claim:

> The knyght mad ay god chere,
> And sayde 'Quat schuld I wonde?
> Of destinés derf and dere
> What may mon do bot fonde?' (562-65).

These, the conventional words of a knight taking the adventure that God had provided, are challenged by Gawain's earlier reluctance and undercut by the court's own pragmatism. The words *mad ay god chere*, translatable as 'put on a good face', suggest the effort required to set up this pretence. Gawain remains a reluctant hero.

The narrator's overt encirclement of his hero continues in two related passages—the account of Gawain's journey to Bercilak's castle and the description of the pentangle. Abbreviating the journey in lines 713-35 the narrator intrudes into his narrative to dismiss material in his fictive source:

> So mony mervayl bi mount ther the mon fyndes,
> Hit were to tore for to telle of the tenthe dole (718-19).

The unconvincing claim that the narrator, and the reader, would find the recital of 'marvels' difficult (*MED tore* [a]) is followed by a list of the opponents encountered by Gawain which suggests to the reader the kind of 'marvel' that is being excluded. Instead, the imagery of conflict is transferred to the weather. Words bond in significant new collocations (*werre/wynter* 726), while the martial terms *dughty and dryye* (724) and *ded and dreped* (725), which seem in sequential reading attached to the list of foes, emerge (*for*, 726) as references to the weather. The transference from martial prowess to elemental suffering is further marked by the conjunction *slayn* and *slete* (729) and, in the same line, the reference to *yrnes* (see Fitter 1995: 220). Gawain's martial prowess is thus translated into patient endurance rather than stirring heroism.

Although in structural terms this abbreviation suggests a determined, if atypical, concentration upon the main narrative-line, it simultaneously suppresses the self-determination of the hero. Conventionally in romance, the journey to the place of combat represents a process of educating the knight and proving him worthy of his quest. The individual contests on the way offer not only intrinsic interest but, more importantly, a revelation of character and fitness. Here, however, Gawain is not allowed space to establish his own knightly credentials. Instead, character is imposed upon him by the narrator through the pentangle.

Whereas the narrator will not deflect his narrative with marvels on the journey, he explicitly stops it, in another act of narratorial autonomy, to compel his reader to read the figure on Gawain's shield in a particular way:

> And quy the pentangel apendes to that prynce noble
> I am intent yow to telle, thof tary hyt me schulde (623-24).

The description of the pentangle is primarily an address to the reader. It is never mentioned again by the narrator or any others, even when Gawain is disarmed or rearmed. It is a sign bestowed upon him by his attendants (*thay schewed hym the schelde,* 619) and by the narrator.[9] Its learned appellation of 'pentangle' (*with lore*, 665) is supplemented by the descriptively vernacular *endeles knot* (630). Knots cannot, literally, be 'endless'. The term, as Nick Davis has shown, points in its abstract sense to the geometric figure as a puzzle (*MED* 2[a]), but the word resonates with the association of binding or fastening.[10] The fact that it is endless means also that it is incapable of being untied. While its enclosed geometry can stand, like other images of enclosure, as an emblem of the poem itself, the pentangle also holds the reader in a conceptual prison. We are henceforth constantly measuring Gawain against the standards arbitrarily attached to this sign by the narrator.

Gawain seems oblivious to the sign's interconnecting qualities as such, but recognizes that having entered this narrative he has been constructed in a particular way. Not only is he held for us within the pentangle; he is bound, for us and for himself, by the alliterative linkage of words, the *lel letteres loken*. The first passing reference to him at Arthur's table contains the formula *gode Gawan* (109), and the form *Gawan* continues to collocate alliteratively with *god* (adjective) and *God* (noun) thereafter.[11] The constant iteration of this collocation reinforces the hero's virtue, until Gawain himself employs it as his defining quality when he reaches the Green Chapel, shouting:

> For now is gode Gawayn goande ryght here (2214).

By then on his lips it has an ironic ring.

In the Temptation, the Lady not only effects the literal imprisonment of Gawain in the bedchamber; she also seeks to confine Gawain within a different identity. She literally imprisons Gawain—locking his door behind her, coming within the bed-curtains, and placing her arm across him, conducting the conversation over a distance of inches. That enclosed space includes

9. On the implications of *schewed* see Lindley (1997: 40): 'indicating that the pentangle is presented to Gawain by his peers rather than claimed by him'. A similar imposition is suggested by *ho bere on hym the belt* (1860).

10. Davis 1993. *MED* lists the *Gawain* references as the sole examples under **knotte**, n 1(e), a pattern of interlacing lines.

11. Lines 109, 381, 633, 692, 811, 842, 1029, 1036, 1037, 1079, 1110, 1208, 1213, 1241, 1248, 1297, 1376, 1498, 1535, 1926, 2031, 2073, 2118, 2149, 2205, 2214, 2239, 2250, 2270, 2365, 2429, 2491.

them and excludes the outside world, as she tellingly points out:

> My lorde and his ledes ar on lenthe faren,
> Other burnes in her bedde, and my burdes als,
> The dor drawen and dit with a derf haspe (1231-33).

Now she seeks to imprison 'her' knight in another identity. She introduces a *doppelganger*, a Gawain identical in name and appearance but different from the narrator's hero, the Gawain of the romances that she has read. Her ostensible purpose here is to write a sequel in which she will occupy the heroine role and Gawain that of the courtly seducer. It will be a story only they two will 'read', and its authoring makes its sexual climax seem almost comically incidental to its construction:

> I schal ware my whyle wel, quyl hit lastes,
>   with tale.
> Ye ar welcum to my cors,
> Yowre awen won to wale… (1235-38).

Gawain evidently finds this proferred role more attractive than the one that he occupies here but recognizes that he is now constrained by another identity:

> 'In god fayth,' quod Gawayn, 'gayn hit me thynkkes,
> Thagh I be not now he that ye of speken' (1241-42).

Here, as at line 2466, *now* refers both to time and to the present narrative. Gawain's responsibility—which, so far as he knows, has no bearing upon the outcome of the Beheading—is to remain within the parameters set for him by the narrator, however uncongenial they may be; but *now* suggests that he is aware of a different possibility. Similarly, in his rejection of the Lady he denies that he loves another:

> In fayth I welde right non,
> Ne non wil welde the quile (1790-91),

where *the quile* is ambiguous, apparently referring to the duration of this adventure, whatever the outcome. Gawain retains that alternative role as a possibility for another story.

The reader does not know what the link between the Temptation and the Beheading may be but expects one to exist, encouraged by the narrator's hints at such a connection (cf. 1550). But to Gawain the Temptation seems an irrelevant distraction, as the narrator reminds us (1284-87), until the girdle suggests to him a way of connecting the two narratives (1855-58). The girdle is a conventional romance-motif, the magic object, which here will modify the narrator's control and empower the hero. Gawain sees in it an opportunity to write his own conclusion to a story seemingly predetermined to a *hevy* end by its narrator (496). And because the Green Knight had also used magic in his story (cf. 2282-83), the narrative transfer seems admissible. It is the only time that Gawain is given space to act autonomously within the adventure of the Beheading, although in so doing he infringes the terms of his bargain at the castle.

At the Green Chapel that autonomy proves illusory. Gawain, believing that the girdle has preserved him, leaps back, turns on the Green Knight, raises his shield and draws his sword. But although there is magic—for the Green Knight's blow, *homered heterly* (2311), would presumably have killed Gawain had he not been chaste—the outcome depends not upon the girdle but upon Gawain's conduct, upon his acting out the identity given him by his narrator. Ironically, he has fulfilled neither role—pentangle knight nor courtly seducer. His identity has now to be reconstructed, by him and by the reader, somewhere between the two. What he was is destroyed (2380); what he is seems misread (2382); and how he excuses it remains a major focus of critical debate (2407-28).

Encircling the Author

Sir Gawain is comically overcrowded with would-be authors. The Lady, working in the tradition of the romances she has read, seeks to write herself into the role of courtly heroine and Gawain into the confining role of courtly seducer. Gawain, as we have seen, resists that role, and she is compelled to adapt her narrative to a different end. The Lady is herself written into the role of seducer by Bercilak (*I sende hir to asay the*, 2362); effectively, he plans the 'architecture' of the plot, but she is to build it. Yet the reader finds it difficult to consider the Lady as mere agent. She seems to know little of the wider purposes of Bercilak (cf. 1550), but she seems to have taken the initiative in inventing the device of the girdle:

> Myn owen wyf hit the weved, I wot wel for sothe (2359)

and in so doing to have taken over the direction of her narrative and played an active part in determining its outcome, and that of the wider plan.

Bercilak himself is written by Morgan. This is evident when he occupies the role of the Green Knight (2456-62), where he is the agent of a narrative that does not move to its desired end, the death of Guinevere. His words to Gawain:

> 'The knyght of the grene chapel men knowen me mony' (454)

have the familiar assurance of the narrator's addresses to the reader—in fact, until he reaches the castle Gawain can find no-one who has ever heard of the man. But we cannot even be sure that Bercilak is not always a construct of Morgan, that his role as lord of the castle is not simply another part that she has written for him:

> Bercilak de Hautdesert I hat in this londe,
> Thurgh myght of Morgne la Faye, that in my hous lenges (2445-46).

The phrase *in this londe* may still imply a temporary identity, and the sustaining power of Morgan in that identity is explicit. His departure for an unnamed destination sounds mysterious, as if he may re-appear elsewhere in a different guise:

> And the knyght in the enker-grene
> Whiderwarde-so-ever he wolde (2477-78).

Yet the sudden revelation of Morgan's authorship has failed to satisfy critics. Bercilak seems too active and autonomous. Like the Lady, he plays his role convincingly and with energy, and seems to have taken advantage of his position within Morgan's unsuccessful narrative to author a story of his own. Part of that impression, by the end of the poem, lies in the fact that he is a figure with two names whose 'identity' the reader feels impelled to construe somewhere between the roles of Green Knight and castle-lord.

Gawain is in a similar situation, although his two identities—of perfect knight and courtly seducer—are borne upon him by two different authors, the narrator and the Lady, and endorsed by the reader in two different capacities, 'fictive' and 'actual'. Yet he contrives to steer a course between the two, emerging as the creation of neither. The simplistic assessments of 'pass' (2362-65) or 'fail' (2385-88) are inappropriate. It is the sympathetic laughter of the court and the honour that they confer upon him that signals our necessary response. To the 'actual' reader, Gawain has finally managed to elude the encircling narratives, write his own story, and emerge as a credible autonomous character.

What, then, of these authors? At all levels, having attempted to trap their characters in an invented action, they find that the narrative does not work out as they intended. Their 'characters' take on an independent existence. Seemingly trapped within their narratives, they manage nevertheless to encircle their own narrators, taking their own initiatives and constructing their own stories. Ironically, it is Morgan, writer of the Beheading, who represents our author here. A remote figure, possessing the power of magic to exercise control over others, she is a goddess (2452); but when we see her, she is a pathetic old woman (946-65), dependent upon others to carry out her biddings. In her power and her frailty she emblematizes the predicament of all authors who create characters only to find themselves finally helpless to contain their own creations.

WORKS CITED

Anderson, J.J. (ed.)
  1996   *Sir Gawain and the Green Knight, Pearl, Cleanness, Patience* (London: Dent, rev. edn).
Batt, C.
  1992   'Gawain's Antifeminist Rant, the Pentangle, and Narrative Space', *Yearbook of English Studies* 22: 117-39.
Blanch, R.J., and J.N. Wasserman
  1992–93   'The Current State of *Sir Gawain and the Green Knight* Criticism', *Chaucer Review* 27: 401-12.
Boitani, P.
  1982   *English Medieval Narrative in the Thirteenth and Fourteenth Centuries* (trans. J.K. Hall; Cambridge: Cambridge University Press).
Burrow, J.
  1965   *A Reading of 'Sir Gawain and the Green Knight'* (London: Routledge & Kegan Paul).
Davidoff, J.M.
  1988   *Beginning Well: Framing Fictions in Late Middle English Poetry* (London: Associated University Presses).

Davis, N.M.
    1993   'Gawain's Rationalist Pentangle', *Arthurian Literature* 12: 37-61.
Fisher, S.
    1988   'Leaving Morgan Aside: Women, History and Revisionism in *Sir
                    Gawain and the Green Knight*', in C. Baswell and W. Sharpe (eds.),
                    The Passing of Arthur: New Essays in Arthurian Tradition (New York:
                    Garland): 129-51.
Fitter, C.
    1995   *Poetry, Space, Landscape: Toward a New Theory* (Cambridge: Cam-
                    bridge University Press).
Ganim, J.M.
    1983   *Style and Consciousness in Middle English Narrative* (Princeton: Prince-
                    ton University Press).
Haines, V.Y.
    1982   *The Fortunate Fall of Sir Gawain: The Typology of 'Sir Gawain and the
                    Green Knight'* (Washington: University Press of America).
Lindley, A.
    1997   'Pinning Gawain Down: The Misediting of *Sir Gawain and the Green
                    Knight*', *Journal of English and Germanic Philology* 96: 26-42.
Mann, J.
    1986   'Price and Value in *Sir Gawain and the Green Knight*', *Essays in
                    Criticism* 36: 294-318.
Matthews, D.O.
    1994   '"A Shadow of Itself"? Narrative and Ideology in *The Grene Knight*',
                    Neophilologus 78: 301-14.
Nuttall, A.D.
    1992   *Openings: Narrative Beginnings from the Epic to the Novel* (Oxford:
                    Clarendon Press).
Putter, A.
    1996   *An Introduction to the 'Gawain'-Poet* (London: Longmans).
Spearing, A.C.
    1997   'Poetic Identity', in D. Brewer and J. Gibson (eds.), *A Companion to
                    the 'Gawain'-Poet* (Cambridge: Brewer): 35-51.
Vinaver, E. (ed.)
    1954   *Malory: Works* (London: Oxford University Press).
Whiting, B.J.
    1947   'Gawain: His Reputation, his Courtesy and his Appearance in
                    Chaucer's *Squire's Tale*', *Mediaeval Studies* 9: 189-234.

The Enduring Popularity of Thirteenth-Century Verse: The *Estorie del Evangelie* and the Vernon Manuscript

Oliver Pickering

Part Two of the monumental Vernon manuscript (Oxford, Bodleian Library MS Eng. poet. a.1), written c. 1390, begins with a fragment of a little-known Middle English narrative poem there called, in French, the 'estorie del euangelie', that is, the story of the gospel.[1] It is fragmentary because the manuscript has here been mutilated for the sake of the poem's pictures. Seven of these, interspersed at appropriate points in the narrative, are preserved on f.105, the sole surviving leaf of the poem,[2] but the *Estorie* is likely to have once occupied up to seven further leaves, which could have provided space for at least 35 additional miniatures (Doyle 1987: 9).[3] The textually-related Clopton manuscript (London, University Library Sterling MS V.17), which preserves most of the 2,400-line poem, has spaces for 33 pictures, never filled in.[4] The opening leaf of the *Estorie* seems to have been one

1. *IMEV* 3194. For editions of the poem see Millward (1998) and nn. 6-9 below.
2. They are reproduced in full colour as plates III-IV in Doyle (1987).
3. Doyle's calculation of 35 miniatures is apparently based on his estimate (p. 9) of 'five or six' further leaves for the *Estorie*. The true figure must be six or seven because the next item listed in the manuscript's table of contents is said to begin seven leaves after the *Estorie*, i.e., on f.112: see f.i verso and Serjeantson (1937: 234) (both of which use the old foliation and so refer to ff.104 and 111). The number of lost miniatures must therefore be correspondingly greater: cf. the next note.
4. But the Clopton manuscript is also fragmentary, at the end, and Celia

of the most decorated folios in the whole Vernon manuscript.[5] There is a formal illuminated border of maple-like leaves, and there was once, before it too was cut out, an unusually large initial capital letter. Present also, in the lower margin, is a blank shield, perhaps for the arms of an owner or donor. It has even been suggested that this leaf, now the beginning of Part Two, may originally have been intended to stand first in the whole volume (Doyle 1987: 8; Turville-Petre 1990: 29).

But what sort of text is it that is placed in such a prominent position in the most important surviving anthology of Middle English religious texts, a manuscript to which, shortly before the end of the fourteenth century, enormous resources of expense, labour and time must have been devoted? It is a prosaic, predominantly unimaginative, predominantly short-couplet narrative of the life of Christ, written a hundred years earlier, which one would have thought hopelessly old-fashioned by this date. Its text is somewhat corrupt, not disastrously so but to the extent that the sense is sometimes lost. At least as significant is the fact that it contains a good deal of archaic vocabulary, some of it from a dialectally distant area. Why was this poem chosen?

To illustrate this point I now print and discuss three short extracts from the *Estorie del Evangelie*, taken from the recent edition by the late Professor Celia Millward (Millward 1998). In the early stage of the poem, which is all that Vernon preserves, there are four relevant manuscripts,[6] namely:

Millward has calculated that the missing leaves would have included space for up to ten additional pictures (Millward 1998: 38). For a list of the likely subjects of the miniatures in this manuscript (and therefore also in Vernon) see Turville-Petre (1990: 31). The table of contents in Vernon makes special mention of the illustrations in the poem: see Serjeantson (1937: 234), Doyle (1987: 9), Turville-Petre (1990: 29), and Hardman (1997: 46-48).

5. For an analysis of the decoration and illustration of the Vernon manuscript see Doyle (1987: 6-9).

6. There are three other manuscripts. The end of the poem is preserved in London, British Library MSS Lansdowne 388 and Royal 17.C.xvii, as a separate Resurrection and Judgment narrative (see Pickering 1972). Extracts totalling 260 lines are inserted into the text of the *Northern Passion* in Oxford, Bodleian Library MS Rawlinson C.655, from where they were printed in Foster (1913-16: II).

B   Oxford, Bodleian Library Additional C.38, early fifteenth century, localized in south-east Worcestershire[7]

D   London, Dulwich College XXII, c. 1300, localized in north-west Norfolk or south Lincolnshire[8]

S   London, University Library Sterling V.17, early fifteenth century, localized in central Worcestershire (the Clopton manuscript)

V   Oxford, Bodleian Library Eng. poet. a.1, c. 1390, localized in northern Worcestershire (the Vernon manuscript)[9]

We have here (apart from Vernon) one manuscript (D) which is much earlier than the others and whose text is likely to correspond closely to the poem's original form and dialect (McIntosh 1987); a second (S) which is so close to Vernon that it clearly derives from the same textual tradition (Turville-Petre 1990: 30-34); and a third (B) of a broadly similar area and date but which shows obvious signs of having had its language updated (although not so much in the early part of the poem).[10]

In the following extracts the three texts are presented in parallel, as they are in Millward's edition. They are arranged here in presumed chronological order of writing, with B, the most altered text, placed last.

7.   See Görlach (1974: 106). B's text was previously edited in Campbell (1915: 545-610).

8.   For this localization see McIntosh (1987) and Laing (1993: 108). D's fragmentary text was previously edited in Campbell (1915: 545-80).

9.   See the summary of opinion on the dialect of the Vernon manuscript in Doyle (1987: 11). In McIntosh (1987: 187) its language (and that of the Clopton manuscript) is located in central Worcestershire, but see more precisely the linguistic profile of the main hand (LP 7630) published in *LALME*, III, 553, which localizes it in central north Worcestershire. V's text was previously edited in Horstmann (1892: 1-11).

10.   Its scribe 'modernised the text linguistically by updating the spelling, morphology, lexicon, and, to the extent that metre and rhyme allowed, syntax' (Millward 1998: 19).

I, lines 65-68 and 145-50

D	For a wis man seiz þat bestis be	65
V	A wys mon seiþ þat bestes weren	
S	A wyse mon seiþ þat bestes weren	
B	A wise man seide þat bestes weren	
D	Hert ant neddre and ern, þis þre	66
V	Hert and eddre, þeos þreo and ern	
S	Hert & addre, þes þre and heren	
B	Hert & addir, þise three & eren	
D	Þat changiz þere lif þoruut þere kinde,	67
V	Þat heore lyf chaungede þorwh here kynde,	
S	Þat here lyf chaungede þorow her kynde,	
B	Þat her lyf chaunge thorou her kynde,	
D	For þus of hem iwrite we finde:	68
V	For þus of hem iwrite we fynde:	
S	For þus of hem iwrite we fynde:	
B	For þus of hem writen we fynde:	
D	Þat kinde giuez il man eginge,	145
V	Þat kuynde ჳifþ vche mon eggynge,	
S	Þat kynde ჳeueþ vche mon eggynge,	
B	Þat kynde gyueth iche man eggyng,	
D	Of god þing to haue ჳerninge.	146
V	Of vche good þing haue ჳeornyng.	
S	Of vche good þynge haue ჳyrnynge.	
B	Of iche goed thing to haue desiryng.	
D	Bot betir þing mai no man finde	147
V	Bote beter þyng ne mai no mon fynde	
S	But betur þyng may no man fynde	
B	But bettir thing may no man fynde	
D	Þan þe louerd of alle kinde,	148
V	Þen þe lord of alle þynge,	
S	Þan þe lorde of alle kynde,	
B	Þan þe lord of al kynde,	
D	Þat best ant fouhl ant alle þinge dihte	149
V	Þat beest and foul and alle wiht	
S	Þat beest & foule & alle wyჳt	
B	Þat beest & al thing dight	

D	To be vndir mannis mihte.	150
V	At wille beoþ vndur monnes miht.	
S	At wille ben vnder mannes myȝt.	
B	At wille to be vndir mannes myght.	

This first passage is the beginning of an extended allegory, with moral application to sinful mankind, of how the hart, the adder and the eagle renew their lives when they feel old age approaching. MS D alone preserves most of the allegory, hence the omission here of lines 69-144.

It is at once apparent that VSB transmit a corrupt text: the change from 'be' to 'weren' in 65 has led to 'eren' becoming the rhyme word in 66, making nonsense of *þeos þreo*[11] which now occurs after only two of the creatures have been named. In 148 V is in isolated error (*þe lord of alle þynge*), its spoiled rhyme presumably the result of carelessness. But the following error, in 149-50, must derive from its exemplar as it is shared with S. The biblical 'who established beasts and birds and all things to be under mankind's control', as in D and partially in B, becomes 'so that beasts and birds and all creatures are, by his will, under mankind's control', which follows much less well from 147-48. The sense of the substituted word *wiht* would normally include mankind.

II, lines 319-28

D	'Þarefore me schal al mankinde	319
V	'Þerfore me schal al monkynde	
S	'Þerfore me shal al mankynde	
B	'Þerfore shal al mankynde	

D	Blisful telle in þeire minde	320
V	Blisful telle in heore mynde	
S	Blysful telle in here mynde	
B	Blisful be in her mynde	

D	Þat he wold in me swo gret þing finde	321
V	Þat he wolde in me mekenesse fynde	
S	Þat he wolde in me mekenes fynde	
B	Þat he wolde in me mekenesse fynde	

---

11. I quote from V unless it is unrepresentative.

D	Þat is of mihte to leyse ant binde.	322
V	Þat mihtful is to lame and blynde.	
S	Þat myȝtful is to loome & blynde.	
B	Þat mightful is to lese & bynde.	

D	Of mercy þanne he was leche	323
V	Of merci he was leche	
S	Of mercy he was leche	
B	Of merci he was þe best leeche	

D	Fram kin to kinde þat dredde his speche.	324
V	From kynde þat dredde his speche.	
S	From kynde þat dredede his speche.	
B	Fro kynde to kynde dred was his speche.	

D	Of þe prude in herte he dide wreche	325
V	Of þe proude of herte he dude wreche	
S	Of þe proud of herte he dude wreche	
B	Of þe pride of hert he did wrecche	

D	Ant dide þe meke on hey to reche.	326
V	And dude þe meke an heiȝ to reche.	
S	& dede þe meke an hi to reche.	
B	& did þe meke on hye to reeche.	

D	Þe hungery in god he made stronge,	327
V	Þe hungri in god he made stronge,	
S	Þe hongry in god he made stronge,	
B	Þe hungry in goed he made stronge,	

D	Ant þe riche he lette alswonge.	328
V	And þe riche he lette alswonge.	
S	& þe ryche he lette alswonge.	
B	& þe riche lete ydel gonge.	

This second extract is part of the poem's rendering of the Magnificat. VS are in error in 322, where they corrupt *leyse ant binde*—that is, 'loose and bind', though the phrase is non-biblical at this point—into 'lame and blind', much less appropriate after *mihtful*. The same manuscripts go astray in 324, where the necessary *From kynde to kynde* ('from generation to generation') is reduced merely to *From kynde*, quite losing the meaning. The final four lines are more straightforward except that they end with the very rare word *alswonge*, with which the scribe of B (or his exemplar) clearly could not cope. It is related to Old Icelandic *svangr*, 'thin', 'hungry', producing here a meaning on the lines of 'he left the rich gaunt and lean'. *MED*, under *swong*, records it otherwise only in two fifteenth-century texts, a treatise on uroscopy and the *Promptorium Parvulorum*, 'a text known to have originated in or near the Fenland area and so at no great distance from where *La Estorie*, as I am suggesting, was written' (McIntosh 1987: 190).

III, lines 463-66 and 471-72

D	Wareof hit were nouht he ne wiste	463
V	Wharof hit were noþing he nuste	
S	Wherof hit were noþyng he nuste	
B	Wherfore it were noght he ne wist	
D	Swo alse he neuir hire muht kiste	464
V	So as he neuere hire mouþ custe	
S	So as he neuere hir mouþ custe	
D	Wiht wille of sinne, ne neuir liste	465
V	Mid wille of sunne, ne neuer luste	
S	With wylle of synne, ne neuer luste	
B	With wille of synne neuer he ne lyst	
D	Hire maidinhod fullic vpbriste.	466
V	Hire maidenhod fulliche vpbreste.	
S	Hir maydenhod folliche vpbrede.	
B	Hir maidenheed fully upbriste...	
D	[A]nt for þat he neuere sauh wiht eye	471
V	And for he neuere ne saiȝ wiþ eiȝe	
S	& for he neuer ne say with ede	
B	And for he neuer sawe with eye	
D	[þ]at scho hire gan to folye beye.	472
V	þat heo to fool dede gon hire beyȝe.	
S	þat heo to foul dede gan hire bede.	
B	þat she to foleheed hir gan beye.	

This final passage is from Joseph's Trouble about Mary, in which both *vpbreste* (466) and *beyȝe* (472) seem to have troubled the scribe of S, which is normally closely allied to V. The first of these words is apparently 'up-burst', not recorded in *OED* before Spenser.[12] We have to take it as an infinitive after the preterite

---

12. *s.v.* **up-**, prefix, 4a. Professor Frances McSparran kindly informs me that the *MED*'s files contain only two references to the word, one the present

luste in the previous line, and the meaning of *fulliche vpbreste* is no
doubt 'foully violate'. S alters the word to *vpbrede*, which, if not
simply a mistake (because the rhyme is so badly destroyed), must
mean something like 'snatch'.[13] The word *beyʒe* in 472, meaning
'incline', 'turn', is not unusual, but is scarcely attested in works
composed after 1300. S's scribe changes it to *bede*, perhaps intend-
ing *hire bede* to mean 'offer herself', but if so it is at the price of the
seemingly meaningless form *ede* in 471. It may more likely be an
escape into some kind of familiarity. V's archaic 'Mid' in 465 may
also be noted here.

To return now to the earlier question: what did the Vernon
compiler think he was doing in including such an elderly poem as
the *Estorie* in his manuscript? Crucially, was he expecting it to
be read and understood?[14] This of course raises questions
about the whole nature of Vernon, its purpose and its intended
audience. The manuscript is likely to have been produced in a
well-equipped religious house, perhaps Cistercian, in northern
Worcestershire, but it is not known for whom.[15] Doyle, combining
the evidence of the book's enormous size with that of the varied
nature of the texts and the presence of illustrations, has suggested
that it could have fulfilled both private and public reading
functions.[16] It was written by two scribes, but one of these, clearly
working towards the end of the whole project, contributed little

text, the other in a life of St Edith of c. 1450 in which it means 'break open
(a gate)'.

13. Cf. *MED* **breiden** v.(1), 6, 'seize', 'grasp'. It may be noted that lines
467-70 legitimately rhyme on *-ede* (in all manuscripts), following which S
apparently disrupts the sense again with two more rhyme words in *-ede* (see
below).

14. The same questions might be asked of the contemporaneous *South
English Legendary* collection, also copied into the Vernon manuscript, but that
at least originated in the West Midlands.

15. See the discussion in Doyle (1987: 14-15).

16. Doyle (1990: 4). There is general agreement that the book would
probably have had to be read or consulted at a lectern; see especially
Robinson (1990), where it is suggested (p. 27) that 'the resulting volume perhaps formed a library copy or reference collection'. Hanna, in his recent
account of the Vernon manuscript's prose texts, states that it was prepared
'for public reading in a religious establishment, probably a community of
nuns' (Hanna 1997: xii), but this remains speculation. A case for the female
readership of Vernon is attempted also in Riddy (1996: 106-107).

more than the preliminary quire, which contains the table of contents and the translation of Aelred of Rievaulx's *De Institutione Inclusarum*.

In the past there has often been comment about how the main scribe of Vernon 'edited' his material, and it seems to be the case that numerous texts in Vernon (although not the *Estorie*) have in some way been altered from the form in which they are commonly found elsewhere. It is now agreed that such editing can hardly be attributed to the scribe,[17] and, speaking generally, it is uncertain to what extent it can be attributed to the compiler or organizer of the volume. The scriptorium where Vernon and its sister volume the Simeon manuscript[18] were produced must have been very well supplied with exemplars, copied from in a variety of ways, but it is unclear how much, if any, editorial or compositional work was carried out there.[19]

It may also be questioned to what extent the guiding hand behind Vernon was exercising real discrimination in deciding which texts should go in. Norman Blake has argued that the small number of texts with illustrations means 'that illustrations as such had no bearing on the choice of texts to include', that texts were chosen purely for their non-visual content, and that the compiler had so much material to hand 'that he did not necessarily include everything which was available' (1990: 46-47). There is deliberate grouping of texts within Vernon, but the motives for their arrangement are not always obvious. One can conclude, with Doyle, 'that there was an intention of broad categorization of the material, better achieved in some parts than others' (1990: 5). What is clear is that the more up-to-date and intellectually demanding material—the Rolle, the Hilton, *Piers Plowman*—is grouped towards the end of the book, in Part Four, which contains almost all the manuscript's prose. Hanna has recently drawn detailed attention

17. See Doyle (1990: 9-10, and his n. 34) for a list of modern editors who have commented on the phenomenon.
18. See Doyle (1990) for the relationship between Vernon and Simeon (London, British Library Additional MS 22283) and references to other studies.
19. Cf. Ayto and Barratt (1984: xviii): 'Like the other texts in the Vernon manuscript, the translation [of Aelred of Rievaulx's *De Institutione Inclusarum*] was clearly not made specifically for inclusion here; the multiple layers of the language of the text show that it must have existed in earlier versions.'

to the modernizing and 'canon-forming' activities of the 'Vernon team' in this section of the volume, suggesting the execution of a deliberate policy (1997: xiii-xv; and see also Hussey 1990). But although the compiler or compilers undoubtedly assembled a remarkable range of texts, their textual quality is a separate question. The presence of Rolle's *Form of Living* may be significant, but according to a recent editor the source of Vernon's copy 'gives a very poor text, with numerous omissions for which there is no apparent reason' (Ogilvie-Thomson 1988: lix).

It may be better to accept that the compiler did not gladly leave things out. He evidently wanted to produce a huge book, and it may be noted that Part Five, a separate quire containing the so-called Vernon lyrics, was very likely added as an afterthought (Blake 1990: 56; and cf. Doyle 1987: 2). The compiler, it might be argued, simply could not stop accumulating texts. Turville-Petre, considering motives, has drawn attention to 'the intense interest in religious writings in English' in the diocese of Worcester around 1400, and has linked it to a possibly deliberate policy, on the part of the local ecclesiastical authorities, of providing books of orthodox religious content to combat the challenge posed by Lollard teaching (Turville-Petre 1990: 42-44). Heffernan has gone furthest in this respect, seeing Vernon as symbolizing 'the values of a resurgent orthodoxy under siege' (1990: 79), and characterizing the choices made by its compiler as politico-religious:

> Viewed from the perspective of the religious dissent of the middle 1380s, the inclusion of texts like the N[orthern] H[omily] C[ycle] and the S[outh] E[nglish] L[egendary] in the Vernon [manuscript] seems to be part of a programmatic effort designed to inhibit greater autonomy on the part of the laity in the life of the church (1990: 78).

But the length of time needed to produce Vernon—likely to have been several years (Doyle 1990: 1-2)—does not seem to square with any sort of planned campaign. Its production was, as Heffernan (1990: 77) says, 'slow, painstaking, encyclopaedic in scope and traditional in outlook', and one of Doyle's suggestions is that its writing might have been undertaken as a pious or even penitential act (Doyle 1987: 15). The achievement of its principal scribe, not least in attaining a high degree of transcriptional accuracy, and in imposing a 'remarkable level of linguistic uniformity' on the texts he copied (Doyle 1987: 11), should not be down-played. But it is noteworthy that there are striking repetitions of material within the manuscript, for example three versions (two verse, one prose) of the *Mirror of St Edmund,* and two virtually identical copies of the *Trental of St Gregory,* a mistake which Doyle (1990: 4-5) associates with the sheer passage of time during Vernon's production. There is also very little sign of correction of the copying, either by the scribe himself or by anyone else. Taking into account Doyle's deduction, from the scribe's steady round anglicana hand quite lacking in symptoms of secretary style, that he had 'probably formed his hand nearer the middle of the fourteenth century, possibly even in the second quarter' (1987: 12), we may posit that the scribe was a trusted elderly man, largely left to get on with his laborious task and supplied from time to time, not always consistently, with exemplars from which to copy.[20] If this was the case it is likely that the compilation of the manuscript proceeded in a less planned way than has sometimes been argued, and that neither the scribe nor his director was always critically engaged with the texts in question.

Once the bulk of the writing was finished the purpose and destination of the manuscript may have become more focused: decorators and illustrators were engaged, and the second scribe was brought in to supply rubrics, foliation and the important table of contents, which entitles the finished book 'sowlehele' and gives its readers detailed access to what it contains.[21] Before then, how-ever, it may not be unreasonable to regard Vernon as a relatively unplanned encyclopaedia of texts, a compilation of enormous potential spiritual value but of uncertain practical purpose.

If it is correct to suggest that the choice of texts for copying into

20. Cf. Doyle (1987: 2), particularly the remarks about speed in com-pleting the work not being of the greatest importance.

21. Cf. Robinson (1990: 16): 'Despite its fine appearance, however, Vernon would not [i.e. at first] have been an easy book for a reader to find his or her way about in'; also Gillespie (1989: 328): 'This [the list of con-tents] transforms the book from a somewhat random collection into a work-ing anthology... It may have been executed sometime shortly after the main task of copying, perhaps as a response to the demands of readers.' The suggestion that the table of contents may not have been added until the early fifteenth century (Serjeantson 1937: 222; followed by Robinson 1990: 16) is strongly challenged by Ayto and Barratt (1984: xvi-xvii).

Vernon was less than wholly discriminating, then the question of a
motive for including the *Estorie del Evangelie* is not so pressing—or
so easily answerable. We can say, at the very least, that the compiler believed the poem suitable for copying, despite its archaic
language and uncertain textual state. Its presence in the manuscript consequently presupposes, on his part, a high level of tolerance of old-fashioned narrative poetry. We cannot know whether
he thought that the recipients of the manuscript—if he had
particular ones in mind—would fully understand the *Estorie*, but it
must be that he believed a life of Christ of this kind an appropriate text to place before them. It is likely that the poem's genre
partly determined its presence.

If so, it does not follow that the compiler had a number of verse
lives of Christ from which to choose. The contents of Vernon
provide a good conspectus of the English religious literature then
in circulation, and the manuscript is distinguished by its inclusion
of both recent and older writing. Broadly speaking the newer
material is devotional, mystical, didactic and allegorical, in a
variety of literary forms, while the older material (except, notably,
the prose *Ancrene Riwle*) is narrative or didactic, and predominantly in simple couplet verse. It is only natural that later fourteenth-century writers should be interested in exploiting different
literary forms and genres from those practised by their earlier
fourteenth-century and later thirteenth-century predecessors. By
the date of Vernon it seems clear, from the paucity of contemporary examples, that the verse life of Christ is, in terms of 'new'
writing, out of fashion; that as a genre it scarcely interested creative writers.[22] Other earlier versifications were in theory available
to the Vernon compiler, for example *Cursor Mundi* and the
Northern Passion, and indeed the manuscript contains on ff.19v-27
a text of the *South English Legendary*'s *Southern Passion* poem, which
might be seen as another instance of its duplication of material.[23]

22. There are isolated exceptions such as the *Stanzaic Life of Christ*, normally dated to the later fourteenth century and extant in three manuscripts.
But by this date prose lives of Christ had begun to take over in terms of serious writing, a trend which culminated in Nicholas Love's *Mirror of the Blessed
Life of Jesus Christ* of the beginning of the fifteenth century.

23. It contains also (ff.6v-9) another *South English Legendary*-related poem
known as the *Vernon Life of Mary*, which, although principally a close transla-

But although originally from the North-East Midlands, the *Estorie* was clearly well known in the West Midlands of the late fourteenth and early fifteenth centuries, for MSS Bodleian Additional C.38 and London University Library Sterling V.17 are also localized in Worcestershire. Despite the poem's antiquity, it would appear to have been the most popular verse life of Christ for copying purposes in the West Midlands of c. 1400.

The age of the poem clearly did not count against it. Heffernan notes how the Vernon compiler included 'texts which typically had the imprimatur of time', in some cases texts which might almost be characterized as 'anachronistic' (1990: 79). He is thinking primarily of the *South English Legendary* and the early fourteenth-century *Northern Homily Cycle*, but the *Estorie* falls into the same category. This traditionalism on the part of manuscript compilers in respect of narrative religious verse, the result of a combination of cultural-historical and literary-historical factors, is not confined to Vernon,[24] but is of particular interest—in terms of assessing its significance—in a manuscript of such wide-ranging and at times 'modern' contents.

In this connection we can return to the question of what Vernon's readers, as opposed to its compiler, may have thought of the *Estorie del Evangelie*. Doyle comments that the manuscript's chronologically diverse contents reflect 'the development from an overwhelmingly oral mediation of vernacular literature, in the thirteenth and the earlier fourteenth century, to the larger share of private reading in the later fourteenth and the fifteenth centuries' (1990: 4). It can be argued that the presence of the *Estorie* in Vernon is a case of a late fourteenth-century compiler, wanting a verse life of Christ, happily making do with a text from the period of oral mediation (bolstered as it is with illustrations), and extending its written life almost beyond the ability of anyone to transmit or even understand it accurately. Elsewhere Doyle (1987: 11) writes of the manuscript's intended readers not being inconvenienced by the scribes' spelling conventions, but what if they

tion of *La Conception Nostre Dame* by the French poet Wace, ends with yet another run-through of episodes from the life of Christ. For the *Vernon Life* see Pickering (1973: 440-42).

24. For example, at least eight of the 26 major *South English Legendary* manuscripts are dated to the fifteenth century.

were inconvenienced by some of the actual texts? It is not unusual for people to enjoy works from earlier times, which may well be easier and more reassuring than modern productions. But although little is known about the ability of 'non-professional' medieval readers to cope with the literature of the past, we may expect them to have had, as in all ages, a limited tolerance of archaic vocabulary and textual corruption.[25]

The *Estorie* tells a story with which all people of any education would have been familiar,[26] and Norman Blake has taught us that medieval readers, when faced with difficult vocabulary, probably 'grasped the general intention of a word by assessing its meaning from the context in which it occurred' (1977: 50). Nevertheless the textual state of Middle English manuscripts is too often considered as a wholly scribal phenomenon, as a source of information to be used when making editorial decisions or working out manuscript affiliations. It must, however, have affected contemporary readers. In some cases scribes will revise the texts they are copying, by modernizing the language or smoothing out difficulties. The result may be harmful from an editorial point of view but would surely have been beneficial at the time. We can see some of this happening with the manuscripts of the *Estorie*, especially in the case of Bodleian Additional C.38, whose scribe, according to Celia Millward, achieved successfully his goals of abridging, modernizing and normalizing his text. His work, she says, 'gives us a clear picture of a competent and usually careful medieval editor at work' (1998: 18-19; and cf. Turville-Petre 1990: 34). Additional C.38 was produced not very long after Vernon, in much the same part of the West Midlands, and yet its text is

---

25. The more extreme case of Old English homilies being copied in twelfth-century England, 'when the major theological, cultural, and linguistic changes would seem to render them obsolete and useless' (Irvine 1993: lii), is different, in that such manuscripts are likely to have been normally made for private or professional scholarly use, at least in the first instance.

26. And so it could be argued that it was more obviously necessary for the compiler to include an updated version of the non-narrative *Ancrene Riwle*. For the modernized nature of Vernon's text of this work see the summaries of studies by Kikuo Miyabe (1979) and Bernhard Diensberg (1992) in Millett 1996 (where they are items 343 and 452).

significantly different.[27] It may be contrasted also with London University Library MS Sterling V.17, which is textually close to Vernon and resembles it also in containing a copy of *Piers Plowman* alongside other narrative religious verse of an earlier period; it was probably made for Sir William Clopton, a man of some importance in the South-West Midlands of the early fifteenth century (Turville-Petre 1990: 36-38). This manuscript, like Vernon, transmits the archaisms and corruptions of the *Estorie* while hardly attempting to update the poem. Would Sir William and his household really have understood all of its detail? Or is it that, in both these cases, a scribe or compiler is relying on the reputation rather than the readability of a well-known piece of thirteenth-century verse?[28]

27. In one way the manuscript is similar to Vernon, in that here too the *Estorie* occurs together with the *South English Legendary*, to the extent that in Additional C.38 the former sits within the latter, almost adjacent to a text of the *Southern Passion* (Pickering 1973: 444, 453). However, its version of the *Passion* resembles its text of the *Estorie* in being noticeably abridged, and Brown remarks on the degree to which its language has been modernized (Brown 1927: xxv, l).

28. An earlier version of this essay was presented at the Second International Conference on Middle English, held in Helsinki in 1997. I am grateful to the organizers for giving me the opportunity to air these thoughts there.

WORKS CITED

Ayto, J., and A. Barratt (eds.)
1984   *Aelred of Rievaulx's 'De Institutione Inclusarum': Two English Versions* (EETS, 287; London: Oxford University Press).

Blake, N.F.
1977   *The English Language in Medieval Literature* (London: Dent).
1990   'Vernon Manuscript: Contents and Organisation', in Pearsall 1990: 45-59.

Brown, B. (ed.)
1927   *The Southern Passion* (EETS, 169; London: Oxford University Press).

Campbell, G.H.
1915   'The Middle English *Evangelie*', *PMLA* 30: 529-613, 851-53.

Doyle, A.I.
1990   'The Shaping of the Vernon and Simeon Manuscripts', in Pearsall
                1990: 1-13 [a revised version of an essay with the same title originally
                published in B. Rowland (ed.), *Chaucer and Middle English Studies in
                Honour of Rossell Hope Robbins* (London: Allen & Unwin [1974]):
                328-41].
Doyle, A.I. (introd.)
1987   *The Vernon Manuscript: A Facsimile of Bodleian Library, Oxford, MS Eng.
                Poet. a.1* (Cambridge: Brewer).
Foster, F.A. (ed.)
1913-16   *The Northern Passion* (2 vols.; EETS, 145, 147; London: Oxford Uni-
                versity Press).
Gillespie, V.
1989   'Vernacular Books of Religion', in J. Griffiths and D. Pearsall (eds.),
                Book Production and Publishing in Britain, 1375-1475 (Cambridge:
                Cambridge University Press): 317-44.
Görlach, M.
1974   *The Textual Tradition of the South English Legendary* (Leeds Texts and
                Monographs, 6; Leeds: University of Leeds School of English).
Hanna, R.
1997   *The Index of Middle English Prose, Handlist XII: Smaller Bodleian Collec-
                tions* (Cambridge: Brewer).
Hardman, P.
1997   'Windows into the Text: Unfilled Spaces in Some Fifteenth-Century
                English Manuscripts', in J. Scattergood and J. Boffey (eds.), *Texts
                and their Contexts: Papers from the Early Book Society* (Dublin: Four
                Courts Press): 44-70.
Heffernan, T.J.
1990   'Orthodoxies' *Redux*: The *Northern Homily Cycle* in the Vernon
                Manuscript and its Textual Affiliations', in Pearsall 1990: 75-87.
Horstmann, C. (ed.)
1892   *The Minor Poems of the Vernon Manuscript*, I (EETS, 98; London:
                Kegan Paul, Trench, Trübner).
Hussey, S.S.
1990   'Implications of Choice and Arrangement of Texts in Part 4 [of the
                Vernon Manuscript]', in Pearsall 1990: 61-74.
Irvine, S. (ed.)
1993   *Old English Homilies from MS Bodley 343* (EETS, 302; Oxford: Oxford
                University Press).
Laing, M.
1993   *Catalogue of Sources for a Linguistic Atlas of Early Medieval English*
                (Cambridge: Brewer).
McIntosh, A.
1987   'The Middle English *Estorie del Euangelie*: The Dialect of the Original
                Version', *Neuphilologische Mitteilungen* 88: 186-91.

Millett, B.

1996   '*Ancrene Wisse*', the Katherine Group, and the Wooing Group* (Annotated
            Bibliographies of Old and Middle English Literature, 2; Cambridge:
            Brewer).

Millward, C. (ed.)

1998   *The Estorie del Evangelie: A Parallel-Text Edition* (Middle English Texts,
            30; Heidelberg: Winter).

Ogilvie-Thomson, S.J. (ed.)

1988   *Richard Rolle: Prose and Verse* (EETS, 293; Oxford: Oxford University
            Press).

Pearsall, D. (ed.)

1990   *Studies in the Vernon Manuscript* (Cambridge: Brewer).

Pickering, O.S.

1972   '*A newe lessoun off Crystys ressurrectoun*: A Second Manuscript, and its
            Use of *La Estorie del Evangelie*', *English Philological Studies* 13: 43-48.

1973   'The Temporale Narratives of the *South English Legendary*', *Anglia* 91:
            425-55.

Riddy, F.

1996   '"Women Talking about the Things of God": A Late Medieval Sub-
            Culture', in C.M. Meale (ed.), *Women and Literature in Britain, 1150–
            1500* (Cambridge: Cambridge University Press, 2nd edn): 107-27.

Robinson, P.R.

1990   'The Vernon Manuscript as a "Coucher Book"', in Pearsall 1990: 15-
            28.

Serjeantson, M.S.

1937   'The Index of the Vernon Manuscript', *Modern Language Review* 32:
            222-61.

Turville-Petre, T.

1990   'The Relationship of the Vernon and Clopton Manuscripts', in
            Pearsall 1990: 29-44.

The Language of Persuasion: *De Clerico et Puella* from London, British Library MS Harley 2253

John Scattergood

In Michael Radford's film *Il Postino* (1995) the issue of the impact of poetry and poetic language on unsophisticated, perhaps largely illiterate, people is given a modern dimension. It is set in about 1952, and concerns Pablo Neruda, the diplomat and poet, exiled from Chile because of his Communist activities, who comes to live on an island off the coast of Italy. Mario Ruoppolo, an auxiliary, part-time postman, impressed by the beauty of Neruda's wife and the fact that most of the letters he receives appear to be from women, decides that the ability to write love poetry is something which would enhance his own attractiveness to women—which in other respects is not great. He asks Neruda to teach him to write love poetry, and, though he never manages to write anything particularly impressive, he does at least begin to appreciate the power of metaphor, contributes an adjective to one of Neruda's own love poems,[1] and is successful beyond his wildest imaginings in his

---

1.   In the fiction of the film Neruda asks him for an adjective to describe fishing nets and Mario comes up with *triste*, 'sad'. The poem alluded to is presumably that which begins:

> Inclinado en las tardes, tiro mis tristes redes
> a tus ojoas oceánicos...
> [Leaning into the afternoons, I cast my sad nets
> at your oceanic eyes...]

See Neruda (1975: 22-23). This is an edition with translation of Neruda's *Veinte Poemas de Amor y una Cancion Desesperada* (1924).

pursuit of Beatrice Russo, a waitress. Beatrice's aunt warns her against listening to Mario's words:

> Quando un uomo comincia a toccarti colle parole, arriva lontano colle mani.

> [When a man begins to touch you with his words, he goes further with his hands.]

Beatrice argues that there is nothing wrong with words, but her aunt maintains that words are the worst things ever. This is an unresolved disagreement, though eventually Mario does persuade Beatrice to become his wife. The film, in its own way, is inter-textual and allusive: behind this Beatrice lie other Beatrices—d'Annunzio's and, above all, Dante's—to whom love poems were addressed. And the argument about the power of poetic language, especially about the power of love poetry in relation to seduction, is an ancient one too, and it seems to me that this is what is centrally at issue in the Middle English lyric usually enti-tled *De Clerico et Puella*, and, indeed, in a number of texts related to it.

This short seduction poem, which has proved popular in mod-ern anthologies, appears on f.80v of London, British Library MS Harley 2253, an early fourteenth-century West Midland anthology, which preserves, amongst other things, the most extensive collec-tion of pre-Chaucerian secular lyrics (see Ker 1965). The poem is untitled in the manuscript, and it is not divided into stanzas. Nor is there any indication as to who speaks which lines—though in this case it is not difficult to work out. In its physical layout there is nothing to distinguish it from the short poems which surround it in the manuscript. Yet it seems to me to be an especially pre-cious text, because it participates importantly in the ongoing liter-ary debate about the power of words, and in particular about the power of love poetry in the winning of love.

I

The view that the language of love poetry is dangerously alluring and that a woman who wishes to preserve her virtue should not listen to it (essentiallly the position assumed by Beatrice's aunt) is expressed most memorably in English in the early Middle Ages in that section of *Ancrene Riwle* which deals with the custody of the

senses. Their advisor recommends that the anchoresses are to
deny their would-be seducer not only the sight of them, but also
the opportunity of communicating with them verbally—and various biblical texts on the danger of listening to certain sorts of
speech are mentioned here as support for the argument:

> Vorði, mine leoue sustren, ʒif eni mon bit fort iseon ou, askeð of
> him hwat god muhte þerof lihten; vor moni vuel ich iseo þerinne,
> & none biheue; & ʒif he is meðleas, ileueð him þe wurse; & ʒif eni
> wurðeð so wod, & so awed, þet he worpe his hond forð tuoward þe
> þurl cloð, swiftliche anonriht, schutteð al þet þurl to, & letteð hine
> iwurden, & also sone ase eni mon ualleð into luðer speche, þet falle
> touward fule liue, tuneð þet þurl anonriht; & ne answerie ʒe him
> nowiht, auh wendeð awei, mit tisse uers, þet he hit muwe iheren,
> 'Narraverunt mihi iniqui fabulaciones, sed non ut lex tua'; ant goð
> forð biuoren ower weouede wit te miserere. Ne chastie ʒe neuer
> nenne swuchne mon bute o þisse wise; vor, mit te chastiement, he
> muhte onswerien so, & blowen so liðeliche þet sum sperke muhte
> acwikien. No wouleche nis so coulert ase is o plaint wis; ase hwo se
> þus seide: 'Ich nolde, uor te þolien deaðe, þenche fulðe touward
> te; auh ich heuede isworen hit, luuien ich mot te, & nu me is wo
> þet tu hit wost. Auh forgif hit me nu, þet ich hit habbe itold te, &
> auh ich schulde iwurðe wod, ne schalt tu neuer more eft witen hou
> me stont'. Ant heo hit forʒiueð him, uor he spekeð þus feire, &
> spekeð þeonne of oðerwhat. Auh 'euer is þe eie to þe wude leie,
> þerinne is þet ich luuie'. Euer is þe heorte in þere uorme speche;
> & þet hwon he is forðe, heo went in hire þuhte ofte swuch wordes,
> hwon heo schulde oðerhwat ʒeornliche ʒemen. He eft secheð his
> point uorte breke uoreward, ant swereð þet he mot nede; ant so
> waxeð þe wo, se lengre se wurse; uor no freondschipe nis so vuel
> ase is fals freondschipe. Ueond þet þuncheð freond is swike ouer
> alle swike. Uorþi, mine leoue sustren, ne ʒiue ʒe to none swuche
> monne non inʒong to spekene. Vor ase holi writ seið, 'hore speche
> spret ase cauncre'. Auh for alle onsweres, wendeð ou ant wencheð
> frommard him. Al so as ich er seide, o none wise ne muwe þe
> betere sauen ou saulen, ant maten, & ouercumen him betere
> (Morton 1853: 96-97).

What is particularly interesting about this is the terminology in
which the argument is articulated. It is not simply the wonderful
image of ashes being coaxed into flame by the breath of words (a
version of the 'fire of love' trope), but the language of persuasion
quoted or travestied here is the language of love poetry. The
would-be lover, in the advisor's fictions, stereotypes himself as the

suffering lover and the anchoress as the cruel mistress, and he uses the tropes of 'dying for love' and 'love's madness' which were evidently familiar enough to be recognized. The idea of 'dying for love' does not appear in extant lyrics until the poems of London, British Library MS Harley 2253, but is frequently found there. The author of *Alysoun* complains:

> Bote he me wolle to hire take
> forte buen hire owen make
> longe to lyuen ichulle forsake
> ant feye fallen adoun (Brook 1964: No. 4, 17-20).

Another complains that his lady has consigned (*diht*) him to death and says 'y deʒe longe er my day' (Brook: 1964: No. 5. 25-6). The idea of 'love's madness', however, appears earlier. One thirteenth-century poet complains:

> Loue is a selkud wodenesse
> Þat þe idel mon ledeth by wildernesse... (Brown 1962: No. 9, 1-2).

And another more memorably encapsulates the same idea in a brief stanza:

> Foweles in þe frith,
> Þe fisses in þe flod,
> And i mon waxe wod.
> Mulch sorw I walke with
> for beste of bon and blod (Brown 1962: No. 8).

Such words, it seems, are held to be dangerously seductive. That the advisor has poetry, and the language of poetry, in mind here is made clear by his reference to the words being spoken *o plaint wis*, which seems to mean 'in the style of a complaint' (a recognized literary genre), and by the quotation of a snatch of verse (a longer version of which appears in the British Library MS Cotton Cleopatra C.vi version):

> euer is þe eie
> to þe wude leie
> þerinne is þet ich luuie.[2]

The best response to these harmful words leading to unchaste

---

2.   These lines are from the text quoted above, but set out as verse. For a more elaborate version of this snatch of verse see Dobson (1972: 76-77). See also Wilson (1970: 164).

love, the anchoresses are advised, is no response of a verbal sort at all: they must close their windows and avoid the man. On no account must they enter into a debate, for to reply, or even to listen, is to risk being persuaded to change one's mind and to act sinfully. Instead of listening to these words, the anchoresses are advised to ponder the words of the Song of Songs:

> Lokeð nu, hu propreliche þe lefdi in Canticis, Godes deorwurðe spuse, lereð ou, bi hire sawe, hu ȝe schulen siggen, 'En dilectus meus loquitur mihi, Surge, propera amica mea, &c' Lo, he seið, 'ich ihere nu mi leofmon speken; he cleopeð me; ich mot gon.' & ȝe gon anonriht to our derewurðe spuse & leofman... (Morton 1853: 97).

The meaning of the Song of Songs is wrapped up and concealed (*bilepped & ihud*), says the advisor some lines later, but he will reveal (*unuolden*) it, and he expounds various passages of the text, in standard exegetical terms, as referring to God's love for the faithful within the church, or, more precisely here, for the individual anchoress, who is instructed to listen only to God's voice and to ignore all others, especially those who try through words to tempt them into worldly love. The language of love poetry is seen as a threat to moral behaviour, and the advisor takes the trouble to warn against it and to attempt to counter it by transferring the desire: the love of God is meant to be a more satisfactory alternative to the love of man.

II

But women, at least in fictions, did listen to the language of love, particularly, it seems, when it came from the mouths of clerics. This is a category which, in English, takes in a notoriously broad range of men—enclosed monks, friars, the clergy in major or in minor orders, and scholars training in the universities—but whose defining characteristic is that they engage in activities which are essentially intellectual. Because of their knowledge, their learning, their intelligence, they are considered to be especially dangerous to women.

Dame Sirith is the earliest extant fabliau in English. It is preserved in Oxford, Bodleian Library MS Digby 86, which was written in the diocese of Worcester between 1272 and 1283—

though the fabliau itself appears to have been East Midlands in origin. The text consists of 450 lines, of which only about 50 are spoken by the narrator: the rest is dialogue. And in places marginal cues are used to denote the speaker (see Tschann and Parkes 1996: ff.165-68). So the poem looks like an embryonic play: it could be performed by a narrator and three other actors, or by one person who spoke all the parts but used different voices and gestures to distinguish the characters. In the poem, Wilekin, a 'Clericus', indicated by a marginal C before some of his speeches, addresses Margery, a merchant's wife whom he is attempting to seduce, in a reduced, but unmistakable version of the language of love. Having initially been refused, he asks the woman to change her mind and look on him favourably:

> Amend þi mod, and torn þi þout,
> And rew on me (Bennett and Smithers 1968: No. VI, 113-14).[3]

And when he speaks to Dame Sirith about his desperate situation, and asks her to be his intermediary, he uses the familiar tropes of 'loves madness' and 'dying for love':

> Bote if hoe wende hire mod,
> For serewe mon Ich wakese wod
>> Oþer miselue quelle (Bennett and Smithers 1968: No. VI, 181-83).

Here the language of love poetry, which the cleric uses in his approach to the woman, is not successful, and he needs Dame Sirith and her stratagems to obtain her compliance. Again, in the *Interludium de Clerico et Puella*, the earliest secular play in English, which appears because of certain verbal similarities as well as similarities of plot to derive from *Dame Sirith*,[4] the Clericus similarly uses the language of love for an attempted seduction, and some of his verbal resources are similar to those used in the earlier text:

> For þe Hy sorw nicht and day—
> Y may say 'Hay, wayleuay!'
> Y luf þe mar þan mi lif;

3. There is no exact source for this poem but several analogues involving wicked intermediaries.

4. On the relationship of these texts see the interesting discussion in Hines (1993: 43-70), though I do not agree with all his conclusions.

> Þu hates me mar þan gayt dos chnief!
> Þat es nouct for mysgilt—
> Certhes, for þi luf ham Hi spilt.
> A! suythe mayden, reu of me
> Þat es ty luf hand ay sal be!
> For þe luf of þe moder of efne,
> Þu mend þi mode and her my steuene! (Bennett and Smithers
> 1968: No. XV, 17-26).

The girl, Malkyn, has rebuffed his first advances, and he here
testifies to his sorrow, and to the long duration of his love. He asks
her to 'mend þi mod', and to have *reu* on him—both of which
ideas appear in the fabliau, and he also uses the 'dying for love'
trope. Later, when he talks to Mome Elwis, who is approached,
like Dame Sirith in the fabliau, to act as his intermediary, he again
uses the language of love to describe his situation:

> Hic am a clerc þat hauntes scole.
> Y lydy my lif wyt mikel dole:
> Me wor leuer to be dedh
> Þan led þe lif þat Hyc ledh!
> For ay mayden, with and schen,
> Fayrer ho lond haw Y non syen (Bennett and Smithers 1968: No.
> XV, 41-46).

The play is incomplete, but it is clear that the language of love has
here failed again. In both these texts the women listen to the
speeches of their would-be lovers, and engage in dialogue with
them, but are firm in their refusals. Margery has no wish for a
man other than her husband:

> So bide Ich euere mete oþer drinke,
> Her þou lesest al þi swinke.
> Þou miȝt gon hom, leue broþer,
> For wille Ich þe loue ne non oþer,
> Bote mi wedde houssebonde...(Bennett and Smithers 1968: No.
> VI, 133-37).

Malkyn wants nothing to do with clerics in general:

> Do way! By Crist and Leonard,
> No wil Y lufe na clerc fayllard...(Bennett and Smithers 1968: No.
> XV, 7-8).

If they are to be won, they are to be won by other means than the
language of love poetry. In the humorous context of these stories

the artificial language of love has no effect: the good sense and practicality of the women see to it that any offer of love based on it is rejected.

It seems reasonable to suppose that the author of *De Clerico et Puella* in MS Harley 2253 knew and used both the fabliau and the interlude in fashioning his own poem: the narrative dynamic of each of these texts—a cleric tries to seduce a woman—is not frequently found in English literature at this date, and there appear to be distinct verbal reminiscences of the earlier texts in the lyric; and, crucially, in all three texts the men draw on a particular set of ideas in relation to love, and a particular diction which clearly belongs to a tradition of writing, an English tradition, which was well-established linguistically. Derek Brewer briefly discusses the poem in relation to these earlier texts and describes it as 'as much a "play" as a lyric' (1983: 58). There is something to be said for this view: the speakers in the poem interact like characters in a play, and the plot moves on as a result of the dialogue. But the lyric does not deliver the same story. The cleric makes no use of female intermediaries: there is no Dame Sirith and no Mome Elwis to make his amorous arguments for him. He uses his own imagination and his own words. If the lyric does bear an intertextual relation to the fabliau and the play, if it is a rewriting of these texts, as I think, then it is a radical and highly individualistic one.

In a sense, though, the associations with fabliau and drama, though real, are somewhat misleading. It seems to me that the more significant generic context of *De Clerico et Puella* is lyrical: it is preserved in that section of MS Harley 2253 along with other lyrics.[5] And, in formal terms, in relation to the alternating speeches of the participants it has associations with the *tenso* (though the contributors are not rival troubadours) and the *debat* (though the matter at issue is not a moral or philosophical question). But it seems to me that it has even more in common with love songs and poems of the pastourelle genre.

In this respect its position in MS Harley 2253 may be significant. It is followed on ff.80v and 81 by *When Þe Nyhtegale Singes*, a love

5.   For some intelligent comments on the shifting principles of organization underlying the structure of MS Harley 2253 see Stemmler (1991: 231-37).

song set in spring, written in the same long-line monorhyming quatrain form, and using extensively the 'dying for love' trope and the associated idea of the lady as 'healer':

> Suete lemmon, y preye þe of loue one speche;
> whil y lyue in world so wyde oþer nulle y seche.
> Wiþ þy loue, my suete leof, mi blis þou mihtes eche;
> a suete cos of þy mouþ mihte be my leche (Brook 1964: No. 25, 9-12).

So similar are the poems in manner and approach that some have argued that they may be by the same author. But *De Clerico et Puella* is preceded on f.80r by *An Autumn Song*, beginning 'Nou skrinkeþ rose ant lylie-flour...' Helen Sandison calls this an 'undeveloped' pastourelle (1913: 61 n. 57), but it seems to me it could be more properly described as an imaginative subversion of the genre. The conventional pastourelle, the genre alluded to intertextually here, is a seduction poem, or a poem about attempted seduction: the poet, or the first-person speaker, riding through the countryside, comes upon a shepherdess or a country girl with whom he engages in conversation and whose love he tries to win, sometimes with success, sometimes not. Here, the poet rides out in the conventional way:

> From Petresbourh in o morewenyng,
> as y me wende o my pleyȝyng...(Brook 1964: No. 23, 11-12).

But it is autumn not spring, and the poet's sense of the transitoriness of things, generated by a contemplation of the landscape, causes his frivolous, sexually inclined mood to turn to seriousness. He thinks of the Virgin Mary instead of a shepherdess, and ponders her role as spiritual healer in place of the secular lady's capacity for relieving the pangs of frustrated love:

> Betere is hire medycyn
> þen eny mede or eny wyn;
> hire erbes smulleþ suete:
> from Catenas into Dyuelyn
> nis þer no leche so fyn
> oure serewes to bete (Brook 1964: No. 23, 31-36).

Fittingly within the logic of the poem, it ends with a repudiation of secular love and a prayer:

Wymmon, wiþ þi iolyfte,
þou þench on Godes shoures.
Þah þou be whyt ant bryht on ble,
falewen shule þy floures.
Iesu, haue merci of me,
þat al þis world honoures.
Amen (Brook 1964: No. 23, 54-60).

This is sophisticated allusive art. The poem is an intertextual mosaic whose pieces have to be recognized for anything like their full meaning to emerge.[6] The poet expects his audience to be aware of certain linguistic clues—that a poem which begins with a poet riding out *o my pleyʒyng* is likely to be a pastourelle; that the idea of the lady as a *leche* dispensing *medycyn* is a trope of secular love poetry; that to mention a lady as being pre-eminent between two geographical points (here Caithness and Dublin) is a topic of praise in love poetry, here applied to the Virgin Mary; that the *rose ant lylie-flour* of the opening lines are the two flowers convention-ally associated with the beautiful complexions of women and that they are the *floures* that will *falewen* metaphorically in line 57, which associates the end of summer and the fading of beauty, again in a conventional way. He probably expects *shoures* also to be read as a pun: it primarily means the 'pains' Christ suffered on the cross; but the context of seasonal changes also suggests that he may have in mind the storms of autumn and approaching winter—the equinoctial gales—which beat down the late-bloom-ing roses and lilies.

III

The poet of *De Clerico et Puella*, it seems to me, has many of these same expectations of his audience. Formally, the poem is a pas-tourelle without the narrative setting. But there are other differ-ences too. The man in this poem is not a knight but a cleric and the girl is not a shepherdess, nor perhaps any kind of country girl. Nor is the dialogue the result of a chance encounter in the coun-tryside when the man is riding out seeking pleasure: it is hard to be sure where it takes place, but the girl twice mentions her *boure*

---

6.   On the intertextual relations of this and other pastourelles see Scattergood (1996a).

(Brook 1964: No. 24, 11, 119) as if the conversation may be taking place there, and a *wyndou* (23), perhaps a window-alcove or perhaps simply a window, where a previous encounter with a cleric took place. Nevertheless, this poem also uses the pastourelle genre allusively, in the structure of its argument. After the cleric's initial declaration of love for the girl she, in the traditional way, categorically refuses him and tries to send him away (9-10). Then she warns him of the scandal which might ensue if their liaison were to be discovered (11). Then comes the argument that her family disapproves of him, that her father and other members of it are on the lookout for him, and that, if he and she were to be caught in compromising circumstances, she might be locked up and he might be killed:

> Þou art wayted day ant nyht wiþ fader ant al my kynne.
> Be þou in mi bour ytake, lete þey for no synne
> me to holde ant þe to slon, þe deþ so þou maht wynne!
> (Brook 1964: No. 24, 18-20).

These are all standard moves in pastourelles. So too, in some, is the girl's change of mind as she accedes to the man's arguments and sexual advances, in some ways against her better judgment (35-36). Though neither the characterization nor the setting is that of the conventional pastourelle, the shape of the argument— proposal, refusal, dispute, compliance—is the familiar one in poems of this genre, and would almost certainly have been recognized by an audience of any literary sophistication.

But there is another aspect of this poem's relationship to the pastourelle genre which is critical. One of the most frequently recurring distinctive features of the pastourelle is the disjunction in power relations between the two speakers—the man is characteristically a knight or gentleman, the girl a shepherdess or someone else from the peasant class—and there is sometimes a marked difference in their linguistic registers: his is more courtly and learned; hers is more demotic.[7] This linguistic disjunction is a characteristic of *De Clerico et Puella*, though with a subtle difference. Social class does not appear to a major issue here, though it is implicit, in a surprising form, in some parts of the argument.

---

7. On this question see the highly informed treatment of Zink (1972: 53-63).

Nothing is said of the cleric's social background. But the girl's does not appear to be menial: she mentions *my boure* as if she had her own chamber or bedroom, so the house in which she lives may be substantial; and the cleric refers to her by the respectful term *leuedy* both when he speaks about her and when he addresses her (1, 21, 32), though he also calls her by the familiar term *lemmon* (8, 16). If there is a social difference between them, there- fore, it would appear that the girl may be more well-to-do than the cleric. But there is also an intellectual difference which goes in the opposite direction: he is a university-trained cleric (*clerc in scole*, 29), like the *clericus* in the earlier play, and he has ready access to a linguistic register and a set of linguistic resources which are highly sophisticated, though the girl eventually adopts some of them herself. Like most pastourelles, this poem deals in power relations between the sexes. But this is not so much about social relations but about the power of language, and in particular about the power of the language of love poetry.

The cleric's opening speech is full of rhetorical devices—a paradox (1), two similes (2-3), personifications (3)—and is highly extravagant in feeling:

> 'My deþ y loue, my lyf ich hate, for a leuedy shene,
> heo is briht so daies liht, þat is on me wel sene;
> al y falewe so do þe lef in somer when hit is grene.
> 3ef mi þoht helpeþ me noht, to wham shal y me mene?
>
> Sorewe ant syke ant drery mod byndeþ me so faste
> þat y wene to walke wod 3ef hit me lengore laste;
> my serewe, my care, al wiþ a word he myhte awey caste.
> Whet helpeþ þe, my suete lemmon, my lyf þus forte gaste?'
> (Brook 1964: No. 24, 1-8).

He invites the girl to participate in fictions: he stereotypes himself as the suffering lover, and the girl as the beautiful and cruel mis- tress, who could, if she so wished, relieve his distress through her mercy and pity. He frames his appeal according to the conven- tional tropes of love poetry—tropes used earlier by the cleric Wilekin and the unnamed cleric of the interlude. Most important is the idea of 'dying for love': the speaker embraces his expected death because of a 'hate' for his existence: he is like a dying leaf; the lady will waste (*gaste*, 8) his life unless she relents. Subsidiary to this trope is that of the 'prisoner of love', the idea that the cleric's sad thoughts fetter him closely (*byndeþ me so faste*). Again this is a commonplace of this period or earlier: one poet complains 'icham in hire bandoun' (Brook 1964: No. 4, 8); another asks his lady to 'les me out of bonde' (Brook 1964: No. 5, 12); another is 'bounde' by his lady's beauty (Brook 1964: No. 25, 18). The author of *Blow, Northerne Wynd*, like this author, runs together the two tropes of 'dying for love' and the 'prisoner of love', interestingly describing the lover's mental state in terms of personifications in a contemporary social situation—they are like *knyhtes* in the lady's service, who persecute him—thus fictionalizing one of the more notorious actualities of bastard feudalism:[8]

> To Loue y putte pleyntes mo,
> hou Sykyng me haþ siwed so,
> ant eke Þoht me þrat to slo
> wiþ maistry, ȝef he myhte,
> ant Serewe sore in balful bende
> þat he wolde for þis hende
> me lede to my lyues ende
> vnlahfulliche in lyhte (Brook 1964: No. 14, 63-70).

And then the cleric uses the trope of 'love's madness' ('y wene to walke wod'), which is developed later in the poem by a reference to suffering for love in the woods ('vnder þe wode-gore', 31)—an ancient idea which achieved wide currency in the Middle Ages, mainly because of its appearance in the Tristan story, but which appeared early in the lyric tradition, as has been shown, and is used by Wilekin and travestied by the advisor in the passage from the *Ancrene Riwle*. And when the cleric speaks of the girl it is in the conventional terms of love poetry: she is *shene* and *briht* as is practically every object of a love poet's affection; and she is a potential 'healer' of the cleric's suffering (7). The cleric ends his opening stanza with a question which implies that if his *þoht* does not help him nothing else will—and his 'thought' largely consists of a deployment of the tropes of love poetry as a means of persuasion.

The girl's reply is not encouraging. It is not only a rejection of the cleric's offers of love, but a categorical refusal to engage in a dialogue on the cleric's 'poetic' terms:

8.   On this aspect of some of the MS Harley 2253 poems see Scattergood (1996b).

'Do wey, þou clerc, þou art a fol, wiþ þe bydde y noht chyde;
shalt þou neuer lyue þat day mi loue þat þou shalt byde.
ʒef þou in my boure art take, shame þe may bityde;
þe is bettere on fote gon þen wycked hors to ryde'
(Brook 1964: No. 24, 9-12).

She takes some of the cleric's poetic tropes, rejects their fictions, and redescribes them reductively in matter-of-fact, everyday terms: the extravagances of 'love's madness' become simply foolishness (*fol*), which she later insists is the correct (*riht*, 17) word; the 'dying for love' trope is reworded into the common asseveration 'you will never live to see the day...' And in her next line she reminds him of contemporary social realities, that to be caught in her *boure* would result in a public loss of honour and a resulting 'shame' for him. She closes the stanza with what looks like a cautionary proverb against dangerous aspiration,[9] but social realities are again implicit here because only the better-off members of medieval society rode horses. She appears, indirectly, to be suggesting to him that she is, in terms of social class, rather beyond him.

This is meant to be conclusive, since in medieval debate poems proverbs were often used to close off arguments. She does not succeed, however, because the cleric takes up her points and turns them round—she perhaps ought to have done as the advisor counselled the anchoresses and have not replied at all:

'Weylawei! Whi seist þou so? Þou rewe on me, þy man!
Þou art euer in my þoht in londe wher ich am.
ʒef y deʒe for þi loue, hit is þe mikel sham;
þou lete me lyue ant be þi luef ant þou my suete lemman'
(Brook 1964: No. 24, 13-16).

If he dies for her love, he says, returning to his main argument, the 'shame' will be hers, since, presumably, it will be known that she has been the cause of it, and therefore, he argues, she ought to 'rewe on me, þy man'. This means literally, 'have pity on me, your servant', and it appears to be a response to the girl's earlier use of a socially loaded proverb. But it also translates what may be a social reality into a poetic trope: the cleric tries to reconstruct the relationship in the fictional terms of contemporary love

9.   For the proverb see Whiting and Whiting (1968: F464)—though this is the only instance given.

poetry. The linguistic and poetic implications of the phrase
emerge if one looks at a passage from the *Way of Woman's Love,*
from the same manuscript, where the same terminology is used:

> Adoun y fel to hire anon
>   ant crie, 'Ledy, þyn ore!
> Ledy, ha mercy of þy mon!
>   Lef þou no fals lore!
>   ʒef þou dos, hit wol me reowe sore.
>   Loue drecceþ me þat y ne may lyue namore'
> (Brook 1964: No. 32, 16-21).

The collocation of the 'dying for love' trope and words like
Ledy, mon, reowe (and its semantically related words *ore* and *mercy*)
demonstrate the similarity with the phrase from *De Clerico et Puella,*
and 'Adoun y fel to hire' suggests the social convention which is
being alluded to—the beloved is seen as a feudal lady, the poet as
a dependent retainer or servant doing homage. It is highly likely
that, at this date, this was no more than a conventional poetic
fiction, and that the poet is inviting the girl to participate in it and
to accept the agenda suggested by the language of love poetry.
For the moment, however, she refuses, tries to get him to cease
(*blynne*) his arguments, and insists on social realities: if the cleric
is 'in my boure…take' her family will not desist from killing him,
though it is a sin, and so the 'dying for love' trope may become a
reality, 'þe deþe so þu maht wynne' (17-20). She sounds very
much like Rosalind in *As You Like It,* who responds to Orlando's
similar arguments about 'dying for love' with a definitive piece of
commonsense: 'Men have died from time to time and worms have
eaten them, but not for love' (IV.i.96-98). It looks, at this point, as
if the fictions of poetry have failed, destroyed by the matter-of-
factness of things as they are.

But the cleric persists, asks the girl to 'wend þi mod' (21), in
much the same terms as those used earlier by Wilekin and the
unnamed cleric of the interlude, recalls a happier time when they
'custe vs fyfty syþe' (23), and reminds her of a promise: 'feir
beheste makeþ mony mon al is serewes mythe' (24). The nuances
of this are interesting. It appears to be a version of a proverb, and
as such is a response to the girl's proverb at line 12: the cleric tries
to clinch an argument in a similar way. But the more usual version
of this saying is 'fayre byhestes maketh foles blithe' (see Whiting

and Whiting 1968: B215); the cleric appears to be accepting the girl's view of him as a *fol* (9, 17), and urging her to keep her promises so that he can be made *blype* (22) again. Whether it is the memory of the 50 kisses which changes the girl's mind, or the skilfully deployed implications of this proverb, is not made clear, but change her mind she does.[10] What is more, she begins to speak the cleric's language and accepts as true the tropes of poetry she had formerly rejected:

> 'Weylawey! Whi seist þou so? Mi serewe þou makest newe.
> Y louede a clerk al par amours, of loue he was ful trewe:
> he nes nout blyþe neuer a day bote he me sone seȝe;
> ich loucdc him bctere þen my lyf, whet bote is hit to leȝe?'
> (Brook 1964: No. 24, 25-28).

The first half of the opening line erases the differences between them: it replicates verbatim his question at line 13. And her use of the word *serewe* in the second half of the line picks up his use of it and its related adjective earlier (in lines 5, 7, 21, 22, 24). She joins the cleric and herself together in a sorrow which is the result of a lack of love. And in the next line she begins to use the language of love on her own initiative: *par amours*, in its French form, is a notable and significant phrase outside the mundane register of everyday which she has so far used. She also begins to use the language and ideas of love poetry. She esteems the cleric because he is *trewe*, a quality everywhere praised in a lover, and accepts his argument that he is only happy when he sees her and that her absence causes unhappiness. This is a common idea in love poetry of this period, and forms the basis of the refrain to the *Way of Woman's Love*:

> Euer ant oo for my leof icham in grete þohte;
> y þenche on hire þat y ne seo nout ofte.
> (Brook 1964: No. 31, 7-8, etc.).

Most importantly, she takes to herself the 'dying for love' trope which she had ridiculed earlier when the cleric had used it: she loves him 'betere þen my lyf'.

10. It is not clear from the wording of the poem whether the girl's previous encounter with a 'clerk' and the exchange of 50 kisses was with the man with whom she is speaking or with some other 'clerk'. Perhaps sentimentally, I incline to the view that she is remembering a previous encounter with the same man. My students usually think otherwise.

At this point the cleric has virtually succeeded in persuading the girl to accept his love. His last speech simply consolidates a position already won: as already shown, he elaborates a little on the idea of 'love's madness' by locating his suffering in the woods; and he repeats his plea that the girl should have *rewe* on him (31-32). But he does add one thing, the idea of 'love's wounds' (30), which appears elsewhere, most memorably in *When þe Nyhtegale Singes*:

> ...loue is to myn herte gon wiþ one spere so kene,
> nyht ant day my blod hit drynkes; myn herte deþ me tene
> (Brook 1964: No. 25, 3-4).

At this point the cleric does at last respond to the girl's requests that he should 'Be stille' and 'blynne' (17) when he says 'nou may y no more' (32). In an academic debate this would be tantamount to an admission of defeat: to be unable to respond to an argument was to concede victory to one's opponent. But since the girl has begun to speak the language of love poetry and has admitted that she has told lies (28) he is confident of her compliance. She responds to his final speech by saying that he will never, because of his love for her, suffer 'woundes...grylle' (34): that is to say that she accepts the role of 'healer' that the fictions of love poetry invest her with, and that she will at last have *rewe* on the cleric. Her last lines, which are also the last lines of the poem, represent another significant *volte face*:

> 'fader, moder, ant al my kun ne shal me holde so stille
> Þat y nam þyn ant þou art myn, to don al þi wille'
> (Brook 1964: No. 24, 35-36).

This reverses the girl's position at lines 17-20, and represents a determination to defy the social realities, in relation to which she had earlier advised caution. She is willing to resist the claims of her family and commit herself to the cleric, as he has committed himself to her—the possessive adjectives (*þyn*, *myn*) signal the proposed reciprocity. She wishes to close out the world of familial obligation and social duty, and accepts as real the tropes and fictions of love poetry, persuaded by the cleric's words.

This is a poem about the power and effectiveness of love poetry and the language of love poetry. Unlike Wilekin in the fabliau and the unnamed *clericus* in the interlude, this cleric succeeds in seducing the girl by the power of words alone. And several features of the poem draw attention to this dimension of its meaning. The most important is the fact that the poet has erased the narrative elements from his pastourelle, leaving only the dialogue: the poem is all about speech, and consists of nothing but speeches. What is more, attention is frequently drawn (see lines 4, 7, 9, 13, 25, 33) to the action of speaking in the poem, and to its importance: *a word* (7) can make all the difference between happiness and sadness for the cleric, and as the girl reflects on the course of the discussion she pays a compliment to the cleric's skill in speech: 'Þou semest wel to ben a clerc, for þou spekest so stille' (33). Quite what *stille* means here is debatable: it could mean 'continually' and refer to his persistence; but more probably it means 'softly'. It has been suggested that the reading should be *scille*, meaning 'eloquently', thus avoiding a rhyme on the same word, but this is unlikely since the manuscript form is more likely to have been *shille*—OE *sc*- is usually spelt *sh*- in this manuscript.[11] But whatever its meaning the line appears to offer a compliment, and it brings this poem into line with other texts which favour clerics as lovers. Andreas Capellanus had argued that since God, through his grace, had conferred a special dignity and nobility on clerics it was inappropriate for them to love:

> Ab omnibus igitur clericus amoris actibus alienus exsistat, et omnis corporalis immunditia eum relinquat, alias enim sua speciali et a Deo sibi nobilitate largita merito privatus exsistat.

> [So the cleric must detach himself as a foreigner from all the processes of love; all bodily uncleanness should go out of him, for otherwise he would be deservedly be deprived of his special nobility conferred on him by God.] (Walsh 1982: 210-11)

However, a whole series of poems written in France, some in Latin some in French, deriving from the mid-twelfth-century *Concile de Remiremont*, debated the issue of who makes the better lover, a knight or a cleric—and the conclusions favour clerics. Clerics are generally preferred for their goodness, their gentleness, their trustworthiness and loyalty. One speaker in the earliest of these

---

11. See Brook (1961: 85) for a defence of the manuscript reading. For an argument for *scille* on the grounds of sense see Dickins and Wilson (1951: 230).

poems, Elizabeth de Faucogney, also mentions their prowess in writing love poetry:

> Clericorum probitas, et eorum bonitas,
> Semper querit studium ad amoris gaudium,
> Sed eorum gaudia tota ridet patria.
> Laudant nos in omnibus rithmis atquae versibus.
> Tales, jussu Veneris, diligo pre ceteris,
> Dulcis amicicia, clericis est et gloria (Oulmont 1911: 137-42).

> [The honesty of clerics and their goodness always prompt in them a study of the joy of love; the whole country rejoices in their pleasures. They praise us in all sorts of rhyme and in all sorts of verse. By the order of Venus, I love such men before others. In relation to clerics there is sweet love and glory.][12]

The clerical wooer of the English lyric, with his skill and proficiency in the language of love poetry, takes his place in this celebrated tradition.

IV

In the late 1380s or the 1390s the question of the effectiveness of the language of love poetry in relation to seduction was treated humorously though with some thought by Chaucer in the *Miller's Tale*: Nicholas, who is described as a *poure scoler* of Oxford, and as a *clerk* (I3190, 3199), and Absolon, a *parish clerk* (I3312), both attempt to seduce Alison, a carpenter's wife, by using, among other persuasions, the language of love poetry. The tale is richly intertextual: it has a recognizable fabliau plot; but it alludes to and parodies the *Knight's Tale*; and it invokes the biblical narratives of Noah's Flood and the Annunciation, and those versions of these stories as they were mediated through the mystery plays. In a justly celebrated essay, E. Talbot Donaldson argued that there were also traces of earlier texts from the English literary tradition which Chaucer called up, particularly in relation to Alison, Absolon and Nicholas:

12. Oulmont (1911), gives the whole sequence of poems. The translation of the passage from *Le Concile de Remiremont* is mine.

> One of the devices he used most skilfully was that of sprinkling
> these characterizations and conversations with cliches borrowed
> from the vernacular versions of the code of courtly love—phrases
> of the sort we are accustomed to meet, on the one hand, in Middle
> English minstrel romances and, on the other, in secular lyrics such
> as those preserved on Harley MS 2253…In their conversation with
> Alison the two clerks talk like a couple of Harley lyricists (1970: 16-
> 17, 25).

He does, briefly, ponder the relationship between Chaucer's tale
and the *De Clerico et Puella* lyric—he stresses the maiden's initial
repulsion of the clerk and compares Alison's initial resistance to
Nicholas (3285-87) and her warning of the possible consequences
in relation to her family (3294-97); and he draws attention to the
importance of windows in both the lyric and the tale. But he is
dubious about the possibility that Chaucer knew the poem: 'In
view of the adverse conditions for the preservation of secular
lyrics, to associate Chaucer with a few survivals seems too large an
economy' (Donaldson 1970: 25 n. 4).

Such caution is proper, no doubt, though it does not seem to
me impossible that Chaucer could have known any or all of the
earlier texts addressed in relation to this issue. Whether he knew
these texts or not, however, he was clearly aware of the issue itself,
of the relationship between the language of love poetry and
seduction. Nicholas's wooing of Alison is set in the following
unmistakably allusive and parodic terms:

> Now, sir, and eft sire so bifel the cas
> That on a day this hende Nicholas
> Fil with this yonge wyf to rage and pleye,
> Whil that hir housbonde was at Oseneye,
> As clerkes ben ful subtile and ful queynte;
> And prively he caughte hire by the queynte,
> And seyde, 'Ywis, but if ich have my wille
> For deerne love of thee, lemman, I spille.'
> And heeld hire harde by the haunchebones,
> And seyde, 'Lemman, love me al atones,
> Or I wol dyen, also God me save!' (I.3271-81).

Here the adjectives *hende* and *deerne* unmistakably suggest that
Chaucer was aware of the earlier traditions of love poetry (see
Donaldson 1970: 17-20) which, incidentally, often used extensive
decorative alliteration—and line I.3279, a perfect alliterative line

on *h-*, appears to be a recognition of this. Nicholas also calls
Alison *lemman* and says that he wants his *wille* with her—both
words common in the earlier tradition—and he uses the familiar
'dying for love' trope to help to make his case. Here, in a manner
which would have confirmed all the worst fears of Beatrice Russo's
aunt, the words are accompanied by actions: in fact, Nicholas
touches Alison with his hands marginally earlier than he attempts
to persuade her with his words. Nevertheless, it seems that the
words have some effect. After Alison has repelled him and refused
his advances we are told that he begged her *mercy*, and 'spak so
faire and profred him so faste' that she at last granted him her
love (I.3288-90). Here words help somewhat, it seems. The language of love poetry has some power to persuade, though the per-
suasiveness is in part enhanced by action.

But this is not the case in relation to Absolon. His preferred
approach is by way of the serenade:

> ...[he] dressed hym up by a shot-wyndowe
> That was upon the carpenteres wal.
> He syngeth in his voys gentil and smal,
> 'Now, deere lady, if thy wille be,
> I praye yow that ye wole rewe on me',
> Full wel acordaunt to his gyternynge (I.3357-63).

He addresses Alison as *lady*, and asks her to have *rewe* on him in
the familiar language of love poetry. But the approach fails, partly
because Alison is in bed with her husband, who also hears the serenade, and partly, no doubt, because she already has an arrangement, which evidently she intends to keep, with Nicholas. Absolon
uses other kinds of approach also—including wooing Alison
through intermediaries (I.3375), sending her presents of 'pyment,
meeth, and spiced ale' and wafers, and offering her money
(I.3378-80). This causes the Miller to reflect on a triad of ways in
which people can be won—wealth, force or *gentillesse*. But none of
these strategies is successful. So Absolon tries the power of language once more:

> He rometh to the carpenteres hous,
> And stille he stant under the shot-wyndowe—
> Unto his brest it raughte, it was so lowe—
> And softe he cougheth with a semy soun:
> 'What do ye, hony-comb, sweete Alisoun,

My faire bryd, my sweete cynamone?
Awaketh, lemman myn, and speketh to me!
Wel litel thynken ye upon my wo,
That for youre love I swete ther I go...' (I.3694-702).

The basis of this appeal is the 'suffering for love' trope. But the striking intertextual feature of this serenade is its dependence on the language of the Song of Songs—without of course its allegorical dimension (see Kaske 1962). Whether Chaucer knew the passage on the custody of the senses from the *Ancrene Riwle*, in which material from the native tradition of love poetry and material from the Song of Songs are adduced, is not certain. But a lot of copies of the rule were extant and it was still being copied in the fourteenth century, so it is entirely possible.[13] If he did know the passage it would not be the first or only time that Chaucer had used a text as a source while at the same time subverting its intention. But this kind of amorous language also fails for Absolon, and Alison initially does as the anchoresses' advisor had suggested, and keeps her window closed and dismisses him: ' "Go fro the wyndow, Jakke fool", she sayde' (I.3708). She eventually opens the window for him to kiss her, but only so that he can be humiliated. It is usually held that the sort of text which lies behind this part of the tale is 'the song of the night-visit', and this, at one level, is probably true (see Baskervill 1921). But because Chaucer is obviously interested here in the question of the effectiveness of the langauge of love poetry, especially when it is used by a cleric, it may be that he was also conscious, at an intertextual level, of earlier treatments of the subject in a rule for anchoresses, a fabliau, a play or a lyric.

When one sets the *De Clerico et Puella* lyric in this context, which in my view is its proper context, its individuality and special qualities emerge. Clerics who employ the language of love poetry as a means to winning love are commonly, in the English tradition, regarded satirically, and the language, for whatever reason, does not work. A strain of anti-clericalism, perhaps of anti-intellectualism, which presents itself as robust good sense, sees to it that the

---

13. For a brief survey of the manuscripts of the *Ancrene Riwle* and their dates see Salu (1955: xxiii xxvi). See also the succinct but informative comments of Shepherd (1959: ix-xiv). For a more lengthy recent treatment see Wada (1994: xlvi-lxiv).

refinements of courtliness, if uttered by clerics or intellectuals, are treated with scepticism, sometimes with derision. The clerical wooer is almost always material for comedy, especially if he uses the conventional language of love poetry. But the cleric in this lyric from Harley MS 2253 is not of this kind: he is a successful wooer who uses, glories in, and persuades the girl to participate in the fictional linguistic world of love poetry. She is persuaded to set aside a social reality which she articulates precisely, because she agrees to give credence to the literary tropes of 'dying for love', 'suffering for love', 'love's wounds' and the like. For a rare moment the English tradition takes seriously a learned clerical wooer whose command of the persuasive tropes of love poetry is compelling.

WORKS CITED

Baskervill, C.R.
    1921   'English Songs of the Night Visit', *PMLA* 36: 565-614.
Bennett, J.A.W., and E.V. Smithers (eds.)
    1968   *Early Middle English Verse and Prose* (Oxford: Clarendon Press, 2nd edn).
Benson, L.D. (ed.)
    1987   *The Riverside Chaucer* (Boston: Houghton Mifflin).
Brewer, D.
    1983   *English Gothic Literature* (London: Macmillan).
Brook, G.L. (ed.)
    1964   *The Harley Lyrics: The Middle English Lyrics of MS. Harley 2253* (Manchester: Manchester University Press, 3rd edn).
Brown, C. (ed.)
    1962   *English Lyrics of the XIIIth Century* (Oxford: Clarendon Press).
Dickins, B., and R.M. Wilson (eds.)
    1951   *Early Middle English Texts* (London: Bowes & Bowes).
Dobson, E.J. (ed.)
    1972   *The English Text of the Ancrene Riwle, edited from BM Cotton MS. Cleopatra C.iv* (EETS, 267; London: Oxford University Press).
Donaldson, E.T.
    1970   *Speaking of Chaucer* (London: Athlone Press).
Hines, J.
    1993   *The Fabliau in English* (London: Longman).
Kaske, R.E.
    1962   'The *Canticum Canticorum* in the *Miller's Tale*', *Studies in Philology* 59: 479-500.

Ker, N.R. (introd.)
1965   *Facsimile of British Museum MS. Harley 2253* (EETS, 255; London: Oxford University Press).

Morton, J. (ed.)
1853   *The Ancren Riwle* (Camden Society, 57; London).

Neruda, P.
1975   *Twenty Love Poems and a Song of Despair*, translated by W.S. Merwin (London: Cape).

Oulmont, C. (ed.)
1911   *Les Debats du Clerc et du Chevalier dans la Litterature Poetique du Moyen Age* (Paris: Champion).

Salu, M. (trans.)
1955   *The Ancrene Riwle* (London: Burns & Oates).

Sandison, H.
1913   *The 'Chanson d'Aventure' in Middle English* (Bryn Mawr College Monographs, 12; Pennsylvania: Bryn Mawr).

Scattergood, J.
1996a   'Courtliness in some Fourteenth-Century English Pastourelles', in J. Scattergood, *Reading the Past: Essays on Medieval and Renaissance Literature* (Dublin: Four Courts Press): 61-80.
1996b   '*The Old Man's Prayer* and Bastard Feudalism', in S. Horlacher and M. Islinger (eds.), *Expedition nach der Wahrheit: Poems, Essays, and Papers in Honour of Theo Stemmler* (Heidelberg: Winter): 119-30.

Shepherd, G. (ed.)
1959   *Ancrene Wisse: Parts Six and Seven* (London: Nelson).

Stemmler, T.
1991   'Miscellany or Anthology? The Structure of Medieval Manuscripts: MS Harley 2253, for Example', *Zeitschrift für Anglistik und Amerikanistik* 39: 321-27.

Tschann, J., and M.B. Parkes (introds.)
1996   *Facsimile of Oxford, Bodleian Library, MS Digby 86* (EETS SS, 16; Oxford: Oxford University Press).

Wada, Y. (ed.)
1994   '*Temptations' from Ancrene Wisse* (Osaka: Kansai University Institute of Oriental and Occidental Studies).

Walsh, P.G. (trans.)
1982   *Andreas Capellanus on Love* (London: Duckworth).

Whiting, B.J., and H.W. Whiting
1968   *Proverbs, Sentences and Proverbial Phrases from English Writings Mainly Before 1500* (Cambridge, MA: Belknap Press).

Wilson, R.M.
1970   *The Lost Literature of Medieval* England (London: Methuen, 2nd edn).

Zink, M.
1972   *La Pastourelle: Poesie et Folklore au Moyen Age* (Paris: Bordas).

Caxton's Copy-fitting Devices in the *Morte Darthur* (1485): An Overview*

Toshiyuki Takamiya

Caxton's *Morte Darthur* of 1485, though not textually identical in the two extant copies, had been the unique authority of Sir Thomas Malory's romance of King Arthur until the Winchester manuscript was rediscovered by Walter Oakeshott in 1934.[1] It was neither Malory's original nor the text that Caxton printed from; if it had been used as Caxton's setting copy, it would have carried cast-off marks for compositors. Until 1947, when Eugène Vinaver issued his critical edition using the Winchester manuscript as copy text (revised as Vinaver 1990), philological analyses of the *Morte* had been based on Caxton's text alone. Examples are the traditional survey by Helmut Wienke (Wienke 1930) and the studies by Charles Sears Baldwin (Baldwin 1894) and Arie Dekker (Dekker

*   This is a revised version of a paper I read at the Second International Conference on Middle English at the University of Helsinki in May–June 1997. I am very grateful to the organizers for inviting me, to the distinguished audience for valuable comments, and to Professor Valerie Wilkinson for improving my English.
  1.   Of the two extant copies, the uniquely perfect one in the Pierpont Morgan Library, New York, is available in facsimile in Needham (1976). The other copy, slightly imperfect and with reset pages, is in the John Rylands University Library, Manchester (*STC* 801). For the Winchester manuscript in facsimile see Ker (1976). As early as 1839 or 1840 W.T. Alchin described it in his manuscript catalogue of the Fellows' Library of Winchester College, p. 446 as 'The History of Prince Arthur. Imperfect'; see Ker (1976: xx-xxi). Oakeshott made a first report of his 'rediscovery' in *The Times*, 26 June 1934, p. 17 and published a detailed account in Oakeshott (1963).

1932), both of whom argued that Malory's language was representative of late fifteenth-century English.

The publication of Vinaver's text immediately drew much scholarly attention to textual discrepancies between the now two extant versions of the *Morte*, particularly Winchester's Tale 2 and Caxton's Book 5, the 'Roman War' episode. Jan Šimko (Šimko 1957), for example, maintained that whereas Malory had used the Alliterative *Morte Arthure* with some freedom, Caxton had revised by regularizing Malory's language. Sally Shaw (Shaw 1963), examined Caxton's editorial procedures of the *Morte*, especially Book 5, suggesting that Malory's very individual style in the Winchester manuscript is flattened in Caxton's more grammatical version. Fumio Kuriyagawa also dealt with the problem (Kuriyagawa 1958), followed by other Japanese Malorians, such as Shunichi Noguchi, Tomomi Kato, Yuji Nakao and Kunio Nakashima, all of whom contributed philological studies of Malory's two versions (Noguchi 1977, 1984, 1995; Kato 1993; Nakao 1987, 1993; Nakashima 1981). In 1968 Arthur O. Sandved presented a mass of data to suggest that Caxton is more likely to have preserved the language which he found in his exemplar (Sandved 1968).

The fact that the two witnesses to the *Morte* have come down to us in different media, that is, a manuscript and a roughly contemporary printed book, provides a unique case in Middle English literature. The existence of a manuscript and a printed copy of one and the same work makes detailed textual and philological comparison possible so as to reconstruct more accurately what Malory originally wrote. It was not until 1975, however, when the Winchester manuscript was permanently transferred to the British Library as Additional MS 59678, that anyone working with Malory's text and language paid serious attention to the physical appearance or layout of the printed page.

At that time Lotte Hellinga made a remarkable discovery when she identified a few letters used by Caxton offset in mirrored type and smudges of printing ink on the Winchester manuscript.[2] The evidence indicates that it was at Caxton's printing shop, where it was probably used by Caxton or his editors ancillary to a setting copy, which must now be lost. It also suggests that the relationship

---

2.   Originally published in Hellinga and Kelliher (1977). Their revised texts were published separately as Hellinga (1986) and Kelliher (1986).

between the two versions is not so far apart as Vinaver claimed. By
good fortune her discovery coincided with the publication of
these two versions in facsimile, thus providing Malory students
with a do-it-youself kit for textual collations.

Hellinga's acute eye in bibliographical observation enabled her
to detect not only the above-mentioned evidence but also printing
anomalies in the layout of some of Caxton's pages. Each printed
page of the *Morte*, which is a folio in eights, normally comprises 38
lines of prose text in a single column, but there are some pages
which end with blank lines and other pages that want more than a
line of text. Perhaps she was the first to observe that various kinds
of copy-fitting devices were incorporated, particularly at most
page ends (Hellinga 1980; 1982, especially 89-94).

One of the most arresting examples that I have detected occurs
in the last three lines of page T3r of Caxton's *Morte*:

> <Caxton's sig. T3r> [paraph mark] Thenne felte he many handes
> aboute hym whiche tooke hym | vp / and bare hym oute of the
> chamber dore / withoute ony almendynge of his swoune / and
> lefte hym there semyng dede to <T3v> *of the chamber dore and lefte*
> *hym there semynge dede to* al pe|ple / Soo vpon the morowe… [italics
> mine]

The countervailing part in the Winchester manuscript, f.401v,
lines 23-25 reads:

> //Than felte he many hondys whych toke hym vp | and bare hym
> oute of the chambir doore and leffte hym þer | semynge dede to all
> people So vppon the morow…[3]

This episode in Caxton's Book 17, Chapter 15 deals with Sir
Launcelot in 'The Tale of Sank Greal'. As soon as he entered the
room in which the Holy Grail was placed, Sir Launcelot felt as if
he were struck by fire, and swooned. The passage cited from page
T3r then follows: 'Thenne felte he many handes aboute hym…',
and so on. Page T3v begins with the italicized sentence above,
which does not correspond exactly with that at the end of page
T3r, but does correspond with that in the Winchester manuscript,
f.401v.

---

3.   This section is reprinted, with some modifications, from Takamiya
(1993).

The reading on page T3r contains two phrases—'aboute hym' and 'withoute ony amendynge of his swoune'—neither of which is found in the manuscript.

It may be possible to reconstruct the decision process of the compositor, though we need not presume that T3r and T3v were set by the same person. When approaching the setting copy for 'of the chambir dore' on T3v, the compositor obviously followed the mark for casting-off in the margin of the setting copy. But why did he find it necessary to complete T3r with 'semynge dede to'? It may be that a cast-off mark in the margin of the setting copy suggested this. Was there then a mark, such as two strokes drawn immediately before 'Than felte he', which suggested to him that this was the spot where a new paragraph should begin? If so, he inserted the paraph mark only to confront another difficulty: he found he needed three lines of text to fill the full page of T3r, although there were only two lines in the setting copy. Whether he actually asked Caxton for advice at this stage we do not know, but at any rate he had to invent the two phrases mentioned above, which he inserted in appropriate places on the page so as to make it look like a page filled to normal length, 'a "seamless" transition to the following page' (Hellinga 1982: 94). This copy-fitting device gives us some insight into the editorial methods and the freedom of the compositor which evidently prevailed in Caxton's printshop.

The expression 'withoute ony amendynge of his swoune' is not found anywhere in the Winchester manuscript. Eugène Vinaver suggested that '[Caxton's] reading may well be authentic, though it is not confirmed by [a French source]' (Vinaver 1990: 1579), but the argument I have just presented suggests the contrary. In addition, my argument has some linguistic support. The gerund *amendynge* is not used anywhere else in the Winchester manuscript but it appears in Caxton's own prose edited by Norman Blake (Blake 1973).[4] Caxton has *amende* as many as 16 times and *amende-mente* and *amendyng* once each, so there may be some grounds to suppose that the phrase was inserted by Caxton himself or a compositor who knew what his employer favoured. According to Hellinga (1980: 96-97), this kind of minor textual change was

4.   For concordances of Malory and Caxton see Kato (1974) and Mizobata (1990).

possibly made at the compositor's discretion.

The printing mistake discussed above occurred simply because the compositor of page T3r assumed that the cast-off mark in the margin of the setting copy indicated the last line of the page, while the compositor of page T3v took it to indicate the first line of a new page.

We are now able to reconstruct just a small portion of the setting copy through the above mentioned process as follows (× represents the cast-off mark):

> //Than felte he many handys whych toke hym up and bare hym ×
> oute of the chambir doore / and leffte hym there semynge dede to
> all people / So vppon the morow...

Caxton's division of the *Morte* into 21 books and 506 chapters in total and his introduction of chapter headings served as the major contribution he made to the text of the *Morte*, and it was for the benefit not only of the reader but also of his compositors (see Takamiya 1996, especially 68-69). Indeed the latter were able to make use of these divisions as a most helpful copy-fitting device by adjusting white space between the lines. This was particularly effective if they fell towards the page break.

Nevertheless, there remain some intriguing chapter divisions which Caxton's compositors found really troublesome in their attempts to set pages properly, with too many lines of the text in hand. Let us take page d1r (see Fig. 1), for example. Here the chapter heading of Book 2, Chapter 7, part of the Balin story, is so squeezed that the compositor had to set *Ca* rather than the full form *Capitulum* and, furthermore, shorten the text drastically and omit the normal white space. For the last line of Chapter 6 Caxton's text reads *that we do ⁊ we wil helpe eche other as bretheren ouʒt to do*, while Winchester has *that ye so do; and I woll ryde with you and put my body in adventure with you, as a brothir ouʒt to do* (f.26).

The constant use of the ampersand rather than the full form *and*, particularly round the chapter division, is also due to the compositors' struggle in copy fitting. But lines 36-38 of d1r suggest, on the contrary, that at the very end of the page the compositor, realizing the need to amplify the exemplar, had to add *the* to *whiche*, and use a slash, a paraph mark, *and* in full form, as well as the longer form *whanne* (rather than *whan*).

Figure 1: Caxton's *Morte Darthur*, sig. d1r (reproduced by kind permission of the Pierpont Morgan Library)

lytel wende to haue met with yow at this sodayne auenture / I
am ryght glad of your delyueraunce and of youre doloous
pryonement / for a man told me in the castel of four stones that
ye were delyuerd / & that man had sene you in the court of kynge Arthur / & therfor I cam hyder in to this countrey / for here I supposed to fynd you / anon the knyght Balyn told his bro-
der of his aduenture of the swerd & of the deth of the lady of
the lake / & how kyng arthur was displeasyd with hym wherfor he sente this knyght after me that lyeth here ded / & the wyfe
of this damoysel greueth me sore / so doth it me said Balan / but
ye must take the aduenture that god wil ordeyne yow / Truly said Balyn I am ryght heuy that my lord Arthur is displeasyd with me / for he is the moost worshipful knyght that
regneth now on erthe / & his loue wil I gete or els I wil put
my lyf in auenture / for the kyng Ryons lyeth at a syege atte
castel Tarabil & thyder wil we drawe in all hast to preue our
worship & prowesse vpon hym / I wil wel said Balan that we
do & we wil helpe eche other as brethern ought to do / Ca viij
Now go we hens said Balyn & wel be we met / the mene whyle as they talked ther cam a dwarf from the cy-
te of camelot on horsbak as moche as he myght & foud
the dede bodyes / wherfor he made grete dole & pulled out his here for sorou & saide which of you knyghtes haue done this dede /
wherby askest thou it said Balan / for I wold wete it said the
dwarfe / it was I said Balyn that slewe this knyght in my de-
fendaut for hyder he cam to chace me & other I must slee hym
or he me / & this damoysel slewe her self for his loue which re-
penteth me / & for her sake I shal owe al wymmen the better loue / Allas said the dwarf thow hast done grete dommage vnto
thy self / for this knyght that is here ded was one of the most
valyauntest men that lyued / and trust wel Balyn the kynne of
this knyght wille chace yow thorowe the world tyl they haue
slayne yow / As for that sayd Balyn I fere not gretely / but
I am ryght heuy that I haue displeasyd my lord kyng arthur for the deth of this knyght / Soo as they talked to gy-
dre there came a kynge of Cornewaille rydynge / the whiche
hyght kynge Mark / And whanne he sawe these two bodies ded and vnderstood hou they were ded by the ij knyghtes

d j

The discoveries, including the above mentioned, that I made (1993–94) have led me to take a fresh look at Caxton's whole text from copy-fitting points of view, by conducting a collaborative and systematic survey at Keio University. I encouraged our graduate students, about ten in number, to select one copy-fitting phenomenon each .[5] Since Caxton's setting copy for the *Morte* is not extant, there has been no other way than using the Winchester manuscript for textual comparison, but with extreme caution.

Our investigation is still under way, but we would already maintain that Caxton's compositors, apparently facing inconsistently scattered cast-off marks in the margin of their setting copy of the *Morte*, had to devise several copy-fitting means such as white space at chapter divisions (see sig. m1r, for example: Fig. 2), parallelisms, titles such as *sir* and *king*, pleonastic *it*, paraph marks (see sig. q3v for an example of the use of as many as ten paraph marks: Fig. 3), *then* and *and* in the beginning of sentences, superscript *n* or *m*, final *e*, and final *d* with a flourish. The omission, addition or manipulation of these all helped to make a 'seamless' transition to the following page.

I would argue, therefore, that some if not all occurrences of multiple negation in Caxton's *Morte* should also be regarded as part of his copy-fitting technique. This theory is in opposition to Ms Ingrid Tieken-Boon van Ostade's rather controversial hypothesis that the relationship between the Winchester manuscript and Caxton's edition is a linear rather than collateral one (1995: 87-97).[6] Her data on Malory's multiple negation, the fruit of long-term research, presents 285 identical cases of multiple negation between the two versions and about one hundred different instances. In Chapter 7 of her book, entitled 'Editor/Copyist and Compositors' she suggests the possibility that Robert Copland was a house editor of Caxton's print shop and that he may have been responsible for the change in multiple negation.

5.   So far the following reports have been printed privately: Nagai 1995; Kato 1995; Kurihara 1995; Kato 1996; Isaka and Shiratori 1996; Nishida and Kashiwabara 1996; Ito and Okada 1997; Takagi 1997; Takahashi 1997; Miyamaru 1997; Kato 1998; Asai 1998; Kobori 1998; Tokunaga 1998; and Mihara 1998.

6.   See Field (1997).

Figure 2: Caxton's *Morte Darthur*, sig. m1r (reproduced by kind permission of the Pierpont Morgan Library)

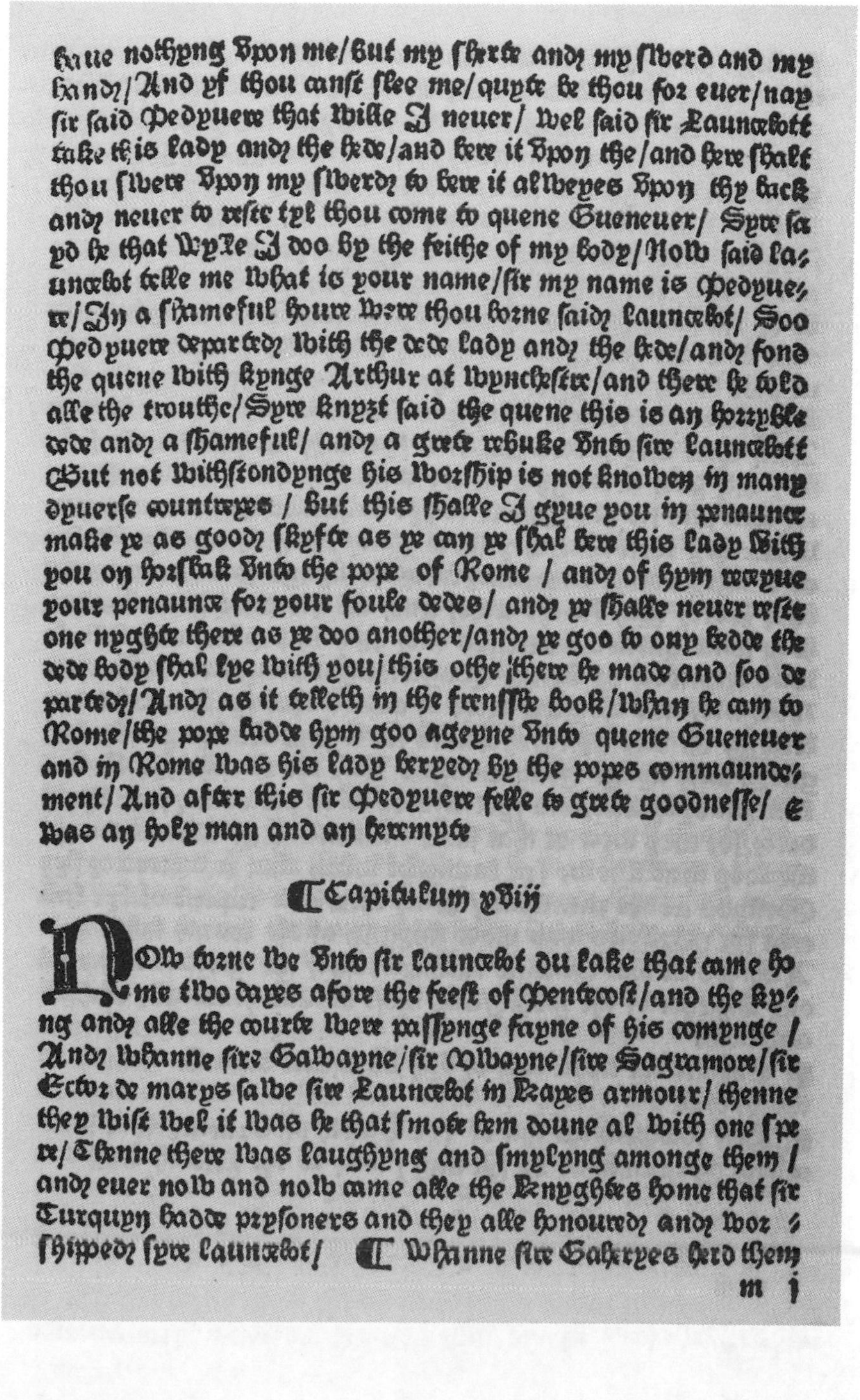

haue nothyng vpon me/but my sherte and my swerd and my
hand/And yf thou canst slee me/quyte be thou for euer/nay
sir said Pedyuer that wille I neuer/ wel said sir Launcelott
take this lady and the hede/and bere it vpon the/and here shalt
thou swere vpon my swerd to bere it allweyes vpon thy back
and neuer to reste tyl thou come to quene Gueneuer/ Syr sa
yd he that wyll I doo by the feithe of my body/Now said La
uncelot telle me what is your name/sir my name is Pedyue
r/In a shameful houre were thou borne said launcelot/ Soo
Pedyuer departed/ with the dede lady and the hede/and fond
the quene with kynge Arthur at wynchestre/and there he told
alle the trouthe/Syr knyzt said the quene this is an horryble
dede and a shameful/ and a grete whuske vnto sir launcelott
But not withstondynge his worship is not knowen in many
dyuerse countrees / but this shalle I gyue you in penaunce
make ye as good shyfte as ye can ye shal bere this lady with
you on horsback vnto the pope of Rome / and of hym werue
your penaunce for your foule dedes/ and ye shalle neuer reste
one nyghte there as ye do another/and ye goo to ony bedde the
dede body shal lye with you/this othe there he made and soo de
parted/And as it telleth in the frensshe book/whan he cam to
Rome/the pope badde hym goo ageyne vnto quene Gueneuer
and in Rome was his lady beryed/ by the popes commaunde
ment/And after this sir Pedyuer felle to grete goodnesse/ &
was an holy man and an hermyte

¶ Capitulum xviij

Now torne we vnto sir launcelot du lake that came ho
me two dayes afore the feest of Pentecost/and the ky
ng and alle the courte were passynge fayne of his compnge /
And whanne sire Gawayne/sir Owayne/sire Sagramore/sir
Ector de marys sawe sir Launcelot in Kayes armour/thenne
they wist wel it was he that smote hem doune al with one spe
re/ Thenne there was laughyng and smylyng amonge them /
and euer now and now came alle the knyghtes home that sir
Turquyn hadde prysoners and they alle honoured and wor
shipped syre launcelot/ ¶ Whanne sire Gaheryes herd them

Figure 3: Caxton's *Morte Darthur*, sig. q3v (reproduced by kind permission of the Pierpont Morgan Library)

regard vnto her / Also she sente hym a lytel brachet that was
passynge fayr / But whan the kynges doughter vnderstood
that syre Trystram wold not loue her / as the book sayth / she
dyed for sorou / And thenne the same squyer that broughte
the letter and the brachet came ageyne vnto syr Trystram / as
after ye shalle here in the tale Soo this yonge
syre Trystram rode vnto his eme kynge Marke of Cornewa-
yle / And whanne he came there / he herd say that ther wold
no knyghte fyghte with syre Marhaus / Thenne gat sir Trystram vnto his eme and sayd / Syre yf ye wylle gyue me thordre of knyghthode / I wille do bataille with syr Marhaus /
What are ye said the kynge and from whens be ye comen / Sir
said Trystram I come fro kynge Melyodas that wedded your syster and a gentylman were ye wel I am

Kynge Marke beheld sir Trystram and sawe that he was
but a yonge man of age / But he was passyngly wel maade
and bygge / Faire syre said the kynge what is youre name
and where were ye borne / Syre sayd he ageyne / my name is
Trystram / and in the countrey of Lyones was I borne /
Ye saye wel said the kynge / and yf ye wille do this batapll
I shalle make yow knyghte / Therfore I come to you sayd
syre Trystram and for none other cause

But thenne kynge Marke made hym knyghte / And there
with al anone as he had made hym knyght he sente a messa-
ger vnto syre Marhaus with letters that said / that he hadde
fonde a yonge knyghte redy for to take the bataile to the vtter
mest / hit may wel be said syre Marhaus / But telle kynge
Marke I wille not fyghte with no knyghte but he be of blo-
ood royal / that is to saye outher kynges sone outher quenes.
sone borne of a prynce or pryncesse /

Whanne kynge Marke vnderstood that / he sente for syre
Trystram de Lyones and tolde hym what was the answer of
syr Marhaus / Thenne sayd syre Trystram sythen that he se
yth soo / lete hym wete that I am comen of fader syde and mo
der syde of as noble blood as he is / For syre now shalle ye
knowe that I am kynge Melyodas sone borne of youre own
syster dame Elyzabeth that dyed in the forest in the byrthe of
me / O Ihesu said kynge Mark ye are welcome faire neuewe

I would maintain, however, that most of the textual changes, particularly minor ones, in Caxton's *Morte*, were probably made at the compositors' discretion as copy-fitting devices. By way of illustration, let us examine Caxton's page Z7r, which is the beginning part of Book XIX, Chapter 7, dealing with Launcelot and Guinevere. The following tables show the Caxton page and the corresponding text from the Winchester manuscript in parallel, with a dash (-) signifying the same reading and a cross (×) signifying the absence of the word concerned:

```
1    [C sig.Z7r]            ¶   Capitulum septimum
     [W f.441v]         ×      ×          ×
2    WHat araye is this sayd       sir Launcelot / thenne syr mel
     -    -     -    -       -    -       ×    -     -    -
3    lyaraunce told hem what he had fonde ꝫ        shewed hem
     -       -      -    -    -    -    - so he    -     -
4    the quenes bed /        Truly said syr launcelot ye dyd not your part
     -    -     -  // Now  -     -    -    -     -   -    -   -    -
5    nor kny3tly to touche a quenes bedde whyle it was drawen / ꝫ
     -    -     -   -    -    -    -     -     -     -   -    × -
6    she lyeng therin / for I dar say              my lord      Arthur
     -    -      -    × And - -   - sayde syr launcelot -   - kynge   -
     hym self wold
     -    -    -
7    not haue displayed her courteyns      she beyng within her bed / on-
     -    -       -         -     -    and  -    -     -    -    - × -
8    les that it had pleasyd hym to haue layne doune by her / and
     -   -   -   -     -    -    -    -     -    -    - × -
9    therfor              ye haue done vnworshipfully ꝫ shamefully
     -    sir Mellyagaunce -   -    -     -        -    -
     to youre selfe
     -    -
10        I wote not what ye mene sayd syr Mellyagraunce / but well
     //Sir - -   -    -    -    -    -    -       - × - -
11   I am sure ther hath one of her wounded kny3tes layne by  her
     - - -  -    -    -  - hurte   -     - with -
12   this ny3te / ꝫ therfor I wil  proue with my handes that she is a
     -   - × -  that × woll I -    -    -    -    -   - --
13   traytresse vnto my lord       Arthur / beware what ye do said  laun-
     -    -   - - kynge  - × -    -    -   - sir -
14   celot / for ꝫ ye say so ꝫ ye will preue it / it wil be taken at your
     - × - - - - × - - - × - ·
```

15 handes / My lord sir Launcelot said sire Mellyagraunce I rede
 -   × - - - - - - - - -

16 yow beware what ye do / for thou3 ye are neuer so good a kny-
 - - - × - - - - - - -

17 ght as ye wote wel ye ar renomed the best kny3t of the world
 - - I - - - - - - - - - worde

18 yet shold ye be aduysed to do batail in a wrong quarel / for god
 - - - - - - - - - - - - × - -

19 wil haue a stroke in euery batail / As for that sayd syr launce
 - - - - - - × - - - - -

20 lot god is to be drad / but as to that I saye nay playnly / that
 - - - - - × - - - - - × -

21 this ny3te there lay none of these ten wounded kny3tes wyth
 - - - - - - - knyghtes wounded -

22 my lady quene Gueneuer / & that wil I preue with my handes
 - - - - × - - - - myne -

23 that ye say vntruly in that now / Hold
 - - - - - // - what sey ye seyde sir launcelot//
  said sir Mellyagraunce
Thus I say - - -

24 here is my gloue that she is traytresse vnto my lord kyng Ar
 - - - - - - a - [f.442] - - - -

25 thur / & that this nyghte one of the wounded kny3tes lay with
 - × - - - - - - - - -

26 her/ & I receyue your gloue sayd sir Launcelot // & so
 - - // Well sir - - - - - - - × - anone
they were
 - -

27 sealyd with their sygnettys / and delyuerd vnto the x kny3tes
 - - - - × - - - - - /

28 At what day shal we do batail to gyders said sir launcelot / this
 - - - - - - - - - × -

29 day viij dayes said sir Mellyagraunce in the felde besyde west-
 - - - - - - - - - -

30 mynstre / I am agreed said sir Launcelot / but now said sir mel
 - × - - - - // - - - -

31 lyagraunce / sythen it is so that we must fy3te to gyders I pray
 - × - - - - - - nedys - - - -

32 yow as ye be a noble kny3t awayte me with no treason / nor
 - - - - - - - - × nother

33 none vylony the meane whyle / nor none for yow / soo god me
 - - - - × nother - - - // - -

34 help said sir launcelot ye shal ry3te wel wete I was neuer of
 - - - - - - that - - -

35 no suche condycyons / for I reporte me to al kny3tes that euer
   - -   -   × - -   - - -   -   - -

36 haue knowen me I ferd neuer with no treason / nor   I loued ne
   - -   - - -   -   -   - × nother- - -

37 uer the felauship of no man that ferde with treson / Thenne le
   - -   -   - × hym -   -   -   - // - -

38 te vs go to   dyner seid   melliagrau*n*ce. *&* after dyner ye *&* þe quene
   - - - vnto -   - sir   -   - - - the quene and ye

The chapter heading was already printed at the bottom of the preceding page, and its repetition in the beginning of Z7r made the compositor squeeze the text in his setting copy within a printed page of 37 lines of text. Comparison of the two versions reveals obvious traces of Caxton's pruning of the text as found in the Winchester manuscript. The case of Caxton's triple negation against Winchester's double towards the page end (lines 36-37) may indicate that the compositor did not have to worry about shortening the exemplar any more, since his printed text was already pruned sufficiently up to this point, or that he felt obliged to add 'no' to the text in his setting copy.

The next example is taken from sig. d6v, part of the tale of Balin, Book II, Chapter 16:

1 [C sig.d6v] Thenne Merlyn cam thyder and toke vp Balyn and
  [W f.31]   -   -   -   -   - - -   -

2 gat hym a good hors for his was dede / and bad hym
   - - - -   - - - - × - - -

3 ryde outе of that countrey /   I wold haue my damoysel
  voyde - - -   // Sir- - - - -

4 sayd balyn / Loo sayd Merlyn where she lyeth dede *&* kynge
   - - -   -   -   -   -   -

5 Pellam lay so many yeres   sore wounded / and myght neuer
   -   -   -   / -   - × -   -   -

6 be hole tyl   Galahad the haute prynce heled hym in the quest of
   -   -   - þat   -   -   -   -   - - -   - -

7 the Sangraille / for in that place was   part of the blood of our
   -   - × - - - - / - - -   - -

8 lord Jhesu cryst that   Joseph of Armathe broughte in to this
   -   -   - which   -   -   -   -   - - -

9 lond / and ther hym self lay in that ryche bed / And that was
   - × -   -   -   × -   -   -   ×   /

10 the same spere that   Longeus smote oure lorde   to the herte / and
   - ×   - whych -   -   -   - with - - - × -

11 kynge Pellam was nyghe of Joseph   kynne /   and that was
    -     -   -   -   - -   his - [f.31v] - - - /

12 the moost worshipful   man that lyued in tho dayes / and gre-
    - - worshipfullist -   on lyve - -   -   - -

13 te pyte it was of his hurte / for thorow that stroke   torned to
    - - - - / - - × - -   - - hit -   -

14 grete dole tray and tene /   Thenne departed Balyn from Mer-
    -   -   -   -   - // -   -   -   -   -

15 lyn and   sayd   in this world we   mete neuer no more
    - for he - nevir - -   -   parte no*ther* - × - -
    / Soo
    × -

16 he rode forth thorowe the fayr countreyes and Cytees *&* fond
    -   -   -   -   -   -   -   -   -   - -

17 the peple dede slayne on euery syde / and alle that   were on ly-
    -   -   -   -   -   - × -   - - evir -   - -

18 ue cryed   O balyn thow hast   caused grete
    - - and seyde a -   -   - done and -   -
    dommage   in these co*n*
    vengeaunce - thys   -

19 trayes for the dolorous stroke thow gauest vnto kynge Pella*m*
    -   -   -   -   -   - gaff -   -   -

20   thre contreyes are destroyed / and doubte not but the vengeaun-
    thes -   -   -   - × -   -   - - -   -

21 ce wil falle on the at the last /   whanne Balyn was past tho
    - -   -   -   -   - - // But   -   -   - -

22 contrayes he was passyng fayne /   so he rode ey3t dayes   or he met
    -   -   -   -   - And - -   -   - / -   -

23 with   auenture / And at the last he came in to a fayr forest in
    - many   -   × -   -   -   -   -   - -   -   -   -

24 a valey and was ware of a Toure / And there besyde he sawe
    -   -   -   -   - - -   - × -   -   - mette with

25 a grete hors of werre tayed to a treee / and ther besyde   satte a
    - -   - × ×   -   - - × - ×   - *þer* -   -

26 fayr knyght on the ground and made grete mornynge and he
    -   -   -   -   -   -   -   -   -

27 was a lykely man and a wel made /   Balyn sayd God   saue
    - - -   -   - -   - //   -   -   - you -

28 yow why be ye so heuy / telle me and I wylle amende it and
    × - - -   - × -   -   -   -   -   - -

29 I may to my power / Syr knyghte said he ageyne thow doest
    - - -   -   - × -   - he seyde ×   -   -

30 me grete gryef / for I was in mery thoughtes and now thou
    -   -   -   - - - - my   -   -   -   -

31 puttest me to more payne /   Balyn wente a lytel from hym / ⁊
    -    - - -   - // Than   - -   - - -   - × -
32 loked on his hors /   thenne herd Balyn hym saye thus / a fair
    -   - - - //   -   -   -   - - -   - - - -
33 lady why haue ye broken my promyse / for thow promysest me
    -   -   -   -   -   -   -   × -   ye promysed -
34 to mete me here by none / and I maye curse the that euer ye
    - -   - -   - - × - -   -   you -   -   -
35 gaf me this swerd / for with this swerd I   slee my self / and
    - - that - × - -   - - woll - - - × -
36 pulled it oute /   and therwith   Balyn   sterte vnto hym ⁊ took
    -   - - // - -   com   - and -   -   - - -
37 hym by the hand /   lete goo my hand sayd the knyght or els I
    -   - - - // - - -   -   -   - -   - - -
38 shal slee the / that shal not nede said balyn / for I shal promyse
    -   - - × - -   -   -   - - × - -   -   -

Line 15 contains one of the five instances of Caxton's double negation against Winchester's triple negation. Ms Tieken-Boon van Ostade explains that 'the adjunct of space *in this world* has been moved to the more prominent sentence-initial position, while the adverb *never* is placed almost at the end of the sentence. Combined with the time relationship subjunct *no more* in sentence-final position, the negative force of the sentence in Caxton is clearly emphatic' (1995: 74). I would like to draw attention to the fact that this page, like the last example, is also printed without apparent copy-fitting techniques such as the use of chapter division, white space or paraph marks. The compositor of this page, who felt obliged to prune the setting copy, produced a clearer meaning.

Thus, anyone who scrutinizes Caxton's prose text, particularly the *Morte*, to observe grammatical or philological features, should certainly bear in mind some of these changes of the text probably caused by copy-fitting problems.

WORKS CITED

Asai, N.
  1998   'Caxton's Use of a Tittle for *m* and *n* in the *Morte*', *The Round Table*
                  13: 73-86.
Baldwin, C.S.
  1894   *The Inflections and Syntax of the Morte D'Arthur of Sir Thomas Malory: A
                  Study in Fifteenth-Century English* (Boston: Ginn).
Bennett, J.A.W. (ed.)
  1963   *Essays on Malory* (Oxford: Clarendon Press).
Blake, N.F.
  1973   *Caxton's Own Prose* (London: Deutsch).
Dekker, A.
  1932   *Some Facts Concerning the Syntax of Malory's 'Morte Darthur'*
                  (Amsterdam: Portielje).
Field, P.J.C.
  1997   Review of Tieken-Boon van Ostade 1995, *Review of English Studies* NS
                  98: 518-19.
Hellinga, L.
  1980   'Two Malory Facsimiles', *Library*, 6th series 2 : 92-98.
  1982   *Caxton in Focus: The Beginning of Printing in England* (London; The
                  British Library).
  1986   'The Malory Manuscript and Caxton', in Takamiya and Brewer
                  1986: 127-41.
Hellinga, L., and H. Kelliher
  1977   'The Malory Manuscript', *British Library Journal* 3: 91-113.
Isaka, H., and Y. Shiratori
  1996   'An Analysis of Conjunction *and* in Caxton's *Morte Darthur*', *The
                  Round Table* 11: 14-30.
Ito, C., and A. Okada
  1997   'Caxton's *Morte Darthur* from the Discovery of Type 4-w', *The Round
                  Table* 11: 31-43.
Kato, Takako
  1995   'The Inconsistent Use of Paraph Marks in Caxton's *Morte Darthur*',
                  The Round Table 10: 17-29.
  1996   'A Role of Paraph Marks in Caxton's *Morte Darthur*: Text
                  Lengthiness', *The Round Table* 11: 1-13.
  1998   'Doublets in Caxton's *Morte Darthur*', *The Round Table* 13: 1-11.
Kato, Tomomi (ed.)
  1974   *A Concordance to the Works of Sir Thomas Malory* (Tokyo: University of
                  Tokyo Press).
  1993   'Some Scribal Differences in Malory', in Suzuki and Mukai 1993:
                  189-99.
Kelliher, H.
  1986   'The Early History of the Malory Manuscript', in Takamiya and
                  Brewer 1986: 143-58.

Ker, N.R. (introd.)
1976   *The Winchester Malory: A Facsimile* (EETS SS 4; London: Oxford University Press).
Kobori, A.
1998   'Caxton's Use of Hyphens in the *Morte*', *The Round Table* 13: 87-99.
Kurihara, R.
1995   'Wooden Decorative Initials in Caxton's *Morte Darthur*', *The Round Table* 10: 30-42.
Kuriyagawa, F.
1958   'The Language of Malory's "Tale of Arthur and Lucius"', *Studies in English Literature* 24: 253-69.
Mihara, M.
1998   'A Further Note on the Morgan and the Rylands Copy of Caxton's *Morte*', *The Round Table* 13: 123-34.
Miyamaru, Y.
1997   'The State of Caxton's Setting-Copy Seen from *sir, king, lord*', *The Round Table* 12: 77-92.
Mizobata, K. (ed.)
1990   *A Concordance to Caxton's Own Prose* (Tokyo: Shohakusha).
Nagai, Y.
1995   'Caxton Reconsidered: Variants Between the Morgan Copy and the John Rylands Copy of the *Morte Darthur*', *The Round Table* 10: 1-16.
Nakao, Y.
1987   'Does Malory Really Revise his Vocabulary?—Some Negative Evidence', *Poetica* 25-26: 93-109.
1993   'On the Relationship Between the Winchester Malory and Caxton's Malory', in Suzuki and Mukai 1993: 201-209.
Nakashima, K.
1981   *Studies in the Language of Sir Thomas Malory* (Tokyo: Nan'undo).
Needham, P. (introd.)
1976   *Sir Thomas Malory, Le Morte d'Arthur, printed by William Caxton, 1485, reproduced in facsimile from the copy in the Pierpont Morgan Library, New York* (London: Scolar Press).
Nishida, K., and K. Kashiwabara
1996   'A Study of Caxton's Punctuation, with Particular Reference to Malory's *Morte Darthur*', *The Round Table* 11: 44-50.
Noguchi, S.
1977   'Caxton's Malory', *Poetica* 8: 72-84.
1984   'Caxton's Malory Again', *Poetica* 20: 33-8.
1995   'The Winchester Malory', *Arthuriana* 5.2: 15-23.
Oakeshott, W.
1963   'The Finding of the [Winchester] Manuscript', in Bennett 1963: 1-6.
Sandved, A.O.
1968   *Studies in the Language of Caxton's Malory and that of the Winchester Manuscript* (Oslo: Norwegian University Press).
Shaw, S.
1963   'Caxton and Malory', in Bennett 1963: 114-45.

Šimko, J.
1957   *Word-Order in the Winchester Manuscript and in William Caxton's Edition of Thomas Malory's Morte Darthur (1485): A Comparison* (Halle: Niemeyer).

Suzuki, T., and T. Mukai (eds.)
1993   *Arthurian and Other Studies Presented to Shunichi Noguchi* (Cambridge: Brewer).

Takagi, M.
1997   'On the Possibility that the Winchester Malory was Caxton's Copy-Text', *The Round Table* 12: 1-66.

Takahashi, I.
1997   'A Study of Page Breaks in Caxton's *Morte Darthur*', *The Round Table* 12: 67-76.

Takamiya, T.
1993   'Editor/Compositor at Work: The Case of Caxton's Malory', in Suzuki and Mukai 1993: 143-51.
1996   'Chapter Divisions and Page Breaks in Caxton's *Morte Darthur*', *Poetica* 45: 63-78.

Takamiya, T., and D. Brewer (eds.)
1986   *Aspects of Malory* (Cambridge: Boydell & Brewer, 2nd edn).

Tieken-Boon van Ostade, I.
1995   *The Two Versions of Malory's 'Morte Darthur': Multiple Negation and the Editing of the Text* (Cambridge: Brewer).

Tokunaga, S.
1998   'Problems in Caxton's Chapter Divisions, Mainly in the *Morte*', *The Round Table* 13: 99-122.

Vinaver, E. (ed.)
1990   *The Works of Sir Thomas Malory* (3 vols.; Oxford: Clarendon Press, 3rd edn, rev. P.J.C. Field).

Wiencke, H.
1930   *Die Sprache Caxtons* (Leipzig: Tauchnitz).

Caxton and the *Polychronicon*

Ronald Waldron

In offering this summary of Caxton's treatment of the text of the *Polychronicon*, I am aware that the most comprehensive account of the subject to date is that of Norman Blake, in various pages of *Caxton and His World* (1969) and in individual journal papers, collected in his *William Caxton and English Literary Culture* (1991). In the last few years, however, I have been studying the relations among the extant manuscripts of Trevisa's translation, and have also had the opportunity of collating Caxton's text of Book VI with that of the 14 manuscripts of the work which survive from the fourteenth and fifteenth centuries, in my preparation of a new critical edition of Book VI based on the Berkeley manuscript that is closest to the archetype of all the witnesses: London, British Library Cotton Tiberius D vii (Waldron, forthcoming). This research tends to reinforce and supplement earlier observations, rather than overturn them, and gives an opportunity for a new overview.

Caxton's Source Text

Any attempt to specify what Caxton did to the text of the *Poly-chronicon* in his 1482 print (here designated **K**) must necessarily address the prior question: in what form did it reach him? If possible, we would like to be able to say whether he based his revision of the text on one or more of the extant manuscripts. This is particularly critical in this situation because on the one hand Caxton claims in his Epilogue to have *somwhat... chaunged the rude and old englyssh* of the original (Crotch 1928: 68) and on the other hand

we can tell from collation that he was working from a copy of the
text in which some revision of Trevisa's South-Western dialect, as
most faithfully represented in the two late fourteenth-century
Berkeley manuscripts, London, British Library Cotton Tiberius D
vii (**C**), and Manchester, Chetham's Library 11379 (**M**), had
already taken place.

Figure 1: Manuscripts of the *Polychronicon*, showing the derivation of
Caxton's print (**K**)[1]

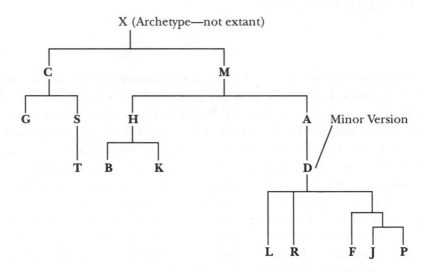

From our current knowledge of the manuscript-relations it
appears that **C** and **M** derive independently of each other from an
archetype close to Trevisa's original copy and that **M** was itself
copy-text for British Library Additional 24194 (**A**),[2] which

---

1.   In the above stemma connecting lines may represent the direct relationship of exemplar and copy (e.g. **M** to **A**), or descent through now-lost
intermediates. It is provisionally proposed that the alternative translation
(Minor Version) of Book VI, Chapters 14 to 26, found in **DLRFJP**, is first
copied in **D**, where it occupies an inserted quire (see Waldron and Hargreaves 1992). The manuscripts in this stemma not discussed in the text are
G: Glasgow, University Library Hunter 367 (s. xv med), **S**: London, British
Library Stowe 65 (s. xv in), and **T**: Princeton, University Library Taylor 6 (s.
xv 3). It should be noted that the sigla used in the present study differ from
those used in Cawley (1948).

2.   The evidence for this is that the exact portions of text contained in

subsequently generated six other extant fifteenth-century manu-scripts: Aberdeen, University Library 21 (**D**), Liverpool, Public Libraries f 909 HIG (**L**), Cambridge, Corpus Christi College 354 (**R**), Oslo, Schøyen 194, formerly Penrose 12 (**F**), Cambridge, St John's College 204 (also H.1) (**J**), and Princeton, University Library Garrett 151 (**P**).

British Library Harley 1900 (**H**), an early fifteenth-century manuscript, also descends from **M** (independently of **A**), and a close affiliate of **H** (possibly a direct copy) is a manuscript of the mid-fifteenth century formerly known as the 'Burghley Polychron-icon', now San Marino, Huntington MS HM 28561 (**B**).

That the text of Caxton's print (**K**) derives from a manuscript of this group is shown by the frequency of variants of the group **HBK** in the apparatus to my published edition of the *Dialogus* and *Epistola*, the two original prefaces which Trevisa wrote for the *Polychronicon* (Waldron 1988). Many further examples of common errors could be cited from the text of Book VI to show the close affiliation of these three copies. For example, in Chapter 1, lines 40-2 (following the lineation in my edition for Middle English Texts, Waldron, forthcoming) in the sentence:

> Also he [i.e. Alfred] sente vor Iohn, monk of Seynt Dauy hys abbay in Meneuia, vor he scholde come to hym out of *þe ottemeste endes of* Wales vor to teche hym lettur & clergy,

HBK (and no other witnesses) omit through eyeskip the phrase *þe ottemeste endes of.* Again, in Chapter 19, lines 66-68, where **C** has

> Duc Robert went to Ierusalem & pasede by Burguyn. Þar, as he went *erliche* out at a ʒate *& was þe laste of alle þe pylgryms,* þe portere smot hym wyþ a staf.

HBK (against all the other manuscripts and the Latin source) omit both *erliche* and the clause *& was þe laste of alle þe pylgryms.*

HBK also agree in several instances where variation may be the result of deliberate linguistic revision or dialect translation in the archetype of this group (possibly **H** itself). For example, in Chap-ter 1 of Book VI, during the wars with the Danes, King Alfred is visited in his hiding-place at Athelney by a pilgrim, to whom he

two consecutive folios of **M** appear in inverted order in **A**. The only tenable explanation of this phenomenon is that **A** used **M** as exemplar and that those two folios were disordered in **M** at the time. See Waldron (1990: 290-91).

gives alms. The pilgrim vanishes suddenly (he later reveals himself in a dream as St Cuthbert), *& non vore was ysene of hys goynge in þe naysch more*. Here the obsolescent word *vore* (OE *fór*) in the sense 'track' or 'trace' (Lat. *vestigium*) is replaced in **HBK** (and—probably coincidentally—in **G**) by *stap, steppe*, whereas in the **A**-group it has been revised to *wey*. Incidentally, a form of *naysch* 'soft' is kept in all manuscripts and in Caxton, though Caxton at least once later substitutes *soft* (Babington and Lumby 1865–86: 1, 333).

Particularly significant are instances where South-Western forms of **M** have been misunderstood or reinterpreted in all three witnesses in this group. An example of this is VI, Chapter 2, 39 *þe best þat hy wolde chese*, where for *hy* all other manuscripts have a form of *they*, only **HBK** reading *he* (i.e. Alfred). There is a similar reinterpreted pronoun (not in this case reflecting dialect translation) in Book VI, Chapter 1, 91-92: *touk þe body of Seynte Werburge þe mayde… & translatede hyt to Chester*, where **HBK** have *hir, her* for *hyt*. Such cases probably go back to the archetype of witnesses in this group (either **H** itself or a predecessor of **H**) and strengthen the hypothesis that **K**'s text derives from this archetype. Conversely, they also show that only those **K** variants not also in **H** can be identified as Caxton's alterations to the text he received.

The Burghley Polychronicon (**B**) is currently under study by Stephen Shepherd, who is preparing an edition of the Middle English *Pseudo-Turpin Chronicle* copied in the volume after the *Polychronicon*. From the arms on f.80 he has identified the owner and probable commissioner of the manuscript as Thomas Myll the younger (b. 1400, d. 1460) of Harescombe, Gloucestershire. In the Wars of the Roses the Mylls were active in the Lancastrian cause. Thomas's elder son William died at the Battle of Towton in 1461; father and son were posthumously attainted as rebels by the first Parliament of Edward IV and the family's property was seized by the Crown. As Ian Doyle has dated the copying of the Trevisa text to 1450–60, Shepherd believes that the death and attainders of Thomas Myll in 1460 account for the incomplete state of the decoration of the manuscript and provide a *terminus ad quem* for the Trevisan texts.[3] My acquaintance with the text of **H** and **B** has made me aware of a close textual and linguistic relationship

3.   Dr Shepherd (in a letter of 27 March 1997) has kindly given me access to his findings, which are to be published in full shortly.

between these two manuscripts. **B** could have been copied from **H** (which is dated on palaeographic grounds to the beginning of the fifteenth century), but in the absence of a feature like that mentioned in note 2 above for **M** and **A** an intermediate between **H** and **B** remains a possibility.

B was not known to A.C. Cawley and therefore not included in his study of the relationships between the manuscripts and Caxton's print (1948). The possibility that Caxton used **B** as his source for the text of the *Polychronicon* is ruled out, however, by the occurrence of errors in **B** not duplicated in **K**. For instance, in Book VI, Chapter 3, lines 62-64: *Lowys, Arnulphus his sone, regnede in Frauns twelf ʒer; bote he hadde neuere þe croune of þe Emper, and in hym was þe ende of þe Emper touchynge Charles hys ofspringe*, there is in **B** an omission through eyeskip *and…Emper*, where **K** has the full text.

The conclusion reached by Cawley on the basis of a partial collation of seven manuscripts was that there is a close genetic relationship between **H** and **K** but that 'it cannot be proved that Caxton used H as his copy. Only printer's marks in H would prove this; and none is to be seen' (Cawley 1948: 478). The collation of the 14 extant manuscripts and Caxton for the edition of Book VI has borne out this link between **H** and **K**, in that it has revealed no decisive errors or omissions in **H** where **K** has the reading of **C** or **M**.[4] The small number of variants in Book VI which might throw doubt on the derivation of **K** from **H** can, I believe, all be explained as coincident or the result of Caxton's own (or his compositor's) editorial choice.[5]

4.   In the Appendix to vol. 7 containing the Harley text of Chapters 15-26 the Rolls Series editor puts in square brackets a passage of 17 words in Chapter 22, noting 'from Cx' (Babington and Lumby 1865–86, 7.523). This is a mistake: the passage is present in **H**.

5.   The instances are:

- *vram þe bryttysche occean* **C**, *vram 'þe' bryttysch occean* (*þe* above line) **M**, *from þe brittisch Ocean* **H** , *from brittyssh occean* **K** (f.282v, Chapter 1.103)
- *dude hys gyst reuerauns* **C**, defective **M**, *dide his gifte reuerence* (*gifte* corrected from *ʒifte*) **H**, *dide his gheste reuerence* **K** (f.284v, Chapter 3.22)
- *vounde þe body* **C**, defective **M**, *fonde þat body* **H**, *founde the body* **K** (f.286v, Chapter 4.68)
- *he ys noʒt yrekened among emperours* **C**, defective **M**, *he is rekened amonge emperoures* **HB**, *he is not rekened among emperours* **K** (f.287, Chapter 5.2)

A few marginal or interlineal glosses in **H** strengthen the case for Caxton's use of this manuscript. For instance, on f.246 (Chapter 13.46) *magnus* (i.e. the German bishopric of Mainz) is glossed *meinse*; **K** reads *menyse/ magunce* (**B** *maguns*). Again, on f.253v (Chapter 20.3) *Noreganes* is glossed above the line *men of northwey*; **K** reads *Norganes that is to sey men of norewey*, **B**: *Noraganes men of Norþwey*. The glosses incorporated into the two later texts could have been independently supplied, or have come from an intermediate copy, but with other instances they support the conjecture that both Caxton and the scribe of **B** copied from **H**.[6]

The absence of casting off marks in **H**, to which Cawley draws

- *on hys wey* **CM**, *in his wey* **H**, *on his weye* **K** (f.290v, Chapter 7.40)
- *Ramesey* **CM**, *Romesey* **H**, *ramesey* **K** (f.292, Chapter 9.12)
- *þe erl hys bast sone* **CM**, *þe kynges baste sone* (*kynges* partly erased) **H**, *þe baste son* **B**, *therles baste sone* **K**, (f.296, Chapter 11.53)
- *in hys bed* **CM**, *on his bed* **HB**, *in his bedde* **K** (f.301, Chapter 14.119)
- *& of mete & drinke* **C**, defective **M**, *and of mete & of drynke* **H**, *and of mete and drynke* **K** (f.306v, Chapter 19.6-7)
- *þat broȝt hym þe knyues* **C**, defective **M**, *þat had brouȝt hym þe knyues* **HB**, *that broughte hym the knyues* **K** (f.307, Chapter 19.26)
- *kynge ouer þe noragenes* **C**, defective **M**, *kyng of þe Noreganes* **HB**, *kynge ouer the norganes* **K** (f.308v, Chapter 20.36)
- *setteþ hyt touore þe cherche dores* **C**, *defective* **M**, *setteþ tofore þe chirche dores* **HB**, *sette it byfore the chirche dores* **K** (f.312v, Chapter 22.86)
- *& went aȝe aȝe in to normandy* **C**, *defective* **M**, *& went aȝen to Normandy* **HB**, *and wente ageyne in to Normandy* **K** (f.315, Chapter 24.57)
- *þe kynge of þe noreganes* **C**, *defective* **M**, *þe kyng of Noreganes* **HB**, *the kyng of the norganes* **K** (f.321v, Chapter 28.74)

6. Other instances are:

- **H** f.247v (Chapter 14.41) *hispalis þat is Cyuil graunt* in margin glossing *hispalis* in the text (there is a similar marginal gloss in **M** beside *hispalis* in line 43): *hyspals/ that is syuyl le grannt* **K**, not copied in **B**
- f.259 (Chapter 25.36) *of schotlond* above (*Dauid þe*) *kyng*: *Dauyd the kynge of Scotlande* **KB**
- f.260v (Chapter 26.51) *a strompet* above (*arayed as*) *an hoore*: *arayde as a strompet* **K**, *araied as a strompet* **B**
- f.260v (Chapter 26.72) *oþer for the feith* above (*for meyntenyng*) *of truþe*: *for mayntenynge of trouth/ owther for the feyth* **K**, *for meyntenynge of truþe oþer for þe feiþe* **B**
- f.261 (Chapter 27.3) *toreyn[e?]* above *Turon*: *Toreyn* **K**, *toreyne* **B**
- f.261v (Chapter 27.71) *pountiff* above *Pontus*: *ponntyf* **K**, *pontus* **B**

attention, makes it unlikely that **K**'s text was set directly from this manuscript (and in any case the nature of the revisions to the text would not encourage us to see this as a possibility). The most acceptable hypothesis, in view of all the evidence, would seem to be that Caxton revised the text of **H** in a manuscript copy and then either he or a compositor set the text up in print from his revised copy.

Description of Britain

The question of Caxton's treatment of the text of the *Polychronicon* is complicated by the publication on 18 August 1480, two years before the edition of the complete work (to which he appended his own 'Liber Ultimus'), of a version of Chapters 32-60 of Trevisa's text, with the title *Description of Britain* (*DB*).

The earlier work considerably rearranges Trevisa's (i.e. Higden's) chapters.[7] In *DB* Caxton numbers his Chapters i-xxix, starting with Higden's Chapters 39-60 (which focus on England), but omitting the list of topics at the beginning of Chapter 39, and continuing after the England section with Chapter 38 (the verse chapter on Wales), Chapter 37 (on Scotland), and then Chapters 32-36 (on Ireland). In the course of this rearrangement he conflates Chapters 47 (ancient cities and towns) and 48 (York) in Chapter ix, Chapters 52-57 (on the bishoprics of England) in one chapter (xiij), and also runs Chapters 59 and 60, on languages and manners and customs, into one new chapter (xv). Conversely the single chapter (38) on Wales is printed as five separate chapters in *DB* (xvj-xx), with English translations of Trevisa's Latin

---

7.   The only portion of text not derived from the *Polychronicon* is a short passage at the beginning of Chapter i supplementing Higden's explanation of the origin of the name Albion:

> <F>Irst as Galfride saith this lande was named Albion after the name of Albyne the oldest doughter of Dioclesian/ and had xxvij sustres/ And they were first that enhabited this lande/ And because she was the oldest suster she named this lond Albion after her owne name as the cronicle reherseth/ Othir saye that [this lond was named Albion, etc., continuing from *Polychronicon*, I, Chapter 39]

The *cronicle* referred to here is *the comyn cronicles of englond... now late enprinted at Westmynstre* (Preface to *Description of Britain*, Crotch 1928: 10) i.c. his own *Chronicles of England* compiled from the *Brut* and published 10 June of the same year.

subtitles as chapter headings, and the first of Higden's five chapters on Ireland (32) is divided into four separate chapters (xxij-
xxv) following divisions indicated by Higden's subtitles (copied in
Latin by Trevisa), which again Caxton translates into English as
chapter headings.[8]

George Painter sees Caxton's motive for his transposition of
chapters as that of a patriotic subordination of the other provinces to England.[9] Caxton himself seems to bear this out in
respect of Ireland when he says in the Epilogue: *bicause Irlonde is
vnder the reule of englond & of olde tyme it hath so continued therfore I
haue sette the descripcion of the same after the said brituyne* (Crotch
1928: 40). It should not be overlooked, however, that Higden
himself wants to give England pride of place—but by leaving it
until last and by homing in on it from the west. Ireland, accordingly, is an important step (both geographically and as subject to
Britain) in the transition from his description in Chapter 31 of
the 'islands' of the Western Ocean (the Canaries, Iceland, Denmark, Norway) to *Britannia* (a term he sometimes uses inter-
changeably with *Anglia* to refer to England alone, as well as for
the whole complex of regions later called the British Isles). His
statement of intention in the *Prefacio secunda ad historiam* (Book I,
Chapter 2) explains how his own arrangement fits into his plan
for the chronicle as a whole. This is its English form in **K**: *And for
this story is trauaylled by cause of brytayne euery prouynce and londe is
descryued vntil we come to brytayne laste of alle as moost speciall And
therin ben conteyned fyften chapytres nedeful to the knouleche of the Ilonde
of Britayne as though it were an Inbryngynge to gretter knouleche in other
bookes that foloweth.* Caxton's rearrangement of chapters for *DB* is

8.   Caxton's rearrangements leave in a couple of places statements which
are no longer true of *DB*: e.g. in *DB* Chapter vj he copies Trevisa (Chapter
44): *Of the meruaylles and woundres of the Ilond Mon thou shalt fynde tofore in the
chapitre of Wales*, though the chapter on Wales is *DB* Chapter xx; similarly the
comment in Chapter xv, part 2 (= *Polychronicon* Chapter 60) that *the maners
and the doyng of Walsshmen and of scottes ben to fore som what declared* is also
rendered untrue by the reordering of *DB*.

9.   Painter (1976: 106 n. 2): 'Higden-Trevisa, however, describes Ireland,
Scotland, Wales, England in that order. Caxton, with his typical editorial zeal
spurred on by patriotic feeling, rearranges the sections in the reverse order,
England, Wales, Scotland, Ireland.'

therefore likely to have arisen from the need to give a geographically more centralized account of England in this separate work.

The *fyften chapytres* on England announced here by Higden are actually expanded to twenty-two in the completed Book I of the *Polychronicon,* but in extracting these chapters for *DB* Caxton reduces them again to fifteen by using the fifteen categories of description at the beginning of Higden's Chapter 39 as chapter-divisions, and he concludes his book with the chapters on the more outlying provinces.

It is clear from changes of spelling and lineation that the text of these chapters was reset for the print of the whole *Polychronicon* in 1482. However, Caxton did not copy the text of these chapters from the earlier printed version when he came to set up the later version—or have it set up by a compositor working under his direction. It would in any case seem improbable that, having begun to print from the beginning of the text, he would put aside whatever copy-text he was using in order to copy from *DB*, but any doubt on this subject is settled by the fact that in the 1482 *Polychronicon* the chapters in Book I follow Higden's (and Trevisa's) order, the passage omitted from Chapter i in *DB* (Trevisa's Chapter 39) is now included, and the chapter headings and subheadings have the original Latin form they have in Trevisa and not the English form of *DB*.[10]

Comparison of the two printed texts shows that, allowing for the sorts of spelling variation commonly encountered in fifteenth-century English and some typesetting errors in each text, they are both printed from the same copy of Trevisa's translation, as revised by Caxton. A few lines from the description of Ireland in each text, together with the same passage from MS Harley 1900, the extant manuscript closest to Caxton's source, will illustrate this similarity.

H, f.70

Þe

lond is nesche reyny & wyndy & lowe by æe see side & wiæi*nn*e hilly and sondy. *Solin(us)* Þere is grete plente of noble pasture & of leese.

---

10. The subheadings in Chapter 38—the verse chapter on Wales—are in English in both printed texts (though in Latin in the manuscripts); this does not, however, seem to me to outweigh the evidence of the majority of the headings, which cannot have been copied from *DB* to the *Polychronicon.*

þ*er*fore bestes mot ofte be ydryue out of her leese lest þei fede hem self
to fulle & schende hem self & þei most ete at her owne wille (Book I,
Chapter 32).

DB [no foliation]

The londe is softe rayny wyndy & lowe by the see si-
de & withinne hilly & sondy/ Solin*us*/ ther is grete plente of noble
pasture & of leese/ therfor the beestes must be oft driuen out of their
pasture leest they ete ouermoch for they shold shend hem self if they
myght ete at their wyll/ (Chapter xxiiij)

K, f. xlij

the londe is soft rayny. wyndy. and lowe by
the see side and withyn hilly and sondy. Solynus/ there is grete
plente of noble pasture and of leese/ therfore the bestes must be of
te dryue oute of theyr pasture leest they ete ouermoche for they
shold shende hein self yf they myght ete at theyr wylle (Book I, Chapter
32)

What is striking in this short passage (and a phenomenon found
throughout the two texts where they run together) is that the
revisions of *DB* (*soft, pasture* for the second *leese* in **H**, *must be oft, ete
ouermoch, for they shold, if they myght, at their wyll*) are repeated
exactly in **K**, apart from minor spelling variations. It is unlikely
that these revisions could have been introduced separately
(whether by two different compositors or the same compositor
working at a two year interval) without varying more than they do.
Given that neither of the printed texts is copied from the other,
there can be very little doubt that the excerpted chapters in *DB*
are printed from the same revised text as was used later for the
setting of the *Polychronicon*.[11]

11. Cawley (1948: 477-78) gives an instance of a reading in *DB* Chapter
xiiij that is closer than the same passage in **K** (I, 58) to the (evidently original) reading of **CS**. The relevant readings are:

C & so þeoues & bribors
S & so þefes & brybors
H And so þese & bribors
K And so these and brybours
DB And so these theuys and brybours

Cawley suggests that this variant is an indication that Caxton might have
consulted an additional Trevisa manuscript for *DB*, though not for **K**. I
believe a more satisfactory explanation for this isolated example would be
that Caxton (or his compositor) at the typesetting stage of *DB* conjecturally

This could have been a marked-up copy of Trevisa like the text Norman Blake has suggested Caxton might have used for his revision of Malory's *Morte Darthur*—as utilitarian a copy as the Winchester manuscript, but one the printer was not afraid of disfiguring, because it was his own property (1991: 202). However, I am inclined to believe that the similarity in small particulars between the two prints should encourage us to reconsider the way Caxton refers to his work on Trevisa's text. He says in the Epilogue:

> Therfore J
> William Caxton a symple persone haue endeuoyred me to wryte
> fyrst ouer all the sayd book of proloconycon/ and somwhat haue
> chaunged the rude and old englyssh/ that is to wete certayn wor
> des/ which in these dayes be neither vsyd ne vnderstanden/ & fur
> thermore haue put it emprynte (Crotch 1928: 68).

I understand Caxton to be saying here that he has exerted himself or taken trouble (*endeuoyred me*) first to copy out (*wryte ouer*) the whole (*all*) of the *Polychronicon*, revising its English, and in addition to that (*furthermore*) he has put it in print. It is noteworthy that the printed text, which Crotch reproduces exactly, has *ouer* and *all* as separate words (though *overall*, 'everywhere, throughout', also yields good sense), making it possible to construe *ouer* with *wryte*, a phrasal verb the *OED* does not record until Shakespeare, but then in a citation from *Richard III* which provides a significant parallel to Caxton's usage here.[12] A Scrivener enters in Act III, scene vi, saying:

> Here is the indictment of the good Lord Hastings;
> Which in a set hand fairly is engross'd,
> That it may be to-day read o'er in Paul's:
> And mark how well the sequel hangs together.
> Eleven hours I have spent to write it over,
> For yesternight by Catesby was it sent me.

emended the faulty reading he had received from **H**, but neglected to emend his copy-text. I have not encountered any other variants suggestive of conflation in my wider collation of the two prints (see n.15 below).

12. *OED* **write** *v*. **18. write ouer a** To write (something) anew or again; to rewrite. *MED* has not at the time of writing reached the letter *w*. *Write* in a context of scribal activity would, in any case, have its common ME sense 'copy'.

It is difficult to avoid the inference that Caxton is alluding to a complete transcription of a manuscript of Trevisa made by himself in revised English to form the basis of his printed edition. But whether this is the case or not, the close relation between the linguistic revisions of *DB* and those in the corresponding parts of **K** makes it possible for us to have confidence that **K** as a whole contains Caxton's revised text, with due allowance for minor spelling changes which may have been introduced by compositors.[13]

Caxton's Process of Revision

Caxton's own statements about the language he uses, in particular the extended discussion in the Prologue to *Eneydos* published in 1490 (Crotch 1928: 107-10), make it clear that his aim was to print his texts in a widely accessible form of the written English of his time; thus two distinct but related criteria would have been before him in revising an English text such as Trevisa's translation of the *Polychronicon*: modernity and regional centrality (i.e. proximity to an emerging formal standard of which he was evidently aware).[14] The first principle of his revising strategy is overtly recognized in his use of the word *old* in reference to Trevisa's English in the passage from Caxton's Epilogue quoted above, and the results are most conspicuous in the area Caxton himself highlights—that of vocabulary. Many of the words Caxton ejected from Trevisa's text were obsolete or obsolescent as lexical items or in the senses in which Trevisa uses them. His recognition of the second desideratum for the English of his edition may be concealed in the epithet *rude*. This is a word he often applies disparagingly to his own style, for instance in the Epilogue to the first edition of *Reynart the Foxe* (1481), where he says that the *dutche* original has been *by me willm*

13. The conclusion that the revisions are those of the printer himself is, of course, special to the *Polychronicon*, for the reasons given, and cannot be extended to other Caxton works such as the *Morte Darthur*, still less to the texts published later by Wynkyn de Worde which Norman Blake has adduced as evidence of the involvement of compositors in linguistic revision (1976: 85-105).

14. I have no evidence that Caxton was concerned to preserve Trevisa's own linguistic characteristics, such as Jeremy Smith finds in the case of Caxton's edition of Gower's *Confessio Amantis* (1986: 63). It may be that the difference between verse and prose is crucial here.

Caxton translated in to this rude & symple englyssh in thabbey of Westmestre (Crotch 1928: 62). Very properly the *OED* cites this under **rude** *a.* and *adv.* **8 a** 'Of language, composition, etc.: Lacking in elegance or polish; deficient in literary merit.' The word has additional contemporary connotations, however, in relation to scenery, manners, etc.: 'rugged, rough, uncivilized, uncultivated'; so it might well have had regional associations of country versus town or court for Caxton in relation to Trevisa's language. Since he elsewhere shows considerable interest in regional variation in English,[15] it seems reasonable to suppose a degree of awareness of a layer of dialect translation in the version of the *Polychronicon* which issued from his press. Both criteria are, in fact, exemplified in the revisions themselves.

In discussing the language of the printed texts it must be borne in mind that, as Norman Blake has persuasively argued, there is no direct pathway from the language of a Caxton print to the speech of Caxton himself, in view of the demonstrable participation of fifteenth- and early sixteenth-century compositors in decisions on the texts they were setting up in print (1976: 85-97). This obstacle is particularly relevant to spelling because of the general variability of spelling in the written language even of one and the same person and also because this freedom was obviously useful to the compositor in the justification of his lines or filling of his pages. Even in two virtually identical texts like *DB* and the corresponding chapters of the *Polychronicon*, which were printed from the same copy, we have seen that there are differences of spelling of this nature. We are fortunate, however, that this partial control enables us to assess the limits of variation in this case, and from extensive collation of the two texts it appears that, in general, variation is confined to a limited number of categories of spelling differences (e.g. single or double final consonants of words, presence or absence of final *-e*, *i/y* and *u/w* alternation), some

---

15. Notably in the Prologue to *Le Recueil des Histoires de Troyes*, 1476 (Crotch 1928: 3-5, esp. 4), with its reference to Kent *where I doubte not is spoken as brode and rude englissh as is in ony place of englond*, and the much-quoted Prologue to *Eneydos*, 1490 (Crotch 1928: 107-10, esp. 108), with its story of *egges* and *eyren*. In that prologue he also couples *rude* and *vplondyssh* in declaring that *this present booke is not for a rude vplondyssh man to laboure therin* (Crotch 1928: 109).

differences in the expression of numerals (e.g. *C.xx* vs. *six score*) and occasional transpositions, some of which may be deliberate, others inadvertent (e.g. *place and stede* vs. *stede and place* , *Of maners of men* vs. *Of men Of maners*).[16]

With regard to spellings that may be dialectally significant in their departure from the form found in **H**, the two printed versions of Book I, Chapters 32-60, do not differ markedly from each other. In a few cases of this kind (e.g. **K** and *DB* agree in having usually *such(e)* for **H**'s *siche* and *hygh/est* for **H**'s *heiȝ/este*) the same spelling can be shown to recur consistently in a later part of the *Polychronicon* (Book VI), and this gives us grounds for thinking that the substituted forms derive from Caxton's own revision of Trevisa's language, as he found it in **H** or a very similar manuscript.

The same can be inferred from the occurrence of chronologically or dialectally significant inflections or other grammatical forms that are common to the two prints (but differ from those in **H**) and also recur extensively in **K**. Such are the present plural indicative, in *-e* or *-en* (**H**'s usual form is *-iþ* from **M**'s *-eþ*), the *-(e)n* (*born, throwen*) form of the strong past participle (**H**, like **C** and **M**, has usually *ybore, yþrowe*, though already some are written with *-en* or *-e* and no prefix), the personal pronouns *I, she, theyr*, beside *her* (**H** *ich, heo, her*), the positive and comparative adjectival/adverbial endings *-ly* and *-lyer* (**H** *-liche* and *-loker*) and the conversion of *-n* plurals of nouns (e.g. *trees* for *treen*). I conclude from these indications that modification of what we may loosely call the 'nonstandard' character of the language of the **H** and **B** manuscripts (in which the language preserves a distinct South-Western/West-Midland colouring) had already taken place in the text used for the typesetting of *DB* and **K**.

It is in the area of vocabulary that the revised language of the Caxton print of the *Polychronicon* has attracted most attention. Churchill Babington, the first Rolls Series editor, printed in the Introduction to Volume 1, lxiv-lxvi, a list of 100 specimens of Caxton's changes to Trevisa's text, compiled from the portion

---

16. The following chapters of *DB* have been collated minutely with **K**: i, ii, xv, xxij, xxiij, xxiiij, xxv and xxix (corresponding to *Polychronicon* I, Chapters 39, 40, 59, 60, 32, and 36); other chapters of *DB* have been tested by random checking.

contained in Volume 1 (Book I, Chapters 1–38). The list is, of course, the product of collation of the Caxton text with his base manuscript, Cambridge, St John's College 204 (**J**) and with BL Additional 24194 (**A**), now recognized as **J**'s ancestor. **H** was not used for collation until Volume 2 and, in any case, Babington was unaware that Caxton's text derives, not from a manuscript belonging to the group containing **J** and **A**, but from **H** or a closely affiliated manuscript. However, the list is confined mainly to vocabulary substitutions and, since **H** and **AJ** agree by and large in preserving Trevisa's vocabulary, most of the items in the list can still stand as examples of Caxton's revisions of Trevisa at the lexical level. This includes such frequent substitutions as *call* or *name* for *clepe, that is to say* for *þat is to menyng, dwelle* for *wone, resseyue* for *fonge, doctryne* for *lore, departe* for *dele* v., *part* for *dele* n., *agayn* for *aȝe, asonder* for *atwynne, take away* for *bynyme*, and *after* for *efte*.

Babington does not claim that the list is complete, and further substitutions (some frequently repeated) come to light in the textual apparatus to that and subsequent volumes. Some examples may be given from Book VI: Caxton substitutes *large* or *grete* for *huge, shette* (past participle) for *ysteke, neete* for *ruþeren, vnto* for *anon to, translate* for *torne, after* for *þerafter, say* for *tell, said* for *quoþ, nonne* for *meynchen, byfore* for *tofore* or *toforehond, enbracyng* for *clippinge, drowned* for *ystoffed, wexe* for *worþe, rodde* for *ȝerde, putte* or *leyde* for *dide*.

Occasionally, even in the area of vocabulary choice, a simple comparison between the Rolls Series word and that in Caxton can be misleading. For instance, Trevisa's usual word for 'commanded' is *hyte*, e.g. in VI, 4.54, *& hyte hys men þat non of ham scholde abyde byhynde.* **H** (or its exemplar) regularly substitutes *bade* for this word (one of its rare revisions of Trevisa's vocabulary) and both **B** and **K** copy this. **A** and **J**, however, accept Trevisa's word and copy *heet* (though some later manuscripts substitute *bade* independently). The result is that from the Rolls Series edition alone we might suppose that **K**'s *badde* is Caxton's own revision of *heet* rather than his acceptance of the word in his copy-text. There is a similar case in VI, 8.53, *into þat helle Cryst alyȝt after*, where **HBK** read *descended*, while **A** and **J** preserve *alyȝt*. On the other hand, **H** has no objection to Trevisa's *yfolled* 'baptized'; **J** and **A** regularly substitute *cristened* and this disguises the fact that Caxton's *cristened* at these points in the text is his independent substitution for the *yfulled* which he probably found in his source.[17]

In some cases (as the Rolls Series editor points out) Caxton shows some hesitation over an obsolescent word: In Book VI, 1.75, he admits *menchon* (**H** *monchon*), for instance, though more often he goes for the synonym that has survived, *nonne* (e.g. VI, 2.74); the same is true of *cleped* (usually changed to *called* or *named*, but retained in VI, 15.41), *poperyche* (usually, but not always, changed to *papacye*), *raper* in the sense 'earlier' (sometimes replaced by *byfore*), and many more. These hesitations and inconsistencies give authenticity to the bewilderment he expresses in the prologue to *Eneydos*.

In addition to substitution of single words there is a sprinkling of examples of minor syntactical change, transposition, and small-scale paraphrase within the phrase or clause. There are many changes of preposition, especially *on* for *in* in expressions of time and place (VI, 6.30 **H** *in a nyȝt*, **K** *on a nyght*, VI, 1.103 **H** *in lond and in see*, **K** *on lond and on see*), periphrastic forms of indirect object expressions (VI, 21.5 **H** *had doon his moder*, **K** *had done to his moder*). **K** will sometimes simplify Trevisa's doublets (VI, 21.4-5. **H** *glemen & mynstrals*, **K** *mynstrals*) and sometimes use this feature of Trevisa's style to add a gloss of his own (VI, 25.63 **H** *to oone*, **K** *to oone and ioyne*—two lines later *ooned* is replaced altogether by *ioyned*). Changes of word order within the clause generally bring the syntax closer to Modern English and further from Old English/Middle English word order, especially where adverbials are involved; so **H**'s (VI, 15.4) *In his tyme came a relygiouse pilgrime* appears in **K** as *in his tyme a relygyous pylgrym cam*; VI, 1.70 **H** *þat ȝer englischemen made*, **K** *englisshmen made that yere*; VI, 2.25 **H** *was ȝursday here*, **K** *yisterday was here*; VI, 13.135 **H** *heo com seelde in his bed*, **K** *she selde come in his bedde*.

Babington draws attention in his introduction to places in Caxton's version where 'the greater part of a sentence has been re-cast more in accordance, it must be presumed, with the

---

17. In at least one place (VI, 13.6), however, he prints *baptysed* where **H** has *folled* (*vullede* **CM**) and the A-group *cristoned*. Probably many of his substitutions are to be seen as a turning away from an expression he deems unsuitable, rather than a positive leaning towards a single substitute.

phraseology of his own day' (Babington and Lumby 1865–86: 1, lxvi). He makes it clear that he had for this reason found Caxton disappointing as a witness to Trevisa's text and this may have led him to exaggerate the extent of Caxton's syntactic alterations. There are, it is true, on the pages listed in the footnote a small number of passages answering this description, but typically the reshaping of the sentence can be seen as the result of a change of conjunction, or other quite local decision.

In Book VI I have found even fewer examples. In reference to King Alfred in Chapter 1.12, Caxton prefers *He was but a symple Gramaryon* to Trevisa's *He couþe his gramer but symplich* (so **H**). In VI, 21.104, **H** reads *In þis henryes tyme was grete strif in þe chirch of Rome þat þre men were chose popes at ones*; **K**'s version substitutes *for* for *þat* producing a different syntax, but it needs to be added that the word *so* has dropped out of the text before *grete*, in the tradition represented by **H**. **K**'s alteration therefore seems to be motivated by a wish to correct an anomaly in the copy-text, rather than a desire for change for its own sake. In VI, 25.73-74 **H** reads *þat rode on an hors vnwiseliche ypriked*, **K** *that rode on an hors vnwisely and spurred hym*; **K**'s change may have originated in the replacement of *ypriked*, as an obsolete word and one which might have an aura of impropriety; in consequence, *vnwisely spurred* may not have seemed idiomatic enough; the insertion of *and* creates two clauses and reassigns the adverb *vnwisely* to *rode*.

In spite of Caxton's declaration in his prologue that in his printed version Trevisa's translation is *a lytel embelysshed fro tholde makyng* (Crotch 1928: 67), a study of Book VI in relation to the Middle English form of the text from which he was working reveals very little positive rhetorical ornamentation or stylistic polishing.

His replacement of Germanic by Latinate vocabulary continues as a matter of course in Book VI. In some cases this is no doubt simply a reflection of a general linguistic change that Caxton wishes to identify with; sometimes, however, one senses a personal leaning to a more formal style, as in *deposed* (of a pope) for *sett doun* (VI, 8.16) or *without yssue* (of King Eadred) for *wiþout children* (VI, 8.35), *take degree or order* for *stye vp* (VI, 1.16) and *auoutrye* for *spousebriche* (VI, 13.52).

There is a distinct tendency to reduce the emphasis, colourful-
ness, and what he perhaps saw as brusqueness, of the original, for
instance in the changes: from *Þe kyng haf vp boÞe his hondes to heuene*
(**H**) to *The kynge lyft vp his handes to heuen* (VI, 2.11), from *Al his lif
from his birÞe to his ende day he schoon* to *Al his lyf to his endynge daye he
shone* (VI, 6.3), from *he byschoon Þese Citees wiÞ lyȝt of riȝt bileue* to *he
caused these citees to be of ryght byleue* (VI, 7.68), from *(Þe walles of Þe
Castel Þat was bysegide) fil doun sodeynlich riȝt to Þe ground* to *fylle
sodenly to the grounde* (VI, 15.17), and, on a smaller scale, from
yloued boÞe of ffader & moder to *loued of fader and moder* (VI, 1.6),
from *to siche & to grone* to *te sygh and grone* (VI, 25).

Another type of revision that might well be regarded as stylistic
is the replacement of terms which Caxton regarded as socially
unacceptable to his putative readers. Trevisa's mode of expression
is notoriously down-to-earth at times and there are signs that even
the Harley copyist balked here and there. For instance Trevisa
comments feelingly on King Alfred's being afflicted with piles: *Þat
ys a schrewede euel vor hyt semeÞ Þat hys bom ys oute Þat hath Þat euel*
(**C**). This very personal remark is omitted by **H**, so that Caxton
was presumably not faced with the choice of excluding it himself.
Again, in VI, 7.57, where Trevisa casually describes the life
together before marriage of Duke Richard of Normandy and
Gunnora as *hourdom,* the Harley text has been roughly altered to
deshonest lif, an expression Caxton accepts in his version. In two
other places the word is replaced apparently on Caxton's initiative
by one he evidently thought more refined: *an hoore* is replaced by
a strompet in Chapter 26, though he had accepted *horedom* in
Chapter 25, while in Chapter 13 the statement that King Ethelred
walwede in lecherye wiÞ strompettes & wiÞ hoores is rendered by
Caxton: *he wallowed in lechery with strompettis/ and with comune
wymmen.*

This brief review of Caxton's changes to the language of the
Polychronicon in Book VI, then, endorses the picture of Caxton's
attitude to stylistic questions painted by Norman Blake in his essay
'Caxton and Courtly Style' (1968; cf. Blake 1969: 171-93). There
he shows by examination of Caxton's comments on style in their
chronological sequence and in relation to his practice that, while
he was eager to pay respect (through terms like *compendious,
enbelissher* and *ornate*) to fashionable criteria as he became aware of

them, and to attribute these skills to other writers while deprecating the *rude* and *old*, his style of translation is directed towards intelligibility and wide acceptability, rather than embellishment as we would understand it.

Conclusion

Caxton's goal (as Norman Blake's many studies make clear) is a courtly variety of contemporary English pleasing to the majority of his customers. To that extent there is already for him an established best kind of English to aim at, though he may not have had a very comprehensive or consistent idea of the nature of that standard. It has long been recognized that the *Polychronicon* plays a key role in our understanding of Caxton's idea of the standard of English writing to be adopted by a printer for a national nobility and gentry. If my hypothesis is correct that Caxton took his text of the *Polychronicon* from Harley 1900 and that he made his own revised copy of that text in manuscript, we can the more confidently see the differences between the extant manuscript and the 1482 print as Caxton's own work. Further study of the language of this print may then enable us to assess more accurately than has hitherto been possible Caxton's own contribution to the development of standard literary English.

WORKS CITED

Babington, C., and J.R. Lumby (eds.)

  1865–86   *Polychronicon Ranulphi Higden Monachi Cestrensis* (9 vols.; London: Rolls Series, Longman Green).

Blake, N.F.

  1968   'Caxton and Courtly Style', *Essays and Studies* NS 21: 29-45.

  1969   *Caxton and his World* (London: Deutsch).

  1976   *Caxton: England's First Publisher* (London: Osprey).

  1991   *William Caxton and English Literary Culture* (London: Hambledon Press).

Cawley, A.C.

  1939/1948   'Relationships of the Trevisa Manuscripts and Caxton's *Polycronycon*', *London Medieval Studies* 1: 463-82.

Crotch, W.J.B.

  1928   *The Prologues and Epilogues of William Caxton* (EETS, 176; London: Oxford University Press).

Higden, R.
  1971   *The Description of Britain 1480* [facsimile of Caxton edition] (Amster-
                dam: Theatrum Orbis Terrarum; New York: Da Capo Press).
Painter, G.D.
  1976   *William Caxton: A Quincentenary Biography of England's First Printer*
                (London: Chatto & Windus).
Smith, J.J.
  1986   'Some Spellings in Caxton's Malory', *Poetica* 24: 58-63.
Waldron, R.
  1988   'Trevisa's Original Prefaces on Translation', in E.D. Kennedy *et al.*
                (eds.), *Medieval English Studies Presented to George Kane* (Woodbridge:
                Brewer): 285-99.
  1990   'The Manuscripts of Trevisa's Translation of the *Polychronicon*:
                Towards a New Edition', *Modern Language Quarterly* 51: 281-317.
  forthcoming *John Trevisa's Translation of Higden's 'Polychronicon', Book VI* (Heidel-
                berg: Winter).
Waldron, R., and H. Hargreaves
  1992   'The Aberdeen Manuscript of Trevisa's Translation of the *Poly-
                chronicon* (AUL MS 21): A Workshop Crisis and its Resolution',
                Scriptorium 46: 276-82.

Index of Chaucer's Works

Index of Manuscripts

General Index